PAVING THE GREAT WAY

PAVING THE GREAT WAY

VASUBANDHU'S UNIFYING BUDDHIST PHILOSOPHY

Jonathan C. Gold

COLUMBIA UNIVERSITY PRESS
New York

Columbia University Press
Publishers Since 1893
New York Chichester, West Sussex
cup.columbia.edu

Paperback edition, 2016

Library of Congress Cataloging-in-Publication Data
Gold, Jonathan C., 1969- author.
Paving the great way : Vasubandhu's unifying Buddhist philosophy / Jonathan C. Gold.
pages cm
Includes bibliographical references and index.
ISBN 978-0-231-16826-7 (cloth : alk. paper)—ISBN 978-0-231-16827-4 (pbk. : alk. paper)—
ISBN 978-0-231-53800-8 (electronic)
1. Vasubandhu. 2. Buddhist philosophy. I. Title.
BQ7529.V367G65 2014
181'.043—dc23
2013043739

Columbia University Press books are printed on permanent and durable acid-free paper.
Printed in the United States of America

c 10 9 8 7 6 5 4 3 2 1
p 10 9 8 7 6 5 4 3 2 1

Cover design: Noah Arlow
Cover image: Three Chortens, Rabdentse, *2009. Courtesy Dhillan Chandramowli*

For my parents

CONTENTS

CONCLUSION: BUDDHIST CAUSAL FRAMING
FOR THE MODERN WORLD

ACKNOWLEDGMENTS

MY INTEREST in Vasubandhu was kindled during a Sanskrit reading course on Yogācāra philosophy taught by Paul J. Griffiths at the University of Chicago Divinity School. The students sitting around that seminar table—especially Mario D'Amato, Richard Nance, Parimal Patil, Dan Arnold, and Trina Janiec Jones—became, and remain, crucial interlocutors for me. This book is only the latest of my attempts to explain myself to them, and over the years they have each read and commented on one or another version of the ideas in this book. I am grateful to them all. Dan Arnold deserves special gratitude for his careful attention to a recent draft. Matthew T. Kapstein, also at Chicago, has had an indelible influence on my education in Buddhist philosophy.

I am grateful for the opportunity to work in the collegial, supportive environment of the Department of Religion at Princeton University. Stephen Teiser, Jacqueline Stone, Jeffrey Stout, Judith Weisenfeld, Leora Batnitzky, and AnneMarie Luijendijk have been especially kind. The department's unmatched staff—Lorraine Fuhrmann, Patty Bogdziewicz, Kerry Smith, and Mary Kay Bodnar—make the working environment here hum with efficiency and just plain fun.

What can I say about the many people who have contributed to my thinking for this book, either in private conversations or by providing comments and evocative questions after presentations? My gratitude, properly elaborated, would fill its own chapter, but fearing prolixity I provide only the root text: Charles Goodman, Christopher Morgan-Knapp, Khenpo Ngawang Jorden, Khenpo Lama Pema Wangdak, Dan Lusthaus,

Christian Coseru, Florin Deleanu, Georges Dreyfus, John Dunne, David Eckel, Owen Flanagan, Jay Garfield, Padmanabh Jaini, Stephen Kaplan, Kristin Beise Kiblinger, Sara McClintock, Karin Meyers, Marlissa Moschella, Changhwan Park, Roy Tzohar, Jan Westerhoff, Marie Friquegnon, Douglas Duckworth, Funayama Toru, Tao Jiang, Andrew Nicholson, Bronwyn Finnigan, Tom Tillemans, Jonathan Ciliberto, Robert Wright, Rick Repetti, and Ram-Prasad Chakravarthi. Mark Siderits and Christopher Gowans each provided incisive, formalized comments. My brother, David Gold, has generously shared his time and his talents as a Sanskritist.

I apologize to those whose names I have neglected to include. And, of course, none of these people should be blamed for the failings of this work; I am not conditioned to follow all of the best advice.

I am grateful to Wendy Lochner and her colleagues at Columbia University Press for their interest, care, and attention to the manuscript.

Since 2011, I have been the beneficiary of Princeton University's Julis Foundation University Preceptorship, which has provided the rarest treasure, a luxurious extension of time (which turns out to have been necessary) to write, meet with colleagues, and complete this manuscript.

Sections 4.1 and 4.3 from my article "Vasubandhu," *Stanford Encyclopedia of Philosophy*, ed. Edward N. Zalta (http://plato.stanford.edu/entries/vasubandhu/ [published April 2011]), have been integrated into chapter 5, and are reprinted here with permission.

This book is dedicated to my parents, with gratitude for their support. I also pause to thank my children, Etta and Milo, for being brilliant and true. To Heather: our love is not for public consumption, so I will only say thank you, again.

ABBREVIATIONS

AKBh	*Abhidharmakośabhāṣya* (= Pradhan 1975; Śāstrī 2008)
AKK	*Abhidharmakośakārikā* (= verses selected from Pradhan 1975)
DhDhV	*Dharmadharmatāvibhāga* (= Mathes 1996)
DhDhVV	*Dharmadharmatāvibhāgavṛtti* (= Mathes 1996)
KSP	*Karmasiddhiprakaraṇa* (= *las grub pa'i rab tu byed pa*; Derge Tanjur 1982–1985; vol. 136 [*shi*]: fols. 134v–145r)
LVP	La Vallée Poussin
MAV	*Madhyāntavibhāga* (= Nagao 1964)
MAVBh	*Madhyāntavibhāgabhāṣya* (= Nagao 1964)
MNS	*Mahānidāna Sutta* (= Walshe 1995b; see also Thanissaro 1997a)
MSA	*Mahāyānasūtrālaṃkāra*
MSABh	*Mahāyānasūtrālaṃkārabhāṣya*
MSBh	*Mahāyānasaṃgrahabhāṣya*
NBh	*Nyāyabhāṣya* (= Jha 1939)
PSP	*Pañcaskandhaprakaraṇa*
SNS	*Saṃdhinirmocanasūtra* (= Lamotte 1935)
SPS	*Sāmaññaphala Sutta* (= Walshe 1995a; see also Thanissaro 1997b)
Triṃś	*Triṃśikā* (= Lévi 1925)
TSN	*Trisvabhāvanirdeśa* (= La Vallée Poussin 1933)
Viṃś	*Viṃśatikā* (= Lévi 1925)
VyY	*Vyākhyāyukti* (= Lee 2001)

PAVING THE GREAT WAY

1

SUMMARIZING VASUBANDHU

Should a Buddhist Philosopher Have a Philosophy?

THIS BOOK is a study of the philosophical work of Vasubandhu, a fourth/fifth-century Indian monk who was perhaps the greatest Buddhist philosopher after the Buddha.[1] Vasubandhu's works are well known in Indian, Tibetan, and East Asian Buddhist traditions. From his time to this day, and without a break, his writings have been widely cited and commented upon, his arguments used and debated, and his accomplishments praised. He is a familiar figure in contemporary Buddhist studies as well. His works have been a constant topic of investigation and translation for more than a century—including being the subject of one of the signature accomplishments in the field, the copiously annotated French translation by Louis de La Vallée Poussin, from Xuanzang's Chinese translation of Vasubandhu's *Abhidharmakośabhāsya*, published between 1923 and 1931. Everyone knows Vasubandhu. What is remarkable, then, is that we do not, by now, know Vasubandhu very well.

We can list his attributed works, and recite his life story, but what exactly was his intellectual contribution? Unlike other Indian Buddhists of comparable stature—Nāgārjuna, Asaṅga, Dignāga, Dharmakīrti—he is uniquely difficult to provide with a tag line. The reason for this is that, as any student of Buddhism knows, Vasubandhu did not stick to one tradition. He was the greatest systematic thinker in the Yogācāra school of Mahāyāna thought, and he defended core Yogācāra doctrines with arguments that are still worth our consideration. Yet before that, he was the greatest advocate for the non-Mahāyāna, Sautrāntika interpretation of Abhidharma thought—a critic of extreme views advocated within the dominant non-Mahāyāna school of the time, the Kashmiri Vaibhāṣika. And even before that, he was the author of the most concise and comprehensive synthetic summary of the Vaibhāṣika tradition itself. Thus, he can be labeled with three distinct scholastic identities—Vaibhāṣika, Sautrāntika, and Yogācāra—none of which applies to the full body of his work. What's more, his contribution to each was unique.

The differences between the distinct scholastic identities represented in Vasubandhu's works are underlined in traditional versions of his biography extant in both Chinese and Tibetan.[2] Vasubandhu, we are told, was the younger half-brother of Asaṅga, the great founder of the Yogācāra school. Asaṅga had meditated for twelve years in a cave before receiving a vision of the future Buddha, Maitreya, and subsequently learning core Yogācāra treatises from Maitreya. Vasubandhu, for his part, is said to have had questions about the details of the Abhidharma traditions, and so he traveled from his place of birth—Gandhāra—to Kashmir, to study with the great Vaibhāṣika teachers there. After mastering the Vaibhāṣika tradition and, according to some accounts, alienating himself from his peers by his too-critical questioning, Vasubandhu returned home and began teaching the Vaibhāṣika tradition. By doing so, he was apparently violating declared Kashmiri intellectual property rights, but the treatise he was composing to accompany his teachings—the *Verses on the Treasury of Abhidharma* (*Abhidharmakośakārikā*, AKK)—was so masterly that, although composed illegally, it was too useful not to be adopted and commented upon.[3]

Yet Vasubandhu's own autocommentary, the *Commentary on the Treasury of Abhidharma* (*Abhidharmakośabhāṣya*, AKBh), was directly critical of numerous elements within the Vaibhāṣika system. To be fair, the AKBh is critical of everyone. Its single most sustained argument is in its last chapter, the "Refutation of the Self," in which the main opponent is not the Vaibhāṣika, but the Vātsīputrīya (*aka* Pudgalavādin), advocate of an ineffable, existent "person." This commentary takes off from the last verse of the AKK, and it may be read as though Vasubandhu, free of the requirement to stick to the Vaibhāṣika system adumbrated in the verses, is able to lay into his main rivals. Still, the majority of the work is a verse-by-verse commentary on the Vaibhāṣika system (sometimes term-by-term), and there are few stones left unturned. The commentary pits the Vaibhāṣika against a great many philosophical opponents, and the winners of the debates are not always clear. When they are clear, however, the victory often goes to a position named

"Sautrāntika"—"those who follow scripture"—which is why this commentary is said to belong to the Sautrāntika school. This is a problematic term, however, because it appears that Vasubandhu was the first to use it as it is used in the AKBh.

To return to the biographies, we see the Vaibhāṣikas of Kashmir expressing their renewed disgust toward Vasubandhu due to this commentary, even as Vasubandhu himself benefits from it by being made court instructor for a Gupta prince. At one point, the great Vaibhāṣika master Saṃghabhadra comes to Ayodhyā to debate him, but Vasubandhu refuses. Notice that the narrative of Vasubandhu's rivalry with his Vaibhāṣika peers and his covert composition of a critical commentary makes sense of the extremely unusual disjunction between the views of the AKK and the AKBh. I will discuss this further in the next chapter, but here we should at least note the characterization of Vasubandhu as two-faced even in his early period as a Śrāvaka (non-Mahāyāna) author.

Meanwhile, we are told, Asaṅga has grown old, and is afraid for his younger brother's future rebirths, given that Vasubandhu is a strident opponent of the Mahāyāna. Asaṅga sends Vasubandhu some Mahāyāna scriptures to study, and some of his own students to instruct him in them. It has the desired effect, and Vasubandhu adopts the Mahāyāna scriptures as legitimate, begins to comment upon them, and composes texts in the Mahāyāna tradition. Notice that this narrative accounts biographically for Vasubandhu's apparent textual transition from Sautrāntika to Yogācāra. Vasubandhu is moved by his brother's dying wish, and by the power of the Mahāyāna *sūtras* themselves, to relinquish his previous views and convert, becoming a vociferous advocate of Mahāyāna. While it is clear that Vasubandhu is said to follow his elder brother's instruction, let us note that Paramārtha's Chinese biography mentions Mahāyāna, but not Yogācāra, as Vasubandhu's final scholastic identity. There is strong reason to doubt that the term "Yogācāra" had its later, doxographic meaning—referring to a particular philosophical school—during Vasubandhu's time.

Nonetheless, with these narratives in hand, Buddhist scholastics have an account of three distinct doctrinal identities into which to ascribe Vasubandhu's diverse body of work. But once we are done explaining the three scholastic traditions in which he participated, there is nothing left to express as the intellectual identity of Vasubandhu himself, or the writings attributed to him. He is just a great scholar, who is able to master, and synthesize, everything he touches. His brilliance alone is what makes him great, as Paramārtha's biography states:

> The sense conveyed in his compositions is fine and excellent; there is no one who, on hearing or seeing it, does not believe and pursue it. Therefore all those who study the Mahāyāna and Hīnayāna in India and in all the frontier countries use the works of Vasubandhu as their textbooks.[4]

Presumably, the point is that those who study the Hīnayāna use Vasubandhu's Hīnayāna works, and those who study the Mahāyāna study his Mahāyāna works. This is the view implicit in the standard Tibetan doxographic categorization of Buddhist doctrine into four philosophical schools: three traditions represented by Vasubandhu's career, capped off by Nāgārjuna's Madhyamaka.[5] When you want to study Vaibhāṣika and Sautrāntika, you look to the AKK/AKBh. When you want to study Yogācāra, you look to Vasubandhu's Yogācāra works (along with those of Asaṅga, of course). This is a fulfillment of Paramārtha's claim that Vasubandhu made good textbooks for the study of each tradition.

As a summary of Vasubandhu's oeuvre, however, this is most unsatisfying. First of all, to suggest that Vasubandhu was merely setting out a doctrinal structure for easy digestion is to entirely ignore his unique contributions to each system, and his vibrant philosophical voice. Peter Skilling describes Vasubandhu's prose style as "confident and learned, replete with citations and allusions to canonical and other literature, and to the opinions of different teachers or schools."[6] We may add, as I will argue throughout this book, that Vasubandhu repeatedly displays a preference for certain specific patterns of argument, certain methodologies in the application of reason and scripture, and remarkably—given the diversity of the topics covered—certain epistemological and ontological claims. These patterns within Vasubandhu's works, I will argue, allow us a glimpse into what drives him as a thinker. Thus, whereas it is difficult to pin down Vasubandhu when we look at him from a doctrinal perspective, he is nonetheless readily identified by the light of his distinctive arguments.

What is missing, then, in the approach to Vasubandhu's texts that divides *his* identity into his texts' purported doxographic categories is an awareness of the continuity in Vasubandhu's philosophical methods, his implicit presuppositions, his argumentative style, his patterns of reasoning, and his uses of scriptural citation and hermeneutics.

When we seek this unity, we find that Vasubandhu's texts are not so easily divided into doctrinal categories after all. And perhaps this is as we should expect, since our best recent evidence is telling us that "Sautrāntika" was not definitively attested as a doctrinal school before Vasubandhu, and "Yogācāra" definitely postdated him. The present study emphasizes the evident continuity of interest and purpose across diverse works attributed to Vasubandhu, and paints a picture of a great thinker's central concerns and philosophical trajectory. It renews our understanding of Vasubandhu as one of the most important Buddhist philosophers of all time.

In the remainder of this chapter I will discuss the vexed question of whether there might be "two Vasubandhus," and describe in more detail the methodology of the present work. The second and third chapters provide fresh, close readings of several passages from Vasubandhu's AKBh. These careful readings are a workbook in Vasubandhu's views and approach, introducing the reader to his characteristic arguments related to causality, time, perception, conceptual construction, ethical responsibility, and the language of Buddhist scripture. It is hoped that, together, they will provide the reader with the skills to identify the distinctive flavor and direction of Vasubandhu's thought.[7] For it is in the next two chapters that these themes are reintroduced as they appear in Vasubandhu's "appearance only" (*vijñāptimātra*) works—chapter 4, focusing on epistemology and scriptural interpretation, and chapter 5, on perception and the nature of consciousness. These chapters argue that Vasubandhu's unique contributions to (what would later be called) Yogācāra enshrine, in a doctrinal system, his unique preoccupations and contributions to non-Mahāyāna Abhidharma. The central chapters of the book also emphasize the many ways in which Vasubandhu's arguments, and his purpose overall, are to be understood as serving a larger project of scriptural interpretation—a fact that is too rarely acknowledged and understood by modern interpreters of Buddhist philosophy. The final two chapters examine some of the significance of my characterization of Vasubandhu's views for Buddhist philosophy more widely construed. Chapter 6 draws upon Vasubandhu's view to clarify vexing issues in Buddhist ethics, in particular the nature of moral agency and the conundrum surrounding Buddhism's apparent disinterest in talk of justice. Finally, the conclusion works toward a more formal statement of this view, which I term "Buddhist Causal Framing," and shows how it may be deployed in arguments regarding idealism and the theorization of culture.

THE TWO VASUBANDHUS AND THE HERMENEUTIC CIRCLE

In 1951 Erich Frauwallner, the great scholar of Buddhism, published his famous article, "On the Date of the Buddhist Master of the Law Vasubandhu," in which he claimed that traditional biographies of Vasubandhu had combined two separate, significant individuals under one name. At the time, Frauwallner pointed out that sixty years had elapsed during which the dating of Vasubandhu, one of "the most discussed questions of the history of Indian literature and philosophy," had failed to settle upon a solution.[8] Although Frauwallner's thesis was intended to resolve the question once and for all, another sixty years has elapsed, and Vasubandhu's identity remains a point of disagreement (though it is perhaps no longer among the most discussed).

While I believe that Frauwallner's thesis has been discredited, it remains of great importance for the light it sheds on the history of the discipline, and, more narrowly, the question of how best to study Vasubandhu. When I tell colleagues in the field that I am writing about Vasubandhu, the question often arises, "Which Vasubandhu?" Sometimes the questioner is asking with sincerity, and sometimes with tongue in cheek. But any scholar hoping to write about "Vasubandhu" must either elect to focus on one or the other of the "Vasubandhus," or do battle with Frauwallner's long shadow. Since this book seeks unity across works attributed to Vasubandhu, I have no choice but the latter option.

I am, however, by no means a pioneer in opposition to the "two Vasubandhus" view. From the moment of its publication, Frauwallner's thesis was under fire. It has had its supporters, but almost immediately, the central significance of the argument—what it was proposed to solve—became difficult to sustain. Frauwallner had argued that the author of the AKK/AKBh was a different "Vasubandhu" from the brother of Asaṅga, and that Paramārtha (or Paramārtha's students) had combined two different life stories in his famous "Life of Vasubandhu."[9] The AKK/AKBh was composed later, Frauwallner said, by *another* Vasubandhu, in the century *after* the Vasubandhu who was Asaṅga's brother. The argument is a sophisticated one, and is primarily based upon a useful observation that Paramārtha's biography is written out of chronological order, in a way that makes it seem like the story of the author of the AKBh was cut and pasted into that of the brother of Asaṅga. As Frauwallner points out, the story of Asaṅga's brother seems also to have appeared elsewhere in Yogācāra circles *independently* of the story of the composition of the AKBh. Two separate narrative streams do seem to have been combined in Paramārtha's biography of Vasubandhu, and Frauwallner's thesis of Paramārtha's *error* accounts for this.[10]

Yet the critiques that have arisen in response to Frauwallner's famous thesis seem far more weighty than the problem of the combination of narratives. P. S. Jaini based his critique on a previously unstudied Sanskrit manuscript, the *Abhidharmadīpa* with its commentary, which includes critical references to the AKK/AKBh.[11] The author of this text criticizes the author of the AKBh for having adopted the Mahāyāna and the "Three Natures" view. Unless this evidence has been misread, it seems to justify Paramārtha's "combination" of the AKBh narrative with the Yogācāra identity associated with the brother of Asaṅga. In a subsequent publication, Frauwallner himself clarified his view to agree that the author of the AKBh certainly wrote *some* Yogācāra texts, but he held onto the two Vasubandhus view as a view of two individuals, *each of whom* started as a Vaibhāṣika and switched to Mahāyāna.[12]

It seems to me that the discussion might well have ended at this point.[13] It is difficult to see how the odd structure of Paramārtha's biography provides any bulwark against a strong textual tradition affirming that the author of the AKBh adopted Yogācāra later on. Even if Paramārtha is assumed to have combined stories about his subject from different sources, he is hardly the first biographer to have done so. What's more, the existence of distinct narratives that emphasize the AKBh and the Yogācāra identity, respectively, can easily be explained by the fact that Vasubandhu's works were, in fact—according to the received narrative—inherited and taught in distinct institutional lines.

In the subsequent decades, a number of authors have sought to counter Frauwallner's thesis—especially its initial version—by describing, sometimes in great detail, apparent continuities across Vasubandhu's works. Lambert Schmithausen argued that two Yogācāra works, the *Twenty Verses* (*Viṃśatikā*, Viṃś) and the *Thirty Verses* (*Triṃśikā*, Triṃś), showed sufficient continuity with the AKBh to be considered as participating in the "Sautrāntika presuppositions" (*Sautrāntika-Voraussetzungen*) of a single author.[14] Akira Hirakawa traced terminology and doctrinal structures from the AKBh to the Yogācāra works via intermediate texts such as the *Analysis Establishing Karma* (*Karmasiddhiprakaraṇa*, KSP) and the *Analysis of the Five Aggregates* (*Pañcaskandhaprakaraṇa*, PSP).[15] Stefan Anacker did the same with closer attention to lines of argument.[16] These are texts that clearly continue the analytical projects of the AKBh, but include, and entertain, terminology classically ascribed to the Yogācāra. Peter Skilling surveyed twelve texts attributed to Vasubandhu, arguing that they share sufficient stylistic commonalities and cross-references to be attributable to the same author.[17] A number of other scholars have done similar work in reconstituting Vasubandhu's oeuvre from various perspectives.[18] In the last decade, Robert Kritzer has advanced the continuity thesis to its extreme, arguing that the AKBh was written under a covert Yogācāra influence.[19] My own reading of Vasubandhu's continuity is influenced by these authors, whose arguments I find largely convincing.

Yet all the king's horsemen and all the king's men have yet to put Vasubandhu together again. Schmithausen still allows that Frauwallner's thesis of "two Vasubandhus" may apply to distinguish, not the author of the AKBh from the Viṃś and the Triṃś, but the commentaries on Maitreya texts. And Skilling sticks to his twelve texts, also refusing to commit on the Maitreya commentaries, the *sūtra* commentaries, and minor works. For his part, Jaini has not pushed the point any further than to say that the author of the AKBh must have written some Yogācāra works. Far from disproving the "two Vasubandhus" thesis, Jaini even went so far as to *affirm* his support for the view.[20] While I have no difficulty admitting that this or that text may be falsely attributed to Vasubandhu the author of the AKBh, we have yet to identify a text that is *legitimately* attributable to the "older" Vasubandhu.[21] Yet he lives on, hovering in the background, and like the ghost he is, scares away many who would otherwise approach a synthetic analysis of Vasubandhu's works.

The evidence that convinced Jaini was not Paramārtha's biography, but rather another point treated in Frauwallner's article: the fact that Yaśomitra, commentator on the AKBh, supposedly *made the distinction between two Vasubandhus himself*. Frauwallner cites a few, rare cases where Yaśomitra refers to *vṛddhācāryavasubandhu* and *sthaviraḥ vasubandhu*, which he says refers to "an older Vasubandhu."[22] As Anacker has argued, these titles could easily mean "eminent" rather than "old," and these passages may be read to foreground the AKBh author's own view amidst a diversity of cited options in a complex discussion.[23] Although I see no mystery here, and no need to accept that Yaśomitra knows of some "older" Vasubandhu, Anacker's analysis has not satisfied all sensitive readers.[24]

A more intricate knot is formed around a passage where Vasubandhu cites a particular approach to the *antarābhava*, the intermediary consciousness of a living being between death and rebirth, and attributes this approach to "*pūrvācāryāḥ*," which Frauwallner translates as "teachers of yore." Yaśomitra explains the phrase *pūrvācāryāḥ* with the gloss, "Yogācaras: Ārya Asaṅga, etc."[25] Based on this gloss, and another example of *pūrvācāryāḥ* used with reference to Asaṅga, Frauwallner concludes, "Asaṅga was therefore for [Yaśomitra] an old teacher in comparison with the author of the *Abhidharmakośa*" and that Yaśomitra believed that "Asaṅga belonged to a considerably earlier time than the author of the *Abhidharmakośa*."[26] Given that Asaṅga was, by traditional accounts, Vasubandhu's *older* brother, a great deal of unnecessary pressure is being put on the interpretation of the word *pūrva*, which means "previous." The passage does not necessarily justify the term "old" in "old teacher," but even if we take it that way, it could still refer to Vasubandhu's older brother. Thus, Frauwallner's "teachers of yore" for *pūrvācāryāḥ* is a selective translation that overstates his case. The phrase "a considerably earlier time" clinches the point, but only by inserting the word "considerably" without justification. Frauwallner's is a sensible reading, but it is only one interpretation. Since Frauwallner will claim to be engaging in a decidedly "scientific discussion" of the topic, let us note for the sake of clarity that no "scientific" method is proposed for determining *how long* before Vasubandhu's composition of the AKBh Yaśomitra intended the "previous" teacher Asaṅga to be stating the views in question. Yet it is upon the interpretation of Yaśomitra that the "two Vasubandhus" hypothesis stands.

Furthermore, Frauwallner mentions, and rejects, a moderating suggestion from Péri: the name Asaṅga might just have been used as an exemplification of "*yogācāra*," since Asaṅga was the most eminent teacher of the Yogācāra school. If Péri is right, "previous teachers" could include Asaṅga's Yogācāra teachers, who might be "older" still than Asaṅga, and thus much older than Vasubandhu. In response to this, Frauwallner writes, "To this we may oppose the fact that Asaṅga is the founder of the Yogācāra school."[27] If we define the Yogācāra tradition as that which stems from Asaṅga's *Yogācārabhūmi*, this "fact" will stand. We may even wish to agree that to identify Maitreya as the source of the school's teachings is a pious fiction. But the question at issue is what Yaśomitra thought Vasubandhu meant by "previous teachers." What is the evidence that Vasubandhu, or Yaśomitra, thought that Asaṅga invented his own view, and had no teachers? Given that the accepted narrative of the founding of the school includes Maitreya's revelations, the scholarly community's assessment of "fact" tells us nothing about what Yaśomitra believed, let alone what he thought Vasubandhu believed.

We might add, as a bit of helpful context, that *every* traditional Buddhist author claims to be passing on inherited teachings. I know of no evidence that Yaśomitra thought Vasubandhu thought Asaṅga had violated this norm. It would, absurdly, follow from Frauwallner's reading that Yaśomitra must think that Vasubandhu thinks that *Asaṅga himself* made up the particular interpretation of *antarābhava* at issue in the passage in question. Even if the Yogācāra school can be traced back to Asaṅga, the views of the *Yogācārabhūmi* did not appear out of thin air.[28] That every author is embedded within his or her context is a "fact" that is implicit in Buddhist doctrine, and that Vasubandhu never forgets.

Furthermore, as it stands, there is no reason to think of a "Yogācāra school" as a "fact" at all during Vasubandhu's time—and this would apply to *any* Vasubandhu. Vasubandhu uses the term *yogācāra* (lit. "practitioner of yoga") in only two instances in the AKBh, and in both cases he is clearly referring to practitioners of yogic meditative exercises, *not* to any philosophical school.[29] This textual fact alone suggests to me that Vasubandhu's AKBh was most likely written before Asaṅga's magnum opus, the *Yogācārabhūmi*, had had time to calcify into the name of a doctrinal school. The fact that Yaśomitra uses the name "Yogācāra" places *him* at a temporal distance after Asaṅga—a distance that is not evident in the AKBh.

If we return to Paramārtha's text, then, under the assumptions of Frauwallner's reading of Yaśomitra—if we ascend to the next round in the hermeneutic circle—we find a contradiction far more puzzling than the question of how to translate *pūrvācāryāḥ*. The AKBh is full of specific names for authors and viewpoints. If it was written a century after the *Yogācārabhūmi*, the flagship treatise of the Yogācāra school, *why didn't Vasubandhu use the term* Yogācāra *when referring to this tradition's views*? Perhaps even more confounding is the same point asked in reverse: why was Vasubandhu comfortable using the term *yogācāra* to refer to a practitioner of yoga, without evincing any concern that it might imply some scholastic identity? In addition, Frauwallner mentions in a note that Haribhadra, still later than Yaśomitra, includes *both* Asaṅga *and* Vasubandhu as *pūrvācāryāḥ* in the Yogācāra. If Yaśomitra knows that the AKBh was written long after the "Vasubandhu" who was a "teacher of yore" of the Yogācāra, why, we may sensibly ask, didn't Yaśomitra include the *vṛddhācāryavasubandhu* in *his* gloss as well? These questions dissolve if we assume that there was one Vasubandhu, who was composing the AKBh at a time when the independent "school" of Yogācāra was still in the process of formation (i.e., the time of Asaṅga).

What would also require explanation, if Yaśomitra were clearly suggesting that there were two Vasubandhus, is the complete and utter lack of awareness of any important "elder Vasubandhu," before the time of the AKBh, in the history of Buddhism, given that so many thousands of eminent scholars of Sanskrit, traditional and modern (to say nothing of Tibetans) have studied Yaśomitra's commentary in the around fifteen centuries since its composition. I do not mean to suggest that there are no systematic misinterpretations of texts. Rather, I wish to call our attention to the fact that these passages, if they *seem to clearly evince another Vasubandhu*, only do so according to a newly imposed set of framing presuppositions. My point is not that every impartial observer would deny Frauwallner's reading; it is that Frauwallner's claim that his own view is one "impartially considered"—and that any similarly impartial reader would be "confronted with the fact" of Yaśomitra's distinction between two different Vasubandhus—is mistaken. We are all conditioned by our interpretive presuppositions. The solution, to the degree that we have one, is to continually test our views for their adequacy to the fullness of the evidence, and to avoid placing too much weight on any given interpretation.

After all of this, though, there is, in fact, a rather elegant solution to the nagging suggestion that Yaśomitra may still be referring to an "elder Vasubandhu." Paramārtha's biography tells not only of Vasubandhu, the main subject, but also of Vasubandhu's two brothers. Before giving the names, though, Paramārtha writes of their shared father, a Brāhman named Kauśika:

> He had three sons, all named Vasubandhu; Vasu means "god" and Bandhu means "kinsman." In India this custom obtains in the naming of children. Though they call all by one and the same name, they, nevertheless, give different epithets in order to distinguish one from the other.[30]

The three children had different mothers, but shared this father, *and the name Vasubandhu*. Paramārtha gives alternate names for the other two brothers: the youngest is called Viriñcivatsa (child of Viriñci, his mother), and the eldest is called Asaṅga. Only the middle son goes by their shared name, Vasubandhu, which means "good kin." So perhaps when Yaśomitra refers to the "elder Vasubandhu," he means Asaṅga. Perhaps, then, we should seek the "elder Vasubandhu's" views in the *Yogācārabhūmi*, and other works of Asaṅga. Still, since the narrative of Asaṅga's life includes a long period of study with the Sarvāstivāda, and mastery of "Hīnayāna," we do not need to be disappointed if we do not find those views there.[31] In fact, by the time Yaśomitra was writing, even Viriñcivatsa would have been an "old" Vasubandhu, and he, too, was a Sarvāstivāda *arhat*. We have, then, *three* Vasubandhus already attested. There is no need to create further mystery by adding a fourth.

ADMITTING THE FALLIBILITY OF THE FRAME

Although I have a strong view about the "two Vasubandhus" hypothesis, then, my goal here is not to defeat it as much as to defeat the hermeneutic methods that support it, and that it promotes. In particular, I'd like to counter the air of scientific objectivity that bolsters the argument on the one side, and closes off alternatives on the other. The historical analysis of medieval texts is an interpretive practice, which requires that we enter the hermeneutic circle—we must admit that our assumptions shape our conceptions, and we may move by degrees toward a more adequate truth, but we are fooling ourselves if we imagine that we have adopted the perspective of absolute objectivity.[32] Given that there is a necessarily subjective element in all interpretation, our search for greater objectivity requires that we pay close attention to the work that is being accomplished by our background assumptions and our interpretive tools. In particular, we are endangering our objectivity when the frame of reference itself appropriates the work of interpretation. When we hold such considerations in mind, the two Vasubandhus thesis reveals itself as a neat but untrustworthy explanatory device. Because of its conceptual structure, it appears as justified based upon too little evidence, and, once in place, it feeds itself on unresolved complexities. It is, in this way, not entirely unlike a conspiracy theory.

The dating of Vasubandhu has been a complex and difficult task for scholars, for reasons that are well attested in Frauwallner's article. A half-century elapsed between Vasubandhu's death and the composition of his first extant biography. That biography was composed in China—or, at least, it is extant only in Chinese—so the distortions attending the composition of hagiographies in India are joined with those attending translations or transitions from Indian languages to Chinese, and from Indic to Chinese culture. The dates for Vasubandhu's birth given in different Chinese biographical accounts differ among themselves. The years 900,

1000, and 1100 after the Buddha's *nirvāṇa* all appear. These may represent different calculations of the date of this event, but even so there is no way to square them. As of Frauwallner's writing, there were two major theses regarding Vasubandhu's dating; these placed him, respectively, in the fourth and in the fifth century. A wide range of minor pieces of evidence was called to account on each side. The major problem for each view was how to account for the evidence adduced by its opponents. The "two Vasubandhus" thesis, conveniently (I am saying too conveniently), represents a fiat that accounts for all of the evidence.[33]

Once the basic argument is in place, Frauwallner's article runs through a variety of problems that are, to his lights, solved by the assumption of two Vasubandhus. One I have already mentioned is the fact that Yogācāra sources tell the life story of the first Vasubandhu (the brother of Asaṅga), *without* the section on the composition of the AKBh. Frauwallner takes it that this is explained by the fact that it is simply the story of the earlier Vasubandhu, not the later. At first glance, this explanation proves satisfying. But as soon as we return to the Vasubandhu narratives passed on by Yogācāra teachers, and attempt to delve deeper into the meaning of these stories, making use of the frame of Frauwallner's new assumptions, we find a host of new interpretive problems. For example, the life story of the brother of Asaṅga always includes the famous event of Vasubandhu's conversion from Hīnayāna to Mahāyāna—it would have to, because that is what happens to Vasubandhu in connection with Asaṅga. The problem, then, is who Vasubandhu was *before* he converted, if he was not the great author of the AKBh.

Inconveniently, the Yogācāra sources are unanimous in expressing his prolific abundance. Vasubandhu is said in one tradition to have composed a work called *Abhidharmasāra* in six thousand verses, and according to another to have written "500 Hīnayāna works" before converting and writing his "500 Mahāyāna works."[34] Recall that the central purpose of Frauwallner's article is to prove that this story is *not* about the author of the AKK/AKBh. Frauwallner knows that the *Abhidharmasāra* itself is the name given for a text attributed to Dharmaśrī, which was a *major source* for the AKK/AKBh.[35] Is it not at least worth considering that this *Abhidharmasāra* with six thousand verses could be taken as a mistaken transposition of the *Abhidharmakośa*, famed for its six hundred verses?[36] If not, one would at least expect some explanation as to *why not*. And, what happened to those five hundred Hīnayāna works (that are *not* the AKBh or its relatives) attributed to this earlier Vasubandhu? When

Frauwallner notes, as explanation, that the Yogācāra author tells us that the Hīnayāna works have been forgotten, we may be justified in wondering what has happened to his "scientific" critical perspective. Of course the Yogācāra authors wish to supplant Vasubandhu's Hīnayāna identity with his Mahāyāna one. But even they admit a vast corpus of material; is it "objective" to accept their narrative as is? Should we trust the Yogācāra authors when they tell us that the great mass of non-Mahāyāna works of this influential author have simply been forgotten?

The central hermeneutic criterion, which I would advocate to avoid this kind of problem, then, is an ongoing, increasing depth of interpretation. There is a surface-level, technical sensibleness to Frauwallner's position—that the five hundred Hīnayāna works are lost, and *Abhidharmasāra* is a name different from *Abhidharmakośa*. Yet in order to accept such a view we must forego a deeper reading of the very texts we are claiming to interpret. The dramatic character of Vasubandhu's conversion, which is central to all of the narratives, is based upon his prior accomplishment as a non-Mahāyāna scholar. If the earlier Vasubandhu *didn't write the AKBh*, then he is not a known, let alone an important, non-Mahāyāna scholar. According to the evidence of Frauwallner's paper, the only non-Mahāyāna accomplishment we know of for this earlier Vasubandhu was that he agreed with the author of the AKBh about three or four points cited by Yaśomitra. The point is that the conversion narrative *itself* clearly unites the AKBh with the Yogācāra texts. It is only the adoption of a lens that seeks to split the evidence in every case that would prevent such a reading from rising to the surface.[37]

The influence of background assumptions shows itself further in how Frauwallner evaluates the significance of particular pieces of evidence. Paramārtha says that Vasubandhu, the author of the AKBh, taught the son, called Balāditya, of one king Vikramāditya. The identification of these kings is crucial to Frauwallner's argument, since we have a fairly good sense of the dating of the Gupta kings. If early Gupta kings can be found to match these names, then this attribution would place the author of the AKBh in the earlier period, the time of the brother of Asaṅga. But these names appear, for Frauwallner, as solid evidence connecting Vasubandhu the author of the AKBh with two *later* figures in the Gupta royal line, properly ordered, and known to be so named: Skandagupta and his nephew Narasiṃhagupta. While other scholars have noted that we know of another Vikramāditya, and hypothesized that other, earlier Gupta rulers might also have been called Balāditya in their youth, Frauwallner cites scientific authority to preclude such assumptions: "A scientific discussion cannot base itself on what name could have been borne by a king, but it must find out who actually bore it."[38]

Of course, assumptions can be dangerous, and all will agree that we should not place too much weight on any given assumption. Yet this very strident comment appears only one paragraph after Frauwallner's claim that "no difficulty is presented" to his interpretation by the admitted fact that there was, in truth, no direct succession from Skandagupta to Narasiṃhagupta, as his interpretation of Paramārtha's text should require. For, he says, the intervening reign of Puragupta Prakāśāditya was so short as to "easily have been forgotten after 50 years," when Paramārtha would have recorded the story. Science allows the assumption that our main authoritative source is wrong in just this way about the line of succession, but does not allow the assumption that we may be missing a name for one of the kings? This is selective leniency, affirmed under a cloak of scientific objectivity. Once we admit that the text's transmission of the royal successions is imperfect, there arise numerous potential explanations of the evidence due to "forgettings"; perhaps the compiler of the biography knew that Vasubandhu taught the son of Vikramāditya, and asked his companion, "Who was it who succeeded Vikramāditya, again?"—and his companion gave him a name for the successor of the wrong Vikramāditya. In such a reading, we end up thinking there are two Vasubandhus because there were two Vikramādityas, and Vasubandhu worked for one of them. I am not saying that this necessarily happened, but it seems just as likely as the specific forgetting that is necessary for Frauwallner's argument.

Later, Frauwallner proposes "another fact which goes against a connection between Vasubandhu and the earlier Gupta rulers," which is that Paramārtha refers to the Gupta capital city as Ayodhyā, whereas the capital at the earlier time might well have been Pāṭaliputra. Frauwallner's account of the dating of the Gupta capitals is by no means certain, and even if it were, couldn't this, too, have been "forgotten" after fifty years—or lost track of in Paramārtha's account? Such evidence is ambiguous. Why not admit that it is ambiguous? There seems to be a disconcerting pattern of claiming "science" when one's own evidence reflects a particular kind of precision—this king was *definitely* named "Balāditya" whereas we're not sure about the other king—and claiming "fact" when there is ambiguity, but only for favorable positions.

Perhaps the most convincing piece of evidence for the early composition of the AKBh, and the most damning expression of Frauwallner's bias, is a verse from the *Kāvyālaṃkāravṛtti* by the grammarian and poetics scholar Vāmana. Vāmana adduces a verse with the phrase "refuge of the wise" (*āśrayaḥ kṛtadhiyām*) referring to "Candragupta's son," as a poetic example of "special intention," or, in Frauwallner's translation, "covert allusion" (*abhiprāya*).[39] The allusion here, Vāmana says, is to Vasubandhu's ministership. The wise one ministering to the son of Candragupta is Vasubandhu. This is clearly saying, from a source outside the lines of Vasubandhu's heirs, that Vasubandhu taught the son of one Candragupta. Unfortunately, since Frauwallner entertains this piece of evidence only *after* he has already concluded that Paramārtha *must* be referring to the kings Skandagupta and Narasiṃhagupta, he says that Vāmana is *in contradiction to* Paramārtha. But surely the goal should be to make the best sense of all of the evidence. It may be that if Vāmana is accepted as evidence, this will require us to go back to the drawing board with our interpretation of Paramārtha. But that difficulty does not mean that it is one or the other.

Nonetheless, Frauwallner pits the evidence from Vāmana against the evidence from Paramārtha, and he proposes two reasons, and a rule of "sound criticism," to prefer Paramārtha over Vāmana. First, he points out that Paramārtha is earlier than Vāmana, by some two hundred fifty years, though the verse upon which Vāmana comments is, he admits, possibly earlier than Paramārtha. Then, he provides an analysis of the general trustworthiness of each text's historical evidence:

> Vasubandhu stands for Paramārtha at the centre of his interest; it is his life, about which he writes. Vāmana writes a manual of poetics, in which he inserts an occasional remark on Vasubandhu, the origin of which remains unknown. We know very well what we should expect from Indian commentators in such cases. Now and then some valuable tradition, but side to side with it the worst examples of superficiality and often the purest nonsense. Under such circumstances we are compelled to say, that according to the rules of sound criticism the authority of Vāmana has no weight at all in comparison to Paramārtha's.[40]

Here Frauwallner's self-contradiction rises to the surface. He admits the possibility of "now and then some valuable tradition" accompanying a verse, which in this case affirms the possibility that Vāmana's reading represents a genuine interpretive tradition reaching back to the time of the Gupta succession in question. Yet this acknowledged possibility is not pursued. But why not? It is clearly not "purest nonsense." What evidence is there that Vāmana, court poet to the eighth-century Kashmiri king Jayāpīḍa, would have chosen a random, "superficial" name as comment to a verse about the education of princes? At the very least, we have with Vāmana a translocal, Indian, courtly affirmation of Vasubandhu's role at the court of someone named "Candragupta." Quite possibly, we have a continuous line of commentary extending back to Candragupta's time. The fact that such a reading *correlates* with Paramārtha's contention that Vasubandhu was court-appointed instructor for a Gupta prince ought to *confirm* the substance of this comment. In such a light it becomes an extremely powerful piece of evidence.

Yet such a confirmation is unavailable, when to confirm the verse would be to contradict details already decided about Paramārtha's history, of which it has already been said that "we may trust in it a high degree, since Paramārtha, according to the results reached up to this point, was separated from Vasubandhu the younger by a comparatively small space of time."[41] In combination with an unjustified tarring of the historical utility of Indian commentarial traditions, this authorization of Paramārtha is leveraged to invalidate Vāmana's comment. Apparently, excepting where it skips one king in a line of succession and, of course, where it unifies two Vasubandhus into one, Paramārtha's history is deemed trustworthy, even to the point that it may be used to thoroughly disqualify otherwise solid counterevidence. Yet, in truth, the thinnest thread distinguishes Paramārtha from Vāmana—the "unscientific" possibility that the name Balāditya might have been used to refer to one of Candragupta's sons.[42] Lacking such evidence of any given son of a king having been called Balāditya, and given that Paramārtha's *purpose* is to write about Vasubandhu, and not about a whole bunch of verses, "the authority of Vāmana has no weight at all in comparison to Paramārtha's." I find it extremely strange that Frauwallner takes it as significant support of the objective quality of Paramārtha as a historical source, that "Vasubandhu stands for Paramārtha at the centre of his interest."[43] The "rules of sound criticism" and "scientific discussion" here are called upon to justify, above all, the linear construction of the argument: first, validate Paramārtha, then use Paramārtha to invalidate Vāmana. A properly circular hermeneutic would double back and engage the possibility of a correlation between Vāmana and Paramārtha.

Anacker advocates the suggestion, from Le Manh That, that the title "Balāditya" was likely not a name for a particular king, but rather a title attributed to a crown prince who has been granted partial empowerment before his father's death and his full ascension to power.[44] This possibility would allow us to read Vāmana's verse and Paramārtha's text as both legitimately referring to Candragupta II, who was famously known as Vikramāditya, and most likely his son Govindagupta. Anacker's thesis nicely solves the Ayodhyā problem as well, but there is no need to rehash that argument here. Florin Deleanu, more recently, has followed up on these arguments and found them somewhat wanting in certainty—but without dismissing them entirely. He provides another series of conjectures that might work as "very fragile missing links" establishing the earlier dating for king Balāditya.[45] Many of the pieces fall into place if we accept, with Deleanu, a dating of around 350–430 CE. Not everything. But notice that we do not need certainty to escape from the "two Vasubandhus" hypothesis; it was certainty that was keeping us trapped within it. With our net less tightly woven, we can cast it more widely, and seek out Vasubandhu, the author, wherever he may range.

VASUBANDHU THE UNIFIER

The "two Vasubandhus" hypothesis that split the works attributed to Vasubandhu between an "elder" Vasubandhu the Yogācārin and a "younger" Vasubandhu who wrote the AKBh, rested from the start on a biased, shaky historical foundation. Once there is acknowledged to be one Vasubandhu who was a brother of Asaṅga, composed the AKBh, converted to Mahāyāna, and composed Yogācāra treatises that prominently advocate the Three Natures—as Jaini showed in 1958—there is very little explanatory power left for the "two Vasubandhus" thesis. There is no longer any biographical detail that is specifically relevant to the "other" Vasubandhu. He is just a catchall, a basket toward which we can throw dubiously attributed texts. But even to call that basket "Vasubandhu" is itself a dubious attribution. For the idea of a "second" Vasubandhu is only a conceptual construction based upon confusion about dates. There could, of course, be many misattributed texts in the received canons; but I see no reason to presume the existence of any unified identity properly called "Vasubandhu" aside from Vasubandhu and his two brothers, Asaṅga and Viriñcivatsa.

The "two Vasubandhus" view's vestigial survival, then, must be attributed to some degree to the resonant authority of its author, and to its comforting utility as a hermeneutic structure. Frauwallner surely deserves his scholarly reputation, but this hermeneutic is undeservedly satisfying and self-justifying. No doubt unintentionally, the view echoes the traditional Buddhist doctrinal compartmentalization of Vasubandhu's works. Ironically, the "two Vasubandhus" thesis, while galling to scholastically trained Buddhist intellectuals, confirms their traditional doxographic categorization, according to which Vasubandhu is declared to have switched sides. Both approaches to Vasubandhu's works reify the apparent divide between the text traditions of the "Sautrāntika" and the "Yogācāra" attributed to him, and both positions explain why Vasubandhu may have been separately valorized by Abhidharma and Yogācāra followers, respectively. Yet this parallel must itself be acknowledged as a methodological red flag.[46]

The scholars whose work upon which I am building here have undermined the strict division between Vasubandhu's traditional doxographic identities. Traditionally, Vasubandhu was a Sarvāstivādin, then a Sautrāntika, then a Yogācāra. But there is no easy classificatory category, for instance, for the KSP; must we call it "Yogācāra" and not "Sautrāntika" just because it includes mention of the "storehouse consciousness" (*ālayavijñāna*)? To do so is anachronistic, as anyone will admit, since during Vasubandhu's time, as I have said, the word "Yogācāra" had not yet taken on its distinctive scholastic meaning. It may be said that, though Vasubandhu never used the term to name his own view, he was a crucial player in the *formation* of what we now call Yogācāra scholasticism. So there is reason to take it as proto-Yogācāra. Yet I believe it is a mistake to set up a teleological directionality for Vasubandhu's works, with the Yogācāra system as its ultimate end. The Yogācāra is surely where his doctrinal work culminates, but his own approach and vision *within* Yogācāra was itself a unique expression of his core values and philosophical interests. There is no satisfactory doctrinal category for Vasubandhu's view, because his ideas cut across, and against, doctrinal identities. Even the AKBh, whose core philosophical position may safely be labeled "Sautrāntika," collects within it countless alternative viewpoints, only some of which are refuted. When we wish to characterize his view, we must call it *Vasubandhu's* Sautrāntika, or *Vasubandhu's* Yogācāra, so as to distinguish it from standard doxographic identities. But given the continuities, let us just call the view "Vasubandhu's."

The goal of this book is, therefore, to set aside doctrinal identities as much as possible, and delve deeply into textual interpretations—to translate and explain the meaning and the core philosophical motivations within works attributed to Vasubandhu. Through this method, it is possible to draw a coherent picture of the broad conceptual structures that underlie Vasubandhu's work as a whole. As I hope to show, it is extremely fruitful to read Vasubandhu's texts *together*, *intertextually*, for their common methods and goals. What they share, it turns out, is a unifying vision that fits a Yogācāra conceptual structure, but is not exclusively associated with *any* individual doxographic category. I take it that there is enough evidence of continuity among Vasubandhu's works that we should no longer expect to draw a stark line between the non-Mahāyāna views espoused in the AKBh and the ostensibly Mahāyāna perspective taken in Vasubandhu's later, explicitly Yogācāra works. On the contrary, we are now authorized, even challenged, to explore philosophical continuities across works previously divided by Vasubandhu's supposed "conversion" to Yogācāra, or his split in identities between "two Vasubandhus." For my part, I believe that Vasubandhu's thinking partakes of, but exceeds, the many traditions in which he played a part, like a flood that overflows the banks of many rivers, coursing over them all. In spite of the intricate specificity of each of his writings, he presents, altogether, a broad mainstream of Indian Buddhist thought.

Finally, this is our best explanation for the complexity of the inherited traditions, and for why no later school adopts Vasubandhu in his entirety. In a sense, Vasubandhu changed his mind, and his stripes, affiliating with one, then another, doctrinal perspective. But during his time these doctrinal identities were not as fixed as they became later on. Perhaps because of his having shifted allegiances and topics, each tradition in which he partook was to see him not just as a great contributor—in fact, their greatest philosophical synthesizer—but also as a renegade, if not a two-faced spy. Each tradition saw its own "two Vasubandhus"—the one that displayed to other Buddhists the radiant quintessence of their position, and the one that betrayed their unique greatness by treating others the same. Vasubandhu's view is a Buddhism that attempts to unite all Buddhists; the very name shared by the three brothers—one a Sarvāstivāda *arhat*, one a Mahāyāna saint, and one who seeks, by appeal to the *sūtras* (Sautrāntika), to unite them—expresses the ideal unity of these "good kin" (*vasubandhu*).[47]

In payment for the arrogance of attempting such a reconciliation, Vasubandhu's very identity has been divided. In spite of Vasubandhu's efforts to cut across schools and scriptural types to unify Buddhist traditions, then, and although Vasubandhu's works and his conceptual structures became a crucial, accepted foundation for Buddhist intellectual work for the next millennium in India, the traditions that he sought to unite were not able to set aside their differences. Of course, this sad condition should not surprise us, and it would hardly have surprised Vasubandhu. He repeatedly articulated the view from the *Scripture on the Clarification of the Intent* (*Saṃdhinirmocanasūtra*, SNS) that equates disputation with the conventional realm—for all views are one-sided and biased. If ever we find ourselves capable of setting aside our differences and accepting the true, ultimate unity behind our disputations, we will know that we have attained the awareness of the Buddhas. But that goal, we can be sure, remains distant.

2

AGAINST THE TIMES

Vasubandhu's Critique of His Main Abhidharma Rivals

Vasubandhu's most important philosophical work by far is his *Commentary on the Treasury of Abhidharma* (*Abhidharmakośabhāṣya*, hereafter AKBh). The careful elucidation of arguments in this text will occupy us in this and the next chapter. As I have discussed in the introduction, I personally do not distinguish the authorship of the verses from that of the commentary, and I will argue, furthermore, that many other works attributed to Vasubandhu show consistency of purpose with these texts.[1] For now, however, let us set aside all considerations of authorship and simply identify the name "Vasubandhu" with the author of the AKBh. In this chapter and the next, my goal is to characterize Vasubandhu's philosophy as expressed in the AKBh by reading his arguments closely. Once we have built an understanding of these views, we will be in a position to discuss how they may have been extended across other works attributed to Vasubandhu.

By Vasubandhu's time, Abhidharma was a well-established genre of Buddhist philosophical and doctrinal analysis, with clearly agreed upon norms and goals. At its root, Abhidharma is intended to draw upon, and reason with, the Buddha's teachings in order to shape a coherent, comprehensive account of the basic, elemental truths of reality. Abhidharma thus deals with every issue of interest to Buddhists, from the nature of the universe and the workings of *karma* to the logistics of the path and the attainment of Buddhahood. Buddhists term the Buddha's teachings the *dharma*, and so the correct analysis of just what is meant in the Buddha's teachings is called the "higher" (*abhi-*) teachings, the teachings as understood by learned people, the "Abhidharma."

The Abhidharma traditions seem to have developed out of a desire, among Buddhist teachers, to coordinate and classify the many terminological lists that appear in the Buddha's teachings.[2] For instance, Abhidharma is centrally concerned with problems such as how to correlate the five aggregates (*skandha*), the twelve sense bases (*āyatana*), and the twelve links of dependent origination (*pratītyasamutpāda*). Over the centuries, however, much of Abhidharma discussion coalesced around the same problematic issues that have concerned every sustained, philosophical attempt to account for human experience: the nature of the person and the mind, time and causality, how perception works, how language works, what happens at and after death, the reality of God and gods, good and evil, and so on.

In Abhidharma, however, based as it is upon the coordination of terminological lists, these issues arise out of asking: *Which elements are the most basic, and how do they account for the rest?* The word *dharma* is therefore used not only as a term for the highest truth of the Buddha's teachings, but also as a term for the *most basic elements of reality*, whatever they turn out to be. After all, the Buddha said that not only is the *dharma* true, but also, whatever is true is the *dharma*.[3] So, for Abhidharma philosophers the *real* truth is not the words the Buddha spoke, per se, but the real entities that exist in the world, which are sometimes expressed in the Buddha's words, and sometimes only implied by them.[4] The majority of Abhidharma argumentation, then, questions the reality and the functionality of specific *dharmas*, the basic elements out of which everything in experience is composed. For this reason, what might appear to be mere terminological quibbles are always also at the same time both scriptural interpretation and basic philosophy. To debate whether the term "arising" refers to a real *dharma* in the Buddha's words "the arising, etc., of conditioned things is discriminated"[5] is to engage in a basic philosophical argument over the nature of causality and its representation in the language of scripture.

In line with the foregoing, Vasubandhu defines Abhidharma in the AKBh in three distinct ways.[6] First, he says that *abhidharma* refers to flawless discrimination (*prajñā*), which he glosses as correct analytical knowledge of the *dharmas* (knowing which elements belong to which categories, and so on).[7] This, he says, is the ultimate (*paramārthika*) meaning of *abhidharma*. Second, he explains the conventional (*sāṃketika*) meaning, which is similar to the first except flawed, or in a text. We ordinarily take the Abhidharma texts, and our limited understanding of them, to be *abhidharma*, but really these only help to produce within us the wisdom that is the true discernment of all *dharmas*. Third, and last, he gives an etymological gloss on the term: *abhi-* can mean "toward," so this is analysis focused "toward" the correct discernment of *dharmas*, or, which is the same, toward *nirvāṇa*. Understanding things correctly leads, eventually, to liberation. Failing to understand, prevents it. Vasubandhu's *Treasury of Abhidharma* therefore claims to synthesize all that is, and must be known, about the basic elements of reality if one is to attain the Buddhist goal of liberation from suffering.

The verses of the text (AKK) present this comprehensive analysis from the perspective of the Kashmiri Vaibhāṣika school. And, Vasubandhu's commentary on the AKK, that is, the AKBh, claims to have for the most part (*prāyeṇa*) explained the Vaibhāṣika position articulated in the root verses.[8] But it is an extremely unusual specimen of the *bhāṣya* style of Sanskrit commentary.[9] Like other such commentaries, it goes beyond simply glossing the terms of the root text, and elucidates their meanings and implications as well. It is not unusual in a *bhāṣya* to find the commentator explaining a single verse in great detail over many pages, and here Vasubandhu follows the norm. In addition, it is standard for a *bhāṣya* to entertain an objection, called a *pūrvapakṣa*, and effectively stage a debate over the established position of the root text, called the *siddhānta*. Sometimes more than one *pūrvapakṣa* enters the fray, and the commentator's job is to adjudicate among the many objections and settle the established view, the *siddhānta*. The purpose is apparently as a guide to topics in debate; one can imagine teachers within a given school using such a text to develop their students' abilities to understand, and defend, their intellectual tradition.[10]

Vasubandhu's *bhāṣya* certainly entertains objections and stages debates. But what distinguishes his commentary is that the *siddhānta* position from the root verses quite often appears to *lose* the debate. Even when the *siddhānta* is restated as though proven at the end of a given line of argument, the best arguments with unmet objections have often been those put forward as a *pūrvapakṣa*.[11] This kind of text would arm students with arguments against their professors. One can understand why, according to Paramārtha's biography, the Vaibhāṣika teachers were upset by the commentary.[12]

Furthermore, as I hope to show in this and the next chapter, the winning arguments in the commentary are not simply disjointed criticisms. They are connected with one another by parallel lines of argument and cross-references, and together they form a coherent, integrated view. There seems, then, to be a philosophical purpose behind the AKBh, which is clearly not simply to illuminate the view in the verses, although neither is it simply to critique and destroy the views within them. That is, the AKBh is not simply an anti-Vaibhāṣika commentary, nor is it a Vaibhāṣika presentation that seeks to damage and eliminate select aspects of the tradition. Rather, it establishes an alternative worldview. It is generally said that Vasubandhu's verses in the AKK summarize the Vaibhāṣika view, whereas the commentary advocates the view of the Sautrāntika. As we will see below, Vasubandhu uses the term "Sautrāntika" to name what seems to be his own view. Still, it should be noted that what Vasubandhu calls "Sautrāntika" may be different from other so-called Sautrāntika positions articulated in other texts.[13] My goal in this chapter is to explain only Vasubandhu's view in the AKBh, not this text's relation to other texts that articulate views named "Sautrāntika." Given the strong possibility that Vasubandhu initiated this term, which subsequently took on a life of its own, I am inclined not to rely upon later summaries and commentaries to understand his own articulation of this view.[14]

In this chapter and the next, then, we will see Vasubandhu establish his own perspective, in contradistinction to the Vaibhāṣika: first, in response to their presentation of the nature of time (in this chapter); and then, of causality (in the next chapter). These issues are interrelated, and they draw together nearly every other major issue of philosophical interest in the AKBh. My goal in presenting these passages, then, is to introduce Vasubandhu's worldview, and at the same time to display the integrated nature of his analyses. These passages will allow us to build a familiarity with Vasubandhu's characteristic lines of argument, his conceptual matrices, and his style. Furthermore, time and causality in the AKBh are central topics that will allow us to develop an interpretive framework for Vasubandhu's oeuvre as a whole.

VASUBANDHU'S SUMMARY OF THE EXISTENCE OF THE THREE TIMES (AKK V.25–27)

Three verses from AKK book V, with their commentary, provide a useful entry into some of the most important core doctrines of Vasubandhu's philosophy. The verses are the launching point for the most extensive commentarial flight in book V—a book in which Vasubandhu tends to stay rather close to the root verses. It is in this passage that Vasubandhu most explicitly names, classifies, and rejects his main adversaries' defining position, their "saying that everything exists"—a literal translation of Sarvāstivāda. "Sarvāstivāda" names the view that things "exist" (*asti*) in "all" (*sarva*) of the three times—the past, the present, and the future.[15] Vasubandhu uses a variety of arguments to defeat this view and establish instead that things exist only in the present—or, to be more precise, that existing and being present are equivalent. While his position is itself significant (especially for its illumination of the doctrine of momentariness), these arguments resonate with, and refer to, a great many important points treated elsewhere, often repeatedly, in the AKBh. I will therefore use this passage here to establish a basic grounding in Vasubandhu's thought, and later as a jumping-off point for other analyses.

The verse text here is characteristically terse, but not (as sometimes) thoroughly unreadable without the commentary.[16] In the first two of the three verses, Vasubandhu names four justifications for the Sarvāstivāda belief in the existence of the three times (V.25). Then, he lists four separate characterizations of the Sarvāstivāda doctrine—four varieties of the "All Exists" position—and declares that the third of the four is best (V.26).

> 25 All times exist: because it is said, because of the two things, because of the existent sense object, because of the result. Since they say that these exist, they are esteemed Sarvāstivāda. They are of four kinds,
> 26 Called differentialists of: being, quality, position, and difference. The third is best, for whom the times are arranged according to activity.[17]

Even in this concise summary, we can see that these verses list eight different views: four reasons to believe in the thesis of the true existence of the past, present, and future, and four varieties of that thesis. Then, in a third verse, Vasubandhu outlines an unresolved conundrum for the Vaibhāṣika tradition, which he claims they address only by appealing to the "profundity" or "depth" of the true nature of reality (V.27).

> 27 What is the obstruction? How can this not be something else, disconnected from the times? Existing in this way, how can it be unborn and destroyed? The basic nature is indeed profound.[18]

Now, Vasubandhu will never try to argue that the basic nature of things is not profound. Yet his commentary expands upon the questions in this verse, which highlight the central problematic in the Sarvāstivāda position, to such a degree that, by the time the end of the commentary comes around, when he says that the basic nature is "profound" he will seem to be implying, ironically, that the Sarvāstivada view is, on the contrary, shallow.[19] To put it very briefly, the unsolved problem is just how to define and identify the differences between past, present, and future without begging the question of the reality of the times.

The *Commentary*, the AKBh, proceeds across these three verses as a single line of argument, beginning with a question: Do things in the future and the past really exist, or not? The entirety of the lengthy commentary on these three verses—including the identification of various named scholars and schools—is expressed as a response to this question. The question of whether existents in the past and the future are truly real is surely of interest on its own terms. Here, however, the issue is particularly important because it is a conundrum raised by the conjunction of two commonly held Buddhist views: all things are conditioned, and so are connected with other things in a causal stream, and yet all conditioned things are impermanent, and so exist for a time and then pass away. The question is then what to say about the future and the past of these conditioned things:

> Does a past and future thing really exist, or not? If it exists, then you have to say that conditioned things [*saṃskāra*] are eternal, because they exist at all times. If, on the other hand, it does not exist, then how is one bound in it or by it, or freed?[20]
>
> The Vaibhāṣikas do not accept that conditioned things are eternal, because that is the point of being conditioned.[21] Instead they clearly accept that **all times exist.** [I.25a1][22]

This opening statement of the paradox is clean and simple. If a thing exists in the past, present, and future, that seems to be equivalent to saying that it always exists, which is again equivalent to saying that it is eternal. It would appear to be straightforward, then, that based upon the doctrine that conditioned things are impermanent, Buddhists should accept the unreality, or nonexistence, of past and future objects. But to say that things are impermanent is also to say that they exist based upon causes and conditions. So, the question arises, if there is no past or future, how do you account for the truth of the statement that present entities are causally dependent upon past ones, and condition future ones? The reality of causes and conditions would appear to necessitate the reality of the past and the future. The central problematic is thus how to reconcile impermanence with time and causality. (Vasubandhu's somewhat surprising choice here, as we will see later on, will be to admit the insubstantiality, the unreality, of causality per se, though not of the causally related entities.)

Vasubandhu identifies the Vaibhāṣika position as accepting *both* the impermanence of conditioned things *and* the reality of the three times. He goes on to identify this position with the name "Sarvāstivāda"—the view that all times exist. For Vasubandhu, if you are a "Vaibhāṣika" you are also a "Sarvāstivāda." Their position is justified by four reasonably convincing arguments, named in V.25. Yet none of the arguments answers to the heart of the conundrum, which is that the reification of past and future entities undermines the doctrine of impermanence in a way that seems non-Buddhist. Vasubandhu will call upon numerous arguments Buddhists have used against non-Buddhists to refute each of the Sarvāstivāda arguments and present his own, alternate position. Before providing his refutation, though, he summarizes each Sarvāstivāda argument in turn, and then summarizes the four varieties of the Sarvāstivāda position. Then, he first refutes the four kinds of Sarvāstivāda, and finally, provides an extensive refutation of each of the four arguments. The passage overall has the following A, B, ~B, ~A structure (the full text is translated in appendix A):

ORDER OF EXPOSITION IN AKBH V.25–27

1. (A) Brief Presentation of Four Arguments for "All [times] exist" (295.2–296.4)
2. (B) Brief Presentation of Four Varieties of "All [times] exist" (296.6–297.3)
3. (~B) Refutation of Four Varieties (297.4–298.22)
4. (~A) Refutation of Four Arguments (299.1–301.16)

In what follows, I will more-or-less follow the line of argument in Vasubandhu's commentarial refutations, inserting citations of the earlier presentations as appropriate. I will first explain the four varieties of Sarvāstivāda, along with Vasubandhu's critiques of each (2 and 3). Then I will analyze the four more general arguments in support of the substantial existence of the three times, explaining Vasubandhu's criticisms in turn (1 and 4).

THE FOUR SARVĀSTIVĀDA VIEWS; OR, WHAT IS MEANT BY "EVERYTHING EXISTS"

One question looms large in Vasubandhu's treatment of the Sarvāstivāda view, the view that things truly exist in the past and the future: namely, can there be a difference between saying that something exists in all of the three times, and saying that it is eternal and unchanging?[23] Vasubandhu would like to show that things in the past and the future do not really "exist"; only things in the *present* exist. There is no difference, he thinks, between saying that something exists and saying that it is present.

In order to prevent all things from being present, then, Buddhists who advocate the "everything exists" position must articulate a theory that distinguishes the times (past, present, and future), each from the others. Without being "one who holds there to be a difference" (*ānyathika*, hereafter "differentialist") among the times—a difference that explains *how* things change in time—there would be no way to articulate the basic Buddhist view of universal impermanence, that everything in time changes. This issue is clearly central to Abhidharma discussions of temporality, and each of the four Sarvāstivāda views Vasubandhu examines is thus associated both with a particular person and with that person's advocacy of a particular way of differentiating among the three times (see table 2.1). For each differentialist view, Vasubandhu provides his critique, in order to show the impossibility of establishing the reality of the times on any basis that is not question-begging.

The first kind of differentialist is described as explaining the difference among the times in terms of their being (*bhāva*):

> Bhadanta [= noble monk] Dharmatrāta is a being-differentialist. Indeed, he says: "A *dharma* proceeding through the times is different in being; it is not different in substance. Just as a golden pot, being broken, when it is changed, is different in shape; it is not different in color. And just as the milk being changed by curdling, loses its flavor, strength, and freshness, but not

TABLE 2.1 Four Sarvāstivāda Differentialists, Based on AKBh V.26

KIND OF "DIFFERENCE" AMONG THE THREE TIMES	NOBLE MONK (*BHADANTA*) WHO ADVOCATES IT
being (*bhāva*)	Dharmatrāta
quality (*lakṣaṇa*)	Ghoṣaka
position (*avasthā*), activity (*kāritra*)	Vasumitra
difference (*anyathā*)	Buddhadeva

> its color. So a *dharma* too, when it comes from future time to present time, loses its being in the future, not its being a substance. So when it goes from the present into the past time, it loses its being in the present, not its being a substance."[24]

Dharmatrāta's point (at least as presented here) is that things exist in the past and future with the same substantial nature that they have in the present. A future piece of gold is as much a piece of gold as is a past piece of gold. What changes is the temporality itself—a thing's mode of being—which inheres in the entity as qualities inhere in a substance.

The point seems reasonable, but Vasubandhu rejects it because of its affinity with the non-Buddhist, Sāṃkhya doctrine of change, or transformation (*pariṇāma*). In response to Dharmatrāta, then, he refers to his own previous argument against this Sāṃkhya view, which appeared in his comment to III.49d:[25]

> But it is not indeed like change for the Sāṃkhyas.
>
> And how is change for the Sāṃkhyas?
>
> Where, possessed by a stable substance, one *dharma* disappears and another *dharma* arises.
>
> And what is the fault here?
>
> That the *dharma*-possessor is not known which is stable, but whose *dharmas* are made to change.
>
> What about saying that the *dharma*-possessor is other than the *dharmas*?
>
> But the substance itself has a change, simply by becoming possessed of difference [*anyathībhāva*]. This is what is illogical.
>
> What here is illogical?
>
> "That very thing is both this way and not this way"—such an unprecedented expression of logic![26]

This argument encapsulates for us Vasubandhu's extremely strict view of the inconsistency of stability and change, which is rooted in the simple dictum that one thing cannot be in opposition to itself. Two opposites cannot logically be said to be the same entity. Consequently, when a thing is said to change, and become its own opposite, it would be a mistake to imagine that this change takes place against the backdrop of some stable entity. There is no stable "thing," but only a changing system.

Why, we might ask, is it not acceptable to say that the backdrop remains the same? For Vasubandhu, the reason is that you must make a choice:

you must declare whether it is a true part of the "backdrop" that it "possesses" the changing entities in question. For, surely that very *possession* changes—first one thing is possessed, then another. If this changing *possession* is a true aspect of the substance, then the substance changes, vitiating its nature as an unchanging substance. If, conversely, the backdrop does not change, then there is no sense in saying that the backdrop "possesses" one thing or another. The backdrop becomes, by definition, irrelevant to any possible changes that may take place.

This strict view ramifies across Vasubandhu's philosophy in a great many ways. It is evident even here that not only change, but in fact all relations to changing things become impossible for an unchanging entity. Vasubandhu will take advantage of this point in his disproof of a creator god, where he points out that an eternal, unchanging divinity, who acts as creator of the universe, ought to be creating the universe always and forever. If such a god stopped creating, he would become a noncreator. So, there should be no time during which the universe might grow or change.[27] Vasubandhu will also take advantage of this point in his argument for universal momentariness. Since things cannot change, he argues, they must either exist only for a moment or exist eternally.[28] This is also the basic argument when Vasubandhu denies the causal efficacy, and the reality, of unconditioned things. Since unconditioned things (such as space and *nirvāṇa*) are by definition independent of the conditioning powers of other entities, they are like a creator god in that they must have no visible effects at all. The only reason we notice them—really, we imagine them—is that we project an absence upon a locus of expectation; there is no separately "existing" unconditioned entity.[29] All of these arguments may be read, like the present one, as arguments against entities that supposedly change, or "exist in possession of a difference" (*anyathībhāva*), and the "differentialists" (*ānyathika*) who defend their existence.

To return to the issue of the three times, we can see how Dharmatrāta's view—that past, present, and future are like qualities that inhere in the unchanging nature of entities—resembles the Sāṃkhya view, and falls prey to the same critique. If an unchanging substance possesses the characteristic *future*, it will never come to be *present*; to be present would contradict its nature as *future*, which it cannot relinquish without also relinquishing its nature as *unchanging*.[30]

Moving on, then, the second version of the Sarvāstivāda view is described as the advocacy of difference in terms of qualities (*lakṣaṇa*).

> Bhadanta Ghoṣaka is a quality-differentialist. Indeed, he says: "A *dharma* proceeding through the times is past insofar as it is connected to the quality *past* but not insofar as it is cut off from the qualities *future* and *present*; is future where it is connected to the quality *future* but not cut off from *past* and *present*. So it is present, too, where it is not cut off from *future* and *past*. In this way, a man desirous of one woman is not devoid of desire for others."[31]

This view appears to have been formulated in anticipation of a critique like Vasubandhu's argument against the first view. It accepts the idea that qualities of an unchanging entity cannot be said to switch out with, and be replaced by, opposite qualities. Thus, even when something is bound to one of the three times, Bhadanta Ghoṣaka claims that it is still "not cut off" from the other two times. Yet this attempt to slip out of the dilemma in fact throws out the baby with the bathwater, as Vasubandhu points out:

> The second leads to a confusion of the times, because everything is connected to every moment. For how is it the same, where the man's desire is enacted for one woman and only possessed[32] for another?[33]

With its analogy of someone who desires many women but is especially focused upon one, Ghoṣaka's theory seems to rest upon the idea that the qualities of past, present, and future might lie dormant in an entity without thereby being entirely absent. Vasubandhu insists that this makes a muddle of the three times: if you use this analogy to say that there is no real change in the entity through time, then you must be saying, absurdly, that the daydreamer who fantasizes about many women, taking each one in his imagination in turn, is in fact *always* daydreaming about *all* of the women. If there is no real difference between the qualities of past, present, and future, then there is no difference between enactment and mere potential.[34]

Next, the third Sarvāstivāda view is the one that Vasubandhu says is "the best"—at least, that is what he says in the verses. He certainly dedicates the most time to refuting it, so it is fair to say that he takes it more seriously than the other three:

> Bhadanta Vasumitra is a position-differentialist. Indeed, he says: "A *dharma* proceeding through the times, reaching one position and then another, is taken as being one thing and then another due to its having another position, not another substance. Just as one and the same mark placed in the

> ones' space is called 'one' and in the hundreds' space a hundred, and in the thousands' space, a thousand."[35]

The analogy of a single token being used to represent different amounts in different contexts suggests that Vasumitra might be a relativist of some stripe. The implication is that past, present, and future are somehow imposed upon an entity by its context. It is the fourth view, however, that presents a true relativism, and as we will see below, Vasubandhu does not give it any credence. This, the third, view is not relativist. The changes in "position" between past, present, and future are considered real, and not mere conceptual constructions.

But what constitutes the genuine difference attributable to a *dharma* in its past, present, or future positions? This view is explained by appealing to the notion of "activity" (*kāritra*):

> For him, indeed, **the times are arranged according to activity.** [I.26c–d] "When the *dharma* is not doing its activity [*kāritra*], it is future.[36] When it does it, it is present. When, having done it, it is stopped, it is past." This encompasses everything.[37]

Here the notion of activity (*kāritra*) explains a thing's temporal identity very straightforwardly. If a thing is engaged in its activity—its *doing what it does*—it is present. If it has done so already, it is past. If it will yet do so, it is future. The question, then, is not going to be whether the idea makes sense; the question is just what is accomplished with this notion of "activity." Vasubandhu will argue that the view fails because it is attempting to explain temporal identity by appealing to a concept that either already relies upon a thing having a temporal identity (and so is a circular definition), or is irrelevant to temporal identity. After all, what could make the thing "activate" its "activity" that does not already assume the notions of past, present, and future?

There is no way, Vasubandhu believes, to establish an intermediate position between entities being eternal and entities existing only in the present. He begins thus:

> But this must be said: If what is "future" exists substantially even as past, why is it called "past" or "future"?[38]

This is a general critique of the Sarvāstivāda view of the reality of the three times. Ordinarily, we would say that what exists is present. If what distinguishes the present from the other times is not its existence, it must be whatever "differences they accept"—in this case, differences of "position," which are further explained as being differences of "activity." To ask this question again is to suggest that *activity* is not going to do the job of differentiating the three times.

In order to advance this suggestion, Vasubandhu first focuses upon what it means for a thing to be "active" in the sense that it may be called "present." The traditional Vaibhāṣika explication had been that a thing's activity is its causal interaction—specifically, its production of some causal result. A thing is present when it is actively causing a result. So Vasubandhu challenges the opponent to explain a present "activity" as bringing about a causal result for two distinct kinds of entity: namely, an eye that causes a subsequent eye, and an eye that is of the same kind as one that does that, but happens not to, because it is at the end of a series—called a *tatsabhāga*.[39] An eye that *does* generate the next in a series is on the surface the simpler case: it may be called "present" when it is generating, or *producing*, its causal result. But if that is the case for an eye that *does* cause a subsequent eye, does this mean that an eye that fails to produce such a result is never "present," simply because it happens to fall at the end of a series? The traditional Vaibhāṣika answer to this is that, on the contrary, what makes a *tatsabhāga* eye organ "present" is not its present causal production of a future result, but its present "taking on" or "grasping" (*pratigrahaṇa*) of its own existence as a result, which is applicable to all eye organs. This is a causal result of a different (technical) kind, but it is considered a sufficient "activity" to give the *tatsabhāga* eye the name "present."[40]

Having drawn out these details of the Vaibhāṣika view, Vasubandhu indicates a problem. Surely the eye that does produce the next in a series also serves as the "grasper" of its own existence as a causal result. But this would mean that its being "present" is causally overdetermined: it has two separate, sufficient reasons for being "present." Yet one entity cannot be caused twice. Even worse, the "activity" that is the cause of the subsequent eye occurs in the past, before the moment in which it grasps its own existence as a result. That means that it is "present" twice, at two separate moments. The more general point behind this rather technical discussion is that the notion of "activity" is far from straightforward. Things sometimes seem to "act" upon entities that exist at the same time they do, while other times they exist at different times. Activity is therefore not going to solve the problem of defining temporality. Or, if it does, then it is an arbitrary construction built specifically to solve the problem.[41]

It would appear that, after Vasubandhu's critique, the orthodox Vaibhāṣika philosopher and rival to Vasubandhu, Saṃghabhadra, altered the tradition somewhat in response.[42] The result is exactly the fiat that Vasubandhu's critique implicitly predicts. For Saṃghabhadra, the "activity" of a *dharma* is dependent *only* on the kind of causality associated in the above argument with the *tatsabhāga* eye—the one that produces no subsequent eye. Thus, in order to elude Vasubandhu's criticism, Saṃghabhadra ends up defining in a strict way the entity, called "activity," that accounts for temporal identity. He distinguishes this technical meaning for "activity" from other aspects of an entity's causal identity. After Saṃghabhadra, it does not matter *when* an entity's causal result comes to fruition; it is called "present" when it *grasps* its own existence as a result. This new, technical formation of the "activity" argument separates activity, and hence temporality, from the nature of a thing. Yet this argument was not apparently accepted by Vasubandhu's predecessors. On the contrary, as I read Vasubandhu, he is the one to credit with the suggestion that, in order to secure an entity's temporal identity, it will be necessary to rely upon an arbitrary, and circular, definition of causal "activity," itself defined in relation to temporal identity.

One way to read Vasumitra's attempt to define temporal identity via "activity" in a noncircular way would be to regard it as an appeal to a linguistic form. We could say that when we refer to an entity in the past tense, as "having its activity completed," this expression is to be accounted for by the fact that that entity is past. This might merge linguistic with ontological claims in a way that seems anathema to all of us who accept Saussure's famous doctrine of the "arbitrary nature of the sign," but the point of such an argument would not be to claim that words grasp and resonate with ultimate reality. Rather, the argument would propose that were there no reality to past and future "activity," there would be no meaning to the linguistic signs that employ verbal tense. Past and future exist, then, because without them our expressions about past and future actions—and, indeed, present ones—would come to naught.

Vasubandhu does not frame, or address, this argument here, so I will hold off on discussing his philosophy of language. I will, however, treat this argument where Vasubandhu does, in the context of his discussion of scriptural passages that make reference to the past and future. (He says that these words are meant figuratively.) Nonetheless, I believe this is a valid potential reading of Vasumitra's view, which hovers in the background here, and so deserves mention. And, Vasubandhu may be considered to be countering *both* the ontological *and* the linguistic argument when he notes the impossibility of distinguishing the "activity" of the entity from its intrinsic nature:

> And this must be said: Where by that very nature the *dharma* exists eternally, in its doing its activity, **what is the obstruction** [I.27a1] by virtue of which, sometimes it does [its] activity, sometimes not? Suppose you say the conditions are not in place: no, because you have conceded that they always exist. And when the activity is said to be past, present, and future, **how can this be?** [1.27a2] Does the activity, too, have another activity? In that case, it is not past, nor is it future or present. Then you would be saying that since it is unconditioned, it is eternal. Thus it cannot be said that a *dharma* is future when it does not perform [its] activity.[43]

If entities are said to exist in past, present, and future, and it is their nature to *be* a certain kind of entity (say, to be eyes, with certain specifiable capacities), then what is it that *prevents* them from being causes sufficient to be called "active"? You cannot say that the necessary conditions are nonexistent, because your view is that everything that has ever existed still exists, and everything that will ever exist already exists. So the conditions that, together with an eye, may some day produce a visual sensation must already exist, to the same degree that the future eye does. Thus, a future eye should be able to see its future visual objects, because they too exist, along with it, as future entities; together, they should then be able to produce the causal result of the contact of eye organ and object. Why can't they, if they all exist already, with exactly the same characteristic natures that they will come to have when they are present? If they cannot, then there is something about their natures that is unable to produce results, which means that they will never be able to produce results without altering their natures. But if they will never "act" any more than they can act now, they are not "future" events, but nonevents.

Notice the resonances between this argument and the argument against the Sāṃkhya view of change. Both rely upon the notion that an entity's own, characteristic nature—its *svalakṣaṇa*—is something that can never change, if the entity is to remain the same entity. Vasubandhu presses this point again and again throughout the AKBh. It is a cornerstone of his worldview, and he adheres to it with unflagging strictness. Here he is using it to argue that the notion of "activity" imposes a false equivocation. Like Dharmatrāta, Vasumitra is trying to have his cake and eat it too. If things genuinely change, then they cannot be said to exist as the very same entities in different times. If they do not change, then the very fact that they are "future" means that they cannot *change* to become active, and hence "present."

The opponent attempts to save the argument at this point by accepting that the activity is identical with the entity (*dharma*), but Vasubandhu points out that this simply isolates the entity from the three times, and makes it unchanging and eternal. In the following passage, which completes Vasubandhu's critique of the third form of Sarvāstivāda, he and the opponent go around in circles, with the opponent repeating commonsense notions such as the past being that whose entities are "destroyed" or "finished," and Vasubandhu repeatedly returning to his core idea: if an entity has a certain nature, there is nothing that can make it fail to express that nature. If, on the other hand, it lacks a nature (such as being "destroyed"), there is nothing that can make it so:

> This would be a mistake if the activity were something else other than the *dharma*. But in fact **it is not something else,** [1.27a3] so this is not a mistake.
>
> So then that very thing **is disconnected from the times.** [I.27b1] If the *dharma* itself is the activity, how can it be that this very *dharma*, existing by its own nature, is sometimes called "past" and sometimes "future"? This is not an acceptable arrangement of the times.
>
> What is not acceptable about it? For a *dharma* is future if it is unborn. It is present if it is born and not destroyed. It is past if it is destroyed.
>
> The response to that is as follows: if the past and the future exist substantially just like the present does, for something **existing in this way, how can it be unborn or destroyed?** [I.27b2–c1] For how can a *dharma* that exists by its very own nature be acceptable as "unborn" or "destroyed"? What did it previously lack, by virtue of whose nonexistence it is called "unborn"? And what does it subsequently lack, by virtue of whose nonexistence it is called "destroyed"? Therefore it is not acceptable that it be here in the three times and also eternal.
>
> If one does not want to say that having not existed, it exists, and having existed it does not exist again, and what one does say is "Because of being joined with the qualities of conditioned things, there is no erroneous entailment of eternality," this is just words, because it is not connected to arising and destruction. To say that "it is eternally quasi-existent, and the *dharma* is not eternal" is an unprecedented expression.

Indeed, he also says:

> *Own-nature [svabhāva] always exists, but its existence is not accepted as eternal.*
> *Nor is there existence other than the own-nature—an expression spoken by the Lord.*[44]

Here we see Vasubandhu riffing on the unbridgeable gulf between eternity and change, a crucial theme of the AKBh. The argument as a whole, we might notice, is taken as an extended gloss on the Buddha's point in the quotation cited to cap the argument. When the Buddha speaks of a thing's own nature, its *svabhāva*, as existing "always" (*sarvadā*), he means that a thing can have no nature other than its own nature, but he does not mean that things with their own nature exist forever. Vasubandhu's arguments are never far from scriptural interpretation, and here we see him drawing upon scripture to justify his position at the same time he is explaining a confounding scriptural passage with extended philosophical reasoning.

The fourth and final version of the Sarvāstivāda view is, as I have already mentioned, a form of relativism, and Vasubandhu dismisses it readily:

> Bhadanta Buddhadeva is a difference-differentialist.[45] Indeed, he says: "A *dharma* proceeding through the times is called one or the other with reference to what is previous and later, due to it having another position, not another substance. Just as one woman is called mother or daughter."[46]

This view Vasubandhu considers to have failed entirely to distinguish between the three times:

> For the fourth, too, in any one time the three times obtain. In the past time, the previous and the later moment are past and future, and the middle moment is the present. So also in the future.[47]

Here the point is that if the difference between events in time is just the perspective from which they are described, then every event may be said to be equally of every time. If one woman may be called mother or daughter, then surely *she is both*. The truth of her relativistically distinct identities is founded on the relationships that allow her to play multiple roles. Yet each of the three times is defined in contradistinction to the other two. For this reason, the notion that one entity may be *all three times* must be rejected as failing to provide a genuine distinction. This is exactly what we find, if we say that the temporal identity of an entity is only to be affirmed relative to other entities. For one entity will be past to later entities, present to its temporal peers, and future to those things that came before it.

It is useful to keep this criticism in mind as we come to understand Vasubandhu's own view, which does take into consideration the great significance that context plays in the appearance of entities. But although Vasubandhu will say that things gain different *names* and *appearances* depending upon the context and depending upon the mental capacities of the observer, he does *not* believe that things *exist* relative to their contexts, as this passage makes plain. To say that a thing differs in different contexts is a proof that it *does not exist*. It is proof that what seems to be a substantial entity is only a convention, a name, or an appearance.

The positions advocated by Vasubandhu's Sarvāstivāda opponents are thus used to display the difficulties with the position that "everything exists"—meaning, that everything that ever has existed, and ever will exist, exists. Vasubandhu also uses various arguments to indicate mistaken assumptions that, once corrected, suggest paths to greener pastures. In particular, his strict view of the unchanging character of every entity's identity comes to the fore in these arguments. He wishes, above all, to distinguish his own view from those views that have a muddled approach to what it means to *exist*, and consequently a muddled approach to the nature of the past and the future. His own alternative, which he believes is not only reasonable but also grounded in a sophisticated view of scripture, becomes clear only in his criticisms of the four major arguments in defense of the Sarvāstivāda view, to which we now turn.

ARGUMENT 1: THE ARGUMENT FROM DIRECT SCRIPTURAL ASSERTION

For a Buddhist audience, the first argument provides an extremely strong basis for the Sarvāstivāda position that past and future objects exist: the Buddha said so.[48] The opponent provides an undisputed, canonical passage:

> Since the Lord said, "O monks, if past form did not exist, then the learned, noble hearer [*śrāvaka*] would not have been indifferent with regard to past

> form. Since there is past form, the learned, noble hearer is indifferent with regard to past form. If a future form did not exist, the learned, noble hearer would not have been pleased with regard to future form. Since there is future form" and so on.[49]

Notice that the opponent quotes a passage in which the Buddha declares that the past and future must exist because otherwise *his own doctrines would not make sense.* The Buddha is saying that he has already said[50] that the "hearers" (*śrāvaka*) are indifferent with regard to past objects and pleased with regard to future ones, so the questioner should trust him to mean what he says, and therefore these things are real. The Buddha is effectively calling upon, or at least underlining, his own authority as the basis of the proof. Such a quotation supports not only the point at issue, but also the argumentative strategy of calling upon the Buddha's authority by citing his words: if the Buddha can call upon his own authority, so can the opponent, no?

In response, Vasubandhu accepts the passage along with the Buddha's authority, but reads it in a way that refuses the Sarvāstivāda interpretation:

> We too say that the there is a past and future thing. But a past thing is what existed before. A future thing is what will exist when there is a cause. Each is said to exist just insofar as this is the case, but not also substantially.[51]

Vasubandhu agrees, from the start, that it is perfectly acceptable to say that past and future things exist. Yet the question is how to interpret the Buddha's words to this effect. What does it *mean* to say that they exist? Vasubandhu believes that his opponents are reading too much into the passage. Past and future, he thinks, are legitimate, convenient expressions, but only *present* entities exist "substantially" (*dravyataḥ*). It is a crucial error of Abhidharma analysis to fail to distinguish real things, which exist substantially, from mere conceptual fictions, which have at best conventional (*prajñapti*) or verbal (*nāma*) reality. The disagreement over the past and future is a typical instance in which Vasubandhu feels that his opponents mistakenly reify what are merely nominal entities.

Yes, Vasubandhu admits, the Buddha believes in the past and the future, but not as *real, substantial* entities. To prove this point, Vasubandhu adduces a counterquotation that shows the Buddha presenting a different kind of position on the nature of the past and future:

> And who says, "It exists as present"?
>
> How else does it exist?
>
> As past and future [*atītānāgatātmanā*].
>
> This is also established for you: "How is it called past and future if it exists eternally?"[52]

The opponent questions the equation of "existent" with "present," and in reply Vasubandhu quotes a passage from the Buddha, which the Vaibhāṣika accepts as authoritative, but that seems to side with Vasubandhu's interpretation of the terms "past" and "future." Perhaps the most straightforward reading of the Buddha's concise argument takes the opponent here to believe that things exist eternally, which is a doctrine of the Nyāya-Vaiśeṣika school. The Nyāya-Vaiśeṣika of course know that ordinary objects are perishable, but they believe that the fundamental entities out of which things are made—atoms—are eternal and unchanging.[53] The Buddha's argument apparently combats this view by making use of the notions of past and future. If you want to say that an entity is past, he is saying, then you cannot say it is eternal—for how could it have passed into the past? If you want to say that an entity is future, then you cannot say it is eternal—for it must always be, so it cannot be a merely future entity. The argument seems to be saying that, for eternal entities, there can only be an eternal present. As I read this argument, the Buddha seems to assume, furthermore, that it is part of the meaning of each of the three times—past, present, and future—that it is distinct from the other two. Such an assumption also lies behind Vasubandhu's criticisms of those who accept what he considers muddled or relativistic distinctions between the times.

As we have just seen argued from several angles, Vasubandhu also believes that something eternal must never change, and so can never impinge upon a temporal causal series. Here he is merely using the Buddha's disproof of eternal entities as proof that while the Buddha believed in the past and the future, he did not accept the *existence of entities* in the past and the future, which would entail a self-contradictory belief in their eternity. To explain this argument further, Vasubandhu provides a reading of the Buddha's approach:

> Therefore, the Lord says, "the past thing exists, the future thing exists," in order to refute the view that denies cause and effect, and in order that one come to know that a previously existent cause existed, and a subsequently existent result will exist.[54]

Past and future existence are only affirmed as a way of explaining the nature of causality, which the Buddha must affirm against those who deny causality. As against the Buddhists, who believe that change and impermanence are fundamental truths, the Sāṃkhyas believed that results were preexistent in their causes.[55] Notice, then, Vasubandhu's translation of the times into causal language: past = "that a previously existent cause existed"; and future = "that a subsequently existent result will exist." For Vasubandhu, "past," "present," and "future" are only names used to pick out different entities in a connected, causal series. Unlike an eternal entity, a causal series is in constant flux. To assert the existence of past and future things, then, is not to affirm hidden additional realities, but only to counter the Sāṃkhya-like denial of cause and effect by emphasizing the necessity of real change through time.

Next Vasubandhu uses the Buddha's distinction between eternity-talk and past-and-future-talk to highlight a special, irregular use of the word "exists" (*asti*).

> This is because the word "exists" is used as a particle [*nipāta*].[56] Just as one says of a light that previously it is nonexistent and subsequently it is nonexistent,[57] and as in, "The light is extinguished, but has not been extinguished by me," the past and future thing, too, is said to exist. For otherwise the existence of a past and future thing would not be acceptable.[58]

Notice the line of argument here. First, Vasubandhu shows that the Buddha has implied, contrary to the opponent's view, that past and future entities cannot exist substantially without entailing permanence. Next, he gives a reasonable alternative interpretation of why the Buddha asserted that past and future entities exist: in order to counter the mistaken denial of causality. Now, he provides a linguistic rule that justifies his correction, and accounts for his opponents' misunderstanding: the reason you think that he is asserting past and future entities when he is not, is that there is an irregularity with the word "is" (*asti*). The word itself often seems to imply an entity when no such entity is really meant. We ordinarily say there is an extinguished light, but this does not require us to believe that there remains some *thing* that counts as the extinguished light that "is."[59]

Vasubandhu uses this commonsense example to make intuitive sense of his anti-realism about merely linguistic or conceptually constructed entities. I will explain in chapter 4 how he develops the idea that destructions and nonentities do not exist (they are, like space, merely conceptual-linguistic constructions imposed where perceptual expectations are unsatisfied) into an innovative proof of the Buddhist doctrine of universal momentariness. For now, though, it suffices to notice how this linguistic rule—"exists" doesn't always mean *exists substantially*—together with the Buddha's belief that the past and future are causal terms, serves to undermine the scriptural literalism that reads the words of the Buddha as affirming the substantial existence of past and future. Vasubandhu's scriptural readings tend to follow this complex pattern of combining philosophical reasoning with counterquotation and the adducement of hermeneutic rules. As we will see, the results of his arguments are generally, as here, to undermine the scriptural literalism and linguistic realism of his opponents.

This pattern of argument is repeated in response to a second quotation adduced by the opponent:

> What then of what the Lord said when speaking to the mendicants of the *Laguḍaśikīyaka*, "Past action lost, destroyed, gone, changed—it exists!" Did he not in this passage intend that each of these actions existed previously?
>
> With regard to that passage too, it was spoken with the special intent [*saṃdhāya*] that what was deposited within that causal series is capable of giving forth a result. For the alternative, that what is existing by its own nature is past, would not be acceptable.[60]

In response to an apparently direct statement from the Buddha that past actions exist, Vasubandhu says here that the teacher's words must be read in the light of a "special intent" (*saṃdhāya*), which is a term used to specify a nonliteral reading of an expression.[61] In accord with his previous identification of the past as spoken of to indicate "that a previously existent cause existed," he says here that what the Buddha intends when he speaks of an action's past is that "what was deposited within that causal series is capable of giving forth a result." He makes the point that a literal, surface reading of the quotation issues in an apparent contradiction. You cannot say that something is past with respect to its own self—that is, it cannot both *be* and *be past* at the same time. So the only sensible reading is Vasubandhu's: to be past is to be a cause of something present. This reading enlivens the overall intent of the statement, for it is surely an exhortation to believe in the "karmic," causal consequences of one's actions, which, once completed, are by no means "gone." We see the very close connection, here, between Buddhist causal theory and Buddhist moral theory; we will see this point return in the fourth argument.

Before turning to the next argument, Vasubandhu once again brings forward a counterquotation, this time one that would appear to clinch the point:

> And this is just what the Lord expressed in the *Paramārthaśūnyatā*: "The eye, coming into existence, does not come from anywhere, nor, being destroyed, does it go to a dumpsite [*saṃnicaya*] anywhere. For, O Bhikṣus, the eye, not having existed exists, and having existed goes away." And if there were a future eye, he would not have said that having existed it does not exist. If you say that "having not existed" refers to its having not existed in the present time: no, because there is no difference in meaning between the existence and the time. If, on the other hand, "having not existed" refers to its having not existed in its own nature, this establishes that the future eye does not exist.[62]

The *Paramārthaśūnyatā* quotation provides, finally, a clear statement from the Buddha that there is no "existence" attributable to past and future entities. The eye does not exist in the future or the past. Vasubandhu pushes the point one step further, to deny even the "existence" of the present. There is nothing accomplished by saying that there is "present" existence, he says, "because there is no difference in meaning between the existence and the time." Whether or not the Buddha ever said so, for Vasubandhu all three times are only linguistic fictions. Bewitched by the word "exists," and zealously attached to a literalistic reading of scriptures, the Sarvāstivāda have come to resemble non-Buddhist philosophers.

ARGUMENT 2: THE ARGUMENT FROM THE TWOFOLD CAUSE OF CONSCIOUSNESS

The Sarvāstivāda opponent's second argument is based on a combination of scripture and reasoning. It introduces a term from the Buddha's teachings—"duality" or "the two" (*dvaya*)—which will be of great interest to Vasubandhu in his later career as an interpreter of Mahāyāna treatises. We can see his early musings about this term here, where the duality is acknowledged to be a condition for consciousness. The opponent cunningly argues that, for this reason, past and future must exist:

> **Because of the two things.** [I.25b1] As it is said, "The arising of consciousness is dependent upon two things." What are the two things? "Eyes and visual forms, up to the mind and mental objects." Also, were there no past and future thing, the consciousness that has it as its object would not be dependent upon the two things. So a past and future thing exists based on scriptural authority and from reason as well.[63]

This brief, causal argument quotes a part of the Buddha's doctrine of the chain of dependent arising (*pratītyasamutpāda*), according to which any given consciousness depends upon a previous pairing of sensory organ and object.[64] The first example of "the two things" given here is eye-and-visual-forms. The "up to" is an ellipsis for the "two things" for the other senses: ear-and-sounds, nose-and-smells, tongue-and-tastes, and skin-and-touchables. The Buddha, like many Indian philosophers, considered the mind to be a kind of sensory organ as well, so the last of the organ-and-object pairs is mind-and-mental-objects. Vasubandhu has a somewhat unique understanding of just what it means for consciousness to be conditioned by this last twosome, and we will have occasion to discuss his view at length below. Here, the Buddha's point being quoted by the objector is that you cannot see something—there can be no visual consciousness—without there being, as a condition of its arising, both a seeing organ (the eye) and a seen object (the visual form). An eye in the dark is insufficient, as is a lamp placed in front of a blind person.

What does this have to do with the question of the existence of entities in the past and the future? Well, the opponent's rather clever maneuver is to note that sometimes we are conscious—aware, thinking—of past and future things. If these awarenesses are to be consistent with the Buddha's rule that consciousness arises dependent upon "the two things," then—the opponent claims—"the two things" must exist in the future and the past. How could a consciousness of something in the future or the past be dependent upon the duality of sense-organ-and-object, unless sense organs and their objects *exist* in the future and the past?

Vasubandhu's response to this argument is to reinterpret what the Buddha must have meant by the term "dependent upon" (*pratītya*), at least for the case of the "sixth sense," the mental sense:

> As to the expression "The arising of consciousness is dependent upon two things," this, first of all, needs to be considered: in the situation where the mental consciousness arises dependent upon the mind and *dharma*, is it that

> the *dharmas* are a condition as a producer [*janaka*] of the mind, or that the *dharmas* are merely experiential objects [*ālambana*]?[65] If, on the one hand, the *dharmas* are producer conditions, how can what will come about one thousand kalpas in the future, or not, bring about a present consciousness? And *nirvāṇa* does not make sense as a producer, since it is the elimination of all activity. If, on the other hand, the *dharmas* are merely experiential objects, we say that the past and the future are also experiential objects.[66]

Vasubandhu sets aside the five external senses and focuses on the mental sense.[67] For him, awareness of past and future are not perceptual events occasioned by existent, past and future sensory organs and objects; it is not that past or future objects are somehow reaching across time and space to create experiences for us. Rather, our envisioning past objects can be accounted for through mental causes only. He asks: When the Buddha says that mental consciousness depends upon the mental organ and mental objects, does he mean that the mental objects (*dharma*) are "producers" (*janaka*) of the consciousness, or merely that they are conditions in the sense that they are the experiential objects (*ālambana*) for the consciousness? Just what Vasubandhu means by this distinction between two kinds of "condition"—a "producer" versus an "experiential object"—is clear both from this argument and from his previous use of these terms.

He says that if we think of, or experience, something that will exist in the distant future, it does not make sense to think of that future thing as the "producer" of the present consciousness. Now, this might be thought to beg the question of the nonexistence of the future. If we believe in the existence of future entities, we might be inclined to believe that those entities are available to produce a present consciousness. Indeed, this is exactly what Sarvāstivādins seem to believe, under a certain interpretation of one of their main arguments (see argument 3). This is perhaps why Vasubandhu employs the term "producer" (*janaka*) here—it means literally "that which causes birth."

In order to place this argument in its proper context, we can see that Vasubandhu uses the term *janaka* in the same way in a parallel argument against the Vaibhāṣika notion of mutual causality (*sahabhūhetu*), of two entities arising by virtue of each causing the other. Vasubandhu wants to argue that the Buddha defends the proper causal directionality of producer and produced; they cannot be switched around. A feeling is produced by a perception, a perception is not produced by a feeling. Since this is always true of every production, there is no possibility of a truly mutual causality; when one entity already exists, there is no longer any need to account for its existence by appeal to an additional causal capacity:

> How can the existence of producer and produced be acceptable for two things arising together?
>
> How is this not acceptable?
>
> Because of the lack of causal efficacy [*asāmarthyāt*]. No *dharma* has a confirmed characteristic of causal efficacy with respect to a *dharma* that is already produced. For just as there is no existent relation of producer and produced for two things arising together, there is none for one *dharma* with respect to an already produced *dharma*. Thus, mutual production is disproven by *reductio*.
>
> There is no fault, because of what we accept. For just that is accepted, that there is the mutual result for things that have arising-together causes [*sahabhūhetu*].
>
> What you accept, the mutual result for contact and feeling, is not accepted in the *sūtra*. For it is said that the feeling that is born from visual contact arises conditioned by visual contact, not that the visual contact arises having conditioned the feeling that is born from visual contact. And it is illogical because of the overextension of the producer *dharma*. For where one *dharma* is established as the producer for another *dharma* it is established as being at a different time from it. In this way, the seed is before, the sprout after; the milk before, the yogurt after; the articulation before, the sound after; the mental organ before, the mental consciousness after—and so on.[68]

Production, here, is clearly understood to be an immediate succession of events; one entity produces the next. This defeats mutual causality on the grounds that if an entity already exists, it needs no cause. Causality as understood in this way, as "production," is a linear, unidirectional relation between separate entities.[69]

To return to the temporality argument, causal "production" in this sense would seem to be not only directional but temporally located; to bring something about would be to cause a "birth" at a particular time. If that is the case, then even a somehow "existent" future entity should not be able to "produce" a present consciousness. Here we may usefully recall Vasumitra's characterization of the distinct "activities" of the three times, and now add that even if an entity is capable of "production" and exists in the future, its *activity* of production should only be available to it when it is in the present. Indeed, its activity is what distinguishes its present from its past and its future. A future "producer" is not yet producing. So it should not be able to produce a present consciousness.

Vasubandhu makes a similar point with reference to the consciousness of *nirvāṇa* (which would include the hope for *nirvāṇa*, the praise of *nirvāṇa*, etc.). *Nirvāṇa* is defined as "the elimination of all activity," so it cannot be an active "producer" any more than a future entity can. If we bring these two points together, we can see that Vasubandhu is suggesting that mental objects cannot be required to engage in any causally efficacious activity with respect to the consciousness that takes them as experiential objects. This is what it means to say that they are "merely experiential objects" (*ālambanamātra*). Whatever existence they may have, they are not *doing* anything.[70]

If mental objects are merely experiential objects, Vasubandhu continues, then future and past objects may also be taken to be merely experiential objects—at least, that is a coherent interpretation of the quotation from the Buddha. Remember, the opponent's point was that since the Buddha said that the six organs and their objects conditioned the consciousnesses, the Buddha would not have allowed the view that we could have consciousnesses of future and past entities unless those entities existed as things that our consciousness "depended" upon. What Vasubandhu has shown is that the Buddha's statement allows for the term "dependent" to indicate merely experiential objects, as opposed to "producer causes." What needs still to be shown, then, for this to be a reasonable view, is that experiential objects, too, fail the test of existence. This will be the challenge in the opponent's next counterquestion. By arguing against the notion that the future and past may be "producers" of consciousness, Vasubandhu has effectively reduced the second objection to the third, to which we now turn.

ARGUMENT 3: THE ARGUMENT FROM THE EXISTENCE OF SENSORY/EXPERIENTIAL OBJECTS

The third argument may seem quite similar to the second, but the distinction between them makes a difference to Buddhist philosophers on both sides of the issue. Whereas the second argument attempted to prove the existence of the past and future by arguing that a present awareness of past and future entities was *conditioned* by such entities, the third argument argues for the existence of past and future entities by equating them with *existent* sensory or experiential objects. That is, whereas the second argument says that consciousnesses must be *caused by* existent mental objects, the third argument says that for consciousnesses to exist, their objects of consciousness must exist as well:

> **Because of the existent sense object.** [I.25b2] Consciousness is engaged with an existent sense object, not a nonexistent one. And if a past and future thing did not exist, consciousness would have a nonexistent experiential object. Then there would be no consciousness either, because it would have no experiential object.[71]

This is an argument that appears to rely upon what contemporary philosophers, following Brentano, call the "intentional" character of consciousness—that it is "about" something. It need not be thought of as anything very complex. The point is that if you are not conscious *of* anything, you are not conscious. Every awareness has an object. The question at issue here is what to say about the existence—the ontology—of the "thing" *of which* you are aware. For Vasubandhu's opponents, since consciousness always has an object, the existence of the consciousness of a future object entails the existence of that future object.[72]

Vasubandhu's response to this argument follows immediately upon his response to argument 2, in which he reduced past and future *causes* of consciousness to *experiential objects* of consciousness. Consequently, he does not provide a direct response to the claim that "sensory objects" (*viṣaya*) exist, but rather conflates that question with the question of the existence of "experiential objects" (*ālambana*). The shift is of potential philosophical significance, in that it somewhat masks Vasubandhu's selective emphasis on mental objects, as opposed to the objects of the other senses. But Vasubandhu has addressed the notion of direct sensory perception of future and past objects in a separate passage,[73] and in any event his argument will encompass ordinary sensory perception along with the mental sense, so he should not be thought to have used an equivocation to avoid a difficult point. The practical consequence, though, is that Vasubandhu does not, here, make direct reference to the argument against "sensory objects,"[74] but instead places the equivalent objection regarding "experiential objects" in the voice of the opponent. The opponent asks how it can be that past and future objects can be "experiential objects," if they do not exist:

> If they do not exist, how are they experiential objects?
>
> With regard to this, we say: If an experiential object exists in this way, how can it be that that experiential object existed and will come to be? For it is not that someone remembering a past form or feeling sees that "it exists," but rather that "it was." For surely, one remembers what is past just as one experiences it when present. And the intellect grasps the future just as it will be when present. And if it exists just as it is, you say it is present, otherwise not. It is established that nonexistents too are experiential objects.[75]

Here the opponent challenges Vasubandhu's notion that past and future objects do not exist by pointing out an apparent contradiction: on the one hand, Vasubandhu says that past objects exist as experiential objects, while on the other hand he says that they do not exist. Vasubandhu's response relies upon a distinction between the experienced object *as it is seen or experienced*, and the experienced object *as it exists.* Although this is something of a subtle distinction, its importance for Vasubandhu cannot be overstated. The point is most easily grasped if we focus first on Vasubandhu's final claim in this quotation, which is that even though a nonexistent object (of course) does not exist, it is still acceptable to say that it exists as an experiential object. This does not mean that the nonexistent thing gains some "reality" for itself by virtue of its apparent existence. Rather, Vasubandhu's point is that although (for instance) thinking of a unicorn will *not* make that unicorn real, the unicorn in our imagination *appears as a real unicorn.*

The crux of Vasubandhu's argument is therefore not simply a statement that a merely experienced entity has no reality. Different philosophers have different intuitions as to the truth of that point, and contrary to appearances (no pun intended), Vasubandhu does not rely upon it here. Instead, he is using a kind of argument based upon the evidence of introspection to reveal a serious flaw in the opponent's reasoning. Although we know the unicorn does not exist, when we think of it, we cannot but think of it as *existent.* The mental image that represents the nonexistent unicorn in fact appears to be an *existent* unicorn. Therefore, what appear as objects of experience may well be nonexistent.[76]

This point is used to refute the claim that we experience past and future objects. When I think of a loved one who has died, I do not think of her in her current, "passed" state; rather, I think of her *as she lived.* It is therefore perfectly fine to say that a certain object, which is itself past, exists as a mental object; but saying that the object is past does not mean that the mental object exists *in the past*. Rather, introspection reveals that what seems to be an existent, past object in fact exists *in the present* in two quite different senses: first, the mental event takes place in the present; second, the past object is experienced as *existing*, not as *past*. This is what Vasubandhu means when he says that we do not experience "a past form or feeling," but rather, no matter when we bring a thing to mind, we experience that thing *as it used to exist* ("It was").[77]

This point dovetails elegantly with Vasubandhu's critique of Vasumitra's "activity" view of temporality, according to which a thing is "past" once its activity is complete. Remember, Vasubandhu claimed in that context that an object that has the capacity, by nature, to be an "active" cause must always have that capacity, and so cannot be said to be the same entity if it becomes "inactive." A thing does not, therefore, come to be past—it simply ceases to exist. Now, if argument 3's defense of the existence of past objects is grounded in our experience of those past objects, then the "activity" view should predict that when we experience past objects, we should experience objects *that have completed their activity*. Yet Vasubandhu points out that when we call to mind past objects, they appear to be *active* and thus, to accord with Vasumitra's view, they ought to be *present*. There is never, in fact, any experience of past or future objects as such—only experience of objects *as existing* that we happen to know are no longer, or not yet, existent. A thing's temporal identity as past or future, he is suggesting, is not an aspect of direct experience, but is rather a conceptually constructed imposition.[78] In sensory experience, entities always appear as though present.

This is one of Vasubandhu's most profound arguments, and he will develop it in establishing his unique presentation of Yogācāra philosophy. We will also have an opportunity to examine the relevance of this argument for contemporary philosophy of mind. For the time being, though, although we might wish to dally here contemplating Vasubandhu's greatness, let us follow him as he moves on. I will not treat here the remaining twists and turns of Vasubandhu's response to argument 3, which draw upon discussions of the relation between parts and wholes, the effectiveness of linguistic utterances, and yet another claim that the Buddha's words must be taken under a special intention (*abhiprāya*). These are issues that I will address at length in other contexts, and the reader will be better equipped to unravel the compact arguments here after more extensive discussions later in the book.

ARGUMENT 4: THE ARGUMENT FROM KARMIC CAUSALITY

The fourth Sarvāstivāda argument put forward to prove the reality of past and future entities calls upon the basic Buddhist view that our morally significant actions (*karma*) bring about positive or negative results for us, depending upon the virtue of the acts:

> **Because of the result.** [I.25c] And if there were no past, how could the result of virtuous or nonvirtuous action come about in the future? For at the time the result comes about, the cause of maturation does not exist. Therefore, according to the Vaibhāṣikas that past and future thing is indeed existent.[79]

The point here is that there is generally a significant temporal delay between an action taken (say, killing someone) and the karmic result (say, going to hell). Everyone agrees that the result is caused by the action. But what connects the action to the result? This is a crucial question for Buddhists, who deny the reality of an enduring self or soul in which the karmic result might abide, and who furthermore deny that *karma* is controlled by an eternal creator god. The question is a version of the problem of continuity, which is central to Vasubandhu's argumentation in the AKBh, as it is central to Abhidharma discussions overall. The Sarvāstivāda approach to the problem takes crucial advantage of their view of the reality of past and future entities. (Indeed, there is reason to believe that the problem of continuity is a central philosophical motive for their view of time.[80]) They say that the past action (the killing) exists, as a *past entity*, from which state it can act as a cause of the present rebirth in hell, once the other appropriate conditions are in place. Vasubandhu has already expressed his misgivings about the idea that a past entity can be causally effective (see his response to argument 2). Yet if Vasubandhu is going to deny the real existence of past entities, he must himself address the problem of continuity as it arises with respect to the doctrine of *karma*.

Vasubandhu did not shy away from the problem of continuity, and his response to argument 4 makes reference to how he resolves this question as a part of his best-known argument, namely, his disproof of the self:

> As to the expression "because of results": no, because the Sautrāntikas do not accept that a result arises from a past action.

From what then?

As we will explain thoroughly in the refutation of the doctrine of self,[81] from a characteristic of the continuum that precedes it.[82]

Here Vasubandhu quite clearly states that his commentary, in denying the various Sarvāstivādin positions *as well as* in its later disproof of the self, is advocating positions of the Sautrāntika. Based on this passage alone, it is fair to say that the philosophical view that Vasubandhu ("we") most definitively advocates in the AKBh is what he is terming "Sautrāntika." This passage also connects the authorship of chapter V with that of chapter IX, for those who have doubt on that question.

In this case, the Sautrāntika view under consideration is the denial that rebirth comes from past actions. Now, all premodern Buddhists accepted *karma* and rebirth, and this is not intended as heresy. Instead, what Vasubandhu is denying is not *karma* per se, but merely the reality of entities called "past actions" that are said to persist, somehow, and provide a causal impetus when they are no longer active. In reply, he says that the karmic result is caused by "a characteristic of the continuum that precedes it." This phrase is explained here only by referring to the later passage disproving the self, but on its own terms it apparently means that what brings about the karmic result is not the past action itself, but a present quality of the person's causal continuum or mental series—a quality that was initiated by the past action.

If we turn to the refutation of the self (AKBh IX), we find that the notion of "a characteristic of the continuum that precedes it" is "explained thoroughly" only in the final paragraphs of this final chapter. It is quite literally the end point of the AKBh, and though the work covers dozens of topics with hundreds of arguments, this is the argument that shows us how the discussions of time and of no-self are integrally related, and morally significant, and that they both hinge on the issue of how to understand the nature of causality. If, then, we notice the place this final argument holds in the refutation of the defining position of the Sarvāstivādins as well as in the refutation of the defining position of non-Buddhists and Pudgalavādins (the preoccupation of AKBh IX), we may be justified in asking whether this is not merely the last, but in fact the *main* argument of the AKBh. It seems to me that this point synthesizes the causal argumentation we have seen in development throughout the disputation against the times and places it at the pinnacle of the AKBh. In later chapters we will see that this argument is the root from which multifarious ramifications grow across Vasubandhu's works. I will therefore introduce the passage here and summarize its significance for the argument in question, but return to it repeatedly in the chapters that follow.

The relevant passage from the refutation of the self may be read in three sections: (1) a presentation of the analogy of seed and fruit; (2) a didactic explanation of the real basis for the analogy; and (3) a refinement of the analogy based upon the more precise definition. I provide here (1) and (2), and I will make reference to (3) in the discussion. Kapstein's fine translation of this passage reads:

> We, in any case, do not say that the fruit arises in the future from exhausted deeds.
>
> What then?
>
> From the distinctive feature of the transformation of that continuum, like seed and fruit. "As the fruit arises from the seed"—so it is said. It does not arise from an exhausted seed, but neither [does it arise] immediately.
>
> What then?
>
> From the distinctive feature of the transformation of that continuum; from the completion of the sequence of sprout, stem, leaves, etc., culminating in the flower [which transforms into the fruit].
>
> If that [fruit] is completed from the flower, then why is it called the fruit of that seed? Because that potency belonging to it [i.e., the seed] [is generated] in the flower only mediately. For if that [seed] did not precede, then there would not be the capacity to arise as a fruit of that sort. Thus, the fruit of the action has arisen—so it is said. And that has not arisen from exhausted action, and also not immediately.
>
> What then?
>
> From the distinctive feature of the transformation of that continuum.
>
> What, then, is the continuum? What the transformation? What the distinctive feature?
>
> That which, preceded by deeds, is an ongoing coming-to-be of mental events, is a continuum. Its arising otherwise is transformation. And, moreover, that potency, which immediately produces the fruit, being distinct from [that involved in] other transformations, is the distinctive feature of the transformation. E.g., a mind at the point of death which grasps for rebirth. And though various sorts of deeds precede, that deed which is weightier, or proximate, or reinforced by practice, is one which has generated a potency that shines forth, but not so another.[83]

This passage repeats several times—and explains—the expression "from the distinctive feature of the transformation of that continuum" (*tatsaṃtatipariṇāmaviśeṣāt*),[84] which echoes the passage presented as an answer to argument 4, "from a distinctive feature of the continuum that precedes it" (*tatpūrvakāt saṃtānaviśeṣād*). The words are not an exact repetition, but the point is clearly the same: a karmic result arises from an action indirectly, rather than directly, and the causal event is mediated by a continuum, a connected series of stages. What actually and directly causes the karmic result is a characteristic of the mental series, which shines forth at the moment of death.

The first explanation goes the route of employing an analogy, that of a fruit arising from a seed. Just as a fruit arises from a seed via the intervention of a sprout and many other stages of a plant, karmic fruit arises from an action indirectly via the intervention of the mental continuum.

ANALOGY OF SEED AND SPROUT FOR *KARMA*, BASED UPON AKBH IX (477.9–20)

seed →	sprout → stem → leaves → flower →	fruit
action →	mental continuum →	rebirth

The initial point of the analogy is to indicate the natural sensibleness of indirect causes. We do say that the seed causes the fruit, even though the fruit is more directly caused by a flower. Why? Because there is something in the seed (the DNA, it turns out), that determines *what kind of fruit* will arise. There are, of course, many different causes and conditions that must be in place for a fruit to arise, and a seed is only one. But the kind of soil and the kind of weather (for instance) do not determine what kind of fruit will arise. Nor can you take any other moment in the series—the flower, say—and pluck it out, and start over with it, and end up with a fruit. You need a seed, where the continuum begins, and you need a particular kind of seed to produce a particular kind of fruit. Here we have a figurative point similar in ways to the Christian idea of "good seed" (Matthew 13:24), if that is a useful reference. In just the same way that good seeds bring about good fruit, good deeds eventually cause good results.

Yet in addition to this basic karmic claim, Vasubandhu's argument uses the seed and fruit analogy to make quite a different moral point. *Karma* appears to imply a kind of determination, in that the seed produced by the action will produce a very specific kind of fruit, and no other. Yet Vasubandhu's emphasis here counters such an intuition. He says that the result *does not* directly arise from the seed, but rather relies crucially upon the mediation of the many stages of the plant. In fact, the notion that the DNA in a seed produces, *inevitably*, a particular kind of fruit is directly contradicted in the final paragraph of the work, when Vasubandhu refines the analogy and points out that a seed that is coated with lac generates a plant that eventually produces reddened flowers. By altering the supporting causes, he is saying, it is possible to have a genuine effect on the fruit of a given seed.

The moral point, then, is that remorse can be crucial, and, as Vasubandhu is pointing out in the passage quoted, one's particular rebirth is not determined by any single act in the past, but by the accumulation of many acts, which together shape and constitute one's mental state at the moment of death. The particular quality of the person's mental continuum at death—the quality that shines forth and causes the particular rebirth—is said to be the "distinctive feature" (*viśeṣa*) only in the sense that it is the one quality that *happens to cause* the resultant rebirth. What makes a particular deed the "distinctive" one is that it "is weightier, or proximate, or reinforced by practice," and so is the one that "shines forth" at death. There is nothing "distinctive" in the past event itself; its causal capacity is entirely relative to the other qualities of the continuum. If a weightier deed had been recently performed, *it* would be the proximate cause of rebirth, rather than the one that ends up being considered responsible for the "distinctive feature of the continuum."

If we feed this observation back into Vasubandhu's larger causal argument, we notice that if the past action were itself the *direct* cause of the result, then no conditioning factors (such as remorse or prayer) could intervene and change the result. It would never be possible to paint the flower with lac and get a differently colored fruit. Vasubandhu's argument rejects this kind of fatalism and implies that it would be true if real past actions somehow remained in existence to cause karmic results directly.

Thus, when the Vaibhāṣika insists that karmic causality is undermined when Vasubandhu denies the reality of past objects, Vasubandhu replies with a defense of a commonsense explanation of how causality works, using the analogy of seeds and fruit, and a good offense, suggesting that the eternal quasi-existence of past actions would vitiate the power of remorse and, perhaps, the Buddhist *dharma* overall. In making reference to this later argument in defense of no-self, furthermore, Vasubandhu is emphasizing how the argument his opponents have proposed against his understanding of karmic causality in fact ends up resembling the non-Buddhist, Nyāya-Vaiśeṣika view of the eternal soul as the basis of karmic retribution. If you are willing to believe in the never-ending existence of past actions, he seems to imply, why not simply accept the eternal existence of the soul, and be done with your quasi-Buddhism?

CONCLUSION

Vasubandhu's concerns in his disproof of the Sarvāstivāda theory of the reality of the three times touch upon a great many themes, all of which will recur in the chapters that follow. He discusses the incoherence of a traditional notion of an entity changing or becoming active (central to my chapter 3); the foolishness of literalism in scriptural interpretation of the Buddha's use of the term "existence" (chapter 4); the distinction between "producers" of consciousness and "mere experiential objects," which is to say the distinction between how entities exist and how they are experienced (chapter 5); and the morally perilous implications of granting proximate causes inevitable, unmediated results (chapter 6). Each section addresses the concerns of a different opponent, but the opponents are not selected arbitrarily and the responses to them are connected. These diverse discussions are woven into a coherent, distinctive approach to one of the, if not the, most fundamental of metaphysical questions: What does it mean to say that something *exists*? And, as the final argument has shown, this question is for Vasubandhu a mirror image of the question of what the Buddha meant when he said that the so-called self *does not exist.*

Given the arguments discussed here, we may state that for Vasubandhu, to say that an entity *exists* means that it is actively engaged in causal relations with other entities. It makes no sense to imagine an existent entity that *fails* to produce its causal result, because in such a situation an entity is not an existent. This is why entities cannot change their states, or their status. There is, he argues, no scriptural basis for a belief in past and future entities. The Buddha did not intend to say, when he spoke of the "existence" of past *karma*, that karmic acts endured like present entities—only their causal results endure, until their fruit is borne. Furthermore, our intuitions about how the mind works can be accounted for without reifying the past and the future. Merely experiential objects do not "exist" because, like unicorns (and unlike perceptual objects), they can never be the "producers" or causes of mental events. And finally, the moral basis of Buddhist belief and practice—the doctrine of *karma*—works better, not worse, when the reification of past entities is removed from the story. In all of these arguments, we see that one of Vasubandhu's main purposes is to establish his decisive equation of causal activity with existence, and to eliminate alternatives to this view, even when they are apparently supported by common sense or direct scriptural citation. To think otherwise, Vasubandhu reasons, is to court a non-Buddhist interpretation of scripture and the universe, and to undermine the Buddha's decisive denial of the self.

As mentioned in the opening of this chapter, the Sarvāstivāda position is one that takes most seriously the claim of the reality of causes and conditions. If causes are real, even when they are past, this would appear to necessitate the reality of the past. So, we might ask, how will Vasubandhu, having refuted the reality of the past and the future, account for the Buddha's fundamental claims about the nature of causal conditioning? How can he believe that existence itself is equated with causal activity, and yet at the same time deny the reality of past and future entities? How can causal activity be real, if the entities that make up a causal series—at least those that are past and future—are unreal? The short answer is that, for Vasubandhu, causality itself is *not* substantially real, and is *not a dharma*. As we have already seen in the seed-and-fruit analogy, what makes one set of entities a "cause" is not something about its inherent nature, but rather a conceptual construction that we formulate by observing multiple entities' behavior through time. Thus, whereas causality is what determines the presence, and the reality of an entity, *causality itself* is not a reality that may be affirmed, over and above the behavior of distinct entities. For this reason, while the determination of causality is how *we judge* what is real and what is not, causality itself is only a conceptual construction. This view of causality, and Vasubandhu's fascinating use of it to distinguish the real from the unreal, is the subject of the next chapter.

3

MERELY CAUSE AND EFFECT

The Imagined Self and the Literalistic Mind

VASUBANDHU'S DISPROOF OF THE TRANSMIGRATING SELF (AKBH III.18)

Vasubandhu is well known for his extensive, brilliant argument defending the Buddha's doctrine of no-self, which takes up the entirety of chapter IX of the AKBh. We ended our last chapter with the finale of that argument, we will begin the next chapter with its opening, and we will refer occasionally to other moments within it as well.[1] For this chapter, our goal is to grasp not the twists and turns of that argument, but only its motivating structure in Vasubandhu's characteristic appeal to the nature of cause and effect. With that in hand, we will be able to see how the same motivation that disproves the self holds together a range of positions across the AKBh. The core of the argument may be discerned in what serves as Vasubandhu's first draft, a kind of compact edition of the argument, which he includes in his chapter III.[2] We will begin with this argument, and then examine two passages—on "view" (*dṛṣṭi*) and on "atoms" (*paramāṇu*), respectively—that will together display how Vasubandhu uses the doctrine of no-self as the touchstone for a properly Buddhist approach to causality, the nature of existence, and the interpretation of scripture.

The concise no-self argument opens with a challenge from a non-Buddhist, who sees an opening, in the context of chapter III, in the fact that Buddhists affirm rebirth:

> Now, in this case outsiders [non-Buddhists], having grasped upon the view of a self, declare: "If it is accepted that a living being transmigrates to another world, then a self is proven."
>
> One counters this: **There is no self.** [III.18a1]
>
> What kind of self?
>
> That kind of internally functioning person does not exist, who is imagined to abandon these aggregates and appropriate others. Thus the Lord has said:[3] "There is action and there is fruit, but no agent is perceived who casts off these aggregates and appropriates other aggregates, because this is counter to the stipulated meaning [*saṃketa*] of *dharma*. In this situation, the stipulated meaning of *dharma* is just what is dependently originated—elaborated as 'when this exists, that arises.' "[4]

What is at issue here is a question that arises often in beginning Buddhist studies: How can Buddhists believe in reincarnation, but reject the soul? What reincarnates, if not the soul? Of course, the Buddhist view is defined by its acceptance of both no-self and rebirth, so Vasubandhu is prepared to explain how this can work. His central point is that there is an erroneous assumption embedded in the question. Not only is the notion of a self or soul mistaken in itself, it is unnecessary. It contributes nothing to the explanation of rebirth. All that is necessary for rebirth is the aggregates, the *skandhas*, which make up what *appears to be* the self. Instead of thinking of a self that takes on a body-and-mind complex, think of a body-and-mind complex working, causally, to produce another body-and-mind complex. This is how the basic elements (*dharmas*) that make up the person work: "When this exists, that arises." One mental event leads to the next mental event. One physical form leads to the next physical form. You don't need an "agent" to account for the succession of events in this kind of linear causal description. You don't need a self that *appropriates* these elements. All you need is the natural, internal functionality of the elements themselves.

What's more, if we imagine that the rebirth of the person depends upon the self or soul's having moved from one locus to the next, then there must not only be a self *over and above* the aggregates; there must be an "internally functioning person" that keeps its identity as a person after death, until rebirth. That is, the soul that is reborn would need to have its own, causally efficient identity that is independent of its previous and subsequent body-and-mind complexes. But outside of the aggregates (which include mental events and karmic imprints), it is difficult to say what such a "person" would be.

In the final chapter of the AKBh, Vasubandhu meets a great many objections to the view that he advocates—defending the notion that the aggregates, understood causally, can indeed account for our intuitions about the nature of memory, personal identity, perception, action, and moral recompense. In particular, he critiques Buddhists who maintain belief in a "person" over and above the aggregates. Here, in chapter III, the point is made concisely by quoting the Buddha's view that a description of rebirth requires action and result, but does not require an agent. This, he says, is the point of the Buddhist teaching of dependent origination.

Vasubandhu moves directly from the basic defense of no-self to a clarification of why this is not, in fact, a denial of rebirth. One might think that if there is nothing to be reborn, then there should be no rebirth. Yet the Buddhist position is not, he says, that there is *nothing at all* that transmigrates; it is that there is no self *over and above* the aggregates. Vasubandhu therefore emphasizes that the self is not "denied" entirely, but is just made into a "figurative designation" (*upacāra*) for the aggregates:

> But then what kind of self is not rejected?
>
> **But that which is only aggregates.** [III.18a2] But if that which is only aggregates is figuratively called "self," it is not rejected. It is thus that the aggregates-alone transmigrates to another world. But it is not that a complete [*prāpta*] aggregates-alone transmigrates there. **Conditioned by defilements and actions, it proceeds to the womb as the intermediate-state continuum, like a light.** (18) [III.18b–d] For the aggregates are momentary; they are not able to transmigrate. But brought into being by defilements and actions, defilements alone approach the mother's womb as a continuum known as the "intermediate state." In this way, it is not a fault to say of a light, though momentary, that it moves to another place as a continuum. Therefore it is accepted that although the self does not exist,[5] the continuum of aggregates, conditioned by defilements and actions, enters the mother's womb.[6]

Once it is established that there is no self, it may be asked whether it is truly accurate to say that the *aggregates* transmigrate. If we are looking to transcend the figurative and provide the literal truth of the matter, Vasubandhu admits that, although when we speak of the self transmigrating we are truly referring to the aggregates, in fact the aggregates do not really transmigrate either. For they are momentary and ever-changing.

No aggregate "transmigrates," for that would mean that it exists in two different places at two different times. What transmigrates, then, is a *continuum of aggregates*. The continuum of aggregates, the causal series, exists, *but never all at once*.

As we have discussed at length in the previous chapter, Vasubandhu differs from the Sarvāstivādins on the reality of past and future events, and so he gives a different account of the figurative reference of a word like "transmigrates," which refers to a continuum. For the Sarvāstivādins, the true referent of such a term is complexly made up of past, present, and future entities in relation to one another. For Vasubandhu, the separate entities are causally related, but they only appear to exist as a unit by virtue of their having been joined through the conceptual-linguistic act of reference. The continuum exists as the figurative reference for what "transmigrates." In reality, though, there is no agent of transmigration and no unified entity that persists through time.

As an analogy, Vasubandhu speaks of how a flame, which is in fact made of countless momentary explosions, and which may be passed from one wick to the next, in fact appears as a single, ongoing "light." In the same way, the countless momentary "defilements," which have originated out of previous actions and defilements, continue and move to a new set of aggregates with the appearance of a single, ongoing "intermediate body." Thus there is no "intermediate body," but there is a continuum of entities that may be said to "transmigrate," in the sense that, joined together conceptually across time, the continuum is said to be in different bodies at different times.

We have here, in brief, the key conceptual nexus for Vasubandhu's AKBh. The self is imposed upon the aggregates, and the aggregates are thus only figuratively referred to, collectively, as an agent acting in time. In the same way, a range of doctrinal positions may be characterized as figurative impositions upon changing elements. Again and again Vasubandhu insists that what appear to be agents and their actions are in fact "merely cause and effect," and must be understood as operating in this way if we are to recognize not how things merely appear, but how things really are. In the next section we will see this causal analysis applied to the apparent unity of the agent of perception and cognition. In the final section of this chapter we turn to Vasubandhu's brief disproof of the eternality of atoms. There, we see how Vasubandhu's notion of "merely cause and effect" works with simultaneous, as well as chronological, groupings of elements. These different kinds of falsely appearing "wholes" are critiqued in parallel terms, even using the same analogies, of whirling firebrands and lines of ants.

Throughout, Vasubandhu is showing that what requires explanation is not the reality of the combination of entities, but only the *appearance* of their combinations. Thus the arguments for atoms based upon their necessity for the support of part-whole relations (*mereology*), like the arguments for the apparent activity of the perceiving eye, will be shown to depend upon an overly literal reading of scriptures and an overly simplistic reliance upon what are ultimately only deluded, conceptual-linguistic constructions. With these issues in place, we will be prepared to proceed, in the next two chapters, to see how this view coalesces into Vasubandhu's distinctive articulation of the relation between words, mind, and reality in Yogācāra.

THE SAUTRĀNTIKA VIEW OF PERCEPTION, COGNITION, AND AGENCY (AKBH I.41–42)

A crucial set of discussions that illuminate Vasubandhu's abstract theory of causality grow as offshoots from a main argument about cognition and perception, and we should not think of them as merely opportunistic digressions. The causal arguments gain their impetus from this frame, and return to reframe it as well. As we have seen and will continue to see, arguments about the nature of causality, scripture, and the mind are conceptually intertwined throughout the AKBh. Attention to this kind of argumentative embedding therefore helps to reveal Vasubandhu's motives and modes of philosophical engagement along with the particulars of his arguments. It is helpful, therefore, to follow Vasubandhu's line of argument quite closely, and elucidate each twist and turn, as I will here (the full passage studied in this section is translated in appendix C).

The framing question is the nature of an element called "view" (*dṛṣṭi*). The *sūtras* include numerous passages in which the Buddha speaks of various views, especially views that need to be abandoned in order to attain liberation, and the correct views of those on the path. Abhidharma takes on the responsibility of explaining and accounting for such statements with technical precision. Since a view is causally relevant in its own distinctive way, views constitute a *dharma* with its own class category. For the Vaibhāṣikas, views are classified as kinds of discrimination (*prajñā*), which is an ever-present mental element. The class of views partially overlaps the class of "knowledges" (*jñāna*).[7] Discrimination (*prajñā*) is the term used for an enlightened being's wisdom once purified of defilements. Until that point, the "ignorance" (*avidyā*) represented by false views remains the root cause of rebirth.[8] Ignorance is, after all, the first of the twelve links in the chain of dependent origination. The causal importance of views on the path should be understood as a crucial motivation behind the well-known Buddhist distaste for a distinction between "reasons" and "causes." This is a complex issue that will occupy us here and in subsequent chapters. We will see here that Vasubandhu's arguments on the nature of *dṛṣṭi* somewhat imply that his opponents have forgotten the crucial, *causal* aspect of a properly understood Buddhist "view."[9]

Vasubandhu begins his study of the *dharma* called "view," which appears in the first book of the AKBh, by asking just what the "views"

TABLE 3.1 Nine Kinds of "View" (*dṛṣṭi*), Based on AKBh I.41

KIND OF "VIEW"	ACCURACY	*DHĀTU* CLASSIFICATION
1. View of the eye	N/A	Eye sense organ (*caksurindriya)*
2. View with respect to the existing body (*satkāyadṛṣṭi*)	False views	*dharmadhātu* elements—i.e., mental objects
3. View that is grasping the extremes	"	"
4. View of negation [of the truths]	"	"
5. View that holds "high" to be "low"	"	"
6. View that considers a cause [of liberation] what is not a cause [of Liberation]	"	"
7. Trainee's view	Relative to attainments on the path	"
8. Nontrainee's (Arhat's) view	"	"
9. Worldly right view	Associated with mental consciousness only	"

are. For the Vaibhāṣikas, they include nine varieties: eight that are mental objects (*dharmadhātu*) and one that is the view of the eye (table 3.1). We, too, use the same term "view" for a doctrine and a visual perspective, and this section interrogates the question of whether such usage reflects a genuinely consequential similarity in nature, or merely two meanings for the same word.[10] The majority of Vasubandhu's discussion here will argue that the *eye* should not count as having a *view*, but before turning to that argument he runs through the eight mental objects (*dharmadhātu*) as a way of framing and characterizing the nature of a *view*. These eight varieties include five false views (about which more in a moment), two views attributable to specific categories of practitioners, and one view that is called "worldly right view," which is defined as "good, defiled discrimination [*prajñā*], associated with the mental consciousness." This definition describes an ordinary being's correct mental observations.

Vasubandhu mentions in this passage that he will treat the five false views later on, in his chapter on the defilements. Let us briefly turn to that later passage to provide further framing for the questions at issue here. The most important, paradigmatic "view" is the *wrong view* called the "view with respect to the existing body," *satkāyadṛṣṭi*, which refers to the mistaken view of self. Vasubandhu explains this view as follows:

> The view of the self or the view of things possessed by a self are "view with respect to the existing body" [*satkāyadṛṣṭi*]. "Existing" means that it is. The point is that the clump, or body [*kāya*], is a combination, an aggregate [*skandha*]. What exists as this body, the "existing body," is the five appropriative aggregates. It is expressed in order to preclude the idea of eternality and the idea of a sum. For this grasping of a self precedes them. The compound "existing-body-view" [*satkāyadṛṣṭi*] is to be understood as meaning "the view with respect to the existing body." All defiled perceptual objects are seen with respect to the existing body. But just the view of the self or of things possessed by a self are called "the view with respect to the existing body." As it goes, "This view with respect to the existing body is neither the self nor the things possessed by a self." As it is said, "Wherever Bhikṣus, Śramaṇas, or Brāhmans perceive the 'self,' all they perceive is the five appropriative aggregates."[11]

The basic error for all unenlightened beings is the false imposition of a self upon the aggregates, which are merely collections of ever-changing entities. This error is given the name "the view with respect to the existing body" in order to foreground the real substratum upon which a false "view" is imposed. Many distinct elements that "exist" only momentarily are taken together, as a sum, to be an unchanging and eternal self. Two mistakes—imposing temporal and psychophysical unity—Vasubandhu says, depend upon the "grasping of a self." In fact, for ordinary beings *everything* is perceived in some way with respect to the self—either as *part of* the self, or as *distinct from but known by* the self. Since everything appears as self or other, *satkāyadṛṣṭi* could, in fact describe every ordinary perception. But the term is used, more narrowly, to describe the more fundamental error upon which the other errors are based. When we discuss "views," then, we must keep in mind this foundational "view," which is the erroneous imposition of a self upon the aggregates.

Notice that the correct title for this error is not the "view of the self" (although that expression is used to explain it) but rather the "view with respect to the existing body," because when we speak of the "view" we are brought into awareness of the error. Here "view" implies the *imposition* over and above what is real. "Existing" (meaning existing only momentarily) and "body" (meaning an assemblage, an aggregate) describe, respectively, temporal and psychophysical characteristics that we fail to see properly when we are unaware that our view is a view. This is the meaning of the Buddha's saying that this view is "neither the self nor the things possessed by a self"; the view *that takes things to be* the self and the things possessed by the self *is really* the view with respect to an ever-changing group of discrete entities. This distinction between what a view *takes to be* and what a view *really views* is evident as well in the other standard false views. I will not detail them all here (see table 3.1), but as a further example we may note how the second wrong view, "the view that is grasping the extremes" is (like all perceptions) dependent upon the more fundamental grasping of the imagined self:

> The view of the permanence or the view of the destruction of that very thing imagined as the self is the "view that is grasping the extremes," because of grasping eternity and destruction.[12]

Here again the term "view" provides the occasion for distinguishing between what is really there, which is an action of grasping, and the apparent reality, which is the permanence or destruction of the imagined self. Even to speak of these as "views" implies an awareness of this distinction between what we might call *appearance* (*viewing-as*) and *substratum* (*viewing-of*).[13]

Vasubandhu's works show an astonishing sensitivity to the ways we ascribe reality and terminology to entities in our experience and perception. A constant theme is the need to distinguish between viewing-as and viewing-of, so often conflated in our ordinary experience and language. In his argument against Vasumitra's view of time, we saw Vasubandhu defend a distinction between an object of a memory, which is a mental object, and the object in the world that is remembered but no longer exists. This is to distinguish two different perspectives upon the same view: the view *of* an object that does not exist and the view *as* a present memory. Now, the essence of "wrong view" is explained as the view *of* the aggregates *as* the self. When we turn to Vasubandhu's Yogācāra treatises, we will see this distinction enshrined in the most fundamental metaphysical structure of that tradition, the Three Natures of reality. But already we can see the conceptual apparatus at work.

To return to the passage from the first book of the AKBh, Vasubandhu presents a critique that will imply that the ninefold list of "views" provided by the Vaibhāṣika (see table 3.1) is incoherent—that it fails to accord with its own rules. It might seem that, in arguing so, Vasubandhu has set himself rather an easy task, for we may question whether the list is really *supposed to be* coherent. It could be just a list of things that one (or, to be more specific, the Buddha) sometimes calls a "view." In fact, to say this would be to come fairly close to Vasubandhu's own position—as he will argue later on. Before that, though, he draws out the details of the list as well as the justification the Vaibhāṣikas provide for their classificatory scheme, displaying thereby how they indeed *purport* it to be systematic and rational. The *Commentary*, in this way, is Janus-faced: it does, in fact, provide a comprehensive and detailed account of the Vaibhāṣika system of Abhidharma philosophy; but in doing so, it lays bare the conceptual limitations of that system.

Here Vasubandhu uses the rather elegant and sensible Vaibhāṣika explanation of the choice of "worldly right view" as a launching pad for his critique of the notion that the *eye* has a *view*:

> Now, why is the worldly right view said to be associated with the mental consciousness? Because: **a thought produced with the five consciousnesses**[14] **is not a view, because of being indeterminate** [*atīraṇa*]. (41) [I.41c–d] For a determinate [*santīrika*] view is arisen from close consideration [*upadhyāna*]. And this is certainly not the case for discrimination [*prajñā*] produced with the five consciousnesses. Therefore it is not a view. So too for the others: neither defiled nor undefiled discrimination is a view.

> In that case, how is the eye, which is indeterminate, a view?
> In the sense of seeing a form. For **the eye sees forms.** [I.42a][15]

This opening gambit begins by asking why "worldly right view" is said to be associated with mental consciousness alone. In the *dhatu* system, there are six consciousnesses, one for each sensory organ and one for the mind. Vasubandhu poses the question why mental objects may be considered "views," but not the other five consciousnesses—those associated with the sensory organs. In answer, the Vaibhāṣika replies that a view is something "settled" or "determinate"; it must have arisen from "consideration" (*upadhyāna*). Objects of perception, whether defiled or not, are not decided in this way as the result of cognitive activity, and so they are not properly "views."

This sensible suggestion certainly fits with the other seven mental objects (especially the wrong views), which are the result of deliberative mental activities. But it sparks the question why, if being "settled" in this sense is their criterion for inclusion in the category, the Vaibhāṣikas include the eye. In answer, the Vaibhāṣika must admit that the eye has a different criterion for inclusion: "In the sense of seeing a form." The eye, unlike the other elements in this category, is included because it sees visual objects—clearly, a legitimate, though different, meaning for the word "view" (*dṛṣṭi*). What you see and what ideas you come to hold in mind seem like different kinds of "view." As a first thought, we might distinguish them by saying that the eye's "view" is a literal meaning of the word, whereas calling someone's doctrinal errors their mistaken "view" is only figurative. As he often does, Vasubandhu will seek to dispense with the literal interpretation.[16] In any case, the fact that both ideas can be expressed with the same words ("vision, perspective, view") is not a justifiable reason to classify different entities under the same head. To classify them together implies that they share the same inherent nature (*svabhāva*), which they cannot if they must be characterized differently. The commentary therefore frames the Vaibhāṣika category as inconsistent on its own terms—or, at best, sloppy.[17] It also sets up a problem in the nature of the term "view" that requires resolution: how to account for, and distinguish between, the view acquired by the eye and the view that is a settled idea.

Vasubandhu's analysis will resolve *both* the problem of the two different classifications, *and* the problem of the proper interpretation of the term. He accomplishes this by reconceiving the ostensibly literal meaning of the term "view" as it applies to the eye as figurative, in exactly the same figurative way that it applies to "worldly right view." Explaining this allows "worldly right views" to include the view—the "vision"—of the eye. The arguments used to establish this reflect the causal reasoning and patterns of scriptural interpretation we saw Vasubandhu employ in his response to the Vaibhāṣika position on the reality of the three times. Here we will see how this characteristic approach weds him to a view of the nature of perception and knowledge that presages his later Yogācāra positions. Yet the way this argument rehabilitates the category "view" (*dṛṣṭi*) under its new interpretation shows that Vasubandhu is not attempting to overturn the systematic, Ābhidharmika approach to the Buddha's teachings—on the contrary, he presents his interpretation as the most consistent and logical system available for Buddhists.[18] Above all, it makes sense of the Buddha's having placed *views* in the causal stream, as *reasons that are causes* of conditioned and conditioning mental events. Thus Vasubandhu's analyses of perception and the mind are intended to facilitate a causally realistic explanation of the relationship between the Buddha's teachings, properly understood, and the attainment of liberation that they are supposed to cause.

FALSE REASONS FOR SAYING THE EYE "SEES"

As Vasubandhu moves into his project to reduce the vision of the eye to the vision of the mental, he begins with a dialogue in which the commentary sets itself against the Vaibhāṣika doctrinal position advocated in the verse. Here is one of the famous moments in which Vasubandhu includes the word *kila*, meaning "so they say," within his verse, indicating that even while writing the verse he was willing to express misgivings about this position.[19] Vasubandhu seems to have been wedded from the start to the idea that it is consciousness that "sees," not the eye organ. Yaśomitra's commentary names this a Vijñānavāda argument—a name that is later given to the Yogācāra tradition.[20] Whether or not we wish to ascribe this doctrinal identity to Vasubandhu at this stage, there is no doubt that he foregrounds this argument with rhetorical panache, and seems thereby to be drawing out a critique implicit in the verse itself. Yet the argument is framed, as I have already mentioned, as a search for a consistent *svabhāva* for the *dharma* called *dṛṣṭi*, and it will culminate in an explicit advocacy of a position attributed, again, to the Sautrāntika.

Instead of attempting to sort out the issues of doctrinal affiliation, therefore, let us examine Vasubandhu's own philosophical procedure:

> If the eye sees, then so also the other sufficient conditions for consciousnesses should see.
>
> Certainly not every eye sees.
>
> Which does, then?
>
> **One with a corresponding [consciousness].** [I.42b1] It sees when it is accompanied by consciousness; otherwise it does not.
>
> Then it should be said that just that consciousness sees, with the eye as the support.[21]

The first line sets up a refusal of the Vaibhāṣika distinction between the eye organ and the other organs—if the eye sees, so should the other organs, since they all provide the conditions for consciousness. Vasubandhu's proof that it must be the consciousness that sees will come later. Yet by using the word *samaṅgin*, which I've translated as "sufficient conditions" (more literally, "that which possesses the requisite parts"), Vasubandhu immediately pushes the opponent to come clean about the fact that the eye is not, in truth, capable of being a "view" just on its own. It must, of necessity, have a corresponding consciousness.[22] Thus it is the opponent who is forced to put forward consciousness as the crucial condition for an eye's being a "view." But if this is the case, Vasubandhu replies, how can you attribute the "view" to the eye, as opposed to the consciousness? Clearly the reason the eye is called "view" is because it is associated with the consciousness, and not the other way around.[23]

Once this argument is in place, the Vaibhāṣika position is fatally wounded. The discussion that follows will not challenge the predominance of the mental in the characterization of "views." Eight of the nine "views" in the Vaibhāṣika list take mental objects, and even the exception relies upon a consciousness for its identity as "view." Instead, the Vaibhāṣika argues against the *possibility* that the consciousness may be what is referred to with the term "view." These arguments reveal further, deeper, mistaken presumptions on the part of this system, and Vasubandhu pursues them to their root.

The initial reason that the Vaibhāṣika believes a "consciousness" cannot be considered a view refers back to characteristics of consciousness itself, namely, that it is formless and therefore unobstructed by physical entities. If consciousness were the one to "view" a visual object, there would be no limitations to its capacity for visual awareness:

> **It's not that with it as support, the consciousness** [I.42b2–c1] sees, so it can be able to be unaware.
>
> Why?
>
> **It does not see form, they say, where there is something intervening.** (42) [I.42c2–d] For, they say, it does not see a form covered by a wall, etc. For if the consciousness were to see, since it is not subject to resistance [*pratigha*], there would be no resistance where there is a wall, etc., so it would see even a covered form.[24]

Clearly vision is limited by the positioning of the eye. The theory of vision at play here holds that the eye organ (made of a kind of subtle physicality, not just the eyeball) comes into contact with the visual object—which is why we cannot see a hidden object. Consciousness, however, is nonphysical. So, the Vaibhāṣika opponent says, if vision were a capacity of the consciousness rather than the eye, it could not be limited by its positioning. We should then expect to be aware of all visual objects everywhere. Such a viewing mind would not be "able to be unaware" of anything. Since, however, we cannot see through walls, we may be sure that it is the eye, not the mind, that sees.

This argument reveals that the Vaibhāṣikas are thinking of the "view" of the eye in terms of its range of sight, its scope of activity. Perhaps we should think of the eye's view as something like the view from your bedroom window. The physical, mechanical limitations of the eye, and its spatial location, provide the scope and character of its view. Yet to take this analogy to its conclusion, we must forget what the Vaibhāṣikas have just admitted, which is that the eye is only called "view" when it is actively engaged with a consciousness. When no one is home, there is no consciousness actively engaged with your bedroom window's "view," so at those times it should *not* be considered, literally, a "view." When you brag that your bedroom has a beautiful view, you are speaking figuratively. Your bedroom sees nothing.

With something like this in mind, Vasubandhu proceeds to show that the supposed problem, that the mind does not share the physical limitations of the eye's range of vision, is a red herring. Since the eye is indeed a crucial, causal condition—the "support" (*āśraya*)—for vision, the eye's limited scope is inherited by the consciousness by which it is supported.

The eye *consciousness* cannot arise with an awareness of anything that the eye cannot see:

> No, the eye consciousness does not arise with respect to something covered, so how will it see what does not arise?
>
> How then does it not arise?
>
> Since the eye is subject to resistance, the state of seeing something does not come about with respect to what is covered. So for the consciousness, too, it does not arise; it operates by means of a single sensory object, which joins it as support [*āśraya*].[25]
>
> Why then would you say that the eye, like the bodily sense organ which meets its object, does not see it to the extent it is covered?
>
> Because it is subject to resistance.
>
> And how is something seen which has an interposition by glass, fog, veil, or water?
>
> That is not a case where, because it is subject to resistance, an eye fails to see a covered form.
>
> What is it then?
>
> The eye consciousness does arise in the case where sight has no impediment even with respect to a covered form. But where there is an impediment, it does not arise. In that case, because it does not arise, the covered thing is not seen.[26]

Here Vasubandhu explains that what is "covered" for the eye will never appear to the eye consciousness, because the eye consciousness only takes its object through its support (*āśraya*), which is the eye. The eye cannot attain a "covered" object,[27] and so cannot pass an unattained object on to the consciousness.

In reply, the opponent raises the question of how, under this interpretation, there can be a "view" through transparent media such as water and fog. This is, indeed, a problem for a theory of visual sensation that relies upon the notion of contact between the organ and its object, but it is not entirely clear why this question is a challenge to Vasubandhu's conceptual reclassification of "view." Perhaps the idea that the consciousness, not the eye, "sees" is being taken by the challenger to imply that an eye under this description is passive and inert. Under such an interpretation, the eye's "view" might ordinarily be thought to be a kind of active motion toward contact with its object. The challenge would then be that a passive eye, which is not an *agent* of sight, should not be able to penetrate a pool of water and gain "contact" with objects (for instance) on the bottom of a river. Alternatively, this challenge may be here simply because Vasubandhu has set up a binary distinction (covered vs. not covered), which invites the posing of exceptions to the rule. In either case, Vasubandhu is able to resolve the quandary without delving into the precise workings of the organ, by making a further distinction for the eye, between what merely "covers" the object (which would include a transparent medium) and what is a definite "impediment" to sight (such as a wall). That distinction, however it works for the eye, will allow the right objects to be transferred to the consciousness.

What this segment of the argument establishes is that although the "range of sight" interpretation of "view" may raise some intuitive problems for the active operation of vision, it is inconsequential to the question of whether it is the eye itself, or the consciousness, that should be granted the "view." With these challenges expended, and Vasubandhu's notion of the consciousness as what "sees" established as the most sensible, the discussion can turn to the interpretation of scripture:

> What then of the *sūtra* that says, "Having seen forms with the eye . . ."?
>
> Here the intent is [that one sees forms] *with this as support*—just as he says, "One should know *dharmas* with the mind [*manas*]," and the mind is not cognizing *dharmas*, because it is past.
>
> What does then?
>
> The mental consciousness. Or, the supported action is referred to figuratively as the support, as in "The stands cried out." And as in the *sūtra* that says, "Known by the eyes, forms are desired, beloved," and they are not cognized by the eyes. And it is said in the *sūtra*, "The eye, O Brāhman, is the doorway for seeing forms"; by this is meant that by the doorway that is the eyes, the consciousness sees. In this case he does not say "doorway into seeing," because it does not make sense[28] to say, "The eye is the seeing for seeing forms."[29]

Here Vasubandhu leads off with a figurative reading of a direct statement from the Buddha that the eye is what sees. What he means, Vasubandhu says, is that the eye is the *support* (*āśraya*) of seeing. To read the text literally would require a contradiction within a clearly unified doctrinal system. For the Buddha also says, in a parallel statement, that the mental organ (*manas*) is what cognizes *dharmas*. But this is not possible, because there is no independent organ called the mental organ; the mental organ is nothing other than the collection of the six consciousnesses from the previous moment.[30] The mental organ is therefore an organ only in the figurative sense that it, like the sensory organs, provides the support for a consciousness—the mental consciousness. Whenever anything is cognized, then, the *manas* is already *past*. As discussed in the chapter on the three times, Vasubandhu denies that a past entity can provide a generative causal action in the present. The mental organ may provide the *support* for cognition, but the cognition itself is performed by the mental consciousness.

Since a direct reading would issue in an inconsistency, Vasubandhu invokes a standard hermeneutic method and suggests an alternative intention. He then provides two further texts that necessitate this very same figurative reading of the Buddha's words about the perception of the eye. In the first case, he presents a passage where the Buddha says that forms are "to be known by the eyes" (*cakṣurjñeyāni*)[31]—whereas knowledge is an activity that is only available to the mental consciousness. In the second, rather elegant, case, the Buddha has called the eyes "the doorway for seeing forms." If the eye performed the seeing itself, then it would hardly make sense to say that it was the doorway *into* seeing; it would be the house. In both of these cases, he says, "that which has the supported action is referred to figuratively [*upacaryate*] as the support." In both cases, the eye is referenced directly, but the evident meaning, the figurative referent, is what the eye supports: the cognitive activity of the mental consciousness.

Ironically, this reading flips our earlier figurative assumption on its head. We said above that the "view" of the eye was literal and the mind's "view" of mental objects was figurative. Now it seems that, given the assumptions of the Ābhidharmika perceptual and cognitive system, we must take the "view" of the eye as a figure for the "view" of the consciousness. It turns out that the view of the eye is, like the view from your bedroom window, only a conduit for consciousness, which is what actually "sees" the form. Yet the word "see" implies an eye, does it not? Is it not, therefore, also figurative to say that the consciousness "sees" forms? Consciousness cognizes; does it also see? These questions would imply, in the view of some philosophers, a vicious circularity in the notion that the *direct meanings* of words can be deemed "figurative," if figurative uses of terms are deemed parasitic on, and hence reliant upon, their direct meanings. But here we see that Vasubandhu is content to describe even the view of the *eye* as a figure for a mental event. In his Yogācāra work, the Triṃś, he says that *all* things are only figurative references to mental events—a clear generalization of this usage.[32] We are not there yet, but already Vasubandhu is using the term *upacāra* to refer to the ordinary use of a term. As Vasubandhu explains next, here the point is that it is important not to get caught up in the words. The "seeing" and the "cognizing" are just two different terms for the activity of consciousness:

> If the consciousness sees, what cognizes, and what is the difference between them?
>
> Consciousness of a form just is "seeing" it. In this way, if it is said that some discrimination [*prajñā*] "sees," it also "discriminates"; and if it is said that some consciousness "sees" it also "cognizes."[33]

For consciousness, as for discrimination, it can be said that it "sees" whenever the object that it takes as a mental object is a visual form. By bringing "discrimination" back into the argument here Vasubandhu brings the full argument home: just as the Buddha refers figuratively to the eye when he means the mental consciousness, he refers figuratively to the "view" when he means discrimination. There is no "seeing" or "view" apart from the mental events that take them as their objects. There is no difference in activity between "seeing" and "cognizing" for a consciousness, or between "seeing" and "discriminating" for a discrimination. The alert reader may sense a parallel here between this argument, which reads "view" as a figure for the activity of mental events, and the argument against the self, which reads "self" as a figure for the continuum of aggregates.[34]

As a last stage in this argument, Vasubandhu responds to a new objector, in such a way as to sharpen his position and clarify its significance:

> Others say: If the eye sees, then what else, aside from the eye that is become the agent, may be called the "action of seeing"?
>
> This is unacceptable.[35] For if it is granted that the consciousness cognizes, and in that case there is no difference between the agent and the action, then for the other case it should be accepted just as it is in that case. It is said that the eye "sees," because it is the support for the seeing eye-consciousness. Just as, it is said that a bell "resonates" because it is the support for the resonance.
>
> But then it obtains that the eye cognizes, since it is the support for the consciousness.
>
> This does not obtain. "The seeing consciousness" is a convention in the world. For when it has come about in this way, it is said that the "form is

> seen," not that it is "cognized." Also, the *Vibhāṣā* says, "'Seen' [*dṛṣṭa*] is said when the eye, completed, is experienced by the eye consciousness." Therefore it is said just that the eye sees, not that it cognizes.[36]

The new objector proposes a distinction between the eye as *agent* (*kartṛ*), which is said to "see," and the *action* of that agent. It seems a logical point. Sometimes the eye sees, and sometimes it does not. What distinguishes these times?[37] More importantly, this objection raises once again the specter of Vasubandhu's seemingly having posited an inactive or inert eye; such an eye would still need some additional element or characterization to bring its nature of "seeing" to fruition. Vasubandhu rejects this distinction based, once again, on an analogy to the mental consciousness. If we grant that the consciousness cognizes (and it is assumed that we do), then we must grant (he says) that in that case, at least, there is no possibility to distinguish between the agent and the action. Why should this be? Well, as we have already seen, the mental organ cannot act as the agent of a present action, because it is past. Only the mental consciousness exists to "cognize," so in this case there can be no distinction between agent and action.[38] But if the mental consciousness can be both agent and action of cognition, the eye consciousness can be both agent and action of sight: "For the other case it should be accepted just as it is in that case."

Then, as explanation, Vasubandhu reiterates the interpretation that the eye is figuratively referred to as the agent because it is the "support" (*āśraya*) for the eye consciousness. To explain this further, he gives the example of a bell, which is said to "ring" even when it is not engaged in any "action," but only provides the "support" for the sound. I find this quite a useful analogy to explain how Vasubandhu makes sense of the critique that sees the eye as passive. He says that an eye sees in just the same sense that a bell rings: they are neither active nor passive; they are causally enlivened supports for further causal results. The language of agency, as we will see him articulate in a moment, is entirely figurative.[39]

The follow-up question provides Vasubandhu an occasion to clarify a methodological issue in the application of his hermeneutic principle. The questioner asks whether, since the eye is said to "see" because it is the support for the eye consciousness, it should not also be said to "cognize," because it is the support (indirectly) for the mental consciousness. This hypothetical is a kind of slippery slope reductio ad absurdum. If we start referring to things by their supports, it asks, does not meaning fall away? We may as well say that eyes know, because the eyes are causal supports for cognitions. Vasubandhu's response here is to cut off the slide with an appeal to worldly conventions. What we see is not, ordinarily, called "cognized," whereas what we cognize *is* called "seen" (as in, "I see"). For good measure, even the Vaibhāṣika's own source text, the *Vibhāṣā*, is cited as an example of this conventional understanding of an eye's "seeing" as referring to the consciousness that it generates.

Vasubandhu is not trying to say that our patterns of linguistic application *must* follow the rule of "refer-to-the-support-as-an-agent," nor is he saying that all support-relations may properly be made into figures of agency. The interpretation of the figurative usage is descriptive and not prescriptive, local, not generalized. The Buddha's language needs to be understood in accordance with the linguistic traditions of his audience members. Thus, this discussion of the nature of ideas, refracted through a discussion of perception, yields a philosophical point about the nature of the contextualization of scripture within linguistic conventions.

Having read the foregoing in this way, we can see that the last section of the argument reconstitutes the full debate as a stand-off between the Vaibhāṣika and the Sautrāntika—the main rivals in the AKBh—on ground that has already been covered:

> But it is said that the consciousness "cognizes" form by the mere fact of its presence [*sānnidhyamātreṇa*], as the sun is the "maker of the day."
>
> On this, the Sautrāntika says: Why carve the ether? For, conditioned by the eye and forms, the eye consciousness comes about. In that case, what sees, and what is seen? For it is passive [*nirvyāpāra*], merely *dharmas*, and merely cause and effect. With regard to this, figurative terms are used by choice with a conventional meaning: "Eye sees, consciousness cognizes"—one should not be attached to them. For the Lord said, "Do not be attached to the popular etymology, nor rush to accept the world's ideas."[40]
>
> But this is the established position of the Kashmiri Vaibhāṣika: the eye sees, the ear hears, the nose smells, the tongue tastes, the body touches, the mind cognizes.[41]

In response to the argument that a "view" is an activity that refers, figuratively, to the causal story of an eye bringing about a consciousness, a final claim is advanced that this somehow violates the nature of consciousness, which is to illuminate whatever appears in its purview by virtue of its nature. This interpretation compares consciousness to the sun, which "makes the day" by its very presence. Here we return to the idea of agent and object, but in this case it is the consciousness, rather than the eye, that performs its agential action upon its object of illumination.[42] This claim may be compared to the fourth argument for the times discussed in the last chapter, which relied upon the subject-object quality of consciousness—that it is "intentional," in Brentano's sense of being "about" something, something that must therefore exist. Here we will see Vasubandhu dismiss the notion that the intentionality of consciousness—at least as it shows up in our ordinary use of words—may be used as proof of the true nature of entities. These words are only figurative, and the consciousness itself is not truly "intentional"—it is "merely cause and effect."

Vasubandhu's response comes from the mouth of the Sautrāntika: across the AKBh, one evident reason, if not *the* reason, for the name of this position is that "one who follows the *sūtras*" (*sautrāntika*) will not accept the authority of the *Vibhāṣā*, which is not scripture (*sūtra*) but scholarly treatise (*śāstra*).[43] So we should expect a *sūtra* quotation to counter the Vaibhāṣika view (though, ironically, Vasubandhu has also just cited the *Vibhāṣā* to support his own view). What is fascinating is that the quotation cited is not about "cognizing" and "seeing," but is rather a hermeneutical principle articulated by the Buddha, which supports a figurative reading of the scriptures: "Do not be attached to the popular etymology, nor accept the world's word meaning." The implication is that the Vaibhāṣika view is a "worldly," popular interpretation—just the kind of critique we would expect from a "Sautrāntika." But perhaps more important than simply citing the scriptures to support his view, this passage *cites the scriptures to justify reading ordinary terms figuratively*. One who truly understands the scriptures, the Sautrāntika says, is one who is not misled by them to construct an edifice out of figurative material: "Why carve the ether?"

The term *upacāra*, which I have been translating as "figure" and "figurative reference," has a uniform meaning here and across Vasubandhu's works. It is, quite simply, reference to an unreal entity. Suppose I say, "That boy is a lion!" There are many potential interpretations of this sentence. What is not at issue, though—what sets us in search of a figurative meaning in the first place—is the clear fact that the boy is not *literally* a lion; there is no lion there. Figurative reference, for Vasubandhu, is where something is intended other than the object of direct reference.[44] As we have seen in each case where this kind of figurative interpretation is proposed, all that is necessary in order to prove that such an indirect reference is intended is a proof that the direct reference would issue in a mistake or contradiction (which we cannot attribute to an enlightened Buddha). In order to prove that the Buddha could not mean to say that the *manas*, the mental organ, "cognizes," all that is necessary is a proof that the mental organ *cannot cognize*. What is left, then, is to decide upon the proper reference, the accurate interpretation of the intention. To attempt to make sense of the direct reference when an indirect reference is intended is to "carve the ether"—to attempt to systematize unintended referents.

Vasubandhu makes the identical complaint ("The Sautrāntika say, 'This is to divide the ether' ") in his second chapter, when he is critiquing the Vaibhāṣika view of the four characteristics of conditioned entities (*saṃskāra*): arising, duration, transformation, and destruction.[45] These four, say the Vaibhāṣika, are distinct *dharmas* that adhere to, and "activate," other conditioned entities (they are what make "future" events come to be "present," "present" events come to be "past," and so on). Vasubandhu critiques this view at length, and we will not engage in the details here. What is of great interest in that passage is how he accuses the Vaibhāṣikas of reifying merely linguistic entities like non-Buddhists do, and he calls this mistaken reification a "non-Buddhist false concept" (*tīrthakara-parikalpitā*).[46] Vasubandhu says there is no distinct *dharma* of arising, but rather many instances of conceptual/linguistic construction (*vikalpa*) in which someone notices a thing that did not exist now come into being, and then says of that thing that it is "arising." The terms *parikalpita* and *vikalpa*, which I translate as "false concept" and "conceptual/linguistic construction," respectively, are crucial terms for Vasubandhu. They indicate conceptual fabrications that play no role in the flow of real, efficient causality. They are, for Vasubandhu, the crux of a characteristically Buddhist view, and they play a central role in his Yogācāra works.

The Vaibhāṣika evidently relies too much on linguistic structures, reifying them rather than seeking the genuine meanings implicitly intended by them. This is equally true in the passage on "view" under current consideration. For Vasubandhu—for the Sautrāntika—there is no reason to say, just because the world speaks of the eye "seeing" and the consciousness "cognizing," that there must be a real activity, performed by the eye, that we call "seeing," and another real activity, performed by the consciousness, that we call "cognizing." Language can be misleading. The truth of the matter, the substratum, is merely the causal story of the eye organ, visual object, and consciousness. These elements are "passive [*nirvyāpāra*], merely *dharmas*, and merely cause and effect." In the end, Vasubandhu does not resist the critique that things under this description are not "active." If entities are properly understood, their transformations can occur without the superimposed, conventional understanding of action-with-an-agent. The "agents" and their "activities" are only figures that, once understood, dissolve, in the same way that the falsely viewed "self and things possessed by the self" dissolve in the light of the true causes of the "existing" things that are brought together into a "body."

I mentioned at the start of this discussion that Vasubandhu's causal argument would apply back to the frame, and we can now round out this section by engaging that application. Recall that the argument about the nature of the eye, which was a "view" only when accompanied by consciousness (*sabhāga*), arose in response to a challenge to the notion that "worldly right views" were limited to the mental consciousness. Now that it has been made clear that *all* views, all viewings, are performed by consciousnesses, and are only figuratively ascribed to agent sensory organs, there is no reason left to limit right views to mental views. That is, whereas surely we will wish to distinguish between views that are "settled" due to deliberative mental activities and views that are generated through perceptions, that distinction does not make one or the other category "worldly right views." Both kinds of "view" are mental events—consciousnesses—that are figuratively referred to as actions performed by an eye.

The implication, which I draw, is that "worldly right views" *should* include all of the consciousnesses—all five sensory consciousnesses, together with the mental consciousness. The distinction between sensory and cognitive consciousnesses was founded on a mistaken understanding of the relation between sensory organ and consciousness; but since the sensory *consciousness* is both agent and object in every act of "seeing," the experience of perceptual objects becomes just another form of ordinary awareness. Ostensibly, the goal in this passage was to prove that the eye should not be included in the view, so the category needs fine-tuning. But the more significant result is that perception is wrapped into consciousness, and words that describe literal sensory activity are to be taken as figurative. As we saw in his denial of the ongoing "existence" of past and future experiential objects, Vasubandhu believes that sensory objects and mental objects have no genuine (present) reality, because they have no causal effects outside the mental events that appear to "appropriate" them. Here we see that in order for a "view" to be *causal*, it must be an aspect of a causally efficient *mental event*. In fact, that mental event *just is* the discrimination of the "view"—the *viewing-as-if* through an eye what is a *viewing-of* an act of awareness. The awareness does not see through the eye, however. It is "supported" by the eye in the sense that it has been caused and hence shaped by it, but the eye itself is in the past by the time the awareness arises. Perception, therefore, contains an inherent falsity: we seem to be perceiving things in the present which are in fact past causes of our present discriminations. This notion, too, will be of great significance when we turn to Yogācāra in the chapters that follow.[47]

CLARIFYING CAUSALITY AGAINST ATOMS (AKBH III.100)

The final passage to discuss in this chapter helps to round out Vasubandhu's notion of causality and its relation to his appeals to figurative reference. In a passage from chapter III of the AKBh, Vasubandhu defends the model of a seed coming from a sprout as the paradigmatic, perhaps the only, true form of causality. In the last chapter we referred to Vasubandhu's *linear* approach to causality in his critique of mutual causality; in this passage we have a clear exemplification of what that means.[48]

The issue in dispute in this passage is the non-Buddhist, Vaiśeṣika view of atoms. We began this chapter analyzing Vasubandhu's argument against the self, which hinges on the fact that it is possible to break down the apparent whole, the combination of bodily and mental events, into its constituent parts, the *skandhas*. The Buddhist tradition rejects as mere designations (*prajñapti*) all entities that can be divided up, either physically or conceptually, into component parts. Abhidharma is centrally focused on identifying just what the basic components are out of which apparent wholes, such as the self, are really made. Things that are substantially real (*dravya*), as Vasubandhu explains, are those things that you cannot break down any further into their constituent parts. Real conditioned things, then, must be partless.

The partless components that make up the physical world are called "atoms" (*paramāṇu*). They are the ground-level reality that accounts for everything that we sense in the world around us. For this reason, atoms and their relation to perception are crucial to the Abhidharma account of the world, and the topic of just how atoms work arises on several occasions in Vasubandhu's oeuvre. Here, the argument begins as a disproof of the eternality of atoms, but in response to the opponent's counterargument, it ends up disproving the possibility of wholes inhering in, or existing over and above, their parts.

Vasubandhu reiterates the main points in this argument in his *Twenty Verses Commentary*, and it was upon that text that the Buddhist epistemologists relied for many centuries in their arguments against non-Buddhists.[49] Here we will see that this crucial argument for Buddhist epistemologists recapitulates points that we have already seen at work in Vasubandhu's view of causality: causality alone is the test of the reality of the entities in question; the relation between perceiver and perceived is reformulated in accordance with a unitary causal line; that causal line is distinct from the way things appear as well as the way we ordinarily talk; and, thus, the way we ordinarily talk is reinterpreted as "figurative," referring only indirectly to the true line of causes.

As with the previous examples, my goal is to reveal the method of argument along with the particulars of Vasubandhu's positions, so we must begin with the frame in which the argument is set. The context here is the discussion of the cyclical creation and destruction of the universe; according to Buddhist belief, the universe collapses at the end of a cosmic era, and this process of collapse includes three successive destructions. After these destructions, for a period no bodies remain, and as Vasubandhu says, no physical entities exist at all, since during this time living beings exist only in mental absorption.[50] In this context, the non-Buddhist raises an objection that atoms, the basic units of all things, must persist even after the universe is destroyed:

> Now, what are the destructions?
>
> **There are three repeating destructions: by fire, water, and wind.** [III.100ab] Since in one absorption [*dhyāna*], living beings equally come together there, it is the "coming-together" [*saṃvartanī*, i.e., destruction]. The heat destruction is from seven suns; the water destruction is from rainwater; the wind destruction is from a tumult of wind. And thereby, not even the subtle parts of the receptacle worlds [*bhājana*] remain.
>
> But with respect to this some non-Buddhists accept: "Atoms are eternal. They remain then."
>
> Why do they accept this?
>
> "Lest there be the appearance of coarse things without seeds."[51]

The non-Buddhist argues that atoms must remain, and exist eternally, because they must serve as the building blocks, the basic elements, out of which things of the next world are to be made. The belief in the eternality of atoms is a Nyāya-Vaiśeṣika view, so we can be sure that Vasubandhu is arguing directly with their position—but the larger question of the nature of atoms in the construction of perceptible objects is of great importance to the Sarvāstivādins as well.

In the last chapter we noted that the Sarvāstivāda approach to time ("block time") served as a response to the problem of continuity (or, as Vasubandhu would say, apparent continuity) in a world made up of impermanent entities. The appeal to *atoms* as building blocks is a way of addressing the parallel problem in space. For both Nyāya-Vaiśeṣikas and Ābhidharmikas, it is crucial to have basic elements that are by definition the smallest entities, but that have particular qualities that allow them to be combined into the larger entities that we perceive. Atoms block an infinite regress in the explanation of the composition of perceptible objects. Without them, you can never build your way back to ordinary objects, what the opponent calls "coarse" objects.

Among Buddhists, there are important controversies about just *how* atoms combine into larger perceptibles (we cannot perceive individual atoms), and just what those perceptibles are. Vasubandhu lays out a range of positions on this topic in AKBh I.43, indicating especially the difficulty of explaining how partless atoms come into contact. For instance, it is argued that if an atom a_1 comes into contact on one side with atom a_2 and on the other side with atom a_3, then atom a_1 has at least two sides, which are parts. On the other hand, if atom a_1 does not have sides, then what would prevent atoms a_2 and a_3 from occupying the same space? In that case, all atoms would end up occupying one point of space.

Vasubandhu declares his own allegiance ("This Bhadanta's opinion should be accepted") to the notion "They do not touch, but where there is no interval, there is the idea [*saṃjñā*] of touching."[52] This is a strange position, since (as Vasubandhu's critic Saṃghabhadra will argue) it may be taken that two things with no interval do, in fact, touch. But perhaps we have learned enough of Vasubandhu's views to discern his point: the notion of "touching" as an activity, in which each entity serves as both the toucher and the touched—all entailed by the verb "they touch" (*spṛśanti*)—is a false construction, unnecessarily imposed upon the mere existence of atoms that happen not to have any space between them. Just as temporal events may succeed one another in a line, without requiring that we call one truly "past" and other truly "present," physical entities may exist without their apparent relations to one another adding new entities to our ontology, which we call distinct actions and events. Thus, although atoms in particular configurations may be implicated, causally, in the production of the *idea* that they touch, it is not required that such a causal story include, as one of its realities, an action called "touching." Such a view of the nature of perception was, of course, adopted by the pointillists Seurat and Signac and others, who argued that their works, made of dots of color visible close up, proved that the image was composed by the eye and mind of the beholder.[53]

The argument on atoms from AKBh III makes no direct reference to this previous argument, but it builds upon the issues by targeting, specifically, the Nyāya-Vaiśeṣikas. The Nyāya-Vaiśeṣikas are realists, meaning that they believe that the combinations of atoms create real things—in this case, the things of the world—and that the atoms out of which these things are made must also exist, eternally. Vasubandhu targets the notion that the combination of atoms is necessary as the basis for larger, perceptible entities—a view that is directed at the Nyāya-Vaiśeṣikas, but takes in any Buddhist who is leaning toward the reification of relations among atoms—by arguing that there is no good way to make sense of the relation of parts to wholes. All that is necessary, he will say, is the causal series of separate atoms, overlaid by ideation, by false conceptualization. Thus he accepts the notion that there must be a "seed"—that is, a cause—of the new universe, but he does not see why that seed must be the atoms:

> Surely the seed is said to be the wind that has sentient beings' distinctive powers, born from *karma*. Or, the wind that is associated with the destruction will become its cause. The Mahīśāsakas cite a *sūtra*, "The seeds were carried by the wind from other worlds."[54]

There is wit in this response. It is an intentional misreading of the Nyāya-Vaiśeṣika opponent's use of the term "seed." The opponent had said that there must be atoms even after the final destruction, because without them there would be no possibility of the world resuming again; atoms serve as the "seed" of the new entities. Vasubandhu suggests that there are other options: the seed might be a wind produced by the karmic imprints of living beings; it might be the wind that caused the final destruction in the first place; or it might be an initiatory cause brought from another world. The idea of a seed is, of course, just a metaphor for both Vasubandhu and his opponents; neither really thinks that the universe starts from a seed, per se.[55] But the irony is that, having said that atoms must serve as the "seed" for new entities when the universe comes back into existence, the opponent has inadvertently endorsed a metaphor of seed-to-sprout causality, which is contrary to the parts-to-wholes causality that Nyāya-Vaiśeṣika atomism in fact supports.

Thus, just as with the passage on "view" discussed above, Vasubandhu sets his opponent in an awkward self-contradiction.[56] First they say you need atoms to exist as seeds for the new combined entities, then they say they do not *really* mean seeds. Since they have used their words carelessly, they are placed on the defensive, and must explain their theory in detail:

> Even so, they do not accept that the arising of a sprout, etc., is from a seed, etc.
>
> What then?
>
> From just their own parts, and from theirs in turn, and so on down to atoms.
>
> What is this capacity of a seed, etc., in a sprout, etc.?
>
> Nothing anywhere aside from drawing together their atoms.
>
> And why, again, do they accept this?
>
> Because it is not logical to have an origin from a different class.
>
> Why is it not logical?
>
> Because it would have no rule [*aniyama*]. It will not come about because of a rule of capacities, as in the arising of sound and what is cooked. For the variegated is a quality but not a substance, because things of a similar class are seen to arise from substances of a similar class, such as a mat from grass, and a cloth from thread.[57]

In response to the idea that the "seed" of the new universe may be some wind or other coming from another universe, the opponent explains that Vasubandhu has misunderstood the point; the argument for atoms is not based upon causality from seed to sprout, but rather from part to whole. This is, after all, the point of atoms—to explain things through their components. The opponent goes farther, however, in response to Vasubandhu's implicit interpretation of his use of "seed," and denies even that sprouts are caused by seeds. Vasubandhu is thus taken as adopting the "seed-to-sprout" analogy as a real example of how causes work. Even this analogy is wrong, the opponent says, because both sprouts and seeds are made up of their parts; there is, for the opponent, *no* linear causality. This is somewhat ironic, of course, because Vasubandhu *also* does not take seeds and sprouts to have causal capacities per se. They provide a metaphor for the linear causality of *dharmas*. Still, seeds and sprouts are the model for Vasubandhu's preferred mode of causality, and they become the opponent's target.

The opponent introduces the notion of causal "capacity" (*śakti*), and says that the only "capacity" that may be attributed to seeds and sprouts is their ability to hold together their atoms. But the seed has no causal capacity with relation to the sprout. The idea that causation works from part to whole instead of from whole to whole is not entirely unfamiliar in contemporary, reductive interpretations of scientific theories. If I say, for instance, that the object *ice* is produced by a particular molecular structure in H_2O, then I am employing the causal mode from parts to whole. We might wish to say that what is really happening when ice melts is that an increase in heat causes the bonds in the molecules to change to a state in which they make up *water* instead of *ice*. To be fair, the notion of *capacity* adduced by the Nyāya-Vaiśeṣika opponent articulates causal directionality in reverse; the ice would be said to have the power to unify the H_2O molecules. I suppose gravity is a better modern scientific example here. To apply the analogies to the Buddhist case, Vasubandhu's position would be that water and ice and the gravitational force of a given planet are only *apparent* realities, with no inherent nature of their own. They *appear to* arise and interact with other objects only because of the accumulated specific states of their molecules.[58]

Why does the opponent think that the notion of a sprout arising from a seed is incoherent? Because it would require that an entity arise from something of a distinct class. The principle adduced here is *Like produces like.*[59] Maybe seeds could produce seeds, and sprouts sprouts. But how can seeds produce sprouts? This rule applies not to qualities, but to substances. Given that sprouts are new entities, distinct from seeds, they are understood as distinct substances, which cannot be produced by substances of a different kind. If causality is a rule-bound function of entities, there must be proper classes in which entities produce their causal results. To have causality traversing those boundaries would be to have a rule-free, and hence irrational, causality with no explanatory power.

Vasubandhu does not argue against this rule.[60] He does not argue that seeds *can* cause sprouts, or that substances can be caused by substances of different classes. Rather, he criticizes the notion that the supposed combinations of entities are, in fact, entities at all. His view is that since we can give *no good account* of causality at this level (agreeing, then, that seed-to-sprout causality is not properly rule-governed), it must not really be happening. (We are here only one step short of the full argument for the illusion-like nature of all things, as we will discuss in chapter 5.) Nonetheless, the opponent's argument provides a crucial opportunity for Vasubandhu to disprove both the realist approach to parts and wholes, and the distinction between substances and qualities. The sprout may not be the causal result of the seed, but this is not because they are both caused by their atoms; it is because both are only *ideas*:

> This is illogical.
>
> What is illogical about it?
>
> That something unproven is taken for the reason.
>
> What about it is unproven?
>
> "That a mat is from grass, whereas a cloth is from thread." For as they are brought together, they are taken as an idea [*saṃjñā*], like a line of ants.
>
> How can that be?
>
> Because one does not conceive of a cloth when there is contact with a single thread. For what in that case prevents the existing thing being conceived of as a cloth?
>
> Given that it is incomplete, a part of a cloth should not be a cloth.
>
> In that case, a cloth must be only an assemblage. What, other than a thread, is a part of a cloth?[61]

This first critique targets the example adduced by the opponent to prove that substances are produced by objects that share their nature: a mat of grass, and a cloth of thread. Here the idea is, apparently, that the same configuration—being woven together—will bring about different entities, when their substance is distinct. Thus it is the substance, not the configuration (or the activity), that determines the produced entity. Vasubandhu is not criticizing the distinction between the two entities, but rather their reality as wholes. He does not think the mat and the cloth exist as more than "ideas" (*saṃjñā*). Let us grant that a "line of ants" is nothing but an appearance, an idea imposed upon many distinct and unrelated creatures (there is no *line* over and above the ants that make it up). In the same way, a cloth can appear to exist over and above its threads, even though it does not. Vasubandhu proposes that a cloth is nothing but an assemblage—what else, he asks *is there* to a cloth, except threads? The cloth, then, is not an additional entity with its own nature and causal capacities. Its unity is an illusion.

In order to support this thesis, Vasubandhu interrogates the causal capacities of a single thread. It may be proposed that the threads alone cannot produce the thought of a cloth, so there must be some other entity there that *can* produce such a thought. But Vasubandhu's point is that we know what is there; it is an assemblage of threads, none of which is capable of producing the thought of a cloth:

> When looking at the contact among multiple supports, where the contact is only with the fringe, one should conceive of a cloth—or never. For the sensory organ does not come into contact with an intermediary power. And when coming into contact by stages with parts that are being touched by the eye, there should not be cognition of parts. Therefore, because coming-into-contact by stages engages with parts, the thought is also with respect to parts, like a firebrand circle.[62]

Given that we only perceive threads in succession, there is no way to justify the perception of a cloth as something additional, over and above those threads. For, Vasubandhu asks, if you do not perceive the cloth in the fringe, when will you perceive it? No matter how carefully we look at a single thread of a cloth, we will never sense the "cloth" until we take in the aggregate; this shows that there is no additional entity that can be sensed with the eyes. At the same time, however, it is noticed that we do, in fact, perceive a cloth, in spite of having only had available to us the distinct threads in a particular formation. What's more, not only do we perceive the cloth, we *fail to perceive* the distinct threads! This fact justifies the comparison with a whirling firebrand. Like the line of ants this is an example where we are expected to agree: there is clearly no real entity corresponding to our perception of a circle of light. Yet what we see is a whole, made up of parts that we know exist, but fail to see. Vasubandhu's readers would not need to be told of the evident similarity here to the false idea of the self.

Next Vasubandhu criticizes as internally incoherent the use of the thread-to-cloth causal structure proposed by the Nyāya-Vaiśeṣika theory as evidence of cause and result sharing the same nature, or class (*jāti*):

> The form of a thread does not appear in cloths that are manufactured [*jātikriyā*] out of different forms (colors), etc. If it has the nature of a variegated form, then there is an origin from a different class;[63] and if it is not variegated, one either does not see the thread among those next to it, or

> one sees variegation.[64] Where the manufacture is also variegated, there is extreme variegation. Furthermore, given the difference in the shining of the glow in the beginning, middle, and end of a fire's radiance, it does not appear from contact with its form.[65]

In Vasubandhu's theory, the combination of different entities is simply a function of false conceptualization. But the opponent believes that there must be real entities that we perceive. Against this view, Vasubandhu proposes a problematic example for the proposed theory: How do you account for a cloth composed of differently colored threads? The cloth must appear as variegated. But what creates the variegated color? The threads are not individually variegated; each thread is its own color. If you have a rule that *like produces like*, you cannot allow that a blue thread produces a variegated cloth. If the solution is proposed that there is one cloth called "variegated" in color, that requires that the opponent ignore the *sameness of the color* of the blue threads next to one another in a blue patch of the cloth. If it is argued that we do not see this patch, but only the whole, this supports Vasubandhu's point that we do not really see entities as they are. If it is argued that we in fact see many different small "cloths," some only blue, some variegated, then this opens up a vicious regress: there is variegation to the construction of variegation (it is inconsistently variegated).

Vasubandhu provides another example, that of a flame, which is similarly variegated—brighter in some parts, dimmer in others. Since we know that the flame is made up of countless tiny explosions of fire, perhaps we will be less likely to regard it as a "thing" or a real unity, than a cloth. But just like a cloth, the flame appears to us as a single entity. We know, however, that its unity cannot be the result of some *perceived* unity, because *we do not perceive any unity*.

A final example pushes the point made through the examples of the line of ants, the cloth, and the flame to a new extreme. Those examples showed that it was necessary that in each case an illusory "idea" be acknowledged to have been imposed upon a basis that consisted only of distinct elements. Just as entities are caused by the multiple conditioning factors of many distinct elements, their perception must be their combined effect.[66] The new example is the mass of hair seen by someone with an eye disease. Here, unlike the other examples, in addition to the mistaken *idea* itself, the atomic entities that seemingly make it up *also* fail to exist. This example brings us closest to reality as Vasubandhu understands it, since atoms on their own are imperceptible, and it is only jointly that they produce anything perceptible:

> Also, given that atoms are imperceptible, perception is of assemblages [*samasta*], like their causal origin,[67] and like the perception of a mass of hair for those with diseased eyes. A singular, atom-like hair for them is imperceptible.[68]

Since there is no hair to perceive, it is certainly impossible that the experience of a mass of hair is due to the atomic units of hair out of which the mass of hair is composed. Masses of hair appear because of damage to the visual apparatus, not because of real hairs. It is clear that in this case, at least, the appearance arises unsupported by any hypostatized atomic units. By noting that there is no reason to believe in a *real* entity that is a "cloth" any more than that there is a "circle of fire" or a "mass of hairs," Vasubandhu shifts the conversation about the nature of composite entities from the external to the internal realm, from the world of real, causal entities, to the world of false mental constructions. I cannot help seeing the connection between this passage and the discussion of "view," in which the supposed "view" of the eye, and all of the senses, was relegated to the consciousness. Furthermore, the false appearance of hairs for the person with eye disease is the opening analogy in Vasubandhu's *Twenty Verses* (Viṃś), his most famous Yogācāra work, and in that text he is again putting it forward as an example of an appearance that arises with no external substratum.

Finally, Vasubandhu brings his argument back home to the original argument about the impermanence of atoms:

> And since the specific idea of the atom applies only to the forms, etc., the destruction of the atom is established when they are destroyed.
>
> Since the atom is a different substance from the substance of the forms, etc., its destruction is not established when they are destroyed.
>
> Its being different does not make sense, as long as there is no way to differentiate earth, water, and fire from their forms, etc., and those things that are grasped through touching the eye are perceived. And since there is no thought of wool, cotton, safflower, and saffron [*kuṅkuma*], etc., when they are burnt,[69] the thought of them applies to differences of form, etc. The ascertainment of a pot with respect to what has arisen as cooked is due to the formation generality, like a line. Because there is no ascertainment for one

> not seeing the mark. What is the point of this childish prattling? Let it stand just so, uncontradicted.[70]

Vasubandhu explains that the destruction of atoms at the end of the universe is proven by the fact that perceptibles—forms—do not survive. Of course, the Nyāya-Vaiśeṣika proponent is still unconvinced, and suggests that it is only the forms, and not the atomic substances, that are destroyed. Vasubandhu responds by pointing out that if you want to say that we perceive real things, you are not permitted also to draw a distinction between the things perceived and their real substances. The reason we fail to see different kinds of cloth when they have all been burned to ash is that the means we used to distinguish them—their different colors—are no longer visible. If the forms were still there, and we could perceive them, then we *would* perceive them. This underlines Vasubandhu's point that what seem to be perceived wholes *must* be only ideas superimposed on imperceptibles. The last example, of the "cooked" food in a pot, transfers this point about conceptually projecting differences across color patterns to conceptually projecting differences within a perceived entity changing over time. Vasubandhu's critique of mereological part/whole identities works exactly the same in reference to characteristics attributed to entities due to their having changed through time, such as "being cooked." There is no single entity, only a line of ants, a *causal line* projected by the viewer across distinct, though temporally adjacent, appearances.

CONCLUSION: VASUBANDHU'S PHILOSOPHICAL MOTIVATION

The notion of a *unitary causal line* is one of the most prominent patterns in Vasubandhu's Sautrāntika argumentation, and it is easily identified across the texts from the AKBh discussed so far. I have entitled this chapter "Merely Cause and Effect" in order to bring attention to this notion: Vasubandhu appeals to causality as a full, satisfactory explanation of entities that only *seem* to be something more. When it appears that there is an agent and an action, and that the agent and the action are two separate entities, Vasubandhu argues that the entirety of the situation can be explained as merely cause and effect, only one entity causing another. Of course, it *looks like* there is an agent; the persistent, mistaken *appearance* of the self is a fact of our situation as conditioned beings in *saṃsāra*. We think we are independent agents, and it is difficult to speak of human behavior without implying that there is an agent self. But the Buddha tells us there is no agent, only actions and results, only strings of discrete, dissociated, if causally related, events.

The same can be said of objects and their qualities or their relations. We tend to think of entities as having specific natures that are unchanging, but also as having aspects to their identities that are changeable. Vasubandhu is extremely strict in rejecting the substantial reality of entities under this commonsense view. It violates the basic principle of Abhidharma, which is to reduce things to their primary units, so that each thing can be described according to its single nature, its one *svabhāva*. Two opposing qualities must, therefore, be attributed to two distinct entities. One entity cannot be described as one way (or at one time) *x* and another ~*x*. One entity cannot be different from itself. Read in this way, a thing *just is* its action, its causal relations, its appearance. This is why an object cannot be distinct from its temporal identity, which means that there can be no difference between a thing that is "present" and a thing that is "past." A thing cannot *not be producing* the cause that it is in its nature to produce. It cannot be inactive and still be what it is. For this reason there is no sensible distinction between a real object and its *present*, its *existence*, any more than it is sensible to say that a thing *exists* in the past. Each thing does nothing but immediately produce the result it is its nature to produce.

It is not that things cannot be described otherwise; things of course *appear* to have agents and qualities and relations. Things *appear* to exist in combination. It *looks like* something exists *over and above* the string of discrete events; it *seems* like we can perceive the unity of causal streams. But Abhidharma analysis rules that if you want to say what is *real*, you must appeal to discrete entities that can be proven through appeal to scriptural authority and causal necessity. When Vasubandhu explains away the entities under consideration by saying that they are "merely cause and effect," he is saying that, like a line of ants, and like the self, they have an *appearance* that conflicts with the reality of their true, causal nature. Those who tag those appearances and reify them, creating false ideas of real substances that persist through time, or of entities such as "arising," which is temporarily a quality of every other entity, are allowing a proliferation of "non-Buddhist false concepts" (*tīrthakara-parikalpitā*).

It is therefore, finally, of great significance that Vasubandhu fells with the same causal reductionism not just the agent and object, and the object and its qualities, but also the *appearance itself and its experiencer*. Thus, the eye and its object, the perceiver and the perceived, are not distinguished in the "view" that is perception. Percepts are not distinct from the eye consciousness that takes them up as objects. This is true both as *real objects* perceived through the senses (because they no longer exist when perceived by the senses) and as *mental objects* that are thought to be distinct from the mind but in fact are, again, part of the *unitary causal line* that is consciousness. Objects, if they exist, do not exist in some new, distinctive way just because they are perceived. If they are perceived, that is because they are in causal relation to the perceiving consciousness. But the object itself *just is*. There is no "perceiver" and no "perceived"; it is merely cause and effect. The causal reduction here connects up a great many of Vasubandhu's arguments.

The inclusion, within this causal reduction, of the perceiver and the perceived, both for sensory organs and for the mind, will reappear as Vasubandhu's crucial contribution to the Yogācāra. It is what I will call the reduction of *subjectivity*. In his Yogācāra works the denial of an agent as distinct from an action, and of a perceiver in contradistinction from a perceived, and of a concept as distinct from its linguistic structuration, will be summarized as the principle of "nonduality" (*advaya*). The link between Vasubandhu's Yogācāra understanding of nonduality and the causal linearity of the AKBh will provide a reliable indicator of the coherence of his oeuvre.[71] The reduction of agency and the reduction of subjectivity are united in Vasubandhu's famous, game-changing gloss of the persistent Yogācāra term "duality" as "grasper and grasped." Before turning to this argument about the nature of perception from a Yogācāra perspective, however, we must, in the next chapter, turn our attention to a second, crucial pattern in association with this causal argument, which is Vasubandhu's insistence on a "figurative" reading of Buddhist scripture.

4

KNOWLEDGE, LANGUAGE, AND THE INTERPRETATION OF SCRIPTURE

Vasubandhu's Opening to the Mahāyāna

AFTER WORKING through the last two chapters, we are in a position to summarize some of the central methods and motives of Vasubandhu's philosophy. In addition to presenting a consistent view, the "Sautrāntika" critique of Vaibhāṣika Abhidharma has a number of characteristic philosophical strategies. Above all, the goal, in argument after argument, seems to have been to dismantle the edifice of the opponent's system that supports one or another false entity (a past/present/future reality, a self, a cloth). In each case, Vasubandhu targets the causal logic of the entity—its contribution to the Vaibhāṣika or non-Buddhist system. For instance, past and future were undermined as realities attributable to entities precisely because their identities contributed nothing to the causal order. Vasubandhu was able to account for everything the "times" achieved without requiring that we affirm their reality. In the end, all that they contributed were *names* we give to entities in order to describe *how they appear* due to their relative positions in a causal flow.

In chapter 2 we discussed, under the heading of "argument 1" from the Vaibhāṣikas, a claim that the three times (past, present, and future) must be real *because the Buddha said so*. That was our first introduction to Vasubandhu's approach to scriptural reinterpretation as "figurative," as not meaning exactly what it says. In reply to the Vaibhāṣika claim, Vasubandhu accepted the passage as an authoritative utterance of the Buddha, but interpreted it as follows:

> We too say that there is a past and future thing. But a past thing is what existed before. A future thing is what will exist when there is a cause. Each is said to exist just insofar as this is the case, but not also substantially.[1]

Vasubandhu accepts that the past exists, *but not substantially*—not as a reality that has legitimate, causal powers over and above its appearance within our conceptual nexus. The distinction between entities that are *substantial* (*dravya*) and those that are merely *conventional* (*prajñapti*) is at the center of Abhidharma analysis, and Vasubandhu will never give it up, even in his Mahāyāna works. It is essential to correct the Vaibhāṣika causal story, and explain the causes of past events in the present and the future without reifying these merely nominal entities.

Yet the contribution of names is not negligible; the Buddha used words such as "past" and "future" with purpose. There must be a significant reason for the Buddha to have used these "figurative" terms, given that their literal referents can be shown to be unreal. Thus, having accounted for reality *without* the entities in question, Vasubandhu left himself two distinct tasks: first he needed to account for the appearance of the entities in question (*Why do they seem to exist?*), and second he needed to account for the utility of their names (*Why do they appear in scripture?*).

The question of an entity's causal reality is a question of its existence, a question of ontology. These additional questions—of what the entity appears to be, and what role it plays in our understanding—are questions of our knowledge, questions of epistemology. Each argument that we have studied thus far tacks between these two types of question. For Vasubandhu, ontological and epistemological questions are intimately related, though nonetheless distinct. In this chapter we will look more closely at Vasubandhu's theory of knowledge, and see how he grounds effective reasoning in his view that existence can only be determined through causality. We will see that, for Vasubandhu, since causality is the touchstone of the real, reason provides a guide to the interpretation of scripture, and not the other way around. Scriptures, for Vasubandhu, contain the path to truth, the means to a valid understanding of ultimate reality. But they were created out of a Buddha's desire to speak to ordinary beings, to aid their understanding at a level targeted to their limited capacities. Those who read them incorrectly are liable to justify the very false constructions for which they were intended, ultimately, as an antidote. Thus the language of scripture, useful as it may be, is still an "appearance" that must be analyzed with the same skepticism as the false appearance of the self. We will see how this view of scripture, logic, and language is grounded in the AKBh, but reaches its full expression in Vasubandhu's masterwork on hermeneutics, the *Proper Mode of Exposition* (*Vyākhyāyukti* [VyY]).

VASUBANDHU'S FOUNDATION FOR BUDDHIST EPISTEMOLOGY

In this section I will treat two passages from the AKBh in which Vasubandhu presents what are for him characteristic and possibly original views. As far as I know, they do not appear in any earlier Buddhist texts, Abhidharma or Yogācāra. Both passages are very much aware of the non-Buddhist, Nyāya-Vaiśeṣika school and its approach to argumentation. The great Nyāya thinker from Vasubandhu's time was Vātsyāyana, the first full-length commentator on the *Nyāya-sūtras*, whom Dignāga would later criticize. Even in the AKBh, Vasubandhu appears to be already in conversation with Vātsyāyana, and Vasubandhu's criticisms of Nyāya perspectives may be seen to have laid the groundwork for a characteristically Buddhist epistemology.

I say the epistemology will be characteristically *Buddhist* not only because the epistemic principles—the views of concepts, language, and awareness—are typical of later Buddhist epistemologists, but also because they emerge from Vasubandhu's defense of the characteristic, Buddhist doctrines of no-self and impermanence. They are also doctrines that Vasubandhu himself says distinguish followers of the Buddha from those who have abandoned his teachings. Vasubandhu's intent overall is, first, to show how a very specific philosophical approach—the methods we have seen him employ in the last two chapters—is embedded within the doctrines of impermanence and no-self and, second, to show how this approach may be used to set the Buddha's teachings above, and against, their non-Buddhist detractors. These arguments establish what I take to be a clear foundation for *prāmāṇika* philosophy within traditional Buddhist teachings—both in its characteristic epistemological views, and in its proper application to the defense of Buddhist doctrine.[2]

To begin with the doctrine of no-self, we can see that Vātsyāyana seeks to refute Buddhism by proving the reality of the self. Vātsyāyana begins his commentary on the tenth verse of the *Nyāya-sūtras* by acknowledging that the self cannot be known by perception. But, he says, this does not mean that the self can only be known through the *pramāṇa*—the means of knowledge—of authoritative testimony. Rather, he says, it is also known through inference. The self can be proven. In order to show this, he runs through a series of proofs, each of which is essentially the same argument brought under six different names: proof by appeal to desire, aversion, effort, pleasure, pain, and awareness. The first, the argument from desire, runs as follows:

> Someone who has attained pleasure in his self [*ātman*] as a result of coming into contact with an object of a particular kind, and sees an object of that same kind, desires to acquire it. This desire [*icchā*] to acquire it is a sign of the self, since one sees multiple things as one because of the remembrance of seeing. For mere distinct thoughts with respect to separate sensory objects do not come together, as in separate bodies.[3]

Let us set aside the question-begging assertion that it is the self that experiences pleasure, and notice that the basic argument here is less about desire than it is about the functioning of *memory*, which appears to require the continuity of the self. When we desire, we are seeking something that we know from past experience to be pleasing. If, as the Buddhists claim, all things are momentary and there is no substantial continuity from one moment to the next, then it is one entity that was pleased and another that desires. But that, he says, is just as absurd as saying that experiences in separate bodies come together. His point is that *you* won't know how something tastes just because *I've* tried it.

It is noteworthy that Vātsyāyana repeats essentially the same argument with reference to aversion, effort, and the others. We might think, for instance, that *effort* (*prayatna*) or *pleasure* (*sukha*) would be opportune examples to show how the self is necessary by appealing to freedom of the will, or to what some call "first-person" subjectivity. Vātsyāyana might have asked, "What enacts actions or experiences experiences, if not the self?" But he does not. Instead, he says that *effort* is a proof of the self because if you make an effort, you must be acting on something you *remember*. And memory requires continuity. Similarly, he says, if you have *pleasure*, it is because you have achieved something you desired, so there must be a single being that desires and achieves the object. Even with regard to *awareness* (*jñāna*), he does not claim that a self is somehow needed to bring consciousness to light. Rather, he says that you cannot have "awareness" unless at some previous time you were *unaware*, pondering "What is this?" and then, while staying the same being, you have *become* "aware" of something new.[4] This suggests that at this stage of the game—that is, around 400 CE in India—the main proof of the self for the Nyāya, and the main perceived vulnerability for the Buddhist view of no-self, was the question of *continuity*.[5]

If, now, we turn to look at our first passage from Vasubandhu, from the ninth chapter of the AKBh, we can see that Vasubandhu thinks he has an answer to this argument.[6] What looks like continuity, he says, is in fact merely an ongoing causal series of separate mental events that only appear to be one thing, like a line of ants, or like fire moving across a field. Where Vātsyāyana uses the argument from memory against the self, Vasubandhu applies this familiar argument against the self to the specific case of memory. A memory, he says, is a "distinct mental event" (*cittaviśeṣa*) that has two qualities: it resembles a previous sensory experience, and it is *causally connected* to that experience.[7] The causal connection accounts for the resemblance as well as the appearance of continuity, and at the same time accounts for the proper functioning of memory. The causal connection also allows Vasubandhu to reject the absurd consequence of my remembering your experience. He writes:

> For there is no connection between these two because of there being no existent cause and effect, as there is for the two in a single continuum. We do not say that what is seen by one mind is remembered by another. Rather, another mind, which remembers, arises from the mind that sees.[8]

What this means is (among other things) that if we try to rely upon the appearance of a memory itself—by examining our own experience, for instance—we can be misled. Resemblance can be brought about by a causal link, and so fails to prove continuity of identity. What seems like unity across distinct events is only apparent, only a conceptual construct, a mere convention (*prajñapti*).

As always for Vasubandhu, this category of conventions, which *seem* to appear, must be distinguished from real or substantial (*dravya*) entities that have specifiable cause-and-effect relations with other entities. As the reader will well recall from the previous chapters, there are, for Vasubandhu, only two kinds of things: causal realities, and conceptually constructed falsities that are absent from the flow of causality. A crucial philosophical result of this very strict formulation is that abstract entities and eternal, unchanging entities (including god, past and future, *nirvāṇa*, space, perceptual objects, and concepts), which have no direct causal impetus, are deemed unreal. Notice that Vasubandhu's proof denies the self any causal impetus in the production of memory, or the *appearance* of continuity. The apparent evidence is accounted for without requiring that it be caused by the ostensible inferential result, the self.

This is the argument that gives Vasubandhu confidence that, contrary to Vātsyāyana's claim, there is *no* inferential basis for belief in the self. This is clear in the opening of the chapter, to which we now turn. Vasubandhu begins this passage with a clear statement that alleviates any doubt that his goal is to distinguish Buddhists from non-Buddhists:

> Is there, then, no liberation elsewhere?[9]
>
> There is not.
>
> Why?
>
> Because of grasping the false view of self. For they do not comprehend the convention "self" as just the continuum of aggregates.
>
> What then?
>
> They conceptually construct the self as a separate substance. And all of the afflictions have grasping after the self as their origin.[10]

Vasubandhu thus frames his refutation of the self in the most consequential terms possible, both for the pursuit of liberation and for identifying the true followers of the Buddha's teachings. The basic cause of the afflictions is the mistaken conceptual construction that sees the self as a separate substance, rather than as merely the continuum of aggregates. Those who defend such a conceptual construction are preventing their own, and their followers', freedom from suffering. We saw in the last chapter that the basic error of living beings, the foundation for all other errors, was the mistaken imposition of a self upon the aggregates (*satkāyadṛṣṭi*). Here we see that the Buddha's teachings are the only antidote to this fundamental error.[11]

Vasubandhu then moves directly into his formal proof of the doctrine of no-self, for which he draws upon the *pramāṇas*, the means of knowledge, of perception and inference.[12] The basis for Buddhism's soteriological exclusivism is here presented as dependent upon Buddhism's take on the means of knowledge:

> And how is this to be understood, that the word "self" indicates only the continuum of aggregates, and does not apply elsewhere?

> Because there is neither perception nor inference. For there is perception—apprehension—of existent *dharmas* where there is no interval. Such is the case for the six sensory objects and the mind. And there is an inference for the five sensory organs. In this case, the inference is that with a cause in place, when another cause does not exist, no result is seen, and when it does exist it does come about, as with a sprout. Or,[13] with the cause in place that consists in a manifest sensory object and attention, no grasping of a sensory object is seen for blind or deaf, etc., people whereas it is for people who are not blind or deaf, etc. So, in that case, too, there is determined[14] to be the existence and nonexistence of another cause. And that other cause is the sensory organ—that's the inference. And no such inference exists for the self, so there is no self.[15]

Vasubandhu's works on *pramāṇa* remain only in fragments, but this passage provides a decisive epistemological perspective.[16] He says that the reason the continuum of aggregates can be admitted, but the self cannot, is that the aggregates are proven by perception and inference, whereas the self is not. Buddhist epistemology is ordinarily said to accept these two *pramāṇas* only, but the truth is that Vasubandhu generally refers to *three* means of knowledge—adding the authority of Buddhist scripture to perception and inference.[17] In a parallel passage from an earlier chapter (mentioned in chapter 3), Vasubandhu had accused the Vaibhāṣikas of adopting a *tīrthika*-like practice of reifying conceptual constructions which were based upon no means of knowledge—not perception, not inference, and not scriptures. Here we see only the first two, possibly because he will deal with scriptures later in AKBh IX;[18] but the result is that the argument stands as a stark, negative reflection of the passage from Vātsyāyana quoted above.

Let us examine Vasubandhu's positive proof for the aggregates, which he says is missing for the self. There is a minor conceptual sleight of hand here, since he actually proves the spheres (*āyatana*), not the aggregates (*skandha*). From my perspective this is hardly a problem worth complaining about, but it does remind us that the AKBh is written for a Buddhist scholastic audience, whose members could easily translate between aggregates and spheres. Vasubandhu distinguishes two kinds of legitimately known entities—those known by perception, and those known by inference.[19] The seven entities known by perception are the five sensory objects, mental objects, and the mind. The inference, then, is intended to prove the reality of the remaining spheres, which are the five sensory organs. Yet, as always, the frame is important to keep in mind. The ultimate purpose of the inference adduced is not so much to prove the reality of the sensory organs as it is to display what a proper inference looks like, so that it may be used to show that no inference for the self is forthcoming. The formal structure of an inference is stated, and grounded in two examples: the sprout, and the inference that proves the reality of the sensory organs. Together, this serves as an epistemic argument for no-self.

The example of an inference itself is fairly simple. When you have someone who wants to see something, and that thing is directly perceptible, one of two things can happen. If she has working eyes, she sees it. If she is blind, she doesn't. The distinction here is between two situations, in which only one thing may be assumed to have changed: the presence of the sensory organ. With everything else kept constant, a change in that one variable changes the target outcome. In contemporary parlance, Vasubandhu's view of causality may be called "manipulationist."

Manipulationism is a theory of causal explanation proposed by James Woodward, a contemporary Anglophone philosopher. To the question of how we should understand causality, Woodward provides an answer by analogy to a kind of scientific experiment. What it means to say that *x* causes *y*, he says, is that there is some, hypothetical, situation in which, holding other variables constant, we could intervene to change the value of *x*—to "manipulate" *x*—and that such a manipulation would indirectly change the value of *y*. When we judge this specific kind of correlation to exist, we say that *x* is a cause of *y*. Thus a causal explanation, for Woodward, describes a specific kind of dependence relation that holds as an empirical fact. As he argues, causality is a dependence pattern that is "potentially exploitable for the purposes of manipulation."[20]

How does Woodward's analysis shed light on Vasubandhu? Vasubandhu was trained as a Vaibhāṣika, and as a result he takes quite seriously their view that to be a real thing, to be *existent* or *substantial*, is to be in some kind of causal relation with other entities. Everything else, for this view, is a mere appearance or a mere conceptual construction. Vasubandhu inherits and adopts this basic rule, which is already quite radical. But he makes it perhaps more radical by changing, and refining, what it *means* to say that something is caused. For in order to make sense of their radical view, the Vaibhāṣika school accepted a great many kinds of causality—like Aristotle. Vasubandhu, on the other hand, rejected their profuse list of types of causes, saying that most of them were insufficient to distinguish truly *substantial* things from mere conceptual constructions. Instead, he proposed a much narrower understanding of what it means to say that *x* causes *y*, and therefore, what it means to say that something *exists*.

I have come to believe that Vasubandhu's theory of causality, his "seed to sprout" approach, is quite close to manipulationism. In particular, there are two significant, characteristic aspects of manipulationism that are reflected in Vasubandhu's theorizing. The first is the primacy of the hypothetical intervention, the manipulation itself, and everything that that implies. The second is the empirical setting, the scientific-like structure that holds other variables constant for the sake of a particular analysis, and everything that *that* implies. Both aspects of this approach to causality are evident in the passage under discussion here.

Notice the structure of Vasubandhu's inference, which is almost a formalization of manipulationist causal explanation: "The inference is that with a cause in place, when another cause does not exist, no result is seen, and when it does exist it does come about." First, the expression "with a cause in place" sets up the controlled scenario, the backdrop against which we are looking for a relationship between particular causes and results. Next, that relationship is defined by appeal to a manipulation of the cause in question: if you do not have the cause, there is no result; if you do have the cause, the result comes about. This is the basis for discovering an unseen entity—it is intrinsic to the notion of "inference," or *anumāna*.[21]

Vasubandhu does not use the term *anumāna* often in the AKBh, but when he does, it always refers to the process of extrapolating a causal series—either predicting results based on causes or, as here, inferring a cause from a result. In one passage Vasubandhu says that when the Buddha has provided a shortened version of the links of dependent origination, one can extrapolate the full series of causes and results by "inference" (*anumāna*).[22] In another passage investigating how the Buddha comes to know the future, Vasubandhu proposes an argument that the Buddha might be able to foresee future events by "inferring" a causal series because he knows how each step works; from one *dharma* comes another, and from that, the next, and so on. Vasubandhu rejects this argument because the Buddha is said to perceive the future directly, not merely to infer it.[23] It is clear that perception is assumed to be more reliable than inference, but only inference, and not perception, is capable of determining causal relationships.[24] Vasubandhu formalizes the structure of rational argumentation through a specifically *causal* system.

Another piece of evidence that Vasubandhu saw causality as the centerpiece of inference is an important extant fragment from his *Vādavidhi*—the initiatory text of traditional Buddhist epistemology[25]—in which he defines an inferential reason in accord with the very same principle of manipulationist causality that he has determined above as the only valid proof of existence for a nonperceived entity:

> The reason [*hetu, gtan tshigs*] is said to be the explanation [*upadeśa, nye bar ston pa*] that a *dharma* is of such and such a kind, in the absence of which it does not come about. Of such and such a kind is the thing to be established, such as the impermanence of sound. If its kind does not exist, no thing at all comes about. Just as impermanence with respect to arising from being produced, and fire with respect to smoke—they are phenomena that do not arise where the thing of that kind does not exist. That this is explained is the meaning of the expression that says it is "the explanation of this." For instance, "Because of the fact of arising immediately from exertion"—such a thing is a reason. Where there is no explanation, it is not a reason. For instance, "It is impermanent because of the fact of it being grasped by the eye."[26]

In the expression "a *dharma* is of such and such a kind, in the absence of which it does not come about" (*de 'dra ba dang med na mi 'byung ba'i chos*) one can hear the echo of "when this exists, that arises" (*satīdaṃ bhavati*)—the Buddha's definition of dependent origination (*pratītyasamutpāda*)—which Vasubandhu mentions several times in the AKBh (esp. III.28), including in the shorter disproof of the self (III.18) discussed in chapter 3. Vasubandhu's phrasing here in fact appears to provide a combination of the two versions of the Buddha's definition (one talking of existence, and the other of causality) discussed at AKBh III.28 and said there to both, together, preclude the possibility of the self, the *ātman*, as a substratum for the *skandhas*. It is a wondrous alchemist's tale if Vasubandhu may be shown to have, in fact, combined these two versions of the definition of *pratītyasamutpāda*, which only *together* disprove the self, into the generative core of Buddhist epistemology. But since the AKBh argument is rather obscure, and the *Vādavidhi* here only a Tibetan translation, lacking the Sanskrit wording required to make the point stick, I will refrain from more than suggesting the possibility.

What seems undeniable, though, is that this first Buddhist definition of the logical "reason" is directly intertwined with the Buddha's definition of conditioned arising. This is a fundamental, Buddhist intertwining of reasons and causes.[27] If, furthermore, we can hear the echo between the two passages below, we can say that Vasubandhu is interpreting the doctrine of dependent origination in accord with a manipulationist theory of causality:

> *Vādavidhi*: "The reason is said to be the explanation that a *dharma* is of such and such a kind, in the absence of which it does not come about."

> AKBh: "With a cause in place, when another cause does not exist, no result is seen, and when it does exist it comes about again."

The *Vādavidhi*'s reference to a thing's arising from the appropriate "class" or "kind" (*jāti, rigs*) is a remnant of the widely accepted criterion of causality according to which *like produces like*, as discussed in chapter 3. Here we see a logical reason—the basis of inference—and inference itself defined in accordance with a very specific kind of causal judgment.

When I claim that Vasubandhu articulates a Buddhist inferential form, readers familiar with the history of Indian logic might object that Vasubandhu's analysis here amounts to no more than suggesting that the "cause" and "result" must be discovered through positive and negative concomitance (*anvaya* and *vyatireka*)—an inferential structure that had been in use in Indian grammar and elsewhere for centuries before Vasubandhu.[28] Furthermore, they might point out that the terms "cause" and "result" are used in Indian logic to refer, figuratively, to the relevant parts of the syllogism. So what here is original, and in what way does it make sense to say that Vasubandhu's view is genuinely (and not merely figuratively) *causal*? My point is that Vasubandhu *always* uses the term "inference" (*anumāna*) to refer to linear, temporally indexed, causal series—not merely logical relations—and that he is reconfiguring the earlier conceptual structure (*anvaya* and *vyatireka*) to fit quite directly with the Buddhist doctrine of dependent origination. Vasubandhu provides a definition of inference as a judgment shaped after the Buddha's definition of dependent origination—the root authority for saying that all things are "merely cause and effect"—and he applies it paradigmatically as a disproof of the self.[29]

The other argument I wish to treat here to extend our analysis of Vasubandhu's view of language and logic will underline this view's connection to the Buddha's doctrine of dependent origination. The passage is again one of Vasubandhu's most influential and original—it is the lynchpin of his contribution to the proof of universal momentariness. The argument concerns the nature of a negative, or nonexistent, entity—or, more properly, an entity's nonexistence or its absence (*abhāva*). Vasubandhu insists that one cannot know the causes of an entity's destruction via perception. As a consequence, he says, one must rely upon inference (*anumāna*) alone to determine whether or not destruction is caused. He then proceeds to show that there can be no such inference, which means that destruction is spontaneous, and not caused.[30]

Before turning to Vasubandhu's argument against the causality of nonexistents, though, it will be helpful to look back at Vātsyāyana, to see how Vasubandhu's views on the nature of *abhāva* or nonexistence have been shaped, once again, by his engagement with Nyāya commonsense realism.

The nature of a nonexistent forms a complex problem for commonsense realists. For such a system purports to affirm our intuitive sense of the referential relation between language and the world. If we say, "That is a cow," the realist says that our language picks out a reality in the world—a thing, which is a cow. And what it means for a thing to *be* a cow, for the realist, is generally to say that there is some qualifying aspect or entity—call it "cow-ness"—that resides in the locus of the thing we're calling a "cow." With that, the metaphysical work is done, very neatly, in fact. Linguistic predication is directly reflected in the structure of the world. We have a locus, that thing, and a qualifier, in this case a generality or "universal" called "cow-ness," and our words accurately describe how we perceive them to be related: "This is a cow."

There are, of course, difficulties with this position, and Buddhist philosophers have taken advantage of the many awkward results of reifying general entities such as "cow-ness." It is clearly this kind of reification of conceptual-linguistic entities that Vasubandhu was calling a *tīrthakara-parikalpita*—a conceptual construction of the kind Tīrthakas, non-Buddhist sectarians, use, and we will see that this term marks, for Vasubandhu, a connection between conceptual reification and the failure to respect the Buddha's no-self view.

For now, though, let us point to a different issue, which is how for realists *nonexistents* provide a special case. If I say, "There is no cow in the field," or "That is not a cow," we cannot simply repeat the theoretical interpretation of our intuition about predication already given. That is, while it may be strange to speak of the "cow-ness" in a cow, it is an order of magnitude stranger to say that there's a thing called "non-cow-ness" that resides in the field. First of all, if "non-cow-ness" is there in this field, then surely it is there in *every* empty field, along with a tremendous number of other absences—in fact, along with absences of *everything* except the few things that are present. That is not necessarily a problem, because realists do tend to accept a great number of real entities in order to secure the ordinary referential capacity of our linguistic and conceptual operations. But it is awkward to admit that entities such as "non-beanbag-ness" and "non-iPod-ness" are in the field in front of me along with "non-cow-ness."

We risk sacrificing the key asset of commonsense realism (its common sense), if, in order to secure our intuitions, we must affirm many infinities of strange, new, previously unknown entities. To notice this is to begin to see the aesthetic advantage of ontological parsimony—that is, affirming as few entities as possible, opting for simplicity, and wielding Occam's razor on everything not verifiable through evident causal linkages. This was, as we have already begun to see, Vasubandhu's preference. The key to Vasubandhu's approach is to accept, from the start, that our intuitions are mistaken; we may be unavoidably deluded about how things appear, but if we refuse to base our speculations on those false appearances, we can at least avoid the conceptual constructions of the non-Buddhists.

One way "non-cow-ness" differs from "cow-ness" is that (and this is even more troubling) if it is there in the field, it is not clear how I might come to know it and speak about it (the epistemological question). For let us say that the simplest way to determine that there is a cow in a field is to look at the field in ordinary light, with properly functioning sensory organs. If indeed "cow-ness" *is* resident in the object in the field, it is at least conceivable that I can perceive the "cow-ness" of the cow—as the Nyāya philosophers say we do. But surely I cannot perceive a "non-cow-ness" in an empty field, can I? If I cannot perceive it, though, how do I know there is no cow in the field? If I *can* perceive it, then why do I not also perceive the "non-iPod-ness" and the countless other absences that are also there in every field? It would seem that we cannot become aware of a thing's absence until we have some familiarity with that thing when it is present. Only when we are looking for something can we *fail* to find it, and find instead its absence.

And so we come to Vātsyāyana's astute theory of absences. He says that absences are revealed by the same methods as positive entities, but they are known via a *failure* of the methods of knowledge that seek after the positive entity. We say to ourselves (following Matilal's translation), "If such-and-such were present, it would have been revealed to us by a *pramāṇa*."[31] This means that when I look *for a cow* in the field, and fail to see one, that is when I *perceive* the non-cow-ness.

This seems to me to satisfy our common sense. Yet it leaves open a crucial charge from the Buddhists, capitalized upon most emphatically by Vasubandhu and, later, Dignāga. And that is that if the intellect is engaged, as it must be if we are not merely looking, but looking *for a cow*, then we need to have the *idea* of a cow in mind, which means that we are no longer simply *perceiving*. Vasubandhu would agree with Vātsyāyana that a nonexistent is only known by the failure of a means of knowledge (*pramāṇa*) that is seeking after something. But Vasubandhu understands that it is one thing to fail to see something and something else to *become aware* of that thing's *absence*. For this reason, he says that a nonexistent cannot be known by perception, only by inference.[32] This is behind Vasubandhu's argument against the possibility of perceiving the destruction of kindling by fire. He proposes an objector's argument based on the venerable nature of perception; do we not simply *perceive* a thing's destruction? Note that Vasubandhu does not challenge the claim that perception is the most venerable *pramāṇa*; he still wants to preserve the possibility of the Buddha directly perceiving reality as it is. But he is deeply skeptical about just what we can know *through* perception. He says that when we think carefully about *just what we see*, we realize that our perceptions do not include what we think of as a "destruction." Some things, which we *think* we perceive, we actually construct with our minds:

> But the destruction of kindling, etc., through contact with fire, etc., is *seen*! And there is no means of knowledge more venerable than seeing. And nothing has a causeless destruction.
>
> How, in that case, can you think, "I see the destruction of kindling, etc., through contact with fire, etc.?" For, on the contrary, there is no seeing of them! This must be considered: Is it the case that things like kindling, etc., are destroyed through contact with fire, etc.? In that case these are not seen. Or, is it that they are destroyed by themselves, and others subsequently arisen? In that case they are not seen either. As with a flame due to contact with wind, or the sound of a bell due to contact with a hand. Therefore, this must be settled through inference [*anumāna*].[33]

Now, looking at the structure of this argument, notice that once again inference is understood to be a causal extrapolation. While it might seem that certain entities appear as nonexistent within *perception*, in fact one comes to know a nonexistent, or an absence, by extrapolating from a positive perception to the absence of its cause—that is, by inference (*anumāna*). It is only once you have hypothesized a causal series that you can talk about a thing's absence. This is directly analogous to the inference that concludes the nonexistence of a sensory organ from the absence of a perception in the case of a blind person; where the result that would otherwise be present is missing, one can infer the absence of some missing cause. But an "absence" itself does not depend upon a cause.

We are also familiar with the two philosophical examples Vasubandhu adduces here, the flame and the bell. Vasubandhu appealed to the flame as an example of an entity that appears continuous, but that we know is made up of distinct, momentary flares. When the flame goes out, this is not because it has somehow entered into a new state; it is just that the fuel has run out, and there are no further flares. In fact, this is exactly the argument Vasubandhu brings against the substantial existence of the "quenching" that is the goal of Buddhist practice, *nirvāṇa*.[34] The same is true with a bell: we say, conventionally, that a bell "rings," but since it is the vibrations of the bell that *are* the ringing, when a hand stops the vibrations, the ringing is no more. It is not as though the hand has trapped the ringing within the bell, or that the bell is now generating silence. The sound of the bell and the light of the fire are gone, but they have not gone anywhere.

Vasubandhu then takes this argument one step further, and points out that it is a mistake to infer, from the absence of an existent entity, some "nonexistent" that causes its nonperception. On the contrary, a nonexistent is only a conceptual construct *generated by an inference*, which does not, in fact cannot, cause anything real. As we have already seen, Vasubandhu draws the ontological line very starkly here, between things that are real, and are causally linked with other things, and things that are mere unreal, conceptual constructions. A manipulationist view of causal explanation poses absence as the value of a variable in a causal system, rather than as a separate entity that acts as a (non)cause of a nonresult. The result of an inference is never a separate entity itself, but merely a value of a variable ("presence" vs. "absence") that represents a conceptual construction *across* a series of interconnected but distinct entities.

This view of inference and its implication of the unreality of nonexistents is central to Vasubandhu's distinctive proof of universal momentariness.[35] Anything that passes out of existence must do so spontaneously, he argues, in the very moment of its coming into being. For no entity can be the cause of another entity's nonexistence. Why not? Because nonexistence, or absence, is not a thing, it is not a reality itself; it is only a conceptual construction projected upon the existent thing once it is no longer present. And my conceptual construction about *x* cannot be caused by another entity *y*'s acting on *x*. Instead, the nonexistence of *x* is inferred, and projected upon the space where *x* fails to appear.

> That might be if momentariness were proven for everything.
>
> You should know that that very thing is proven.
>
> How?
>
> **By the fact that** destruction **is spontaneous** [IV.2d2] for conditioned things. For the destruction of existents is uncaused.
>
> Why?
>
> Because a cause is of a result. And destruction is a nonexistent. And what is to be done with respect to what does not exist?[36] If a just-arisen existent should have no uncaused destruction, then later, too, the existent should have none, because of its being the same.[37]

The logic here centers, again, around Vasubandhu's strong identification of *reality* with *causally engaged entities*. To say that something is a "cause" or a "result" is to say that it is a *real thing*. To say that it is *not* a real thing is to say that it is not associated with any identifiable *cause* or *result*. On such a view, destruction is not a thing; it is simply the nonexistence of a recently past thing. Combine this fact with the notion that things cannot change and remain the same entity, as Vasubandhu proves in his argument against "change for the Sāṃkhyas."[38] If entities are to be destroyed, their destruction must be a part of their essential nature, their *svabhāva*, from the start. Things must, therefore, instantaneously self-destruct in the moment of their origin.

Needless to say, this does not mean that things do not *appear* to be destroyed. It certainly seems like I can break a vase, or die. But Vasubandhu's point is that when we think in terms of real causal series, in which each entity is conditioned by what comes before it, what actually occurs below our awareness is not properly described by the language of "destruction." Just as there is no self, there is no vase, and so there is nothing to be destroyed. What happens when something is apparently destroyed is an alteration in its causal continuum so that the entities that are the support (*āśraya*) of the appearance of continuity no longer arise. "Destruction" is figurative. Change is only an appearance.

Notice the connection between Vasubandhu's proof of momentariness and his proof of no-self. There is no need to posit continuity between past experiences and present memories for the same reason that there is no need to posit a real nonexistent to take up the space when an existent entity passes away. And what is the reason? The work of connecting separate events and entities is performed by false conceptual constructions. The result of this discussion is that Vasubandhu has spun a distinctive Buddhist epistemology out of his proofs of no-self and momentariness. For Vasubandhu, inference is a process of extrapolation of a causal series that issues in a potentially valid, but merely conceptual projection. This view, furthermore, is bolstered by the need to distinguish between Buddhist and non-Buddhist views of continuity. Impermanence and no-self are interconnected and derive equal necessity from their shared association with a causal interpretation of inference and a strict conceptual anti-realism. To violate this conceptual anti-realism is to violate the causal interpretation of inference, and in turn to violate Buddhism's most basic teachings.

A NEW THEORIZATION OF BUDDHIST SCRIPTURE

We have seen that in his "Refutation of the Self," Vasubandhu refers to perception and inference—the two traditional Buddhist *pramāṇas*, or means of knowledge—and he says that perception observes one set of objects, that inference determines a second set of objects, and what fails to be found by either does not exist.[39] This epistemic bifurcation of the real world into objects of perception and objects of inference is generally attributed to the great Buddhist epistemologist, Dignāga. But it is at least implicit in Vasubandhu's argument.[40] Next, we have seen that the inference that proves imperceptible entities is a causal inference, which, as we have also seen, is for Vasubandhu the only kind of inference that a Buddhist should allow as proof of an entity's reality. Thus, two principles often attributed to the second great Buddhist epistemologist, Dharmakīrti, are also quite prominent in the *Commentary*. The first is that inferences are essentially formalizations of causal stories, and the second is that without establishing causality we cannot establish reality—or, to say the same thing, that causality is the touchstone of the real.[41] What this means is that Vasubandhu's view of causality was not only the basis for his masterful interpretation of Buddhist selflessness and its relation to Abhidharma. It was also, crucially, the foundation for the epistemological traditions that would dominate Indian Buddhism in the centuries to follow.[42]

I mention this connection between Vasubandhu's no-self proof passage and the origins of Buddhist epistemology not only because it allows us to sing praises of Vasubandhu's significance, but also because it highlights for us that Vasubandhu's argument explicating the Buddha's ontological position of no-self is centrally about *knowledge*. As I have said above, it is an *epistemic* argument for no-self. It establishes no-self at the fulcrum between *what it means* that something exists (it means that that thing has causes), and *how we can know* that something exists (we know because we can measure its causes). Given that Vasubandhu's theory of causality, which we have called "manipulationist," is serving *epistemic* goals, it will do us well to expand our understanding of the epistemic implications of a manipulationist view of causality. Once we have understood the epistemological implications of the manipulationist view, we will see the connection between Vasubandhu's view of causality and his approach to the knowledge gained from Buddhist scriptures. This approach to scriptural knowledge is employed in the AKBh and theorized in the Yogācāra-influenced work *The Proper Mode of Exposition.*

On Woodward's manipulationist view, causality is a mode of explanation that describes not laws, but patterns of invariance—what he calls "patterns of counterfactual dependence."[43] Importantly, these are patterns that only become visible when we are looking to solve particular practical problems. Our causal judgments depend crucially on just how we define our intervention, or manipulation, and on what we take to be the relevant background context against which we are willing to describe a cause. Woodward allows that the contextual framing of the causal scenario in this way introduces a degree of subjectivity to the assessment of causal structures; this is unavoidable. He points out, for instance, that different causal explanations of the same phenomenon may well target different levels of "explanatory depth," depending upon what counts as evidence. An example of such a difference in explanatory depth is the difference between explaining a car's forward motion as caused by (1) turning the key, putting the car in gear, and pressing the gas pedal and (2) the mechanics of the relevant car parts.[44] Thus, just what we call "causes" hinges on what kinds of evidence we are "willing to take seriously." Yet Woodward insists that the relativity that such framing introduces does not prevent the structures from providing evidence of objective realities:

> Causal judgments reflect both objective patterns of counterfactual dependence and which possibilities are taken seriously: they convey or summarize

> information about patterns of counterfactual dependence among those possibilities we are willing to take seriously. In other words, to the extent that subjectivity or interest relativity enters into causal judgments, it enters because it influences our judgments about which possibilities are to be taken seriously. However, once the set of serious possibilities is fixed, there is no further element of arbitrariness or subjectivity in our causal judgments: relative to a set of serious possibilities or alternatives, which causal claims are true or false is determined by objective patterns of counterfactual dependence.[45]

A manipulationist view is therefore willing to acknowledge that causes are inevitably human constructions, named and identified as "causes" because of their relevance to human interests, and selected from among what the interpreter deems "serious possibilities." But that fact does not make causal descriptions merely subjective.

We have seen Vasubandhu bring various arguments—against static entities, against causal overdetermination, and against mental objects and ideal entities—based in the central, manipulationist notion that the dependence relation in causation can only be determined via a hypothetical *intervention.* The fact that this intervention need only be *hypothetical* points to the second aspect of manipulationist causal theory that Vasubandhu adopts, which is the crucial, mentally constructed quality of this quintessentially empirical mode of analysis. For a hypothesis is always only a conceptual construction. We do not need to actually *perform* the manipulation or the experiment in order to hypothesize a cause.[46] Yet even a conceptual construction can be "fixed" and manipulated so as to structure a properly causal inference.

A causal inference is imperfect—it is not as certain as a Buddha's omniscience—because it must appeal to our conceptual constructions. Nonetheless, the entity whose existence is proven by this kind of inference is to be deemed "real" because without it there is no explanation for specific regularities in our experience. This is what it means for an entity to be "substantial" (*dravya*). On the other hand, not all conceptually constructed, experienced regularities are viable as evidence of real entities, because the regularities may be resident within the conceptual construct. There must, therefore, be a means of verifying input from the objective world. For this reason, the subjective aspects of the scenario must be held constant—"fixed"—across the manipulation process for a cause to be properly determined. Scientific experiments use controls to prevent shifts that arise *along with* the manipulation from appearing to be causal results of the manipulation itself. This kind of thinking should help us understand why Vasubandhu denies the substantial reality of entities he believes only appear to exist due to reified shifts in subjective perspective. Such entities violate the requirement of keeping the subjective aspect "fixed." The unique interplay, in this view, of the subjective aspect of causal framing with the objective nature of the results *within* that frame helps to explain how Vasubandhu—and the Yogācāra epistemologists to follow—could employ causally based reasoning (which is necessarily conceptual) even as they cast doubt upon the ultimate reality of all conceptually constructed entities.

In this way, Vasubandhu's detailed arguments throughout the AKBh—against what he takes to be conceptually constructed Vaibhāṣika *dharmas* and the Vātsīputrīya's purported "person"—provide not only a justification for a set of doctrines, but a motivating structure for Buddhist epistemology. I find the convergence of Vasubandhu's conceptual structure with that of a manipulationist view of scientific reasoning about causality quite remarkable. Vasubandhu was not a modern scientist, setting up experiments and articulating their principled guidelines. Why did he adopt this complex, relativistic framing, while at the same time affirming the (relative) truth (substantiality) of the causally derived entities *within* the frame? The reason, I believe, is that Vasubandhu's approach to causality is motivated not only by its benefits in Buddhist metaphysics, but also by what it provides Buddhist scriptural interpretation. Often, in South Asian thought, the needs of scriptural interpretation may be seen to "wag the dog" of the supposedly more fundamental aspects of doctrinal analysis.[47] This was apparently true of Vasubandhu, for whom philosophical reasoning is always motivated by scriptural analysis, and whose most extensive writings include a major treatise on scriptural interpretation. The epistemological implications of his manipulationism are intrinsic to Vasubandhu's unique form of scriptural ecumenism.

As soon as we attend to it, we see that one of Vasubandhu's principal philosophical concerns was to combat dogmatism and literalism in the interpretation of scripture. This has already become a theme of our investigations; criticism of his opponents' false reifications of entities named within Buddhist scriptures that are, more properly, to be understood as mere "figures" with "special intentions" appear in nearly every argument we have studied thus far:

1. In the argument against the three times, he explains that the Buddha said that the past and future exist in order to combat those who do not believe in cause and effect, not to affirm additional entities; "past," "present," and "future" are only names we give for elements understood in a series;
2. In the discussion of the past and future "dualities" of sensory organs and objects that cause consciousness, Vasubandhu says that the Buddha does not mean that these objects are literally "producers" of consciousness, only that they are mental objects (*ālambana*);
3. In the argument against the self, he explains that there are actions and results, but no agent—and that the "self" sometimes referred to by the Buddha is merely a figurative designation (*upacāra*) for the aggregates;
4. In his exposition of "view" (*dṛṣṭi*), he explains that the "view" of the eye is in fact a term for the awareness of the eye consciousness, and that all "views" are therefore figures for consciousness;
5. In his discussion of momentariness, he declares "destruction," and "absence," to be mere words for things when they are perceived as no longer present.

From the very beginning, then, Vasubandhu defended the notion that the Buddha's words *quite often* need to be read figuratively. Vasubandhu was a defender, in the AKBh, and then elsewhere, of flexibility in scriptural interpretation. The AKBh commentary mocks the Vaibhāṣika opponent for showing an understanding of the words, rather than the meaning, of the scripture cited.[48] In truth, the Vaibhāṣika positions that Vasubandhu criticizes are often based in Ābhidharmika philosophy's centuries of gradual systematization of the Buddha's words. Vasubandhu advocates not just a different system of *dharmas*, but also a new interpretation of the scriptural passages that are used to support the older *dharmas.*

For instance, one traditional view, based on a standard reading of the Twelve Links of Dependent Origination, has one *dharma*, "contact" (*sparśa*), as the basic entity of perception. A Vaibhāṣika position is that the coming together of the perceptual organ, the object, and the consciousness produces the *contact*, which in turn brings about *feeling*, and so on. In response, Vasubandhu cites an alternate scriptural source, which validates his position that the contact described in the Twelve Links *just is* the coming together of the perceptual organ, the object, and the consciousness (or, alternatively, simply the organ and the object).[49] There is, he says, no separate entity to label "contact" over and above the activity of these *dharmas*. Here Vasubandhu is using his reasoning about linear causality to decide between two scriptural interpretations.[50]

In another passage (to add to the list), Vasubandhu criticizes the Vaibhāṣika *dharma* of "possession," *prāpti*, which he says has no substantial reality. When the Buddha is cited as having said that the "possession of greed" prevents one from cultivating the foundations of mindfulness, Vasubandhu argues that the "possession" referred to in this passage means some specific, momentary causal event with respect to already established *dharmas*, such as "consenting to greed" or "not rejecting greed."[51] It is superfluous to posit a new *dharma* called "possession," because the causal efficacy described by that term is already taken care of by these other means.

So, we can guess how Vasubandhu will deal with the Vātsīputrīya, who sees an ineffable "person" where Buddha spoke of the "bearer of the burden" of the aggregates (*skandhas*).[52] He explains that what is meant by "bearer" is not some separate entity in addition to the aggregates, but instead is just the causal result of suffering brought about by the aggregates. Once again, Vasubandhu takes a scriptural passage that might otherwise seem to be reifying a distinct, new entity—a personal subject—and reinterprets it as referring, figuratively, to mere appearances that only seem to exist when one imposes a conceptual construct upon a succession of distinct entities. Vasubandhu is, of course, a highly skilled reader of scripture, and he is able to prove his interpretation by citing the Buddha's own explanation of just what he *means* by the "bearer of the burden"—which is just the five aggregates. When we have a direct explanation, Vasubandhu says, how can you justify the claim that the person is "ineffable" (*avaktavya*)?

In light of these passages, and the others we have already studied, we may identify how Vasubandhu's employment of scripture in the AKBh follows a particular, complex pattern. Of course, he sometimes simply proposes a source to defend or explain a given view. But more often[53] than that, he sets up a debate between proponents and opponents of a given view, in which the interpretation of scripture plays a very important role—a central role. Many times there is a debate over the meaning of a particular passage or kind of passage, and very often (and here is where it gets complicated) one side will adduce a counterquotation in order to justify or overturn a particular interpretation of the initial passage. In this kind of complex debate it is common, perhaps even inevitable, that questions will arise about just how scriptures are to be used. It is in this kind of context that, in a number of cases, Vasubandhu presents what may be called "interpretive principles"—rules for the proper application of scripture.

These principles serve as a kind of punctuation in a number of the debates staged in the AKBh; often they provide an endpoint to a particular line of argument. These rules are not intended to provide anything like a comprehensive methodology. In each case, Vasubandhu is simply stating a rule in order to point out where his opponent has failed to interpret scripture in a reasonable way, or in a way that coheres with common sense and common custom. Nonetheless, when we bring these rules together, we can see that Vasubandhu does indeed have a consistent view of the nature of scripture and its relation to the project of Abhidharma philosophy. Furthermore, if we look at the way that Vasubandhu reframes the *sūtras* in general and, more importantly, in countless particulars, we can see how his work paves the way from an acceptance of the full range of Śrāvaka scriptures to what will be a Yogācāra approach to scripture.

A few of these principles include:

POINTS ON THE SELECTION OF SOURCES

1. *A reasonable disputant must accept widely recognized sūtras.* Scriptural acceptance, Vasubandhu argues, may not be dogmatically limited by lineage or school. ("To say that a book which is transmitted in all the other traditions, and which contradicts neither *sūtra* nor reality, is not the Buddha's utterance because 'we do not recite it' is mere recklessness."[54] See below.)
2. *Point 1 does not mean that just any doctrine may be hypostatized to have been accepted by the Buddha.* It is a valid point that the Buddhist doctrine cannot be taken to be closed: "Many *sūtras* have disappeared, so how can one be sure that this was not said?"[55] But this is not sufficient support to contradict direct scriptural evidence.
3. *The following is the proper hierarchy in textual evidence*: (1) sūtra; (2) vinaya *or* abhidharma; (3) śāstra. *Śāstra* may not counter evidence from perception, reasoning, or the authority of the Three Baskets (*tripiṭaka*). Poetry (*kāvya*) may not count as evidence in an argument.[56]

POINTS ON LEGITIMATELY DISCOUNTING SCRIPTURAL EVIDENCE

4. *A* sūtra *with multiple interpretations cannot be used to prove one of them.*[57]
5. *Where scriptures contradict reason, they must be accounted for under a secondary, "figurative"* (upacāra), *nonliteral meaning.*

6. *Nonliteral meanings include idiomatic phrasings.* For example, "ordered" (*yathākramam*) expressions that refer to the result as the object of an activity, as where the Buddha speaks of descent of the "egg-born" into the womb, or "grinding the flour" (which only becomes *flour* via grinding).[58] As another idiom, future *dharmas* which have not yet been produced may still be referred to as "produced in dependence." If one takes such idioms literally, absurdities multiply. To imagine that it is a mistake to say that one "grinds flour" because the flour must already be ground for it to be flour (otherwise it would be seeds), or to imagine that *nirvāṇa* is conditioned because one desires it, is to impose a mistaken terminological realism.
7. "*What has a special intention [belongs] in* sūtra; *what is definitive [goes] in* abhidharma."[59] Although *śāstras* may not be used to counter a direct, authoritative statement from a *sūtra*, it is important to differentiate the intentions of *abhidharma* treatises (such as the AKBh and the *Vibhāṣā*), whose purpose is to describe the definitive nature of real entities (*dharmas*), from those of *sūtras*, which were spoken with a wide range of specific intentions, each targeted to the needs of a specific audience.[60]

POINTS IN APPLIED HERMENEUTICS

8. *Use reason to determine the meaning.* You may not just take a list from a *sūtra* and claim that it affirms a set of separate entities. There needs to be some reason for interpreting elements in the list as either distinct entities or not. Sometimes they are intended that way, but sometimes they are simply collections of names without a defining purpose. See the list of *dṛṣṭi dharmas* discussed in chapter 3. Another example has the Vaibhāṣika citing a list of seven *bhavas* that includes the five *gatis* (rebirths) *and* two more: the *karmabhava* and *antarābhava*, and using this passage as proof that *antarābhava* is separate from the *gatis*. Vasubandhu agrees with the conclusion, but does not consider the scriptural reasoning definitive. In reply, he adduces the list of five *kaṣāyas*, which includes both *dṛṣṭi* and *kleśa*. Clearly *dṛṣṭi* is a *kleśa*, he says, so you cannot just use the list of *bhavas* as evidence that things in the list are separate entities.[61]
9. *Multiple scriptural sources may be used to provide interpretive context for a given passage.* For instance, eight of the Twelve Links of Dependent Origination must refer only to the *kāmadhātu*, because in other *dhātus* we do not have all of the sensory organs.[62] Here the larger point is to take a more holistic approach to scripture, placing every view in its proper context.

10. *Explain what the sūtra tries to teach. It is not acceptable to insert missing elements to "correct" a sūtra passage.* First of all, the meaning is not always intended to be literally accurate. Second, once one begins inserting missing elements, it becomes possible to attribute whatever one would like to a scriptural passage. An example is a passage in which a series of options are floated to explain the cause of the *first* link in the chain of dependent origination, ignorance (*avidyā*). For clearly the links go on forever, but they also seem to *start* with ignorance. One idea is floated that notes two separate scriptural passages, one in which ignorance is said to have "improper mental activity" (*ayoniśomanaskāra*) as its cause, and the other in which improper mental activity is said to have ignorance as *its* cause. This allows for an unending reciprocal causality between these two elements. Vasubandhu rejects this interpretation on the grounds that it ignores the fact that "improper mental activity" is not named as one of the Twelve Links. Even if "improper mental activity" may be extracted from one of the links, this is not *the point* of the *sūtra* in question. Instead, he explains, the reason for the presentation of the Twelve Links was to display the relation between past conditions and present existence, and among present conditions and future existence. There is no reason, in such an explanation, for filling in the blanks. Thus the teaching's *context is everything.*

These points make up only a small selection from a vast variety of scriptural rules adduced in the course of the AKBh, but already they cohere into a clear set of principles for determining the place of scriptures in Buddhist doctrinal theorization. This may be summarized as a preference for the utility of reason and the legitimacy of figurative interpretation over literalism and terminological reification. One might imagine that this would allow the philosopher to simply impose a doctrinal position upon any given scriptural passage. Yet the preference for reason is paired with the requirement to accept, and account for, all widely used scriptures—accounting for them by explaining the Buddha's intention as a teacher. This crucial criterion, given the diversity of scriptural sources available, means that the interpreter must become a skilled analyzer of the Buddha's diverse intentions. The Buddha's words must be judged not as literal, frozen truths, but as enactments in time, with specific causal effects. Vasubandhu's project of reasoning (*anumāna*) by appeal to causal series applies not only to the world, but also to the language of scripture. Even the Buddha's intentions must be determined according to the likely, local causal effects his words would have for his audience members.[63]

Scripture, like all entities, must be understood in its proper frame. Vasubandhu was promoting, at the same time, a particular view of the world and a particular approach to scriptures.

The proper mode of scriptural exposition (*vyākhyāyukti*), then, is to clarify the intentions of the Buddha (*saṃdhinirmocana*). One must determine the meanings of scriptural passages by appealing to the likely motives behind them—motives that must be gauged by a combination of reason together with a broad familiarity with the possibilities of the Buddha's intentions. Given this framework for Vasubandhu's overall approach to scripture, it is not surprising that his treatise on scriptural interpretation—the *Proper Mode of Exposition* (VyY)—draws its impetus from the seminal scripture of Yogācāra interpretation, the *Scripture on the Clarification of the [Buddha's] Intent* (*Saṃdhinirmocanasūtra*, SNS). The goal of that scripture is to provide a new explanation of the Buddha's "intent" in propounding a diverse range of scriptures, focusing in particular on the most contentious among Buddhist scriptures, the Perfection of Wisdom scriptures, which are the central texts of the Mahāyāna. Vasubandhu's VyY synthesizes the scriptural approach summarized above with the hermeneutic theory of the SNS. The two approaches, though evidently based in different scriptural sets, are in fact quite intentionally coordinated.

The first principle of scriptural interpretation mentioned above was Vasubandhu's advocacy of an openness to a diversity of scriptures and traditions of interpretation. He wrote the following in the AKBh IX (in Kapstein's translation):

> To say that a book which is transmitted in all the other traditions, and which contradicts neither *sūtra* nor reality, is not the Buddha's utterance because "we do not recite it" is mere recklessness.[64]

This position of openness to a diverse range of the Buddha's words might well have played a part in propelling Vasubandhu to defend the Mahāyāna scriptures. Nearly the same argument about the nature of scriptural interpretation that we see in the AKBh appears in the VyY:

> Furthermore, if it is said, "The Great Vehicle is not the Word of the Buddha," then we should dispute and investigate, "What is the definition of the Word of the Buddha?"
>
> Suppose someone should say, "The definition of the Word of the Buddha is what is accepted by the 18 Schools."

> In that case, scriptures associated with selflessness such as the *Emptiness of the Ultimate* [*Paramārthaśūnyatā*], which are not accepted by the noble Sammitīyas, and for instance the seven existences including the intermediate state, which are not accepted by those such as the Mahīśāsakas, will not be word of the Buddha.[65]

We see in these passages a principled openness to a diversity of doctrines, and an unwillingness to accept the circular reasoning that would exclude views because they are not already accepted within one's own lineage or school. Indeed, one of the more remarkable and most commented upon aspects of the AKBh is its citation of such a wide range of arguments from so many perspectives. Vasubandhu clearly believed that a Buddhist philosopher ought to take account of the widest possible range of sources, whether scriptural or doctrinal.

Yet if a genuine openness to all widely read scriptures motivated Vasubandhu to take account of the Mahāyāna *sūtras*, he would have to take into account an extremely different and challenging doctrinal perspective. Such scriptures call the practices of other Buddhist traditions "The Degraded Way" (*Hīnayāna*), and explicitly deny and undermine the claims of Abhidharma philosophy:

> Therefore, O Śāriputra, in emptiness there is no form, nor feeling, nor perception, nor impulse, nor consciousness; no eye, ear, nose, tongue, body, mind; no forms, sounds, smells, tastes, touchables, or objects of mind; no sight-organ element, and so forth, until we come to: no mind-consciousness element. There is no ignorance, no extinction of ignorance, and so forth, until we come to: there is no decay and death, no extinction of decay and death. There is no suffering, no origination, no stopping, no path. There is no cognition, no attainment, and no nonattainment.[66]

The negations here, and the doctrine of universal "emptiness" that they express, stand as an open challenge to the authority of previous scriptural and interpretive traditions. It is clear from critiques leveled against the Mahāyāna that many who rejected these scriptures considered them to amount to a nihilistic rejection of the Buddha's key doctrines of *karma* and *nirvāṇa*.[67] Advocates of Mahāyāna, for their part, critiqued the earlier traditions as blind and selfish. Openness to a diversity of such source texts requires a nuanced theoretical framework and a subtle attention to interpretive detail, in order to prevent it from devolving into self-undermining and self-contradiction.[68]

Vasubandhu's works may be read as a great effort to balance diversity with systematicity. If in the AKBh Vasubandhu combats the dogmatism of the Vaibhāṣikas and Vātsīputrīyas, in the VyY we see this approach applied in its most comprehensive fashion. Vasubandhu stakes his claim to a view of scripture that maintains the importance and the validity of *both* Śrāvakayāna *and* Mahāyāna. In order to make this work, however, he must counter the scriptural exclusivism that each "vehicle" levels at the other, and at the same time counter each tradition's claim to the whole truth. Vasubandhu argues that all truths, even the truths of the Perfection of Wisdom scriptures, are relative and conventional. The ultimate truth, beyond all concepts, is inexpressible:

> I exist conventionally as a person but not substantially, because of the imputation of that upon the aggregates. *Karma* and results exist substantially, conventionally. They do not exist ultimately, because they are objects of mundane knowledge. Supreme [*dam pa*, **parama*] is wisdom beyond the mundane, and its object [*don*, **artha*] is the ultimate [*don dam pa*, **paramārtha*]. That object is not the specific character of those two, because that object is an inexpressible [*brjod du med pa*, **anabhilāpya*] general character.[69]

Let's work through this slowly. "I exist conventionally as a person but not substantially, because of the imputation of that upon the aggregates." This is a statement of the basic argument against the self with which we began chapter 3. Going on: "*Karma* and results exist substantially, conventionally." This is an acknowledgment of the Śrāvaka, non-Mahāyāna position, but the addition of the last word, "conventionally," shifts us into a Mahāyāna view. Śrāvakas do not distinguish between *substantial* entities and *ultimate* ones. But notice how Vasubandhu explains why *karma* and results are not ultimate: "They do not exist ultimately, because they are objects of mundane knowledge." They are real, but they are not *ultimately* real, because they are ordinary concepts. He glosses the term "ultimate" by saying: "Supreme [*dam pa*] is wisdom beyond the mundane, and its object [*don*] is the ultimate [*don dam pa*]." The ultimate is thus *by definition* an object of supra-mundane awareness. This is why "that object"—meaning a supra-mundane object—"is not the specific character of those two"—meaning *karma* and results—"because that object is an inexpressible general character." The nature of an ultimate is inexpressible—that is in fact what it *means* to say that it is ultimate.

This passage explains why, for the Mahāyāna, it is essential to reject the ultimate nature of the conventions of the Śrāvakayāna. But more than that, it sets up an explanation of why the scriptures and treatises *of the Mahāyāna as well* are only conventional. For anything that is an object of mundane knowledge—anything that ordinary worldlings can understand—is by definition merely conventional. Thus all scriptures, of all schools, are only conventional. This must be true even when the scriptures are attempting to articulate views that are beyond the conventional. This view recognizes a diversity of doctrines and views, but only by placing them all within the realm of the conventional. Vasubandhu poses the question of whether mundane, worldly knowledge or ultimate awareness should count as valid means of knowledge, and he says that of course ultimate awareness is nothing but valid, but even mundane knowledge only reaches the level of genuine validity by following directly from that awareness. Even direct sensory perception fails, from this perspective, to rise to the level of valid awareness.[70]

Vasubandhu is therefore acknowledging the ostensibly Mahāyāna position that all words and concepts are mere conventions, but without acknowledging that this fact vitiates the scriptural sources of the Śrāvakayāna. On the contrary, if the point is that all entities as we conceive them are conventional truths, then the Mahāyāna scriptures must also be conventional truth only. Therefore, there is no argument based upon the distinction between conventional and ultimate that might undermine the *conventional* nature of the truths Abhidharma philosophers base upon Buddhist scriptures:

> Also, for some Mahāyānists who say that whereas all things, in their natures as a specific character, simply do not exist, this argument will also arise: what is being taught, conventionally, in those expressions where the Lord speaks of the existence of a thing just as it is, in the words, "The very existence of *dharmas* is taught"?[71]

Notice here Vasubandhu's use of the tenth point of scriptural interpretation adduced above, namely, the requirement to *explain what the sūtra tries to teach*. Whereas it may be the case that, as the Perfection of Wisdom scriptures teach, from an ultimate perspective even what Abhidharma determines to be *substantial realities* are unreal, there *still* must be some explanation for the Buddha's having taught this or that *dharma* as real. Whereas the ultimate nature of things is beyond intellection, the conventional nature of things must still be adjudicated based upon the full range of scriptural resources available.

Vasubandhu's view is thus an extremely confident affirmation of the utility of conventional language in articulating the fullness of the conceptual universe, though always with an acknowledgement that reality itself, its causal ways *as they really are*, is beyond language and conceptualization:

> Where all *dharmas* are inexpressible characteristics, by speaking as with the conceptual constructions of fools, following their understanding, it is suitable even for the Āryas to express with words what has no words.[72]

If even Āryas must speak in conventional terms (because there are no other kinds of speech), then surely philosophers are granted leave from the requirement to speak ultimate truths. The acceptance of an ineffable ultimate, beyond the limits of ordinary language, in fact *sequesters it there.* It amounts to a defense of Abhidharma, and at the same time, an opening to the development of logic and epistemology—the tools of reasoning—within the larger framework of a doctrinal acceptance of the Mahāyāna. This was the view of what was to be called the Yogācāra, propounded in the SNS, which is why Vasubandhu punctuates his argument with a quotation from that scripture:

> In this way, the following passage from the *Saṃdhinirmocanasūtra* applies:
>
> Noble son, "conditioned" is a term designated by the teacher. This term designated by the teacher is a conventional expression arising from conceptual construction. And that which is a conventional expression arising from conceptual construction is a conventional expression of various conceptual constructions that is not thoroughly established. Therefore, it is not conditioned. As with the conditioned, so it applies in the same way to the unconditioned as well.[73] Also, whatever is said about anything not included within the conditioned and unconditioned will also be like this. Moreover, an expression is not simply without substance. And what is that substance? It is that to which the Āryas, with Ārya knowledge and Ārya vision, are inexpressibly, perfectly, and completely awakened.[74]

The view of the SNS is that the ultimate nature of all *dharmas* is inexpressible. Yet the inexpressibility itself poses an ironic, self-undermining quality. From the perspective that acknowledges the ultimate emptiness of all concepts, the statement of the *conditioned nature* of all things—the teaching that is the basis of their being recognized as merely imputed—is itself undermined by being a mere conceptual construction. Since it is only an appearance, there is no real causal basis for its arising (appearances have no causal impetus), which means that *it is not a properly conditioned entity*. Thus all entities are both conditioned and unconditioned, or neither, depending on the perspective one takes on their apparent reality. Thus once all concepts are undermined, there is no way to say anything with finality; while things are ultimately empty, they may still have substance.

The point of the final sentence, though, is that for Āryas, for enlightened beings, this is not a problem; they see things as they are, without engaging in false expressions. This is what it means to say that things have an inexpressible nature. It is also what it means to chastise the extreme advocates of Mahāyāna for imagining that their declaration of universal emptiness undermines the non-Mahāyāna scriptures and treatises. For to speak from the ultimate is not only to undermine ordinary conventions; it is to undermine all conceptual-linguistic structures and hence to transform an ordinary hermeneutic circle into the event horizon of meaning's black hole. To read the above is to recognize the difference between talk of the ultimate and talk of conventions, and to see how meaning is undermined when the inexpressible leaks into our conventions. It is a strong motivation, therefore, to sequester the inexpressible where it belongs—beyond the horizon—and therefore to allow substance to play a part in our ordinary explanations. Arguments must be conventional.[75]

Thus the SNS and Vasubandhu posit an ultimate reality that is beyond conceptualization, and is articulated in terms that explicitly prevent the ordinary mind from being convinced that it has grasped the truth of the matter. From the conventional side, on the other hand, this view lays the ground for subsequent Indian Yogācāra—for Dignāga and Dharmakīrti—with their emphasis on the conventional utility of epistemology (*pramāṇa*), and their notion that there are multiple levels of conventional truth—what has been called their "sliding scale" view of truth.[76] What is surprising, then, is the notion that this view of the ultimate is cogently aligned with the theory of causality as the basis for the conventions of reason and logic. Because causality is at the center of all conceptual constructions, the determination of the real is dependent upon causality, and therefore, all of reality—including talk about ultimate reality—is a conceptual construction.

We may summarize Vasubandhu's critique of the Mahāyāna extreme view of nihilism with the same passage he uses to critique the reificationism of the Vaibhāṣikas, namely, where he accuses his opponents of "carving the ether" and reifying the Buddha's words, and making a mere *vijñapti*—a mere linguistic appearance—into a *tīrthakara-parikalpita*—a conceptual construction of the kind Tīrthakas, non-Buddhists, use. The Buddha's words, he says, need to be interpreted. They are not meant to be understood merely for their most direct, surface meaning. They are not like the eternal *Veda*, uncreated, or created by a god, or gods. They are the foundation for great faith, but they do not in themselves provide an unmediated access to reality as it is. For Vasubandhu, an intelligent and lively analysis of the nature of reality—a reasoning about what appears to be causing what—must be part of any proper analysis of scripture. For that reason, the meaning of the *dharma* is always going to be subject to dispute, and thoroughly embedded within the realm of conventions.

The notion of the inconceivable—what cannot be known—plays a part in the AKBh as well. There are some things that cannot be known. In a passage discussing the story in which there is a giant mass of meat, the size of Mount Meru, decomposing, and it changes into a mass of worms, Vasubandhu poses the question of what karmic causes could have allowed all of these beings to be born here, all at once? This is a version of the question of how to account, karmically, for the world's population increase—a question that arises in nearly every attentive first-year Buddhism class. Vasubandhu considers a few possibilities, but ends up saying, "And with respect to this the Lord has said, 'The karmic ripening of living beings is incomprehensible.' "[77] In a passage disproving the reality of a reflection (for instance, as an entity that exists on the surface of the water), he points out that people looking from different sides of a lake see different reflections, and that, furthermore, you do not see a moon *on the surface* of the water—you see it recessed *below* the surface, like you are looking down a well. How does this happen? He does not claim to know: "The different powers of *dharmas* are incomprehensible."[78] And, as I have mentioned above, in one passage Vasubandhu considers inference a second-rate *pramāṇa* by comparison with perception, and the omniscience of a Buddha is direct, not inferred. He says that Sautrāntikas accept that merely by intending it, the Buddha knows whatever he chooses to know. They base this view on the scripture that says that the qualities of a Buddha's awareness are incomprehensible.[79]

We may contrast these cases, which acknowledge the limits of ordinary knowledge, with the "unspeakable" person advocated by the Pudgalavādins in AKBh IX. There, the nature of the person—which they say is neither identical to, nor distinct from, the *skandhas*—serves the role of a kind of "mystery," a phenomenon that exceeds our comprehension by its very nature. Vasubandhu does not argue against the idea of the ineffable per se; instead, he points out that (1) such a view flies in the face of countless scriptures which deny the self; (2) the scriptures upon which the supposed mystery is based can be more straightforwardly explained; and (3) most importantly, the explanatory role of the ostensible "person" (explaining continuity) is entirely unnecessary once we understand fully the causal capacities of the *skandhas*.[80] As with every other false entity opposed in the AKBh, the "ineffable person" is defeated by explanation discounting: given what we know must already exist (the *skandhas*) it need not exist, so it is eliminated by Occam's razor. A causal line of discrete events, each completely distinct, dissociated from any unified "person," explains all the evidence. This does not prevent us from using the word "person" conventionally, but in those cases there is nothing "unspoken" about the meaning. The rule that leads to Vasubandhu adopting the notion of the incomprehensible or the unspeakable seems to be the *priority* of causal reasoning, in that he is willing to give up on knowledge before giving up on causality. This is quite different from the attempt to use ineffability as a cover for vagueness.

In the SNS, the realm of the inconceivable expands, for sure, but under Vasubandhu's careful application of the device, it is not allowed to encompass and nullify what *can* be known. When the Bodhisattva speaks of "no eye, no ear, no nose . . . ," we may accept this as an expression of the ultimate, but one that cannot be taken to provide the end of the story for our ordinary use of concepts. We must still make use of our eyes and ears, for without them we are left spiraling in a void. As in every argument throughout the AKBh, the reasonableness of the Buddha's words, gauged in accordance with his likely pedagogical motives, provide the touchstone for the proper interpretation of scripture and, in turn, the world. Even with regard to the ultimate, then, this is essentially a pragmatic view of scripture, in which certain ends are being effected *through* scripture, and the proper explanation of a passage therefore must appeal to the intended goal to be effected thereby. Such a view may be contrasted, once again, with a linguistic realism that would affirm that words are associated with specific meanings (eternally, as some non-Buddhists have it) that are existent realities—universals. A pragmatic view of scripture presupposes that the Buddha's words are never expressive and effective *in themselves*, but are tools deployed by the Buddha in accord with localized goals. Vasubandhu's view of Mahāyāna scripture therefore fits perfectly with his critique of the Vaibhāṣikas for their *tīrthika*-like, literalistic reification of linguistically constructed entities.

5

VASUBANDHU'S YOGĀCĀRA

Enshrining the Causal Line in the Three Natures

VASUBANDHU IS famous for having converted from Śrāvakayāna to Mahāyāna between writing the AKBh and his Yogācāra works. In the last chapter we saw that Vasubandhu's approach to scripture in the AKBh left him open to considering Mahāyāna scriptures, and that when he does integrate these scriptures, he constructs a hermeneutics that accounts for multiple places on the path under the view of reality as ultimately inexpressible. Although I would caution against placing too much faith in the historical veracity of Buddhist hagiographies, the transition that I have traced is fairly well symbolized by the famous episode in which Vasubandhu is converted to Mahāyāna after studying scriptures sent to him by his elder brother, Asaṅga. Apparently, Vasubandhu never took Mahāyāna scriptures seriously until his brother insisted that he do so. What we have not yet discussed, then, is the doctrinal shift that comes with the adoption of the interpretive perspective of the SNS—a shift that accounts for not just the *validity* of Mahāyāna scriptures and treatises, but for the adoption of many specific doctrines *within* those scriptures. In this chapter we will see just what this transition would have entailed, by illuminating in detail Vasubandhu's distinctive Yogācāra philosophy. We will see that Vasubandhu's transition to Yogācāra and his transformative contribution to it were prefigured, if not yet fully enacted, in the AKBh passages already discussed.

As a paradigmatic example of Vasubandhu's doctrinal shift, let us begin with a comparison of two passages, one from the AKBh and one from the *Exposition Establishing Karma* (*Karmasiddhiprakaraṇa* [KSP]). The KSP is often sensibly considered a transitional text, since it collects and collates many of the arguments on the nature of *karma* from the AKBh, but includes as well a number of additional points that seem to prefigure a full Yogācāra philosophical flowering.[1] For our purposes, however, a crucial shift may be said to have already taken place in a KSP argument that follows the AKBh in every way except in some illuminating specifics of its language.

The argument in question is concerned with the disproof of the reality of a *dharma* called "shape" (*saṃsthāna*). Given what we already know about Vasubandhu's view, it will not be difficult or surprising to follow Vasubandhu's arguments against the view that "shape" is a substantial entity (*dravya*). I will cite the two parallel passages together, and then discuss the crucial difference between them:

> Shape does not exist substantially, say the Sautrāntikas. For when a color comes about facing chiefly in one direction, it is designated [*prajñapyate*] a "long form." Regarding the very same thing as small, "short." When coming about in four directions, "square." The same everywhere, "circle." So for all. In this way, the firebrand in one place seen immediately, without interval, in the next place, is admitted [*pratīyate*] to be "long"; seen everywhere, "round." But there is indeed no separate class, shape. (AKBh IV.3)[2]

> With respect to the multiple appearance [*snang ba*] of an assemblage facing a single way, the thought "long" arises. With respect to short, the thought "short" arises. With respect to the equal appearance from all [four sides], the thought "square" arises.[3] With respect to equal from all around, the thought "circle" arises. With respect to many in the center, the thought "elevated" arises. With respect to few, the thought "low" arises.[4] With respect to an appearance with one position all around, the thought "level" arises. With respect to the way of various positions, the thought "uneven" arises. . . . With respect to the specific situation of the object that is a particular color, thoughts such as "long," etc., arise. For instance, it is as they arise for arrangements of trees, birds, and ants, etc. (KSP D:135a–b)[5]

Both passages argue, similarly, that "shape" is not a thing in itself, but a construction, based upon the perception of multiple discrete entities of color, arranged in one or another fashion. There is no shape "long," but only a linear arrangement of color entities in a single direction. There is no shape "round," but only an arrangement of color entities that are not in one direction alone, but equally expanding in all directions. And so on. The two passages give different philosophical examples, but the idea is clearly the same. For a whirling firebrand, there is no "circle," but only the single flame, taking up adjacent positions in space in sequential moments. The same may be said of a line of ants or a cloud of birds. The full causal story can be accounted for by appeal to the parts alone. To say that there is some substantial "shape" over and above the separate points is a false imposition.

Where the two texts differ is in their language about what to call that imposition. The Sautrāntika in the AKBh says it is a *prajñapti*, a conventional designation—as is argued about all unreal entities in the Abhidharma system. "Round" is merely a linguistic item that refers, indirectly, to the many assembled *dharmas* of color, just as "person" is merely a linguistic item that refers, indirectly, to the assembled *skandhas*. The KSP describes the process of imposition quite differently. For the KSP, "round" is an *idea*, a *thought* (*blo*), which arises with respect to an "appearance" (*snang ba*).

It might appear that the whole doctrine has changed, when a designation is called a thought, and the designated thing is called an appearance. The shift from language-talk to mind-talk might be taken to be fundamental. But it is at least possible to read this as simply a more fine-grained, close analysis of a causal process that was already implicit in the AKBh description. For what did it mean, in fact, to say that the directionally oriented color *dharmas* are "designated" as long? Surely there must be visual perception involved in this procedure; can the notion of "appearance" be entirely anathema to the implicit scenario? If we look closely, we see that the KSP's word "appearance" in fact merely gives a name to the various classes of directional organization of separate entities: there is the appearance "of an assemblage facing a single way," or "the equal appearance from all [four sides]," and so on. This gives a perceptual name ("appearance") to how things are said to be "coming about" in the AKBh passage, and so implies that this directional organization is something that is perceptible, or knowable. But it is not saying that the *shape* is perceived, only the directional organization—that is, we do not see "roundness," but we do see bits of color extending uniformly from a central point. This provides new language, and precision, but is not in evident contradiction to the AKBh position.

The second shift, from saying that these entities are "designated" to saying that with respect to them "a thought arises," is similar in that it appears to impose something new, but might in fact simply uncover implicit assumptions. If we say we "designate" something, can we do so without also assuming some kind of mental event, some kind of intention that goes along with that designation? Granted, the way that meaning gets assigned to words may be characterized as independent of any one person's intentional choice, but here we are talking about the "designating" of a particular perceived object. Surely, just as a perceptual process is implicit here, so also is a mental event of conceptualization.[6]

I am trying to suggest that the shift may not necessarily be a disavowal of previous beliefs. But it would be difficult to deny that we see a marked change in emphasis. In the AKBh the description of the imposition of a term "round" on a distinct set of color *dharmas* says nothing at all about the mental processes that make that imposition possible. In the KSP, the process is described in *entirely mental terms*. The perceptual "appearance" causes a conceptual "idea" or "thought" to arise. Furthermore, the AKBh describes the process as an activity of an agent—a *designating* agent—rather than a dissociated causal process. This is not to say that the Sautrāntika by any means believes that an agent is necessary for the operation of language; but the shift in the KSP allows for a clear, dissociated causal line to be developed in the formation of linguistic entities. Between the arising of discrete *dharmas* in a particular directional formation and their being "designated" as "round" or "long"—the two events named in the AKBh—the KSP inserts two additional, mental events: the "appearance" of the directional formation, and the "arising" of a thought.

This shift may be seen as an application of the logic of no-self, and its attendant causal dissociation, to the operation of linguistic signification. Where Vasubandhu has had no trouble, up to now, eliminating the "agent" from the activity of the eye and describing other apparent "activities" as merely "passive" (*nirvyāpāra*) *dharmas*, he had not yet described *linguistic acts* in this way. Instead, the passage from the AKBh in which Vasubandhu's commentary criticizes the Vaibhāṣika reification of linguistic elements—syllables, words, and phrases—reveals some internal problems in their view, but provides a rather unsatisfying reduction. Words, he says, are not a new, distinct kind of entity; they are merely vocalizations that cause people to understand a meaning.[7]

So far so good: as is his normal practice, Vasubandhu turns an abstract entity into a linear causal story. Yet the question remains just what words are, and why they function in this way. And the reason he gives for why the words work in this way to provide for people to understand a meaning is that "here a word is a sound that is delimited with respect to a meaning."[8] Words, then, are conventional designations that work *because people agree upon their meanings.* This is linguistic conventionalism, a sensible, Buddhist advance over the Vaibhāṣika realism that says that words are real entities that have, like *karma*, invisible effects. Yet it is unsatisfying for two reasons. First, while the Vaibhāṣika view must reify invisible causes in order to explain how words work, at least it is seeking to explain how they work. The position Vasubandhu provides does nothing beyond naming what we can see; but we want to know *why* words can be so delimited to indicate meanings (whereas other sounds, such as the barks of dogs and the patter of raindrops, cannot). Vasubandhu's focus in the AKBh on the absurdities of the Vaibhāṣika position leaves this question unanswered. Second, Vasubandhu's notion—that agreement, or delimitation, provides the causal force—leaves the crucial functionality of language in the terms of personal agency: people must decide what the meaning is. Yet if there are no people—and of course, if we are seeking a Buddhist Ābhidharmika explanation, there *are* no people—then the AKBh has not sufficiently reduced the causal explanation to *real dharmas.* It has traded in one kind of hand-waving for another. What is needed is an explanation of linguistic causality that is *dissociated* from an apparent self.[9]

In the KSP these problems are resolved by shifting the causal story from the real objects and its "designation" to these entities' associated *mental events.* Instead of appealing to an invisible "word" that is expressed or enlivened by sounds, we have a perfectly workable notion of linguistic functionality in the concept of an *idea.* By jettisoning the word-to-world connection, and focusing on the mind, Vasubandhu's KSP arrives at a significant advance over the notion that meaning functions simply through conventional designation. He is no longer obliged to speak of how one "designates" an object, which implies that there is *someone* who engages in the activity of designation. He is now able to say that the mind operates in certain ways, forming concepts (mistaken concepts, as it turns out) based upon particular appearances. This makes better sense of the operation of language in the mind, it transforms linguistic appearances into linear causes along the paradigm of Vasubandhu's explanation of memory, and it accounts for the crucial Buddhist perspective on just why it is that we are so wrong about our ordinary beliefs (in a self, for instance). For all of these reasons, the shift from A to C in table 5.1, expanding the causal story by adding the intervening mental events, may be said to make for a marked improvement.

The problem with my explanation, however, is that whereas the AKBh provides us with the reductive "A," the KSP, which does include the

TABLE 5.1 Comparison of KSP and AKBh Views of "Long"

A (AKBH)	B (KSP)	C (AKBH + KSP)
Color comes about, facing in one direction	. . .	Color comes about, facing in one direction
		↓
. . .	Appearance of an assemblage facing in one direction	Appearance of an assemblage facing in one direction
↓	↓	↓
. . .	Thought "long"	Thought "long"
		↓
Designated "long"	. . .	Designated "long"

mental, does not expand upon the AKBh to give us "C." Instead it gives us only the terms in "B." Thus it is not accurate to say that the KSP's description of a "shape" provides for a mental explanation of the transformation of a perception into a conceptual construction; it *eliminates* the perception, and *replaces it* with the stages in a conceptual construct—and it is sufficiently content with its explanation that language is accounted for by the conceptual construction that it does not bother to explain the *designation*, either.

What happened to the ordinary entities—the perceived entities and the words used to designate them—that were the topic of the initial explanation? If the KSP provides mental events implicit in the movement from perceived object to linguistic designation, what happened to the *objects* that those mental events, those thoughts, were *about*? Well, while I have attempted to delay the inevitable, it is perhaps finally necessary to acknowledge that Yogācāra is generally considered to deny, or at the very least direct our attention *away from*, all events in our causal explanations that are *not* mental. Yogācāra, for Vasubandhu, provides a causal mode of explanation that accounts for all events as "appearance only" (*vijñapti-mātra*). What appears and its designation are, therefore, *only apparent*, and since they have no causal reality in themselves, they are *gone*.

Vasubandhu's basic Yogācāra insight is that mental events account for all perception, conception, and language; there is no need to appeal to anything beyond the mind. In fact, he says that the fullness of the Buddhist universe, the whole world, is only appearance. This means not just that we perceive objects to exist where they do not exist; it also means that we are not even the subjects of our own experience. Vasubandhu in the AKBh was focused on disproving the apparent self (and its accoutrements), which we falsely project over and above the aggregates. In his Yogācāra works, Vasubandhu is focused on eliminating, in addition, a subtler form of self-projection: the subjective self that appears within every apparent perception and consciousness. The false projection of subjectivity—of the distinction between one's mind and the mental objects that it seems to take on, and project—Vasubandhu calls by the name "duality," and calls us to disavow.[10]

The term "Yogācāra" means "practitioner of yoga," and in Buddhist texts it does not by any means always refer to a distinct doctrinal school or philosophical approach. It is most likely that the Yogācāra as a "school" was never distinguished from its later rival the Madhyamaka until at least a century or two after Vasubandhu. It is therefore essential not to impose a later, frozen category system on the works of Vasubandhu. Nonetheless, a number of doctrinal positions that are associated with the term "Yogācāra" do fit together conceptually in Vasubandhu's oeuvre. It makes sense to read the "appearance only" doctrine, for instance, as directly connected, in Vasubandhu's works, with the notion of "nonduality," the "inconceivable ultimate," the "three natures of reality," and the "storehouse consciousness."

This is a complex and counterintuitive view. It is difficult to understand, let alone to prove. Yet Vasubandhu's works provide an excellent guide: a gradual development from AKBh to systematic Yogācāra, in manageable stages. Vasubandhu's works pave the way. First we must understand what justifies the most counterintuitive aspect of the "appearance only" view, which is that the best explanation of everything begins by eliminating external, physical entities. This argument is the focus of the next section, where we provide a summary of Vasubandhu's tremendously influential *Twenty Verses* (*Viṃśatika* [Viṃś]). Then, once this idea is in place, we will begin to examine what is unique, and distinctive, about Vasubandhu's approach to Yogācāra philosophy. We must understand how Vasubandhu presents the concepts of the "three natures" and, most crucially, "duality." I will argue that Vasubandhu's distinctive interpretation of duality is a natural outgrowth of the discussions of perception and conceptualization in the AKBh, which we have already discussed. Finally, with the main conceptual structures in place, we will be able to see how the innovations of the AKBh, the VyY, and the Viṃś are synthesized in Vasubandhu's crowning Yogācāra work, the *Three Natures Exposition* (*Trisvabhāvanirdeśa* [TSN]). Through a reading of that work, we will see how Vasubandhu unifies all of Buddhist doctrine in a crystalline conceptual structure, the Three Natures.

THE CAUSAL INFERENCE FOR A MIND-ONLY UNIVERSE (I.E., MAHĀYĀNA)

Recent scholarship has honed in on a line in the eighth chapter of the SNS as the likely "initiatory passage" of the "appearance only" (*vijñānavāda*) doctrine.[11] While other scriptures espousing Yogācāra philosophical doctrines preceded this text, this was likely the first Yogācāra-*vijñānavāda* passage (and we have already seen that this scripture was a crucial source for Vasubandhu's views).[12] The context of the passage is an instruction on meditation techniques, given by the current Buddha to Maitreya, the next Buddha (and the ostensible author of five classic Yogācāra *śāstras*). Maitreya poses the question of whether mental objects envisioned during meditation are the same, or different, from the mind that envisions them. The Buddha's response is to say that the mind and its images (in this context) "are not different" (*tha dad pa ma yin*). And why not? "Because the image is but appearance only."[13]

Let us set aside the future history of this phrase, "appearance only," and examine how it works for the Buddha's argument here in the SNS. The fact of an entity being "appearance only" is being brought forward as *proof* of the *nondifference of mind and mental objects*. Maitreya does not question the premise that a meditative image is "appearance only"; but his next question does expose a potential problem for the conclusion that there is no difference between minds and mental objects. Since the context is meditation, presumably the purpose of meditation is to examine the mind with the mind. So Maitreya asks: If there is no difference between the imagined object of concentration and the mind, "How can the mind investigate the mind?"[14] "Appearance only" understood in this way would seem to undermine the basic activity of meditation. In response to this, the Buddha provides a wonderful clarification:

> Maitreya, it is never the case that one *dharma* investigates [*rtog pa*] another *dharma*. Rather, in whatever way a mind comes about, so it appears. Here's an example, Maitreya. Although one is looking at a form itself in the circle of a very clean mirror that relies upon the form, one thinks one is seeing an image. The form there and the image appear to be different things. It is the same with the mind that comes about in a particular way and the object of concentration. Although the one is a so-called image of the other, it appears as though it is a different thing.[15]

The Buddha defends the nondifference of mind and mental objects with the remarkable statement that the notion of "investigating" or "conceiving" (*rtog pa*) is in fact not an activity enacted by one entity with respect to another. Instead, he translates the apparent action-with-an-object into a dissociated, unitary causal line. The apparent mental object is just *an image of the mind itself.*

The correlation between this explanation and Vasubandhu's view of the causality of perception and memory, which we have discussed at length in chapter 3, is close. When I read the SNS's description of an image, that "in whatever way a mind comes about, so it appears," this seems to me to reflect quite directly Vasubandhu's "figurative" reading of "view":

> Why carve the ether? For, conditioned by the eye and forms, the eye consciousness comes about. In that case what sees, and what is seen? For it is passive [*nirvyāpāra*], merely *dharmas*, and merely cause and effect.[16]

The Buddha's point in the SNS seems to be exactly Vasubandhu's point here. We can provide a linear causal explanation for what appears to be an action, and relinquish the need for an agent, if we eliminate the apparent distinction between the appearance *within* a mental event and the mental event itself. If the mental object *just is* the mental event's appearance, then there is no need to say that the mental event "sees" and the object "is seen." What *is* necessary is that we acknowledge that the way that the mental event seems to appear—as a mind with a distinct mental object, a perceiver and a perceived—is just an illusion, a mistaken image, "appearance only." If we acknowledge that this apparent division between separate entities, the seer and the seen, is just an illusion, then we can say that the mental event is unitary, it *just is* this appearance. We have no need to say that one mental event "investigates," and another mental event "is investigated." They are merely cause and effect.

The difficult point, that the distinction between the mind and its objects is an illusion encapsulated within a single "appearance," is beautifully illustrated in the mirror analogy. If I walk into a hall of mirrors, I may be momentarily convinced that I am surrounded by countless replicas of myself. But in fact they all *just are* myself. I am not seeing *replicas*, I am seeing my own body, through a perceptual distortion—as is evident when I lift up my hand, and all of the supposed replicas *also* lift up *their* "hands." In just this way, the Buddha says, our ordinary perceptual apparatus gives us the impression that the things that we experience are distinct from ourselves, and that in addition to them *we exist as well*. Thus, there are always two poles to our experience: our minds, and the things our minds experience. The implicit meditative exercise here involves the acknowledgement that meditative *objects* are just *how the mind appears* in its constructing activity, and so they are by nature nondifferent from the mind that constructs them. The fact that things seem otherwise (that we think our minds are one thing, our thoughts and visions something else) is a trick of the perceptual apparatus. We live in a mental hall of mirrors, in which we see ourselves reflected back at us in our every encounter with a mental object, our every "view."

This point coincides not only with Vasubandhu's view of "view," but also with his disproof of the "existence" of past and future experiential objects, which we discussed in chapter 2. There, Vasubandhu first reduced all experience of past and future entities to experience of "experiential objects"—so that they may not be taken to be sensory perceptions. When I think of a beautiful ocean view from last summer, I am not "seeing" something in the past, I am engaging with a mental object. There, Vasubandhu cleverly pointed out that an experiential object *appears to be present*, even when it is past or future. The consequence of this was that we cannot trust introspection as evidence of the nature of an entity—even when it is apparently a mental object. The "past" or "future" or even "real" character of an experiential object, he shows, is not a quality of that object, but in fact an imposition that reflects the conceptual nature of the mental event in which it plays a part. Vasubandhu makes a similar argument when he counters Vātsyāyana's claim that there must be a self, due to the fact of memory: we can account for memory by appeal to a unitary causal line, he says. While we appear to ourselves as the "same" self when we are seeing something as when we are remembering that act of seeing, we do not actually need to *be* the same entity in order for it to *appear as though* we are the same entity. In the latter case, all that is necessary is the right kind of causal connection to the previous appearance.[17]

The Buddha's mirror analogy tells us that the apparently *separate existence* of mental objects is yet another aspect of the conceptually imposed illusion. But this too is hardly entirely new for Vasubandhu; it may be read as simply a restatement of the basic fact that the root, mistaken "view"—the view of self (*satkāyadṛṣṭi*)—is implicit in all other views, all unenlightened perspectives. Vasubandhu denied any real difference between "seeing" and "cognizing"; both were activities of the consciousness, he said. So every "view" participates in this false view of self.

Thus the Buddha's instruction shows how the meditative practice that recognizes the nondifference of mind and mental objects may be used, therapeutically, to observe how the mind's conceptual construction is involved in the creation of the whole world of experience. In response to the Buddha's clarification, Maitreya asks whether, if meditative appearances are nondifferent from the mind, this applies to everything else as well—the world, and living beings, too? In answer the Buddha expresses the radical result of this worldview: yes, *all* objects of experience are nondifferent from the mind that experiences them.[18]

> Lord, as to the appearance of forms, etc., of sentient beings, which are established as natures reflected in the mind—are they too nondifferent from the mind?
>
> He replied: Maitreya, they are no different. Fools with erroneous ideas do not know these reflections to be, as they really are, only appearance, and so they think wrongly.[19]

This expansive claim that all cognized objects are nondifferent from the mind, which arises out of a meditative practice (to see all things *as if* they are nondifferent from the mind), is a radical departure from the Vaibhāṣika, in the direction Vasubandhu had pointed in his AKBh. Yet it is perhaps still another step beyond this claim to the notion that not only all cognized objects, but *all things in the world* are nondifferent from the mind. This, nonetheless, is the point with which Vasubandhu opens the Viṃś, citing not the SNS, but the *Ten Stages Sūtra* (*Daśabhūmikasūtra*): "In the Mahāyāna, the three realms are established as only appearance."[20]

Given that the AKBh was dedicated to the establishment of *some* entities as substantial and *others* as mere designations, the notion that *all entities are only apparent* seems to many readers of Vasubandhu's works to embody a complete departure. I am arguing that we can find a path to the Yogācāra in Vasubandhu's openness to Mahāyāna scriptures, his prior skepticism about experiential objects, and, most broadly, his dedication to the causal priority of reasoning. We have already seen that Vasubandhu's hermeneutics preserves the Abhidharma within a conceptual frame that admits all things to be empty. As we follow the argument in the Viṃś, we will see that Vasubandhu continues to pursue his relentless AKBh practice of rejecting perspectives and entities that can show no causal contribution to the arising of experience. By providing a defense of the "appearance only" doctrine in terms continuous with the causal logic of the AKBh, Vasubandhu's Viṃś paves the way for the Mahāyāna critique of all reification of entities—and the scriptures in which these views arise—to appear both sensible and quintessentially Buddhist. It is the first stage in the path to a Yogācāra synthesis.

The Viṃś is Vasubandhu's most readable, and evidently analytic, philosophical text, and it has consequently drawn a significant amount of modern scholarly attention.[21] Its central argument defends the simple opening statement that everything in the three realms is "only appearance" (*vijñaptimātra*). The three realms are the three states into which Buddhists believe living beings may be reborn. For all beings except for Buddhas and advanced bodhisattvas, the three realms make up the universe. Vasubandhu glosses this statement with citations from scripture that make it clear that he means to say that there are no things (*artha*), only minds (*citta*) and mental qualities (*caitta*). He says that the experience of the three realms is like the appearance of hairs in front of someone with eye disease. It is the experience of something that does not exist as it appears, a distortion of the perceptual apparatus. Although the term has a history of controversy among interpreters of Yogācāra, it seems safe to say that the Viṃś defends at least some form of idealism.[22]

After stating his thesis that everything is "only apparent," Vasubandhu immediately voices a potential counterargument, which consists in four reasons that the three realms being appearance only is impossible. First and second, why are things restricted to specific places and times, respectively? Apparent objects can appear anywhere, at any time. Third, why do beings in a given place and time experience the same objects, and not different objects according to their distinct continua? And fourth, why do objects perform causal functions in the real world, when merely apparent mental objects do not? These objections arise from a commonsense realist perspective on physical causality, and so, combining them with the frame within the "threefold world," we can be certain that the primary objector is a non-Mahāyāna Buddhist, whom Vasubandhu is attempting to convince to accept the Mahāyāna.[23]

The four objections aim to prove the impossibility that the world is merely apparent by arguing that the elements of ordinary experience behave in ways that what is merely apparent does not. Vasubandhu sets up, and meets, these objections in order to prove the possibility, and hence the viability of the theory, that everything in experience is appearance only. He shows, essentially, that the objector has a narrow view of what is possible for merely apparent things; appearances are not *necessarily* limited in the ways the objector thinks.

Note that it is not incumbent upon Vasubandhu here to prove that *all* instances of the merely apparent transcend the limitations assumed by the objector. He has not set up this objection in order to try to prove, absurdly, that *all* mental images, for instance, are spatially restricted, or that *all* mere appearances perform observable causal functions in the real world. On the contrary, one significant upshot of the recognition that things are appearance only will be that things do not have the cause-and-effect structure that we ordinarily take them to have. In any event, the positive argument that ordinary experience is in fact illusory comes later and takes the form of an argument to the best explanation. Before an explanation can be the best, though, it must be a possibility. So here all Vasubandhu must do to counter these initial objections is provide, for each, a single example of a mental event that exemplifies the behavior that the objector claims is only available to physical objects.[24]

To defeat the objections that mental objects are not restricted in space and time, Vasubandhu provides the counterexample that in dreams objects often appear to exist in one place and time, as they do in ordinary waking reality. In a dream, I can be looking at shells on a beach on Long Island, during the summer of my eighth year. It is only upon waking that I come to realize that the dream objects (the shells, the beach) were only mental fabrications, temporally dislocated, with no spatial reality. Thus, what is merely apparent *can* sometimes have the character of appearing in a particular place and time. To say they do not is to misremember the experience.[25]

Next, to defeat the objection that unlike ordinary physical objects, merely apparent objects are not intersubjectively shared by different beings, Vasubandhu provides the counterexample that in hell, demonic entities appear to torment groups of hell beings. This is a case of a shared hallucination. When the objector wonders why the demons might not in fact be real, Vasubandhu appeals to *karma* theory: any being with sufficient merit—sufficient "good *karma*"—to generate a body capable of withstanding the painful fires of hell would never be born into hell in the first place. Any creature in hell that is not suffering must be an apparition generated by the negative *karma* of the tormented.

Finally, to defeat the objection that merely apparent objects do not produce functional causal results, Vasubandhu provides the memorable counterexample of a wet dream, in which an evident, physical result is produced by an imagined sexual encounter with a nonexistent lover.

The initial objection to the mere possibility of the "appearance only" theory quelled, Vasubandhu turns to his main positive proof. This consists in a systematic evaluation of every possible account of sensory objects (*viśaya*) as physical, which ultimately leads Vasubandhu to conclude that no account of physicality makes more sense, or is more parsimonious, than the theory that it is appearance only.

Before turning to Vasubandhu's treatment of physics, it is worth stopping to note the crucial importance that Buddhist *karma* theory plays in Vasubandhu's argument overall. First, the proof of shared hallucinations in hell depends upon the particulars of the Buddhist belief in the hells. Of course, we might have believed in shared hallucinations even without believing in *karma*. But the tormentors in hell play an important, double role in Vasubandhu's argument. He has the objector raise the question again, and suggest, as a last-ditch effort, that perhaps the tormentors are physical entities generated and controlled by the karmic energies of the tormented. At this, Vasubandhu challenges his objector: if you're willing to admit that *karma* generates physical entities, and makes them move around (pick up swords and saws, etc.), so that they might create painful results in the mental streams of the tormented, why not just eliminate the physical? Isn't it simpler to say that the mind generates the mental images that torment it?[26] This is a crucial question, because it resonates beyond hell beings, across Buddhist karmic theory.

In AKBh IV, Vasubandhu expressed the widely held Buddhist view that in addition to causing a being's particular rebirth, *karma* also shapes the realms into which beings are reborn, and the contents of those realms. Such a belief provides Indian religions with answers to questions often thought unanswerable by Western theisms, such as why the mudslide took out my neighbor's house, but not mine. But this view of karmic causality requires that the physical causes of positive or negative experiences are linked back to our intentional acts. Vasubandhu does not say so explicitly, but if it is easier to imagine the causes of a mind-only hell demon than a physical one, it should also be easier to imagine the causes of a mind-only mudslide—assuming that both are generated as a karmic repercussion for the beings that encounter them. The background assumption, that any physical world must be subject to *karma*, therefore places the realist on the defensive from the start. Can the external realist adduce a theory intellectually satisfying enough to counter Vasubandhu's suggestion that we throw up our hands and admit that what appears to be out there is only in our minds?[27]

In response to this, Vasubandhu allows the opponent to cite scripture, asking just why the Buddha would have taught about sensory objects in the first place, if such things did not truly exist. Vasubandhu answers, as we might have guessed, with an interpretation of the relevant passages as expressing a figurative meaning, a "special intention" (*abhiprāya*). Yet the opponent is not satisfied. You cannot simply interpret a passage in any way you want. Vasubandhu must do better than provide an alternative reading. He must explain why his figurative reading is substantially better than the direct, literal reading; the figurative interpretation's more parsimonious ontology is not sufficient reason to reject a well-known, broadly accepted scriptural passage.

The opponent's basic respect for scripture here reflects Vasubandhu's position as articulated in the AKBh and the VyY: point 1 among our interpretive principles discussed in the last chapter was a requirement that widely accepted scriptures be acknowledged; and point 5, which allowed that a scripture be taken figuratively, did so in the light of a literal reading issuing in some contradiction or inconsistency. Vasubandhu's argumentative turn here is an expression of respect for the non-Mahāyāna scriptural traditions, which he defended in the VyY as still viable even within a Mahāyāna worldview. As always, reason is called upon to adjudicate between differences in scriptural interpretation.

It is this debate over the viability of a figurative interpretation of central scriptural passages, then, that motivates what is one of Vasubandhu's most celebrated arguments, his mereological disproof of sensory objects—his disproof of sensory objects based in the relation between parts and wholes. We have already seen an earlier version of some of this argumentation in chapter 3, and the full argument is available elsewhere, so I will only sketch an outline here.[28] The point is that no viable rational explanation for the physical existence of perceptual objects can be found. Given the failure of any rational explanation of physicality, the only remaining position *must be* that *there can be no real sensory objects.* Thus the Buddha *must have* meant his statements figuratively.

Vasubandhu argues that anything that is a physical object of perception must be either a whole made up of parts, a bare multiplicity, or an aggregate. The first two options are eliminated by an appeal to perception. There is no whole, he says, because there is no perception (*agrahaṇāt*), no "grasping" of the whole.[29] We never see a whole that cannot be divided into parts, and once the parts are separated, there is no sense of a "whole." But we also do not perceive a bare multiplicity of partless parts; we cannot experience the individual parts separately.[30] We only perceive parts when they come together into certain formations to create aggregates (we can always divide something visible into smaller and smaller parts). As to what is imperceptible, the question must be answered by appeal to reason alone: how can imperceptible, partless entities be aggregated in such a way that they become perceptible? Vasubandhu provides a logical argument proving that there is no way that this could happen. If you say they line up side to side, then they have sides, which means they have parts. If they have no sides, hence no dimension at all, then more than one of them can occupy the same spatial location, which means that no matter how many you bring together, the aggregate will never achieve spatial extension, and can never be perceived.

A final proposal is the possibility of a unitary sensory object that is extended in space but not divisible into parts. Vasubandhu's argument against this possibility is the physical corollary to his argument for the impossibility of change, which we discussed in chapter 2. If something is extended in space, he argues, it should have different qualities at its different points or sides (at least, different spatial location); but if it is only one entity, then to touch one "end" should be, simply, to touch *it*—to touch *all of* it. That's what it means to be one thing! This kind of argument was what drove Buddhists to the idea of partless parts in the first place, but that's already been disproven. Consequently, there is no good causal account of perceptual objects. The Buddha's position of "nondifference" from the SNS is proven: there is no conceptually coherent reality that can account for the world as we experience it, in which we exist as distinct from the objects of our experience.

One counterargument raised by the non-Mahāyāna opponent is based in the fact of perception. We have already seen that Vasubandhu's views on perception from the AKBh reflect the view from the SNS that all mental objects are "appearance only." By looking closely at how Vasubandhu handles the non-Mahāyāna opponent's challenge regarding perception, then, we can see the essential role of the theorization of perception in forging this connection, for Vasubandhu, between non-Mahāyāna and Mahāyāna Abhidharma.

The opponent opens up the section by declaring the primacy of perception as a means of knowledge (*pramāṇa*), and saying that if all things are "appearance only," then the epistemic benefit of perception is undermined:

> Existence or nonexistence is ascertained by means of knowledge [*pramāṇa*], and among all means of knowledge, perception is the best. So, where a thing does not exist, how can a thought with respect to it be a "perception"?
>
> **Perceptual thought is just as in a dream, etc.,** [16a–b1] even without the thing—as has been shown before. **And when it exists, the thing is not seen; how can it be considered to be perceived?** (16) [16b2–d] And when the perceptual thought, "This is my perception" exists—at that point the thing is not seen, because [the thought] is discerned just by the mental consciousness, and at that point the eye consciousness is finished. How is it accepted as perceived? But especially for a momentary sensory object, at that point its form or taste, etc., is truly finished.[31]

Vasubandhu's first reply is to reiterate his previous point that when we are dreaming we often *think* we are perceiving things. So it is certainly possible that the things we imagine ourselves to be perceiving when we are awake are not really there as they appear.

Next, rather than defending the *pramāṇa* of perception, he casts doubt on the entire idea. When you have the idea that you are perceiving something, he says, that is an idea; it is an activity of the mental consciousness, not the sensory organ. This coheres beautifully with his discussion of "view" from chapter 3: what we take to be a "perception" is really just a mental event that *looks like* a perception. And by the time we think we are perceiving something, the actual sensation that precipitated our awareness of a sensation is always in the past, as are the sensory organ and the sensory object with which the organ came in (ostensible) contact. Everything is momentary, so whatever causes an awareness must be gone by the time its causal result—the perceptual awareness—arises.

In reply, the opponent tries to leverage Vasubandhu's idea of the ostensible perception arising in the mental consciousness as an indirect proof of direct perception. Without a perception of an object, the opponent says, you cannot have a *memory* of a perception of an object, and so you cannot have the mental consciousness' awareness of the perception:

> What is not experienced is not remembered by the mental consciousness. Thus, the experience of a thing exists necessarily, and the "seeing" [*darśanam*] is what is considered the perception of the form, etc., of the sensory object.
>
> It is not established that it is a memory of the experienced thing, since [it is], **as already explained, an appearance with its image.** [17a–b1] Just as an appearance—an eye consciousness, etc.—arises even without the thing, with an image of the thing, so, it is said, **memory is from that.** [17b2] For from that—from the appearance—arises a mental consciousness with a construction of form, etc., that is taken as a memory, having just that image. So the perception of a thing is not established based upon the arising of a memory.[32]

The opponent's challenge mirrors two arguments of Vasubandhu's that we have studied in earlier chapters. In structure, it mirrors the argument against the self from the opening of AKBh IX, which established the case of perception where there is a sensory organ as the manipulationist paradigm for inference of a cause from a result. There Vasubandhu said that since for a blind person there is no sight, whereas for someone who can see there *is* sight, there must be some difference between them—i.e., the sensory organ. Here, almost exactly the same inference is used by the opponent to defend the reality of sensory perception based upon memory. One can have memories of what one has perceived, but not of what one has not perceived—so there must be perception. The structure of the argument, then, is fine, and may even invoke AKBh intentionally.

The error comes where the argument resembles, though inadequately, Vasubandhu's view of "seeing" from AKBh I.42 (see chapter 3). The opponent says that where there is a visual memory, there must have been something we call "seeing"—and this Vasubandhu would have to accept. But just what is that "seeing"? Vasubandhu says that memory does not guarantee that the "seeing" provides access to a genuine perceptual object. Recall from our discussion of AKBh I.42 that Vasubandhu does not believe that "seeing" occurs in the sensory organ; it is an activity of the sensory *consciousness*, a discrimination (*prajñā*). So he is in a good position here to point out that memory comes about from the eye consciousness, not from the eye itself. What this meant there was that it was possible to say that there is no difference in activity between "seeing" and "cognizing" for a consciousness. They are both acts of construction. Here the same argument can be used to show that we cannot depend upon our memory of a perception as proof of a sensory contact. Rather, since we can *imagine* ourselves to be perceiving an object when we are not (as in a dream), we could also be *remembering* our imagination as a real perception. The inference that proves "seeing" does not prove *seeing*.

It may seem odd that Vasubandhu would draw attention to the parallel structure between this argument and AKBh IX, since if he is arguing against the fact of perceptual objects, he would appear to be arguing as well against his own inference that proved the sensory organs. If memories do not provide valid evidence of perceptions, then surely we cannot know the reality of a sensory object's having been perceived by a sensory organ, or not, by interviewing a blind person and a seeing person. Does the paradigmatic causal inference then stand as disproven? And, even worse, if there is no inference that proves the sensory organs, does that inferential failure devolve upon the argument for no-self as a whole? For the argument for no-self was essentially that it had no inference; but if there is no proper causal inference for *anything*, does this mean that the self is no more, or less, dubious than anything else?

That these questions are at issue here is evident not just from the structural parallel to AKBh IX, but from the immediate frame, which was to question the validity of the means of knowledge—the *pramāṇa*—of perception. If things are not as they appear, and what we take to be perception is actually only mental consciousness engaged in conceptual construction, then we may ask Vasubandhu what he asks his opponent: how can this be considered to be perceived? If things are not as they appear to perception, and what we imagine to be perception is only false construction, *why* should we trust it as a *pramāṇa*, a valid means of knowledge? If I understand Vasubandhu's point here, he is saying that *we should not* trust our perception to be giving us direct impressions of real objects. Thus, even if perception has its place as the first means of knowledge, it is by no means indubitable, or even *accurate* in any standard sense.[33] The parallel with AKBh IX tells us that this is true of inference as well. The "appearance only" doctrine would appear to call our means of knowledge into question; if nothing else, the fact that we are fundamentally deluded about everything we see and think ought to issue in some epistemic humility.

But remarkably, epistemic humility does not mean that perception and inference cannot have pragmatic utility—in fact, the most reliable utility to which we have access. Notice that Vasubandhu *accepts* the structure of reason that proves "seeing" based on its patterned association with memory; what he questions is just what kind of "seeing" is justified by the fact of memory. There may still be a useful pattern to our sensory experience, even if it is not caused in the way it seems to be caused. Similarly, in AKBh IX Vasubandhu did not, in fact, prove the sensory organs based on *interviews* with blind people. The premises of his inference were the presence and absence of sight for these people, not their memories. Thus the connection between his premises and the conclusion he draws is valid. Vasubandhu does not shy away from the humiliating implications of a doctrine that affirms that we are living within a hall of mirrors, in which our every mental event is shot through with delusory self-projection. The Copernican revolution has nothing on Vasubandhu. Mahāyāna does, indeed, skirt the abyss. But given how the argument goes next, we can see that Vasubandhu is not at all convinced that such a view undermines our responsibility, and our capacity, to assess to a relative degree our positioning in the world and direct our actions in a way that is proper, productive, and meaningful.

Although this is surely a quite different account of entities than we find in Śrāvaka Abhidharma, the very same principles of ontological parsimony and linear causality, premised on a manipulationist view of causal reasoning, determine the truth of Mahāyāna for Vasubandhu. "Appearance only" is not a skeptical rejection of the evidence of the senses; rather, it is the *best explanation* of the evidence, based upon a careful consideration of observable, conceivable relations of causes and effects.

Vasubandhu's final arguments are against a new objector, who claims that his view leads to moral nihilism or solipsism. Vasubandhu reminds the opponent of his opening argument that it is a mistake to imagine that we need physicality for intersubjectivity. His argument has shown that the world cannot be the way it appears to our senses, but this does not necessarily prevent us from interacting meaningfully with other beings and having morally responsible relationships. Whatever reality we affirm is delusory; we are bounded within the pragmatic frame of how things appear. But the appropriate conclusion to draw from the recognition of universal emptiness[34] is not the extreme views of solipsism or moral nihilism, but epistemic humility: a position that prioritizes the best-known, localized causal results of one's actions over inherited doctrinal schemata.[35] This view has significant applications to contemporary ethics and cultural theory, which we will examine in the final two chapters.

THE MIND IN A CAUSAL LINE: THE THREE NATURES AND NONDUALITY

Vasubandhu did the work of defending the controversial Yogācāra thesis of appearance-only (*vijñaptimātra*) in his Viṃś. In his short poetic works, the *Thirty Verses* (*Triṃśikā* [Triṃś]) and the *Three Natures Exposition* (*Trisvabhāvanirdeśa* [TSN]), he does not entertain objections.[36] Instead, he draws together the basic doctrinal and conceptual vocabulary of the Yogācāra tradition and forms an elegant, coherent system. The Triṃś includes a complete treatment of the Buddhist path from a Yogācāra perspective. In order to understand Vasubandhu's contributions in this text, it would be necessary to place it against the wide backdrop of previous Yogācāra doctrine on the path. This scholarly work is ongoing.[37] Here let us focus instead on introducing the basics of the intricate conceptual structure as formulated in the TSN.

The TSN takes as its topic, and its title, the "Three Natures" of reality from a Yogācāra perspective: these are the fabricated nature (*parikalpita-svabhāva*), the dependent nature (*paratantra-svabhāva*), and the perfected nature (*pariniṣpanna-svabhāva*). In Yogācāra, things no longer have only one nature, one *svabhāva*; rather, things have three different, if interconnected, natures. We may note immediately how fundamentally this differs from the AKBh, in which the apparent purpose is, at all times, to determine the singular nature of each entity (*dharma*). In that context, to discover that an entity must be admitted to have more than one distinct nature was to discover that that entity was an unreal fabrication. An entity that changes, for instance, or an entity that is variegated in color shows an internal inconsistency by exhibiting multiple natures. Like a "self," such entities are only conceptual fabrications (*parikalpita*).

One of the basic distinguishing features of Mahāyāna metaphysics is the affirmation that not only the person, but *all* entities (*dharma*) are empty of a "self" or an inherent nature (*svabhāva*). That means, in the terms laid out in the AKBh, that *all dharmas* are only conceptual fabrications. By defining *svabhāva* itself as inherently threefold, the Yogācāra provides a direct means to see how all things must be subject to this critique. To be multiple is to be a false conceptual construction; to have an inherent nature is to be multiple (threefold); therefore, all inherent natures are conceptual constructions. Q.E.D. What remains is only to define and prove the "threefold" nature of a *svabhāva*.

Thus, to say that all things have *three* inherent natures is not to take back the Great Vehicle's denial of inherent natures ("no eye, no ear, no nose . . ."), but rather to explain it. It is to say that, what we ordinarily take to be a thing's individual character or identity is best understood from three angles, so as to explode its unity. All ostensible "natures" (*svabhāva*) are in fact threefold. The first nature is the fabricated nature, which is the thing as it appears to be, as it is erroneously fabricated. Of course, to use this term ("fabricated") is to indicate the acceptance that things do not really exist the way they appear. This is a thing's nature as it might be defined and explained in ordinary Abhidharma philosophy—its traditional *svabhāva*, but with the added proviso that we all know that this is not really how things work. It is to accept the Mahāyāna framework of universal emptiness *around* the Abhidharma. The second nature is the dependent nature, which Vasubandhu defines as the causal *process* of the thing's fabrication, the causal story that brings about the thing's apparent nature. The third nature, finally, is the emptiness of the first nature—the *fact* that it is unreal, that the appearance does not exist as it appears.

Let us take the most important example, for Buddhists, of a thing that appears real but has no nature: the self. With this as our example of something mistakenly thought to have a nature (*svabhāva*), we may run through its *three* natures. The self as it appears is just my self. I seem to be here, as a living being, typing on a keyboard, thinking thoughts. That is the first nature. The second nature is the causal story that brings about this seeming self, which is the cycle of dependent origination. We might appeal to the standard Abhidharma causal story, and say that the twelve sense bases or the five aggregates, causally conjoined, bring about the basis upon which I superimpose a conceptually fabricated self. Yet in the Yogācāra this causal story is entirely mental (see the Viṃś), so we cannot appeal to the sense bases themselves as the real cause. Rather, the sense bases only *appear* to be separate from my mind due to karmic conditioning in my mental stream. In fact, like the demons in hell, the things of my experience only appear at all because of karmic conditioning. For this reason, the second nature is the causal series according to which the mental seeds planted by previous deeds ripen into the appearance of the sense bases, so that, as a result, there is the appearance that I am sitting here typing and thinking things. As the Buddha in the SNS explained with his mirror analogy, every experience reflects back the appearance of a subject who seems to be, but is not really, distinct from the appearing object. So this appearing occurs in two different stages: my karmic conditioning generates an appearance, and that appearance has the mirror form of a seeming distinction, so I take it that I have a self, distinct from my experiences. This whole causal story is called the "dependent nature." Finally, the third nature is the nonexistence of the self, the fact that it does not exist where it appears. Of course, if there was a real self, I could not have provided a mind-only explanation of how it comes to appear to be there (if it were real, it would be more than merely apparent).

Vasubandhu's TSN draws upon a number of prior formations of the three natures, but it has one clear goal, which is to display the unity and interconnectedness of the three natures. In Vasubandhu's telling, the three natures are all one reality viewed from three distinct angles. They are the appearance, the causal process, and the emptiness of that same apparent entity. (Here I use the word "emptiness" as a shorthand for what is always, for Vasubandhu, simply the nonexistence of what appears to exist in a particular way.) With this in mind, we can read the opening verses of the TSN:

> 1 Fabricated, dependent, and perfected: so the wise understand the three natures as profound.
>
> 2 What appears is the dependent. How it appears is the fabricated. Because of being dependent on conditions. Because of being only fabrication.
>
> 3 The eternal nonexistence of the appearance as it appears: that is known to be the perfected nature, because of being always the same.[38]

These verses emphasize the crystalline, internally unified structure of the three natures. "What appears" is one nature (the dependent), whereas "how it appears"—how it looks—is the fabricated. "The eternal nonexistence of the appearance as it appears" is the perfected. These are, self-evidently, ways of talking of the same appearing entity, or event, from different perspectives.[39]

Whereas some Yogācāra authors describe the three natures as stages in intellectual or meditative development, for these verses they are clearly one unified reality. Each nature logically entails the parallel existence of the other two. The causal event of something appearing that is not really there implies the reality of both the appearance and the unreality of what it seems to be. This formulation enshrines the distinction, which was at the center of Vasubandhu's AKBh, between mere appearances and true causes. The fabricated nature is the aspect of a view, or an idea, that we falsely believe to be real, what we called in earlier chapters *viewing-as*.

The dependent nature, on the other hand, is the actual causal story that is unseen but accounts for the appearance, what we called in earlier chapters *viewing-of*. What the Three Natures doctrine does in the TSN is to unify these into a single conception. It may be described from different angles, but it is one reality.

The fourth verse summarizes all three natures again in one verse, and brings in a crucial new concept, the notion of "duality":

> 4 What appears there? The unreal fabrication. How does it appear? As dual. What, accordingly, is its nonexistence? There being no duality there.[40]

The fabricated is said to appear as a "dual self" or "with a dual nature," whereas reality (*dharmatā*) is nondual.[41] Here, and across Vasubandhu's Yogācāra works, the term "duality" is used to refer to the merely apparent distinction between mind and mental objects—the point illustrated in the Buddha's mirror analogy from the SNS. In TSN 9, Vasubandhu refers to the erroneous duality with the instructive phrasing, "the activity of the seeing intellect and what is seen" (*dṛśyadṛgvittivṛtti*), which neatly combines the SNS mirror passage with the AKBh on "view."[42] Since the false "view" of *satkāyadṛṣṭi* is inherent within every conceptual construction, in TSN 4, above, Vasubandhu puns on the "nature of duality" as the "dual self"; duality is the false appearance of a self that is implicit within any "view." Things and selves mistakenly appear "dual" when they are in reality "nondual," in reality merely *images of the mind itself*.[43]

The central meaning of "nonduality" for Vasubandhu in the TSN, and also in the commentarial works attributed to him, is thus the false, apparent "difference" between mind and mental objects that we saw the Buddha deny in the mirror analogy. As in the AKBh, for Vasubandhu what needs to be denied is always anything that is not reducible to what we have been calling a unitary, causal line—anything requiring an *agent* or a *view* understood literally. Both concepts ("view" and "agent") may be called "dual" in that they are conceptually structured so as to be in relation to some object, with which they interact at a particular time, but which is distinct from them.

Since Vasubandhu's Viṃś was intended to convince non-Mahāyānists of the viability of the Mahāyāna, the text is user-friendly and uses many figures—false perceptions, dreams, illusions, etc.—to exemplify the fundamental error of mistaking an appearance for an independent, objective reality. In order to explain and justify the point, Vasubandhu relied almost entirely on mistakes of perception as the model for the false reification of what is "appearance only." Yet across Yogācāra texts, perception is only one kind of false "duality," and in fact it is the mistakes of *conceptualization*—mistaken "views"—that are taken to be most fundamental and most dangerous. Vasubandhu brings perception to the fore, and thereby makes "duality" more easily understood, but the deeper point is still the false *conceptual duality* of a *cognitive* "view," and we must see how this kind of duality in fact lies behind *perceptual duality* if we are to understand the intricate structure of the TSN.[44]

Conceptual duality is a kind of bifurcation of the universe (or a part of the universe) that appears necessary in the formation of any concept. When we say of any given thing that it is "physical," we are effectively saying, at the same time, that all things are either "physical" or "not physical." We create a "duality" according to which we may understand all things as falling into either one or the other category. This is what it is to define something, and to ascribe it its characteristic nature (*svabhāva*). This is why every "self" is "dual." To say something is *what it is* imposes a duality upon the world. Yet all of our concepts depend upon a pragmatic, selective frame being placed upon what is at root a changing, interconnected, fundamentally inconceivable world. Until we approach it from within our perspectival frame, the world does not accord with any conceptual construct. So every concept imposes a false duality upon the world. To illuminate this with regard to the person, when I say that "I" exist, I am dividing the universe into "self" and "other"—me and not-me, internal and external. Since, for Buddhists, the self is unreal, this is a mistaken imposition, and of course many ignorant, selfish actions follow from this fundamental conceptual error.

A second type of conceptual fabrication, which follows a commonsense interpretation of language and reifies conceptual-linguistic entities that have no true referent, is also called "duality" in Yogācāra contexts. This *linguistic duality* appears when we make the mistake that Vasubandhu calls "carving the ether." Recall the dualities of the Vaibhāṣika system that Vasubandhu criticizes as taking literally the notion that "the eye sees, the ear hears, the nose smells, the tongue tastes, the body touches, the mind cognizes."[45] In fact, as he has argued, these are only figurative expressions for the causal activities of consciousnesses. Yet we take them to be agents acting, as subjects, upon a world.

The following passage from the Yogācāra treatise *Distinguishing Entities from True Natures* (*Dharmadharmatāvibhāga* [DhDhV]), with Vasubandhu's commentary (DhDhVV), translates the Buddha's "nondifference" between mind and mental objects into a "nondifference" of conceptual-linguistic entities and *their* objects:

> The definition of true nature [*dharmatā*] is: **the suchness** [*tathatā*] **which is the nondifference between grasped and grasper, expressed and expression—that is the definition of true nature.** What is the nondifference of grasped and grasper and what is the nondifference of expressed and expression: that is suchness. That is also the definition of true nature. Nondifference itself is, in its proper order, because of not being dual, and because of being inexpressible. With respect to what has no existent difference, it is called nondifferent.[46]

We will have more to say about the expression "grasped and grasper," which Vasubandhu's commentary here correlates with the term "dual." For now, let us just read this passage as saying that the "true nature" (*dharmatā*) or "suchness" (*tathatā*) is explained as the nondifference between the concept and the conceiver, or the word and its meaning. This is why the ultimate is "inexpressible": Every expression, by virtue of *it* expressing *something*, is structured to divide what is properly nondifferent. The meaning is just an image of the expression; the concept is an image of the conceiver; the grasped is an image of the grasper. Like the SNS, the root verse does not contain the term "nonduality" to express this idea, but *conceptual-linguistic duality* is the concept at the center of this passage.[47]

Different, but closely related to both conceptual and linguistic duality, is *perceptual* duality. This is the distinction between sensory organs and their objects, which appears in perception. When I see a tree, I have the immediate impression that there is a distinction between that tree, which I see, and my eye organs, which see the tree. I take it that my eyes are "grasping" the tree, and furthermore I understand that the eyes (my eyes) are part of me, whereas the tree is not part of me. The same is true of all of the sensory organs and their objects. The Abhidharma system calls the sensory organs the "internal" sense bases, and the sensory objects the "external" ones. It is the combination of the "internal" sense bases upon which I impose the false construction of self. Thus perception provides the basis for the conceptual distinction between self and other, the root of all false views, the "view with respect to the existing body" (*satkāyadṛṣṭi*).

For Yogācāra Buddhists, then, sense perception is just as false a "duality" as are false conceptual-linguistic constructions. Given that the external world must be only mind, the sensory experience that we have of a world "out there" is only a figment of our imagination. The self/other distinction implicit in perception is as much a false imposition as is the self/other distinction implicit in the concept "self." Perception, like conceptualization, is only a matter of the mind generating "dual" images. As counterintuitive as this sounds, it may be clarified by analogy to the idea of a multiplayer virtual reality game. In a shared virtual reality experience, the first thing the computer system must be able to track is where, objectively, everything is (where the various players are, where the castle with the hidden jewels is, where the dragon is hiding, etc.). Then, when any new player logs in, the system can place that player somewhere in the multidimensional, virtual world. At that point, the computer must generate a sensory perspective for that individual. Immediately that person experiences herself existing in a world of a certain kind, with certain abilities to move around, and fight, and so on. But this is only a trick of the software. The world is unreal, and so is the player's subjective perspective on that world.

For the Yogācāra, our sensory experience is something like this. All of our causes are only mental, and so the apparent physicalities that intervene between us are merely false constructions of our deluded minds. If this seems like a far cry from the Abhidharma perspective of the AKBh, recall that Vasubandhu had argued that shapes and movements were conceptual constructions. Thus anything that we take to be an ordinary, midsized object of perception is a mental construction *even in pre-Mahāyāna Buddhism*. The shift applies not to the "mind only" nature of ordinary objects, but to the "mind only" nature of *the dharmas that support* our experience. Vasubandhu argues in the Viṃś that the *concept* of a sensory object (*viṣaya*) is a mistake, because nothing can exist as we imagine sensory objects to exist, outside the mind. But he is starting from a position that accepts that sensory objects, if they exist, might well be invisibly small, and momentary.

Furthermore, the physical body that we take ourselves to have, as we negotiate the world, making use of our senses, is also not there. Both external and internal realities are mistaken to the degree that we see them as "two" and not "nondual" constructions appearing within a single mental stream. Recall that in the AKBh Vasubandhu had argued for the conceptual unity of a "view" of the mind, and a "view" of a perceptual organ—both are conceptual constructs that falsely distinguish an *agent* from an *object*. Vasubandhu's notion of "nonduality" in the Yogācāra context works in exactly the same way, smoothly combining the *perceptual* with the *conceptual-linguistic* varieties of nonduality.

After laying out the basic terminology of the three natures, the TSN turns to examine the causal story, the *dependent nature*, which is the basis of the other two:

> 5 What is this unreal fabrication? Mind. For it does not exist at all in the way it is fabricated or in the way it fabricates a thing.[48]

As I read this verse, it contains a concise version of the argument in the Viṃś. There Vasubandhu argued that all things must be "appearance only," because they do not exist—they *cannot exist*—as they appear. Mere appearance is the only ontological option for things that appear but do not exist *as* they appear.

Vasubandhu then spends four verses explicating the Yogācāra terminology of mental causality.

> 6 Mind is regarded as twofold, being cause and result:
> The consciousness called "storehouse," and the seven called "activity."
>
> 7 It is called "mind" [*citta*] because of being "full of" [*citatvāt*] the seeds of defiled tendencies.
> So for the first. But the second because of acting as "various" [*citra*] appearances.
>
> 8 In short, the fabrication of the nonexistent and the thought of three kinds:
> Matured, thus being caused, or else appearing.
>
> 9 The first is the root consciousness, for having the nature of maturation,
> The other the activity consciousness, from the activity of the seeing intellect and thing seen.[49]

Non-Mahāyāna Abhidharma systems describe six consciousnesses: five sensory consciousnesses and the mental consciousness. The Yogācāra system denies the real causal reality of the sensory organs and their objects, but it adds two additional consciousnesses: what Vasubandhu here calls the "root consciousness" or the "storehouse consciousness" (*ālayavijñāna*), and the "defiled mind" (*kliṣṭamanas*). The causal story becomes extremely simple, which is why Vasubandhu prefers it to the notion of physical causality (see the Viṃś). All things are mere appearances, but that does not mean that things are uncaused. Rather, things *are* caused, but are caused in a different way than they appear to be caused. What *actually* causes things to appear as they do is previous *karma*. Your morally significant actions shape your consciousness, which is described as planting mental "seeds" for your future experiences. When the conditions are right, those seeds "mature" into "active" appearances. We are never aware of these "seeds"; the "storehouse consciousness" is subliminal. When activated, though, the seeds "mature" into the full "dual" appearance of "seeing intellect and thing seen."[50]

The seven "active" consciousnesses, caused by the storehouse consciousness, include the six ordinary consciousnesses and the "defiled mind." It is worth remembering that these consciousnesses are what have the "dual" appearances: eye consciousness appears as eye-and-visual-form; mental consciousness appears as mind-and-mental-object. It bears repeating, as well, that each consciousness appears "dual" but is in fact just a unitary, causal line. This is what it is to say that the consciousnesses are caused not by sensory contact, but by subconscious "seeds" in the storehouse consciousness. This may be taken, furthermore, to be a natural extension of Vasubandhu's description of all "views" as forms of consciousness. Yet since each of the six consciousnesses is generated in this way with a particular appearance through a unitary, causal line, there is no place within it for the *error* aspect of duality. Thus, the "defiled mind," the seventh consciousness, is generally taken to be the aspect of mind that *mistakes* the subject for subject, and the object for object. It is one thing to have the *appearances* that have the form of duality (which is just what occurs in the mirror), and it is something else—an entirely separate consciousness—to *take those appearances as really dual*. It is a causal result, and not itself a cause, because it is generated, like the other appearances, by prior karmic conditioning. The goal of Yogācāra mental cultivation is, apparently, to eliminate the "defiled mind"—that is, to recognize the nature of appearances as "dual" without *accepting* duality to be the true nature of things as they really are.

These verses describe the *causal nature* of the mind. Since the AKBh, we have seen Vasubandhu foreground causality as the basis for every entity's identity, the touchstone of the real. Here we have a full account of everything real, then, as only mind. For earlier Abhidharma, to say that something was a false construction or a fabrication, a *parikalpita*, was to say that it was irrelevant to causality—a *mere appearance*. In Yogācāra, the Mahāyāna universal denial of the ultimate reality of all *dharmas* is expressed in the declaration that *every svabhāva is a parikalpita-svabhāva*. Yet this is not the whole story. This does not mean that no entities exist, because nothing is truly caused. Rather, the emphasis shifts from causality of *dharmas* to causality of the mind *to which dharmas appear*. For whereas the entities do not exist as they appear, *their appearances do exist*.

The phrase "fabricated nature"—*parikalpita-svabhāva*—may appear at first to be an internal contradiction, a square circle. For the AKBh, a "*parikalpita*" was the "false construction" that non-Buddhists affirmed, whereas a *svabhāva* was the true nature of a genuinely substantial *dharma*. So there is definitely an irony in putting the two terms together. But *parikalpita-svabhāva* is not a square circle. It is not quite true to say that it does not exist. It does exist, but not as it appears. It is an illusion, a mirage—and it has definite causes that can be studied and, in time, transformed. The Yogācāra system turns us away from the causal story of apparent entities, and toward the causal story of our false conceptualizations. In practical and historical terms, this means new attention to epistemology (*pramāṇa*) and new meditative approaches that seek control of the mind's causal capacities for self-construction and world-generation (*tantra*).

Vasubandhu's clearest, most evocative, and most famous explanation of the three natures appears when they are analogized to a magician's production of an illusion of an elephant, using a piece of wood and a magical spell:

27 It is just as [something] made into a magical illusion with the power of an incantation [*mantra*] appears as an elephant [*hastyātmanā*]. A mere appearance [*ākāramātra*] is there, but the elephant does not exist at all.

28 The fabricated nature is the elephant; the dependent is its appearance [*ākṛti*]; and the nonexistence of an elephant there is the perfected.

29 In the same way, the fabrication of what does not exist appears as dual [*dvayātmanā*] from the root mind. The duality is utterly nonexistent. A mere appearance [*ākṛtimātraka*] is there.

30 The root consciousness is like the incantation. Suchness [*tathatā*] is understood to be like the piece of wood. Construction [*vikalpa*] should be accepted to be like the appearance of the elephant. The duality is like the elephant.[51]

No analogy does better than the magical illusion of an elephant in expressing how there are specific *causes* of an appearance (a spell, some wood) that are quite obviously entirely different from the *apparent causes* (someone has brought an elephant onstage).[52] Notice the two different elements here in the ending of verse 30: the "appearance of the elephant" is "construction," that is, the ongoing process of imagination that arises from the karmic causal stream. The real problem, though, "duality," the dangerous, false distinction between self and other, is analogized to the illusory elephant itself. If I am at a magic show, I should expect to see the "appearance of an elephant." That will make the show worth attending. But if I am not a fool, I will not imagine myself to *actually see an elephant*. That would be to construct duality.

For Vasubandhu, this is a crucial distinction. The basic problem for living beings in his view is not that we *experience* an illusory world; the problem is that we are fooled into *grasping the reality* of our perceptions and our concepts. Once we no longer believe, once we see the falsity of the illusion, the illusion goes away and we can come to experience the truth that lies behind the illusion—the ineffable "suchness" (*tathatā*), the piece of wood.

VASUBANDHU'S COMMENTARIAL INNOVATION: DUALITY AS "GRASPER AND GRASPED"

I have been arguing throughout this book that Vasubandhu has a distinctive approach to causality and scripture, which appears across his AKBh, which motivated his movement toward Yogācāra, and which, further, explains some of his Yogācāra innovations. As summarized in the introductory chapter, the unity of Vasubandhu's oeuvre has been challenged in recent decades, but in the last few years a number of scholars have gravitated toward a view that accepts a single author for nearly all of the texts studied in this book thus far (excluding the TSN and the DhDhVV). One category of texts that has yet to be decided upon by those who nonetheless accept a unified authorship for the AKBh and several Yogācāra treatises is the Yogācāra *śastra* commentaries attributed to Vasubandhu, which include the DhDhVV, just mentioned, the *Mahāyānasaṃgrahabhāṣya* (MSBh), *Mahāyānasūtrālaṃkārabhāṣya* (MSABh), and the *Madhyāntavibhāgabhāṣya* (MAVBh).

While I do not feel I can decisively, "scientifically" ascertain the unified authorship of all of these materials (see chapter 1), I believe that there is reason for their ascription to a common authorial intention. In this section, therefore, I would like to shed some light on Vasubandhu's unique contribution to early Yogācāra in a way that ties the Yogācāra commentarial texts attributed to Vasubandhu back to his overall approach to scripture and causality. I have just pointed out that Vasubandhu calls the "grasper and grasped" distinction "dual" in the DhDhVV, and I have elsewhere argued that Vasubandhu's MSABh underlines this parallel as well.[53] My goal here is to expand upon this point again, by highlighting some interpretive distance between the MAV and its commentary, the *Madhyantavibhāgabhāṣya*, attributed to Vasubandhu, and thereby to correlate some distinctive Yogācāra views with the name "Vasubandhu." I will then argue that those views fit with the approach of the author of the texts we have been studying thus far.

The MAVBh opens with the commentator paying homage to the verses' author, Maitreya, as well as the speaker who revealed Maitreya's text in our world, Asaṅga. In that verse of reverence, Vasubandhu, the commentator, places himself in the audience of those to whom Asaṅga "spoke" the text. He calls Asaṅga "the vocalizer to me, etc."—meaning "to myself, among others."[54] The commentary thus claims for itself an extremely short lineage: I heard the text, it says, from its initial speaker, who heard it from its celestial author, Maitreya.[55] From the tradition's perspective, then, there is essentially no temporal distance between the root text and its commentary.[56] My purpose here is to show how, nonetheless, these texts may quite definitely be distinguished conceptually.

The MAVBh is a complex text, full of terminology that has been developed and argued about across a range of other texts; for the most part the arguing is not taking place in this text. As a general practice, Vasubandhu simply glosses and defines terms laid out in the MAV verses. Of course, glossing and defining can have quite important philosophical consequences. Yet it would be difficult to say that much of the text finds Vasubandhu really doing constructive philosophical work that might distinguish the commentary from the root text. That said, the opening verses, which are front-page Yogācāra metaphysics, supply us with a significant philosophical innovation.

The basic difference between the root text and its commentary is most evident in the very first verse. The root text reads:

> **There is construction of what does not exist. Duality there is not real. Emptiness there is real. [The construction of what does not exist] is real there [in emptiness] too. (I.1)[57]**

The topics here are, self-evidently, the construction of what does not exist, duality, and emptiness. What the verse discusses about these three things is how they are related and how they may each be characterized as existent or nonexistent—real or unreal.[58] Before trying to understand this in any specificity, let us turn to Vasubandhu's commentary:

> The construction of what does not exist there is the conceptual discrimination of grasped and grasper [*grāhya-grāhaka*]. Duality is grasped and grasper. The emptiness of that construction of what does not exist is its lack of existent grasped and grasper. The "[it] is real there too" refers to the construction of what does not exist.[59]

The sore thumb sticking out here is the phrase "grasped and grasper," which is Vasubandhu's repeating, drone-like gloss on the term "duality." As we have already mentioned, it appears to have been in Vasubandhu's commentaries that the term "duality" was for the first time universally tagged to the terminological pair "grasper and grasped." Notice that while the term "duality" appears once in the verse, its gloss as "grasped and grasper" appears three times in the commentary. The commentary therefore uses this expression to tie the three other terms together. The result is that, while Asaṅga's verse is primarily about reality or existence, Vasubandhu's commentary is primarily about grasped and grasper.[60]

It might be thought that I have overstated things by saying that Vasubandhu's commentary is about something different from the verse. Surely the point of the gloss is to indicate that duality *simply is* "grasped and grasper" (*grāhya-grāhaka*); these are the two things, called a "duality," which are not existing in the construction of what does not exist. Vasubandhu's analysis merely uses that gloss as a placeholder for both "duality" and "nonexistence," so as to make all the connections clear. How can that be considered changing the meaning of the verse? My point is that, while this is surely Vasubandhu's view as a commentator, there is reason to doubt that this view of "grasper and grasped" is consistent with the original intent of the root verses.

First of all, "duality" (*dvayam*) is *never* explained as "grasper and grasped" within the verses. The term "duality" in the opening verses seems to me to refer to the duality between existence and nonexistence, using the pair of terms *bhāva* and *abhāva*, and a bit later, the pair *sat* and *asat*.[61] More directly, if we suspend Vasubandhu's commentary and skip immediately from the first to the second verse, we notice that it begins with what could easily be read as its own gloss on "duality does not exist there" from the first verse, saying: **"Therefore everything is established as neither empty nor nonempty."**[62] Now, "neither empty nor nonempty" looks on its surface like a denial of a duality. If indeed the duality denied in the first verse is that between "empty and nonempty," the first verse seems to say that the construction of what does not exist contains both a nonexistent duality between being empty and nonempty and an existent emptiness in which it—the construction of what does not exist—also exists.

The compact poetry of these verses rests in how they use and display an appearance of duality between emptiness and nonemptiness to exemplify nonduality. We find ourselves in a vertiginous, recursive self-referentiality which might indicate a misinterpretation were this feeling not a familiar one from Mahāyāna *sūtra* literature.[63] But this interpretation is cut off when Vasubandhu explains "duality" not as "empty and nonempty" but "grasper and grasped." The comment rescues us from the recursive cycle and therefore, at least temporarily, from the abyss of meaninglessness, and indeed, we may be thankful for Vasubandhu's gloss; but that does not mean it is justified in the terms of the root verses.

When we look at the root verses' own uses of "grasper and grasped," we find that these terms do not have the kind of front-page billing that Vasubandhu gives them, but they do appear: twice in chapter III (III.4, III.17) and twice in chapter V (V.24, V.26).[64] The difference between the use of these terms in the root verses and in Vasubandhu's commentarial gloss on "duality" is quite striking. The verses provide two lists taken from the *Ratnakūṭa-sūtra*—eight conceptual extremes and seven mistaken conceptual pairs (V.23–26)—and "grasper and grasped" appears in the middle of each list. At the very least, then, Vasubandhu seems to have chosen one among many mistaken "twosomes" in the text and made it the privileged gloss for the verse's primary use of "duality." But why choose this particular duality? I believe that the commentary uses this gloss intentionally

(1) to tame and sequester the paradox as already mentioned, and (2) to unify and rationalize Yogācāra around its causal story.

Since we are familiar with the doctrine of the Three Natures, the difference can be summarized concisely by noting that, whereas the MAV verses repeatedly associate the denial of "duality" with the "perfected nature" (as in I.5), they associate the mistake of "grasper and grasped" with the "dependent nature." Vasubandhu's gloss therefore represents the foregrounding of the dependent nature, which is a victory for causal explanation. Same as it ever was: to lack an essence is to fail to meet causal criteria.

The two uses of "grasper and grasped" in the verses of chapter III provide clear evidence of the terms' long association with Buddhist causal reductionism—the use of a causal account of perception to undermine the false view of the self. The second half of verse 17 (III.17c–d) employs the terms "grasper and grasped" as part of a threesome, not a duality, adding "the grasping of those" to "grasper and grasped."[65] This appears in a series of verses addressed to ten mistaken conceptions of a self. This particular half-verse explains the second of the ten, which is billed as explaining the mistaken self as it relates to "causality" (*hetutva*):

> With regard to the next one [i.e., causality,] it should be understood to refer to the seeds of the grasper, the grasped, and the grasping of those.[66]

The verse is telling us that "the grasper, the grasped and the grasping" refer to how a false view of the self is based upon a mistaken understanding of perception. What is really happening is fully accounted for by reference to the causes of sensory organs, objects, and consciousnesses.

In the AKBh, as here, the term "grasper" refers to the sensory organs. The term "grasped" refers to the objects of the sensory organs, which they grasp. So, for instance, one of the "graspers" is the eye, and one of the "grasped" is a visual object—a patch of color. The "grasping," then, which here represents a third term, refers to the sensory consciousnesses: the visual consciousness that is produced by the contact of the sensory organ and the sensory object. Ordinarily, when we think of seeing something, we consider *ourselves* to be seeing something. When we say, "I see that," we tend to think of our eyes, the producers of the experience, as a part of our embodied self. But the Buddha's system allows for the causes of experience to be discrete entities. None is a "self," and none need be in any special relation to a "self." Perceptual grasping of sensory objects by perceptual organs produces visual consciousness. Where is the need for a self? This basic point is evident across the AKBh, as we have seen, and Vasubandhu considers it to be one of the Buddha's most important, characteristic arguments. The MAV, sensibly, calls it an argument regarding "causality" (*hetutva*) and declares that the complex of "grasping" terminology represents it.

Now, although the Buddha's special perceptual causal story provides the conceptual apparatus that allows one to deny the self, it turns out that, in Yogācāra, the "grasper and grasped" explanation is not technically correct either. It is not as bad to think in terms of sensory organs and their objects as it is to think in terms of a permanent self; but "grasper and grasped" is still mistaken. In fact, as a mind-only system, Yogācāra denies the causal story of the sensory organ, object, and consciousness in favor of consciousnesses that arise from other consciousnesses without any intervening sensory organs. This was proven in the Viṃś. Thus from one perspective the "causality" of the Buddha's perceptual account (organ–object–consciousness) frees one of the error of self-construction, but from another perspective it is still erroneous to imagine that the sensory organs and their objects are the *actual* causes of perception and experience. There are no organs and no objects, only consciousnesses.

The idea that "grasper and grasped" is a *mistaken causal explanation* appears in the MAV verses as well. These verses provide three distinct pairs of terms, correlating each to one of the three natures—actually, in this case, not the three natures (*svabhāva*), but the three defining characteristics (*lakṣaṇa*) of reality:

> Views involving the imputation or denial of *dharmas* and persons,
> grasper and grasped, or existence and nonexistence,
> do not occur when there is awareness of the defining characteristic of
> reality. (MAV III.4–5b)[67]

The point of this verse is to explain the benefits of understanding the three characteristics of reality. Correct understanding of each prevents misconstruing things in terms of a specific pair of objects. We may summarize the verse in table 5.2 (which is in agreement with Vasubandhu's commentary).

The term "duality" is nowhere in sight, but the author is clearly structuring each error as a mistaken twosome.[68] All three of these terminological

TABLE 5.2 Pairs of Terms from MAV III.4–5b

SEEING THIS DEFINING CHARACTERISTIC	PREVENTS MISTAKEN VIEWS ABOUT
Fabricated	*dharmas* and persons (*dharma-pudgala*)
Dependent	grasped and grasper (*grāhya-grāhaka*)
Perfected	existence and nonexistence (*bhāva-abhāva*)

pairs are subject to the more generalized conceptual-linguistic mistake represented by a fourth pair of terms, namely "imputation and denial" (*samāropa-apavāda*). These are conceptual-linguistic actions. They consist in either accepting or rejecting the meaningfulness of each pair of terms. They represent two actions that are *both* considered mistaken with respect to *all three pairs of objects*. In a sense, then, conceptual-linguistic imputation and denial are another *duality* that needs to be transcended. But, more accurately, the *way* that conceptual dualities are transcended is by transcending their imputation and denial.

The point of these verses is to relate the proper understanding of the three characteristics to the different kinds of false "views"—views that dissolve once one sees the different "defining characteristics." When one understands that things are illusory, that they are "fabricated," one no longer affirms or denies "persons" or "*dharmas*." When one understands that things are caused, that they are "dependent," one no longer affirms or denies "grasped and grasper." When one understands that things are devoid of ultimate reality, that they are "perfected," one no longer affirms or denies "existence or nonexistence." Note this: for the MAV, the denial of "grasper and grasped" is the characteristic of understanding the *second nature*, whereas the denial of "existent and nonexistent" is the characteristic of understanding the *third nature*.

If this is the case, what is the point of Vasubandhu's commentarial innovation? What is the significance—what is the difference—when Vasubandhu glosses all of the "dualities" as "grasper and grasped"? In order to understand this, we need to see that Vasubandhu is not simply adopting the terminology of the MAV's usage of "grasper and grasped" and applying it to all dualities. Rather, as Vasubandhu explains in his comment on MAV I.3, "grasper" for him refers quite specifically to the consciousness (*vijñāna*) and "grasped" refers the objects (*artha*) that appear to consciousness. Thus, whereas for the root verses these two terms—consciousness and its objects—are not a "duality" in any of the senses we have seen (they do not appear, for instance, in the two lists from chapter V), Vasubandhu's commentary names them as the fundamental mistaken "duality" of Yogācāra. The root verse makes the point that since mental objects are unreal appearances, the consciousness of them is also to be deemed unreal. By glossing these terms as "grasper and grasped," Vasubandhu reminds us that the mind and its mental objects are just as much *perceptually structured* as the eye and its visual objects. The central point of the Viṃś, therefore—that there are no real perceptual objects—is here underlined as a point about the mind: *it too has no perceptual objects.* The denial of all dualities as "grasper and grasped" gives a causal reading of exactly what is denied in the mirror analogy from the SNS. The mind, like your bedroom window, does not take in, or enact, a "viewing" as subject to its object; it is a dissociated line, merely cause and effect.

As I have been arguing throughout this book, Vasubandhu's causal theorizing is thoroughly integrated with his scriptural hermeneutics. Thus, once we see that the term "grasping" refers to *mental perceptual grasping*—exactly what is denied in the SNS mirror analogy—and that it foregrounds the causal *dependent nature*, we can see how this term is intertwined with Vasubandhu's distinctive understanding of the causal functionality of doctrinal analysis—the point with which we ended the last chapter. In MAV III.15–22, which D'Amato calls the section on "skillful reality," the verses first list ten kinds of "self-view,"[69] and then proceed, in subsequent verses, to correlate a doctrinal "antidote" with each false view. Here Vasubandhu's commentarial gloss on "self-view" (*ātmadarśanam*) is "grasping the existent self" or "grasping the self as existent" (*ātmasadgrāha*). Every "view" is a false "grasping." We could hardly hope for a closer connection between Vasubandhu-as-commentator's obsession with the "grasper-grasped" gloss of "duality" and Vasubandhu-as-AKBh-author's obsession with the linear, causal sequencing of "view." We have, however, an embarrassment of riches, since, as I have already pointed out, the specific "false view" countered by talk of "grasping" is the self *as cause.* The purpose of each doctrine, then, is to act as the causal *antidote* to a given version of the false "grasping" of an apparent *self.*

In the context of the teaching that tells us that the specific doctrine countered by talk of "grasping" is the false view of the self as *cause*, Vasubandhu's gloss of *darśanam* with *grāha* is a way of countering the notion that doctrines are held as *intentional objects* of a consciousness. It is, again, the translation of *agency*—even in thought—into a unitary, dissociated causal line.[70] The *grāhya-grāhaka* gloss, which first appears in the MAVBh and the other Yogācāra commentaries attributed to Vasubandhu (DhDhVV and MSABh), becomes prevalent (nearly universal) in later Yogācāra. This gloss unites Yogācāra's central terminological innovations—"appearance only," "duality," and the "Three Natures"—around the view of causality that Vasubandhu foregrounds throughout the AKBh.[71] This suggests to me that these commentaries *do* reflect Vasubandhu's views.[72]

To conclude this section, my reading of Vasubandhu here may benefit from some philosophical clarification. When I say that Vasubandhu's "grasper–grasped" gloss of the term "duality" foregrounds perception in the context of the Three Natures, I do not mean to suggest that he is privileging perception in epistemic terms, as a guarantor of knowledge.[73] Rather, my point is that he privileges perception *as the best model for the basic structure of erroneous awareness.* For Vasubandhu, quintessentially Buddhist philosopher that he is, the fundamental question is always how to root out our erroneous self-construction. In his view, self-construction is rooted in the construction of subjectivity, which is, in turn, mistakenly rooted in perception. Imagining the mind and mental object as two separate entities in relation to one another is a *perceptual model* of the mind—as if the mental object were taken in, acted upon, by the mind the way a visual object is taken in by the eye.[74] "Duality" is shorthand for this "perceptual" structure, and Vasubandhu argues that although it appears in every mental event, it is as false with regard to consciousness as it is with regard to perception; both are, really, "merely cause and effect." When it is said that all things, in this appearance-only world, have a mistaken, "dual" structure, that means that everything in our awareness is mistakenly divided into experiential "subject" and experiential "object." To proceed toward liberation, we must overcome this fundamental delusion.

Furthermore, in addition to sensory perception and cognition, we have seen (with regard to the DhDhVV) that the *grāhya-grāhaka* gloss applies to *conceptual-linguistic* dualities as well. It is standard scholastic Sanskrit to use the term *grahaṇa* ("grasping") to indicate the *use* of a word or a grammatical form to refer in a particular way—that is, its *grasping* is its *taking* a meaning under a particular usage.[75] Vasubandhu thus unites two fields of meaning for this term: its linguistic usage and its traditional Buddhist perceptual meaning. Given this, we may, with fairness, affirm that Vasubandhu's understanding of "duality" encompasses all of what contemporary philosophers, following Brentano, call "intentionality"—the "aboutness" of consciousness and linguistic meaning—their inherent, ineliminable relationality.[76] Of course, there are important differences: Brentano considered intentionality the quintessence of consciousness, whereas Vasubandhu considers duality the root error of all sentient beings. What's more, Vasubandhu's term includes within it further false "dualities" not ordinarily considered "intentional"; his concept extends to include, as well, the mistaken appearance of relationality within *action* (agent and action are also "merely cause and effect"), and perhaps also the relationality of substance and quality—and so on.[77] "Duality" is the fundamental delusion of ordinary beings, whereby things appear in a relational, as opposed to a causal, structure—and for Vasubandhu, like Brentano, the most basic form of relationality is the apparent relation between the mind and the objects it seems to "take."

To claim that Vasubandhu's view of "duality" amounts to a suggestion that we overcome what many philosophers consider the essential nature of consciousness and language might appear to embroil Vasubandhu unnecessarily in contemporary debates. Perhaps more importantly, it might appear to burden Vasubandhu with a highly implausible position. How could Vasubandhu deny the obvious fact that we have experience that is structured as—as he puts it—"dual"? How could that be an illusion? And, how can he be denying all but the causal reality, if he advocates not one, but *three natures,* only *one of which* (the second) is the causal nature? To use John Searle's famous terminology, how could one plausibly deny that there is a difference between the *first-person ontology* of consciousness and the *third-person ontology* of ordinary causality?[78] In answer to this, I would say that Vasubandhu's view is not implausible if we take into consideration the thoroughgoing nature of his antirealism. I am not denying that Vasubandhu allows that the *first-person ontology* is how we *experience* the world; the "first person" perspective, the perspective of there being a world as experienced by a subject, is the construction named as "dual" and glossed as *grāhya-grāhaka.* Vasubandhu does allow that this exists, but *only as an appearance.* This is why, along with the "third person" perspective that is the causal nature (the dependent nature) and the "first person" perspective that is the "dual" construction (the fabricated nature), Vasubandhu as Yogācāra includes a *third nature,* which is just the fact that the "first person" is not real as it appears (the perfected nature).

Therefore, this is not to deny that we *seem to have* a "first personal" perspective—and that this appearance, this "seeming," is part of reality as properly described. One reason that philosophers such as Searle believe that the first-personal perspective is irreducible is that there is no way to explain what we experience without at some point at least implicitly appealing to the subject of experience, which means that you must always bring in a first-personal perspective by the back door, if not the front. But Vasubandhu has provided us a way to describe this *apparent* "first person" fully from a *third-personal* perspective: to be specific, we can speak of the *figurative* perspective, as we have discussed with respect to time, person, and view. View is closest to the case at hand, so let us take this as our example. Recall the distinction we made between the consciousness, which literally "views" a visual object, and the "view" from your bedroom window, which sees nothing—it is only an angle of approach, a perspective, figuratively a "view." What Vasubandhu now tells us, following the Buddha's teaching in the SNS, is that *even the consciousness* only has a "view" *figuratively*.

This is not to deny that there is something called "consciousness"; it is only to deny that its "perspective" is truly an intentionally structured relationship between two distinct entities (the subject and the object). In truth, like the light passing through your window—or like a camera pointed at your window—the "consciousness" takes the form of the visual data and passes it on, in a new form, to other mental events. There is no need here for a human subject; it is only cause and effect. Just as with the eye's "view" or the "view" out your window, the fact that there is a perspectival point—an originating center—makes it seem that there is a subject, or self. Your town can be seen from countless angles; your window has one specific perspective on your town. Of course, no one would mistake your window for a human subject; but there is a danger, if we write of your window's "view," that an overly literalistic reader might mistakenly think we are crediting your window with intentionality. In the same way, the perspectival quality of all perceptions fools the mind into assigning subjectivity. Since I can only see through my eyes, it seems to me that I must exist somewhere behind my eyes. Vasubandhu's denial of subjectivity, then, amounts to the claim that, whenever we *think* we are subjects "viewing" something, in fact there are only a series of perspectivally shaped moments of consciousness. Although our experiential world is "dual" in appearance—it appears as though it is being processed by a subject—in fact the *reality* and the *unity* of the subject are only a habitual, conceptual imposition after the fact.[79]

If Searle and company answer that introspection tells us otherwise, then it may be submitted that the Yogācāras (lit. "Practitioners of Yoga") claim to have worked quite extensively on introspection. Look again, they may say—this time with the idea in mind that perhaps what you think is a subject's perspective on an object is in fact a picture painted *as if* from a given perspective; perhaps the subject you think is self-evident is actually conceptually superimposed, after the fact. Perhaps you are looking at a photograph and assuming that there must be a photographer behind the lens. Whatever the case, though, by the time any given "experience of subjectivity" makes it into the argument in defense of its existence, it must have taken shape in language, and we have already granted that language is inherently "dual." Therefore, there is no argument from the experience of subjectivity to its reality.[80] A computer with no introspective capacities could be programmed to defend the reality of "its" subjectivity. What evidence do you have that *you're* not similarly programmed?[81] I certainly have no need to trust your claim.

CONCLUSION: YOGĀCĀRA AS A PARADIGM FOR THE INTERPRETATION OF SCRIPTURE

Many Tibetans, and some modern scholars, argue that Yogācāra philosophers, including Vasubandhu, affirm the ultimate reality of the subjective mind.[82] This is a textbook error that comes from reading the denial of duality as equivalent to the denial of external reality.[83] We see duality being denied all across Yogācāra texts, and we see in Vasubandhu's Viṃś an argument against external sensory objects, the *viṣayas*. But denying external reality is not the same thing as denying duality. They are two separate stages in an argument, or, better, two separate, causally related stages in the elimination of "wrong view." The difference between the two moments can be stated plainly: duality is two things, and external objects (or mental objects) make up just one of the two things being denied. Also to be denied is internal reality, the mind itself as subject.

This is easily demonstrated by looking to the concluding verses of TSN, where it is quite evident that duality, *dvaya*—here translated "either"—includes both mental objects and the mind itself:

> 36 As a result of perception of only mind, there is no perception of knowable things.
> As a result of no perception of knowable things, there can be no perception of mind.

37 As a result of no perception of either [*dvaya*], there is perception of the *dharma* realm.
As a result of perception of the *dharma* realm, there can be the perception of liberation.[84]

The Yogācāra causal story of liberation is here depicted as a successive release from the "grasped" and the "grasper": first, eliminate the false conception of perceptible objects ("grasped"); then, the perception of mind ("grasper") will fall away. The result of the elimination of both (the nonexistence of grasper and grasped) is the attainment of liberation.[85] The nonperception of duality in TSN 37 picks up on the previous two nonperceptions—the nonperception of knowable things, and the nonperception of the mind. So the two things you have to get rid of in order to attain liberation are (1) knowable things—mental objects, and (2) the mind itself. There is no possibility, here, that the mind is being affirmed as ultimate. The denial of duality is quite clearly intended to deny *the subject together with the object*.

We can see in these verses as well that *cittamātra*, or "only mind," which is one name given to the Yogācāra tradition, is just the starting point for development toward final liberation. It is as though the TSN is picking up where the Viṃś left off. Yes, everything is only mind, but that's just the start. Understanding "mind only" just means that there are no knowable *things*. "Knowable things," of course, are not just physical, "external" things, they are anything you can know. So that includes ideas. Just like other objects, ideas are not going to make it to the last stage. Ideas are not the final reality.

I believe that the best reading of the term "knowable things" (*jñeyārtha*) here actually refers to all of the class categories of the *dharma* system, whatever system you want to use (aggregates, spheres, components, or the three natures themselves). So the point of the first line of verse 36 is that understanding "mind only" (*citta-mātra*) or "appearance only" (*vijñapti-mātra*) amounts to understanding that all of our ordinary perceptions and concepts are mistaken. The sentence "As a result of perception of only mind, there is no perception of knowable things" provides a concise explanation of the intention behind negations in the Perfection of Wisdom *sūtras* ("No eye, no ear, no nose . . ."). What we ordinarily take to be real is unreal. Mahāyāna scriptures express the inconceivable nature of a great being's visionary experience by negating "knowable things."

But that again is just the start. Once you see that all of your ordinary perceptions and concepts are false, something else falls away: namely, the perceiving mind. Thus recognizing *mind only* leads directly to recognizing *no mind*. And you need the nonperception of both of those—"no perception of either"—in order to attain the liberating transformation that is called the "perception of the *dharmadhātu*." This last is a term for the realization of *nirvāṇa*.[86] These stages may succeed one another logically, or causally, but they are distinct stages. First, recognize *mind only*. Then, recognize *no mind*. Finally, having seen *nonduality*, attain *nirvāṇa*.

CORRECTIONS TO TRADITIONAL ERRORS ON VASUBANDHU'S YOGĀCĀRA

1. Denying duality ≠ Denying external objects
2. Nondual ≠ Purely mental
3. Denying the mental object → Denying the mental subject
4. The mental subject is not ultimately real

It is sometimes claimed that Vasubandhu has somehow slipped in an ultimately real nature in his description of the "causal" stream, the dependent nature of the mind, or that he is perhaps affirming an essence in the "storehouse consciousness." This too could not be farther from the truth. First of all, we have seen in previous chapters that Vasubandhu determines the causal nature of entities *always* through conceptual constructions alone. Given a manipulationist view that acknowledges the subjective aspect of the frame in any causal story, there can be no *ultimate* description of a *causal* nature—even though it is only through appeal to the "objectivity" of causal structures that substantially real entities can be affirmed. But more obviously, Vasubandhu is everywhere advocating a mainstream Mahāyāna view that takes all concepts as mistaken from an ultimate perspective—no matter how you parse them. Even the Three Natures view itself, although it names, as if from outside, the construction, the emptiness, and the ongoing causal story of mind—it is still a "view," which is expressed in language.

Vasubandhu's self-awareness on this is quite clearly expressed in his commentary to verse 10 of the Viṃś. There he answers the criticism that if everything is only apparent (*vijñapti-mātra*), then so too, his view must be only apparent, as well. His reply is that yes, of course, all things are only apparent, including the view under consideration. This may seem a bit squirrelly, and I have seen admirers of Nāgārjuna roll their eyes at this apparent mimicry of the master.[87] But it is quite consistent with Vasubandhu's view overall. The final verse of the Viṃś (verse 22) says that the "appearance only" doctrine is "not in every way conceivable"[88] and that "those like me cannot consider all its ways, since it is beyond the reach of reasoning."[89] Instead, "It is the range, in every way, for Buddhas, Lords, because they are unobstructed with respect to all objects of knowledge in all their aspects."[90] The doctrine of mind-only points beyond itself; to prove that what we take to be one way must be only appearance is not to affirm the ultimate reality of the appearance, it is to impose epistemic humility.

Across his Yogācāra works, Vasubandhu consistently affirms the view that, as he cites in the VyY, "all *dharmas* are without words, and are expressed with words."[91] We can, and must, use conventional language to investigate the world of our experience, but the world as it really is is beyond language and conceptualization:

> Where all *dharmas* are inexpressible characteristics, by speaking as with the conceptual constructions of fools, following their understanding, it is suitable even for the Āryas to express with words what has no words.[92]

When we read Vasubandhu's Three Natures view, then, we must understand that its purpose is not a literalistic reification of the structure of ultimate reality; rather, it expresses, pragmatically, the figurative character of all expressions. It is premised on the idea that all conceptual constructions are false, including the three natures themselves, to the degree that we imagine we understand them. Nonetheless, the doctrine of the Three Natures still provides a supremely elegant summary of the view of causality, scripture, and experience that we have studied throughout this book. We may not be able to affirm it as *ultimate*, but it is surely a very good—because useful—explanation of our situation, given the limits of human knowledge, and the unavoidable fact that even our best ideas are conditioned by ignorance.

Just to cement this last point—that the three natures themselves are subject to self-referential self-undermining, and so are not in any way to be taken as an exception to the Mahāyāna claim of universal emptiness (*ngo bo nyid ma mchis pa*)—I will conclude by summarizing the verses from the TSN that we have yet to discuss.[93] For, the bulk of the TSN is dedicated to the idea that the three natures are interconnected and inconceivable, beyond the dualities of conceptualization. In fact, the three natures are best understood not as things in themselves, but as a method for contemplating how *everything* is, at its root, inconceivable.

The tenth verse opens a discussion of why "the natures are profound"—echoing the opening verse's declaration that "the wise understand the three natures as profound."[94] Thus, these eleven verses (of a thirty-seven-verse text) make up the section we turn to for profound wisdom: the central point of the text. The word I translate in both places as "profound" (*gaṃbhīra/gabhīra*) has the literal meaning of "deep," but it is also used to mean "inscrutable" or "mysterious"—as is "deep" in English.[95] The reasons for this profundity, or incomprehensibility, are explained in four topics, each of which represents a way in which we conceive of divisions among the three natures, where divisions do not really exist. The first three are pairs of opposites, natural "dualities": reality and unreality; duality and unity; affliction and purity. The fourth is simply "nondifference in quality" (*lakṣaṇābheda*).

Verses 11, 12, and 13 explain how each of the natures "is said to have the character of reality and unreality." For each, it has a quality of "reality" from one perspective, but "unreality" from another. "Reality" and "unreality" are terms that can be made to apply to each of the three natures, by shifting the frame of reference. Verses 14, 15, and 16, similarly, explain how each of the natures is considered "to have the nature of duality and unity." For each, it is "dual" from one perspective, but "unified" from another. Just as the notion of "three natures" explodes the entire concept of *svabhāva*, here the notion that the three natures are *both* nondual and dual should undermine their having any definable, essential nature. If they are *ultimate*, it is not because they *are* the essential nature; rather, it is because they point in the direction of the inconceivable. They are a moving target, a flexible structure that no "dual" conceptual structures can pin down.

The exception that proves the rule is the third pair of terms, "affliction and purity." Verse 17 says that both the *fabricated* and the *dependent* are associated with affliction, whereas the *perfected* is associated with purity. Here we might expect to find ourselves in a quandary, since to say that two of the natures are afflicted and the third is pure is to ascribe different qualities to them, and therefore to affirm some decisive "nature" to each. Yet the four verses that follow, 18–21, are dedicated to explaining how the three natures are "nondifferent." Verses 18 and 19 tell how the *perfected* is nondifferent from the *fabricated*, and verses 20 and 21 tell how the *perfected* is nondifferent from the *dependent*. Since the *fabricated* and the *dependent* are both called "afflicted," there is no need to say how they are "nondifferent." The upshot, then, is that every entity may have an *afflicted* and a *pure* characteristic, but at the ultimate level these are inseparable, and indistinguishable. When, in verses 22–25, the three natures are finally explained from the perspective of practice, in order to cultivate how they are to be *seen* in stages of meditation, they are called "conventional." The natures *as experienced* must be admitted to be only conventional, because their true natures are inconceivable—they are by nature beyond any nature.

As Vasubandhu explains in the MAVBh, any given doctrinal structure from the Abhidharma may be contemplated in this way, and seen to be subject to all three natures. The three natures are an interpretive schema for all doctrines.[96] If you see the Buddha affirming the reality of the five aggregates, this may appear on its surface as an affirmation of the doctrine as it appears. We may wish to take the five aggregates as real. This is the fabricated nature of the aggregates. But there is a causal story, a special intention, behind the Buddha's action: he speaks in this way (figuratively), as the MAVBh tells us, in order to release living beings from grasping onto the self as a unity. The doctrine arises as an antidote, a causally structured method for transforming the mental continua of deluded sentient beings. As such, the teachings are not merely straightforward affirmations of content. The content is inseparable from the causal stream of the mind that produces it, and the mind or minds toward which it is directed. The content arises as a conceptual construction due to causes and conditions, an inseparable aspect of a unitary, mental causal line. This is the dependent nature. To affirm this causal nature, therefore, is to undermine the reality of the apparent doctrinal affirmation itself. It is to recognize the "emptiness" of the doctrine. Every view, every doctrine, contemplated in this way, is subject to the apparently negative claims of the Mahāyāna ("no eye, no ear . . ."), that its nature is to be empty, *niḥsvabhāva*. This is the perfected nature.

I have said that in the TSN Vasubandhu enshrines his brilliant, early AKBh distinction between how things *appear* and how they are *truly caused* in the doctrine of the Three Natures. What was missing was why, if he wanted a doctrine to enshrine that distinction, he should end up with *three* rather than *two* natures. Now we can answer: the third nature is the Mahāyāna doctrine of universal emptiness, which he has come to see as playing a crucial part in every view, every conceptual construction, that is not as it seems. The scriptures of early Buddhism contained numerous, diverse doctrines, and the Mahāyāna brought in a set of texts that undermine and deny the ultimate truth of those doctrines. Vasubandhu's Yogācāra provides an interpretive method that, by appeal to linear causality, integrates these scriptures into a single, conceptual whole.

The TSN, above all, weaves, presses, and kneads the three natures together. This integrated structure undermines any claim that Abhidharma *dharmas* can avoid universal emptiness (because they are all merely concepts held by their advocates' minds, generated as antidotes by the Buddha), while at the same time undermining the idea that Mahāyāna is superior and ultimate and legitimates a wholesale abandonment of the Abhidarma categories (because its core doctrine applies most decisively *to the Abhidharma*, and it is, furthermore, self-referentially subject to exactly the same directional thrust toward the inconceivable). The TSN therefore establishes a doctrinal path laid, for the interpretation of scripture, in the VyY. It provides an explicit method for displaying the *dharma*'s utility in the light of what is by nature incomprehensible, the inscrutable mystery comprehended only by the Buddha's omniscience.

The doctrine of the Three Natures brings to mind the fact that all of our concepts, though they appear to be independent objects of our thought, are rooted in the history of our own conceptual structures, and shaped out of our own personal baggage, our *karma*. When we note the causally conditioned nature of our own ideas, we are humbled; we cannot but see the fabrications for what they are. This teaches us that all doctrines, even Buddhist doctrines, are potentially dangerous for their capacity to reify self-construction; even Buddhist doctrines can be *tīrthakara-parikalpita*, false conceptual constructions of the kind that non-Buddhists affirm (this was, after all, Vasubandhu's accusation against Buddhist Vaibhāṣikas).[97] Yet we are not forced to give up our pragmatically beneficial views just because we acknowledge their nature as fabricated. There is a "pure" side to simply recognizing fabrications for what they are, which is that we are made, at least temporarily, free of grasping.

The TSN, like the SNS, presents the key value in Mahāyāna as the freedom from views, the freedom from egotistical self-construction that comes of seeing things one way, our way. To seek this purity is to acknowledge, with humility, our own epistemic limits. This acknowledgment itself—based as it is in causal reasoning—calls attention to our ability to test our knowledge, and to gain ever greater control over its causes.[98] Thus, in this way, the doctrine of universal emptiness can move us forward toward the possibility of genuine freedom, in which all apparent views are seen as the linear, nondual, causally generated mental events that they are.

6

AGENCY AND THE ETHICS OF MASSIVELY CUMULATIVE CAUSALITY

> We are reluctant, of course, to treat birth as a scourge: has it not been inculcated as the sovereign good—have we not been told that the worst came at the end, not at the outset of our lives? Yet evil, the real evil, is *behind*, not ahead of us. What escaped Jesus did not escape Buddha: "If three things did not exist in the world, O disciples, the Perfect One would not appear in the world . . ." And ahead of old age and death he places the fact of birth, source of every infirmity, every disaster.
>
> —E. M. Cioran, *The Trouble with Being Born*

CIORAN WAS a cynic and rejected the possibility of salvation, but his reading of Buddhism here is apt. We are trapped, and destined to suffer, by the fact of our birth. Our suffering has, in fact, beginningless causes, and is properly conditioned to continue endlessly. What's more, the Buddhist denial of the personal self—ordinarily the seat of freedom—seems to deny as well the possibility of meaningful human agency. Vasubandhu, as we have seen, is repeatedly found denying agency—even agency in a single momentary event. Yet salvation is possible. It is proposed not through a new kind of agent, but through the very causal, karmic effects that have kept us imprisoned for so long. This chapter seeks to explain how this can work.

For Buddhists, the kind of agency that is available to us sits very close to moral nihilism, but rather than being a rejection of morality, it is best read as a reframing of ordinary action so as to take in the full range of causes and conditions in which one participates—both more than and less than the imagined self. Morally significant acts may, on the one hand, take place within causally efficacious, individual moments of self-aware action (*cetanā*), and on the other hand, provide a limitless potential for gradually transforming nearly deterministic nihilism into boundless freedom and beneficence. This chapter will interrogate the moral underpinnings of the views of causality and knowledge discussed thus far. We will see how turning away from the agent self and adopting a stance of epistemic humility allows one to focus on the true causes of suffering and the true potential for freedom.

BUDDHISM AND RESPONSIBILITY

Who is responsible for my actions? Ordinarily the answer would be, "I am." If I kill someone, I'm the one to put in prison. If I write a popular novel, I'm the one to get the royalties. But how can this be understood without a real "self"? For Buddhists, there is no aspect of the person that is the same—exactly the same—when "I" kill and "I" go to prison. By the time the murder trial comes around I might well regret what I've done. By the time I'm on my book tour, I've forgotten the names of the minor characters in my own novels. Should a regretful murderer have to go to jail? Does a forgetful novelist deserve royalties? We might say so for conventional purposes, to discourage murder and encourage good writing, but the simple truth is that if there is no self, then there's no one who is truly responsible him- or herself. There can't be, because there isn't really anyone *at all*, responsible or not. Given the complex causal chains through which every event is conditioned, the responsibility for every action may be spread across a wide range of potential culprits.

The Buddhist doctrine of *karma* therefore provides a full and sophisticated explanation of moral culpability, but it leaves one wondering whether it is really very fair, if the one who is punished is *not* the one who has done evil.[1] What makes murder punishable, and novel-writing praiseworthy? (The two extremes of human action.) Most scholars today would say that morality-talk, for Buddhists, takes a descriptive perspective that is only conventionally, but not ultimately, real.[2] We use conventions of language and law to impose rules on conventional persons who, we know, are really only conceptual constructs. You don't need to declare the ultimate truth of the author's identity through time just to know where to send the royalty check.

Yet for many observers of Buddhism and many modern Buddhists, such a view is very unsatisfying, because by denying the ultimate reality of moral agents, it seems to undermine the genuine effectiveness of moral actions: I may not be exactly the same person when I'm in a murderous rage as I am when I'm put on trial years later, but such conceptual abstractions pale against the tangible reality of the knife I plunged into another person's body, and the bars that slam shut when I'm finally put away for good. These are real things—knives and bars—and the fact that their moral significance does not exist at the ultimate level seems to deny that their relationship is morally significant. The denial of the ultimate reality of the person seems, then, to deny the moral quality of moral actions, which are by their nature temporally extended.

The response I will propose in this chapter in order to alleviate this feeling is to notice that (based upon a reading of Vasubandhu) although the person has no ultimate existence, what *is* "substantially" real gains that status by its participation in causal relationships. There is a very definite causal connection between the knife and the bars. What we conventionally take to be a person is a string of events integrated only as a causal stream. I may have no ultimate unity, but the causal results of my actions have ramifications within "my" causal continuum. Still, I place the "my" in quotation marks to highlight the primary difficulty to be addressed here. If I do not exist as an ultimately real self, then there is no single entity that may be named as the murder victim and another called the perpetrator. To distinguish "myself" from others, and so to privilege the interests of my own continuum over those of others is, to put it bluntly, the quintessential mistake of living beings. Yet it would appear that without such a distinction, we are left without any ground for moral attribution.

Vasubandhu has provided, if not a solution, a way of thinking about this quandary, which will be our topic in this chapter. Vasubandhu is, of course, always an advocate of the view that we are each merely a series of ever-changing parts that come together to generate the illusory appearance of a self. As I will explain, however, Vasubandhu nonetheless characterizes the universe as quite powerfully charged with moral significance. The moral significance of the universe, it turns out, does not depend upon the existence of temporally extended events. Instead, every element that makes up the person, moment to moment, is *individually* morally charged in accordance with its orientation toward or away from liberation (*nirvāṇa*). Each element of reality, each *dharma*, is accordingly either "defiled" (*kliṣṭa*) or "undefiled" (*akliṣṭa*). As Vasubandhu writes in the AKBh, all *dharmas* are "defiled" except those that are on the path, or conducive to *nirvāṇa*.[3] Thus, while persons are not by nature morally culpable, or morally charged, the elements that make up individuals, and which lead the personal continuum either toward *nirvāṇa* or away from it, are.

This way of putting things makes Buddhism seem pragmatist, because morality is relative, in a sense, to the pragmatic goal of attaining *nirvāṇa*. We might be inclined to think that this is countered by the notion of *nirvāṇa* as an unmoving, literally "unconditioned" (*asaṃskṛta*) goal, which provides an ultimate, not merely pragmatist, test of morality.[4] Yet for Vasubandhu, as we know, what is "unconditioned" is by definition disconnected from the causal flow of conditioned entities, and so must be admitted to be a mere conceptual construction, not an ultimately real entity. Furthermore, as we have already seen of causality more generally, the notion of an entity as placing one on a *causally conditioned path* to liberation is clearly a conceptual construction. If change is itself unreal, surely moral valuation that is dependent upon change is unreal as well.

Yet this way of undermining our ordinary concepts of morality is hardly unique to Vasubandhu. Even without Vasubandhu's denial of the ultimate reality of change and *nirvāṇa*, I think it is important to acknowledge that the Buddhist denial of the conventional self veers quite close to moral nihilism.[5] For the significance granted to momentary events on the path to *nirvāṇa* may, when viewed from the proper perspective, *compensate* for the loss of meaning of an ordinary life. But momentary events do not ever *return* meaning to conventional constructs; on the contrary, Buddhist teachings emphasize, in a very extreme way, the meaninglessness of ordinary cyclic existence (*saṃsāra*). Except in a particular interpretation of Madhyamaka philosophy—which I believe postdates Vasubandhu—Buddhist thinkers do not resuscitate or enliven the value of ordinary lived experience.[6] As a simple example, I offer the following humorous poem by the much-beloved Tibetan saint, Milarepa:

> In the beginning a daughter is a smiling little goddess,
> Imperiously monopolizing your best possessions.
> In the middle, she endlessly asks her due:
> She openly demands things from her father,
> And steals them from her mother on the sly.
> Never satisfied with what she's given,
> She's a source of despair to her kindly parents.
> In the end, she's a red-faced ogress:

At best, she's an asset to someone else,
At worst, she'll bring calamity on you.
How frustrating she is, this ravaging monster!
I've cast off this incurable sorrow.
I don't want a daughter who'll lead me to ruin.[7]

Granted, Milarepa never met my daughter. But the purpose of this poem, and similar teachings about sons, and friends, and other loved ones, is to place these apparent goods within a larger context that drains them of value—really, exposes their lack of ultimate value. Hearing this, and thinking about it, I am supposed to realize that my attachment to my daughter is deluding me and preventing me from renouncing my home and family and pursuing *nirvāṇa*. But from a conventional perspective, the actual perspective from which I view my own life, to see my daughter (or my son, or my wife, or my work, etc.) as a fetter would be to deny what I experience to be the meaning of my life. This is a stark example, and that makes for some of the humor in Milarepa's poem. Surely there must be some positive karmic benefit from caring for a daughter.

For traditional Buddhists, however, there is a genuine divide between the ultimately meaningless pursuits guided by what are considered worldly concerns—whether involving this life or the next—and a life with purpose, namely, a life where one has renounced such concerns and taken up the path to liberation. Renunciation, therefore, as the crux of the Buddhist path, serves to illustrate well the location of meaning within a Buddhist worldview. With regard to ordinary life, it appears to be largely negative; but that is only part of the story. For this reason, before returning to Vasubandhu's discussion of *karma* and dependent origination, I will take a detour and examine the most famous and widely discussed Buddhist text on the meaning and purpose of renunciation, the *Sāmaññaphalasutta* from the Pāli canon.

LEVELS OF FREEDOM IN THE *SĀMAÑÑAPHALASUTTA*

In the *Scripture on the Benefits of Renunciation* (*Sāmaññaphalasutta* [SPS]), King Ajatasattu asks the Buddha whether there is any benefit to becoming a renunciant—a homeless, wandering seeker—that is evident *in this life*.[8] The question shows us that the king is somewhat cynical and spiritually deficient. He is not interested in any future or potentially invisible benefits; he is concerned about this world, and he is not ready to trust any teachers until they can provide evidence that the life of a renunciant is worthwhile. But it is also a pragmatic question about the lifestyle that the Buddha advocates. Carpentry and soldiering make something of a man, help him gain wealth and respect, raise a family. What does renunciation do for him?

The Buddha's response is to speak of freedom. He asks the king how he would treat a slave in his keeping who decided to become a renunciant. Would the king recapture the new monk and order him to be a slave once more? No, the king admits. In such a case, the king would bow down before the former slave and present him with gifts. Well, the Buddha says, *there's* a benefit you can see in this life. Then he asks the king how he would treat a taxpayer in his realm who decided to become a renunciant. Would the king order the new monk to go back to work and resume paying taxes? No, the king admits again. The renunciant is free from the burden of taxation.

Freedom from slavery and taxation are political liberties. These are examples in a language the king can understand, and they get the king's attention. He asks for more examples, and the Buddha shifts from speaking of political freedoms to what we might consider psychological freedoms—freedoms from cares and concerns, and freedom from guilt. He speaks of a householder who, after encountering the Buddha, says to himself that whereas "household life is close and dusty, the homeless life is free as air. It is not easy, living the household life, to live the fully perfected holy life, purified and polished like a conch shell." So the householder leaves home and joins the monastic community. Then, eventually, as the Buddha says, "he dwells restrained by the restraint of the rules, persisting in right behavior, seeing danger in the slightest faults, observing the commitments he has taken on regarding body, deed, and word, devoted to the skilled and purified life, perfected in morality, with the sense-doors guarded, skilled in mindful awareness and content."[9]

Now Ajatasattu has killed his own father, meaning he's a regicide, and he needs a good lesson on morality. The Buddha goes into quite some detail about what it means for the mendicant to be "perfected in morality." At the end of it, he summarizes the this-worldly benefit of virtuous behavior quite pointedly for the king:

> Just as a duly anointed Khattiya king, having conquered his enemies, by that very fact sees no danger from any side, so the monk, on account of his

> morality, sees no danger anywhere. He experiences in himself the blameless bliss that comes from maintaining this Ariyan morality. In this way, sire, he is perfected in morality.[10]

Earlier in the *Sutta*, Ajatasattu had discussed both his restlessness and his fear of his enemies—so it is clear that the king is tormented both by his own political instability and by his lack of virtue, and should understand very well the appeal of the psychological freedom expressed as the "blameless bliss." This is a very deep psychological freedom that comes from confidence in one's own moral rectitude.

The Buddha then explains the other points too—guarding the doors of the senses, mindfulness and clear awareness, and finally, contentedness:

> And how is a monk contented? Here a monk is satisfied with a robe to protect his body, with alms to satisfy his stomach, and having accepted sufficient, he goes on his way. Just as a bird with wings flies hither and thither, burdened by nothing but its wings, so he is satisfied.[11]

It is difficult to think of a more apt analogy for freedom than that of being free as a bird, but the former householder's path of increasing liberation is still only beginning. As his meditative skills advance he is able to conquer the five hindrances, attain various blissful meditative states and supranormal powers, and eventually reach the ultimate freedom: *nirvāṇa*.

The Buddha uses some remarkable analogies to explain the experience of being freed from the five hindrances. He says that (1) conquering worldly desires is like being freed from a debt; (2) conquering ill will and hatred is like being freed from a long sickness; (3) conquering sloth and torpor is like being freed from prison; (4) conquering restlessness and anxiety is like being freed from slavery; and (5) conquering uncertainty and doubt is like being freed from the anxiety that comes during a journey through a desolate and dangerous wasteland. Each of these analogies deserves more attention than I can give here, but I list them to emphasize once more the theme of freedom, in this case freedom from the various burdens of our ordinary mental life. For the Buddha, on the far side of that liberation, our ordinary mind seems, by comparison, imprisoned, enslaved, sick, deep in debt, and in constant anxiety.

My purpose here is to show how we may read the Buddhist path to *nirvāṇa* not simply as a path *to* freedom, but as a path of increasing freedoms, where each new form of liberation paves the way for higher attainments. Ever-increasing attainments of virtue, knowledge, power, and bliss are themselves understood as new freedoms that may be exercised toward attaining still further liberating transformations. Many of the higher powers attributed to Buddhas and near-Buddhas, such as the abilities to create multiple bodies, to fly, and to swim in land or walk on water, express freedom as well: freedom from the physical limitations of embodiment.

The SPS thus affirms the value of freedom at every level, including ordinary political and psychological freedoms, as well as the self-mastery and moral control that are characteristic of Platonic and Augustinian views of free will.[12] Its main affirmations, however, go well beyond these traditional freedoms to assert the possibility, and the benefits, of pursuing freedom from essentially all mental and physical limitations. This is the positive, optimistic side of Buddhist teachings. The Buddhist path is one of limitless liberation.[13]

After King Ajatasattu retires from the Buddha's presence at the end of the SPS, however, the Buddha tells the assembled monks that were the king not a regicide, a murderer of his own father, he would have attained the "dhamma eye" that very night while listening to the Buddha's teachings. That is, the king would have had a significant realization of the meaning of the Buddha's teachings, which would have put him firmly on the path to liberation. But since the king was "damaged," as the Buddha says, that was simply not possible.[14] Because of his previous deeds, because of his accumulated negative *karma*, the path of liberation was apparently not yet open to him. Even a Buddha could not liberate him.

We are left, then, with two sides of a coin. Extraordinary freedoms are possible. Yet ordinary beings are subject to karmic conditioning that prevents them from seeing things clearly and that clouds their judgments with intense emotions such as desire and rage. This is especially true of those who are morally compromised. Even a Buddha cannot open their "dhamma eyes." Ignorance leads to bad choices with negative consequences that reinforce the ignorance. Cycles of suffering, rebirth, and redeath are thereby perpetuated without our knowledge and with hardly anyone having any truly effective ways out. It appears that what we take to be ordinary freedoms are misleading, if not simply unreal. The Buddha described this cycle of rebirths in causal terms—his theory of *dependent origination*—that have the ring of inevitability and causal determination. Sentient beings go wherever the winds of their *karma* blow them. It seems very much like, at least for the most part, living beings are not free.

And yet, as I will argue, the Buddhist theory of *dependent origination* is not metaphysical determinism. On the contrary, while Buddhists believe that freedom for ordinary beings is quite restricted, and that we are generally deluded about the meaning of our own lives and actions, freedom and meaning are never entirely lost in the viciously circular causality of *saṃsāra*. The Buddhist view of *karma* is, rather, premised on the idea that every mental event—every moment in our mind—is invested with the potential to initiate a line of transformation. As we will see, this sense of possibility is explicitly woven into Vasubandhu's philosophy of mind as he describes it in the AKBh. The freedom it grants is minute and momentary, and appears to leave very little room for what we take to be an ordinary meaningful life. Yet it is the wedge that can open up the mind to a universe of literally infinite freedom.

In line with the ideas discussed in previous chapters, we will see that the most quintessential, decisive "freedom" is the freedom from false views. Our narration of the story of Ajatasattu above began with the Buddha's instruction on the benefits of renunciation. But the story includes a preface. Before meeting the Buddha, Ajatasattu had asked the same question of numerous other renunciant masters, none of whom gave him a satisfying answer. He says of each that it was "just as if on being asked about a mango he were to describe a breadfruit-tree, or on being asked about a breadfruit-tree he were to describe a mango."[15] The English expression is "apples and oranges," but the point is clear; the other teachers failed to address the king's question. Remember, the king's question was a practical one: what is the benefit of this practice? What all the other teachers provided were abstract, doctrinal statements, and the result was that none of the other teachers engaged the king, who left each previous teacher disappointed.

Only the Buddha provided direct, practical answers to the king's question, rude though it was. The Buddha, then, is not able to open the king's "dhamma eye," because of his karmic defilements. But he is able, uniquely, to move the king forward. King Ajatasattu is unable to see the truth. But he is agitated by the world as it is, and he is interested in results. This practical standpoint seems to have provided him with a special protection against (egregiously) false views, and the ability to see the superiority of the Buddha's teachings. What propels him to find the Buddha, initially, is his dissatisfaction with his own mental state, and his unwillingness to accept things as they are presented to him. In this way, in his imperfection, he is a model for us ordinary beings, who—until our dhamma eye is opened—must rely upon our wits to reject false constructions wherever they arise. Only such skepticism, even cynicism, is capable of putting us on the path from false views to freedom. All the cynic lacks is the ability to see his own false views, and apply his method to his own mind.

BUDDHISM AND DETERMINISM

Modern discussions of freedom of the will and the capacity for moral responsibility are persistently centered around the problem of universal causal determinism. One standard way of posing the question is to ask whether I can be held responsible for an event today that, given the state of the universe one hundred years ago and the lawful progression of natural causes, was determined to happen. If everything is fully determined by natural laws, how can I be granted any agency, or causal power?[16] The nature of free will therefore depends upon the still larger question of the nature of causality. Agreement is difficult to find on either topic. Most philosophers today are compatibilists, believing that free will is compatible with determinism, but many have been, and remain, incompatibilists, believing either that we are not free, or that the universe is not deterministic.

It is a widely shared assumption among modern philosophers that libertarian views of free will must attribute freedom to some kind of causally independent *agent* or *self*—and this would appear to be exactly what the no-self doctrine denies.[17] When we see the Buddha not only denying the self but also affirming a doctrine of universal causality (everything in *saṃsāra* is the result of causes and conditions), we can understand why some modern interpreters believe he is advocating causal determinism. Mark Siderits, for instance, argues that Abhidharma philosophy denies the self at the level of *ultimate reality* by reducing it to a causal account of non-self parts. Yet Siderits emphasizes that at the level of *conventional reality* the self still plays an important role in explaining our ordinary experience and knowledge. At the level of conventional truth, then, there is a self that acts freely. This, for Siderits, amounts to a Buddhist reductionist version of compatibilism.[18]

Furthermore, Charles Goodman has argued that Buddhists should be (and often are) unrepentant determinists. In one passage, Goodman argues against the libertarian interpretation of Buddhism advocated by

Paul Griffiths, who argued that, for Vasubandhu, karmic causality provides important conditions, but not a deterministic causal account of action.[19] Goodman writes in response that, in fact, there is no nondeterminist reading of Vasubandhu. To state the argument very briefly, he says that the cause of an act for Vasubandhu can be only "one of three things": (1) the *parameters* generated by *karma* actually cause the act (which is determinism); (2) *nothing* causes the act (which is randomness); or (3) something else causes the act, which must be either (3a) a self (which is denied) or (3b) not a self (in which case, Goodman says, go back to [1] or [2]).

For a number of reasons, I am reticent to call the Abhidharma account a determinist one. First of all, I believe that Vasubandhu provides another option not mentioned by Goodman, and it is one that allows us to envision an alternative, quasi-libertarian event of willing that is enacted without an enduring self. That is, there is a (3b) option that is neither determined nor random. In the Abhidharma, mental events are determined to be "volitional" by nature. For Abhidharma philosophers, one omnipresent characteristic of all *citta* (mind) is *cetanā* ("volition" or, to preserve the verbal sense of the term, "intending").[20] So, I will argue, it is a mistake to say that, once we eliminate the self, we must choose between determinism and randomness. Mental events, in this schema, are by nature actions.[21] Goodman's argument neglects the possibility of a momentary, causally efficacious yet in a sense free, individual *cetanā*. This is, of course, not really a live option within contemporary philosophical circles, so it is hardly surprising that Goodman neglects it. Furthermore, we might well doubt that Buddhists themselves held to such a thing, were it not the case that *cetanā* so evidently plays the role of a causally efficacious element (*dharma*) in which the Abhidharma tradition locates both goal-directed intentionality and responsibility (though not the responsibility of an independent agent). And finally, even once convinced that Buddhists believe(d) in such a thing, we might simply dismiss it as an absurd and useless holdover of an ancient scholasticism. However, although I do not intend to defend it here at great length, it is my belief that *cetanā* represents a sensible, distinct option.

Perhaps the most insightful and comprehensive treatment of *cetanā* and its application to a reading of the problem of free will in Buddhism has been put forward by Karin Meyers. Meyers argues, quite sensibly—against an embarrassingly long history of mistaken interpreters—that the notion of *cetanā*, since it is conditioned, momentary, not-self, and, especially, sometimes operating *subconsciously*, is entirely insufficient to support an ordinary conception of free will.[22] My contention is not that *cetanā* supports an ordinary conception of free will. Rather, I will argue that *cetanā* provides the only kind of will to which Vasubandhu can acquiesce, which is a subtle thread, meditationally available, and effective only through accumulation.

One way that I see Vasubandhu's view as differing from the still helpful constructions of Siderits and Goodman is that he recognizes severe limitations on our psychological freedoms, but never entirely closes in on metaphysical determinism. It seems to me that Vasubandhu simply did not have the concept that would deny freedom as a metaphysical possibility.[23] Impersonal, metaphysical, causal determinism, according to which all of our actions and experiences are caused, mechanically, by nonsentient forces outside of our will—even down to the degree of attention and effort we dedicate to each given experience—may be a modern invention.[24] I say this in full awareness of the Buddha's definition of Dependent Origination—"When this exists, that arises" (*satīdaṃ bhavati*)—discussed in chapters 3 and 4, and Vasubandhu's adoption of this formula as the basis for knowledge.

I have shown that Vasubandhu believes that anything we wish to say *exists* must be subject to this kind of analytical, causal analysis. But as I have argued in chapter 4, causality is itself always determined through a conceptually constructed frame, which means that no causal frame is final. From an ultimate perspective, there is literally nothing to be said. The question, then, is whether the causal frame in which Dependent Origination is articulated—the Twelve Links—is a deterministic frame. As we will see, there are actions in this list that are responses to ideas—which we know, for Vasubandhu, are conceptual constructions themselves. Therefore, there can be no "ultimate" causal layer articulated in the Twelve Links. If there were causal determinism in the Twelve Links, there would be no possibility of freedom. Yet, as we will see, the actions that take place on the Twelve Links are described as ordinary choices—they are not described as determined.

An interesting comparison here with our apparent Buddhist determinism is the Sāṃkhya system, in which philosophers posit an elaborate psychophysical causal series (*prakṛti*) with which the soul (*puruṣa*) mistakenly identifies. *Prakṛti* is an inevitable outpouring of mind and matter—as we have seen, the Sāṃkhya philosophers even advocate the idea that the result resides in the cause, so causality is simply an unfolding of destiny.

The body and mind of each person is only a thoroughly embedded part of the larger flow of *prakṛti*. Yet at the same time, the *puruṣa* may be liberated from its entanglement with *prakṛti* through its clearly free development in self-awareness and knowledge. This is why, in the *Bhagavad Gīta*'s presentation of this set of ideas, Krishna explains to Arjuna that living beings reel, mechanically, like puppets on a string. In the same breath, however, he urges Arjuna to accept his role.[25] Where's the sense in that? If the causality that will bring about Arjuna's acceptance is predetermined, why bother with the urging? It would seem to be at least a pragmatic contradiction. The answer is, evidently, that when Krishna suggests that all of existence is inevitable, he does not mean to include the intentions of living beings.[26] The key to Krishna's famous *karma-yoga* method is the directive to disentangle one's intention from one's action, and thereby act without regard for the result. The historical flow of the world is inevitable, but intentions are still free.

I would submit that the Buddhist Abhidharma element (*dharma*) that accounts for intention (*cetanā*) preserves this assumption of metaphysical freedom, and I will explain some consequences of looking at things this way. The result is a reframing of the question of free will in Buddhism from a conversation about metaphysics into a larger discussion of the causes and conditions of one's mental life. The purpose of talking about the causes of the mind is not to convince us to ignore these minute, momentary events and shift our attention to the conventional level.[27] Rather, the purpose is, precisely, to *choose to act where we can really have an effect*. The Buddha's doctrine does, intentionally, call attention to the problem for our apparent freedom that arises with the awareness that our bodies and minds are *causally conditioned*—with disturbing effect, as Cioran intimates. For the causal story of our mental life, as told in the Twelve Links of Dependent Origination, and as elaborated in Abhidharma, shows that much of our worldview is, indeed, deluded and beyond our control. Consequently, we cannot simply change our perspectives directly—we are not acting freely in a traditional sense. But we *may* act in a way that slowly, incrementally, and indirectly conditions new future possibilities. This takes advantage of the unique place that our actions—minute as they may be—have in shaping our mental life. The moral lesson of Buddhist metaphysics is not that we are not ultimately responsible, but on the contrary that we can, and should, hold ourselves responsible for shaping our mental streams, and how our mental streams in turn affect the world.

ACTION (*KARMA*) AND VOLITION (*CETANĀ*) IN THE AKBH

Cetanā is a tremendously productive concept in Abhidharma philosophy. The word itself is derived from the common verbal root √*cit*, which means "perceive, know, appear."[28] The same root is also credited with producing the very common noun *citta*, a central term for mental events in Buddhist philosophy generally translated "mind" or "consciousness." As an adjective, *cetana* is occasionally used to mean "aware, conscious."[29] As a verbal noun, though, it is a technical term, and if we must translate it literally, inelegantly, we might say it means "being aware," "being conscious," or even "mentalizing."

But calling *cetanā* "mentalizing" certainly does not tell us much beyond its being likely to play a central role in the concept of mind. Within the AKBh's system, it is in fact the second of ten concepts categorized as universal "mental aspects" (*caitta*), that is, aspects of every mental event.[30] The other nine are crucial as well for a full understanding of the nature of mind in Abhidharma, but life is short, and I hope to make it clear why *cetanā* is particularly relevant to our discussion. Vasubandhu defines *cetanā* as "mental action that shapes the mind."[31] It is both *what a mental event does* ("mental action") and *the cause for a mind taking on a particular shape or aspect* ("that shapes the mind"). To understand *cetanā* properly, we will need to examine both aspects of this definition, but especially understand how they are conjoined in a single concept.

First, then, is *cetanā*'s definition as "mental action," which points to its crucial role in the explanation of *karma*. The hint that it was a kind of *karma* was there even in our noticing the verbal, active quality of the term *cetanā*; *karma*, after all, means "action." *Cetanā* as mental action is called the quintessence—the *svarūpa*—of *karma*.[32] As the modern Tibetan teacher Geshe Rabten puts it, it is "karma itself."[33] Vasubandhu defines *karma* as being "*cetanā* and that which arises from it."[34] This in fact includes three kinds of *karma*: actions of mind, of speech, and of body. Actions of body and speech are actions that arise from mental actions.

It is this connection between *cetanā* and other actions of body and speech that explains the common translation of *cetanā* as "volition." It is mental action, and it is capable of bringing about physical and vocal actions. This seems very much like an intention or will, in the sense of a purposeful and effective controlling aspect of mind. As Karin Meyers puts it, explaining her fine translation of *cetanā* as "intending," "most would agree that intention is a kind of pro-attitude directed towards an action or goal."[35] I will keep it to "volition," to prevent our confusing it with *āśaya*, which is explicitly articulated as a linguistically formulated intention.[36] *Cetanā* is an action, which can be a speech act, but to shape the wish to act in language is not the same as to perform the act.

In the context of his treatment of action and volition, Vasubandhu engages in some debate about whether bodily actions may persist through time, and this is resolved eventually by his argument that in fact *all things are momentary*. This entails the conclusion that all things disappear in the very moment of their birth. Apparent continuity is a false conceptual projection, like the appearance of the temporal unity of a flame that is in fact made up of countless minute explosions. We have seen this discussion already in chapter 4, but we did not note there that this argument sits right in the thick of the discussion of actions, and it allows Vasubandhu to conclude that what appear to be fluid bodily movements are actually just successive momentary events, better described individually as the "shape of the body just as it is under the force of mind."[37] Here I only bring this up to point out that Vasubandhu says that the body in a certain position must be so "under the force of mind" because without the mental impetus, the body would be "lifeless" (*jaḍa*) and therefore would not qualify as "action" (even granting that there is no motion in a momentary body).[38] This "force of mind" is surely the *cetanā*, the cause of bodily action.

What is important to note here, then, is that (at least for Vasubandhu) the momentariness of the action—the fact that it is only a particular shape of the body—does nothing to detract from its being called "action" or its being determined as caused by the mind. Nor is there any worry about "whose" *cetanā* is doing the causing, or the intending. The attribution of responsibility for these mental actions is entirely unambiguous: the *cetanā* is the action, and it does the causing. Agency and volition, then, are attributed to a momentary event. That fact in itself, I believe, allows our study of Vasubandhu to provide a new contribution to the known history of the philosophy of action. It will take some work, though, to decide how something momentary can be an action, let alone a morally significant action. Does it even make conceptual sense to call the *cetanā* "free"? There are reasons to doubt it.

First of all, the fact of momentariness also helps us understand an interesting characteristic of Vasubandhu's definition of *cetanā*, namely that the two parts of the definition use two different, but often interchangeable (as is declared at the opening of the Viṃś), terms for "mind"—*manas* and *citta*—to represent the agent mind of "mental action" and the patient mind of "shapes the mind," respectively. Under a general theory that everything is momentary, it makes sense that Vasubandhu would be reluctant to imply an equation of these two minds by using the same term for both. He is not saying that the mind shapes itself. Rather, he is saying that the mental action of *cetanā* at time t_1 shapes another mental event at some later time t_2. But if the mind is shaped by prior mental events, how can it be acting in any sense freely? How can it be "acting" at all?

This question brings us from the notion of "*karma*" as an activity enacted for a purpose to the more widely known notion of Buddhist *karma* as the mental impressions that bring about the positive or negative "karmic" results of morally significant actions. "*Karma*" as "action" is also karmic *conditioning*, or *saṃskāra*, which is the cause of a particular kind of rebirth. Here once again the concept of *cetanā* plays a central, defining role.

The Buddhist causal account of karmic conditioning—how it is that beings are unendingly trapped in birth after rebirth—is of course most famously encapsulated in the Twelve Links in the Chain of Dependent Origination. "Conditioning" (*saṃskāra*) is the second of the twelve—it is caused by the first link in the chain, "ignorance," and, in turn, it is the cause of the third link, "consciousness." The idea is that, out of ignorance, we are constantly acting foolishly in such a way that we generate karmic impressions on our mental stream, which in turn leads to our taking on the particular form of consciousness of our next rebirth. For example, if I kill someone out of vengeance, thinking that I have really taken care of things, that ignorant act can generate a karmic impression that causes me to be reborn as a hell being—and so after my death I may take on the specific consciousness of a hell being and be reborn in hell. In a general sense, though, "conditioning" (*saṃskāra*) may be said to sit in for all twelve of the Twelve Links. Everything in *saṃsāra* is impermanent and subject to the flux of causes and conditions. Only space and *nirvāṇa* and "cessations" are unconditioned (and, for Vasubandhu as a commentator, none of these count as real entities, since they have no recognizable causal capacities).

Vasubandhu explains the Twelve Links from several different angles in the AKBh (only one of which was accepted by the Vaibhāṣikas),[39] and in one explanation, he shows how the twelve links may be understood to represent activities over the course of three separate lives—the first two in a past life, the next seven in the current life, and the final three in a future life.[40] In that explanation, he says that when *saṃskāra* is understood to exist in a previous life, it should be understood as *all the karma of that life*. Thus one's karmic conditioning (*saṃskāra*) is the combined karmic result of one's previous actions.[41] This brings to mind the final argument of the AKBh, which we discussed at the conclusion to chapter 2. In that argument, Vasubandhu says that the specific, next rebirth results from whatever *karma* predominates amongst all of a living being's previous actions; here, he gives this accumulation the name *saṃskāra*.

In another explanation, Vasubandhu says how the links may be understood as, all twelve together, always real in every single moment. There, "conditioning" (*saṃskāra*) is described simply as *cetanā*. Clearly, then, *cetanā* is fundamental to *saṃskāra*. It is *cetanā* that is caused by ignorance (*avidya*) and, in turn, causes consciousness (*vijñāna*) to take on a particular form. It is *cetanā*, volition, that enacts the conditioning of conditioned existence.

In a third analysis of the twelve links, illustrated in table 6.1, Vasubandhu divides them into three separate categories: "defilements" (*kleśa*), "actions" (*karma*), and "things" (*vastu*).[42]

Here Vasubandhu classifies *saṃskāra*, of course, as an "action" (*karma*), which once again underlines its identification with *cetanā*. I find this characterization particularly useful, because to call a causal source an "action" as opposed to a "defilement" or a "thing" suggests, of course, agency. Recall, in this context, the difference between the "shape" produced by the body, which was not to be called an "action" since without a mental cause it was deemed "lifeless" (*jaḍa*). This would be true *even of*

TABLE 6.1 AKBh III.26 on the Three Classifications of the Twelve Links

DEFILEMENT (*KLEŚA*)	ACTION (*KARMA*)	THING (FOUNDATION) (*VASTU*)
ignorance (*avidya*)	*saṃskāra*	consciousness (*vijñāna*)
thirst (*tṛṣṇā*)	being (*bhava*)	name and form (*nāmarūpa*)
attachment (*upādāna*)		six sense organs (*āyatana*)
		contact (*sparśa*)
		sensation (*vedanā*)
		birth (*jāti*)
		old age and death (*jarāmaraṇa*)

a moving body, since the issue is not whether a body moves (because in a universe of momentary events nothing truly moves), but whether it is a particular kind of momentary entity called an *action*.

As an extension of this third analysis of the twelve links, Vasubandhu lists how the causal flow from each link may be understood under the classes of defilements, actions, and things. Here what makes something an action is helpfully clarified by noting the categories through which actions operate. I have summarized this classification here:

AKBH III.27 ON CAUSAL RELATIONS AMONG DEFILEMENTS, ACTIONS, AND THINGS:

DEFILEMENTS THAT CAUSE DEFILEMENTS

thirst → attachment

DEFILEMENTS THAT CAUSE ACTIONS

attachment → being[43]

ignorance → *saṃskāra*

ACTIONS THAT CAUSE THINGS

saṃskāra → consciousness

being → birth

THINGS THAT CAUSE THINGS

consciousness → name and form

name and form → six sensory organs

[*should be here*: six sensory organs → contact]

contact → sensation

birth → old age and death

THINGS THAT CAUSE DEFILEMENTS

sensation → thirst

Implication: old age and death → ignorance

Notice that both of the elements that are said to cause actions are "defilements"—that is, negative mental qualities. This represents the standard story that we act out of desire and ignorance. In all, defilements cause both (subsequent) defilements and actions, actions cause only things, and things cause both (subsequent) things and defilements.

Note that defilements do not cause things; things do not cause actions; and actions cause neither (subsequent) actions nor defilements. I do not want to overstate the significance of this revelation, but it seems to express a view of causality among elements that preserves our traditional intuitions about which aspects of our experience are willful, and which are not. If the twelve links expressed a deterministic inevitability—if we were robotically impelled by their causal impetus—then actions might just as well be caused by "things" as "defilements"—but they are not. In the categories supplied, it is only once a "thing" generates a "defilement"—a cognitive and emotional distortion—that it becomes capable of conditioning an action. I do not think it is too much of a stretch to say that this interpretive structure affirms that our actions, even at the level of momentary mental events, are "caused" by responses to cognitive *content*.[44] This is not be taken as a declaration of libertarian free will, but it certainly foregrounds the decision-making power of mental action. To me, this suggests that actions are causally conditioned by knowledge (or lack thereof). Our *actions* are our (willful?) responses to how we feel and what we know.

The fact that the *content* that conditions our actions is called a "defilement" supports a reading of "actions" as causal events with this peculiar structure. For it is *false* conceptualizations that condition actions. Yet here we see the window for conventionally "free" action closing even further. If it is our cognitive content that conditions our actions, our actions are *always* deluded responses to mistaken self-constructions. In fact, this may be not so much a closing of the window as an explanation of why Buddhists feel the window is already so nearly closed. The false view of self conditions our choices, and the ubiquity of this false view—the fundamental fact that, in *saṃsāra*, our every "contentful" thought is deluded—explains why we remain trapped. The only properly free "volition" in such a case would be one that is unfettered by "content"—that avoids acting on such a false view. With all content under suspicion, it is difficult to imagine any proper action, before enlightenment, except perhaps a choice to *refrain* from action. Only such a *negative* "volition" would seem capable of stopping the cycle. It is perhaps unsurprising, then, that the vows taken by Buddhist monks and lay followers are primarily lists of actions *not to be taken*. The vow-taker replaces his or her ordinary response to a cognitive or emotional defilement—an action—with a nonaction enjoined in the wise rulings of the Buddha.

The Three Natures view has a similarly "negative" perspective on the content of our awareness—the fabricated nature—and perhaps the equanimity we are instructed to cultivate, in order to see beyond the bias of views, is another expression of the principle already at work here, in the definition of *cetanā* as conditioning action: the best attitude to cultivate toward one's own views is detachment.

Central to our delusion is that we tend to overestimate the degree of "intentional" control we exercise over our actions when we perform them (the illusion of the self as controller), while we underestimate the degree to which we can cultivate ourselves and change our capacities to perform actions in the future (the illusion of the self as unchanging). Given our cognitive and affective weaknesses, we would expect that to correct for our delusions we should not be told to engage in world-changing acts of heroism, but rather to engage repeatedly in acts that condition our future possibilities. That is, we would expect that instead of being taught to calculate and enact as best we can whatever action will have the greatest positive result, we should be taught, once again, to take vows.

Vows may be thought of as preventing negative actions by intervening in the causal stream of dependent origination between defilements and actions; but they do so through a peculiar conditioning structure, whereby a physical and verbal act is taken to condition a future mental stream. When you take a vow, you are not performing any obviously beneficial act at that moment, but you are transforming your mental continuum so that when the occasion for a moral act arises, you are "conditioned" to act properly. And it is not the good action itself but the *taking of the vow*, of course, which is *the key Buddhist moral act*—the act that the Buddha enjoined for his followers more than any other act, including generosity and meditation.[45] Similarly, the central moral distinction in Buddhist life, between those who are on the path and those who are still, definitively trapped in *saṃsāra*, is that between those who have taken monastic vows and those who have not.

Paradigmatic as they may be, however, vows are only one of many practical methods prescribed by the Buddha to help his disciples advance toward liberation in spite of their (our) ignorance and self-destructive tendencies. Surely all of the Buddha's teachings can be taken this way, especially when they are understood from the Mahāyāna perspective as "skillful means," as the appropriate teachings for given disciples—appropriate although false, because those disciples are not really capable of understanding the ultimate truth. And no disciples are capable of understanding the ultimate truth; it is by its nature inconceivable. The Buddha's doctrines are, therefore, "right view" in the sense that when they are properly internalized, they counter false tendencies. In the language of the previous chapter, we could say that they are false from the intentional perspective, but *causally* beneficial because, like vows, they appear in the mental stream of the person to whom they are directed in such a way that at the appropriate time that person's mental stream, under their influence, leads to good actions.

To return to our opening point, we can see that the Ābhidharmika account of mental action—as a momentary, apparently willful event that has future consequences—preserves the moral responsibility we ascribe to free choices without calling the agent a person or a self. It is only actions (*karma*) that have moral recompense; birth leads inevitably to death, but such a causal result is in no way morally charged. Of course, the tragedy and pathos of life within the cycle of *saṃsāra* are captured here in the reduction of our perceived freedom of choice to momentary responses to limited, almost completely distorted, impressions. It acknowledges the extreme *lack* of freedom that results from our cognitive and emotional limitations. For the most part, since we do not understand how *karma* really works, we act blindly, and because we do not understand the big picture, we place inordinate value on relatively meaningless things. Yet our whole karmic situation—in fact, all of conditioned existence—is brought about by nothing but the combined conditioning (*saṃskāra*) that just is this willful activity (*cetanā*). The appropriate response, therefore, is not to throw up one's hands and declare all decisions meaningless or unfree, but to seek to take charge of the situation by moving onto the path to liberation.

Notice that this kind of advice would be an entirely irrelevant and useless response to a recognition of ultimate meaninglessness or a *metaphysical* lack of freedom, in the same way that it would be entirely inappropriate to say to Arjuna that he should accept his inevitable role, were the acceptance just as inevitable as the role. But as I read both traditions, small acts of volition are available options, and their consequences accumulate, massively, over time. My view is, therefore, that the question of metaphysical necessity—so crucial to modern discussions of free will—plays no part in Vasubandhu's work. Admittedly, it is tempting to say that Vasubandhu's is a new form of compatibilism—one that recognizes free agency within momentary thought-events, and therefore accepts the possibility, at least in principle, that meaningful freedom needs no changes, options, or temporal extension. But what makes this compatibilism and not simply a rejection of the question—or a failure to ask it?

Modern compatibilism generally reinvigorates our commonsense views of agency against a backdrop of metaphysical determinism. What Vasubandhu does, on the contrary, denies commonsense agency (as stymied by ignorance), but leaves open a small window in order to allow for the justness of karmic recompense and the gradual, cumulative effectiveness of the path. Thus Vasubandhu would reject modern compatibilism *both* for its retention of commonsense agency *and* for its affirmation of metaphysical determinism (probably). Yet there is no argument here in favor of *incompatibilism*, either—denying the possibility of meaningful freedom in a deterministic world—except to the extent that Vasubandhu, with all Buddhists, rejects fatalism.[46] Premodern Buddhist thought simply does not engage with the problem of free will in this sense. Our bondage is the conditioned ignorance and attachment that make us act in ways that, if we saw things more clearly, we would not act.

CUMULATIVE *KARMA* AND THE LINE OF ANTS

Rather than worrying further about the superimposed question of free will and determinism, then, a more fruitful direction here is available in Vasubandhu's discussion of the moral significance of action in his argument against the notion of an "agent" (*kartṛ*), which we discussed at the end of chapter 2. In that passage, which I called the "end point" of the AKBh, Vasubandhu explained that the action that "shines forth at death" and so quite literally *makes you who you are* (in your next rebirth) is just whichever *karma* (read *cetanā*) is "weightier, or proximate, or reinforced by practice." Thus, since every result is conditioned by many causes, each *cetanā*, which conditions the mental stream, is always only *one action among many*. In order for a *cetanā* to gain its status as "cause" of a proper result, it is necessary for it to be conjoined in causal potency with other *cetanās*. Unless you do something very dramatic just before you die, it is the accumulation of numerous actions throughout your life that will shape your consciousness at death, and therefore the specific kind of body you take on in your next rebirth. Let us call this Vasubandhu's theory of *cumulative karmic causality*.

In chapter 2 I discussed the significance of this fact for Buddhist religious practice: if every act had its own individual, inevitable result, it would be impossible to alter *karma*'s results through repentance and prayer. Here I would like to apply the same point to the wider question of moral agency—what shape moral agency takes under this reductionist view—and tie it back to what I take to be Vasubandhu's most evocative metaphor for the apparent, but unreal, combination: the line of ants.

The theme of Vasubandhu's Yogācāra writings is the careful distinction between the way things appear, which is shot through with a false reification of the self, and the way things are truly caused. As emphasized in the last chapter, the Three Natures doctrine distinguishes two causal stories—the apparent causal story (how an elephant is born, caught, and brought to the stage; or, the person is born), and the true causal story (how a magician produces the trick; or, the mental seeds in the karmic storehouse bring about an illusory appearance). Since I have claimed that this distinction harkens back to the distinction between false conceptual constructions and real causes in Abhidharma, it ought to be possible to think through this distinction using not just the metaphor of the magical elephant, but the line of ants as well.

When Vasubandhu brings forward the analogy, he says that just as where ants make up a line, but in fact there is no "line," only a group of ants, so too all ordinarily apparent entities that have some "shape" are only structured in this way due to a mental construction, an idea (*saṃjñā*); in truth, they are made up of distinct parts that, when considered closely, cause the "shape" to dissolve. Other examples similar to the line of ants are elephants or armies arranged in a mass, which can appear to have some distinct shape, but in fact are *just* the individuals. There is no "whole" there, except as a mental construction.[47] We adduced in chapter 3 the further example of the Pointilist paintings of Seurat and Signac, which act as proofs of the mental construction of shape, depth, and color. As I indicated there, this argument about apparent wholes is internally connected to Vasubandhu's argument about the apparent wholeness and continuity of the self. The issue of personal identity, for Buddhists, is at stake in their claims that wholes do not exist over and above their parts, for otherwise there could be no denying that people are real entities, at least as defined as the wholes resulting from the combination of the *skandhas*.

It is entirely sensible to accept the *appearance* of the self, though, without accepting that there is any basis to the unity of the many parts that are taken together in that whole. In this context the unity of the self *across time* is no different from its apparent unity across distinct physical and mental parts. The analogy of the whirling firebrand, which makes a circle, or the flame seeming to move across a field, makes this point clear: we can have motion, and change, and the appearance of a singular identity across that change, while acknowledging that the entities that underlie the apparent unity are distinct, even if they are causally related. It is, as Vasubandhu says, only cause and effect.

Where the question for this chapter—the question of moral agency—comes into play, then, is in the relation between *cetanā*, which is a momentary, *real* mental cause, and the higher-level, false constructions of conscious will and human agency. If I normally think that I act freely, in the conventional sense of choosing everything about how I live, and how I react to situations presented to me, then I am deluded. Ordinary free will is clearly a false projection: the agent self that sees itself as acting is a false projection; the cognitive activities that we ordinarily take to make up a choice—reviewing options and selecting among them, for instance—are complex and therefore reducible to numerous parts, out of which no "whole" may be reconstructed; and, as we have discussed above, most of my choices, if not *all* of my choices, "free" though they may seem, are limited to the narrow range of possibilities that my human mind, with its particular tendencies and training, is capable to enact. Attached and deluded, my thoughts are constrained to the range of their conceptual contents. I see the world and react, always, within the field of my own capacities, interests, and biases. Thus, if the Buddha is right, what I take to be a "free" decision is a false appearance, and the actions that I undertake based upon such decisions are conditioned by countless factors beyond anything like "control," at least in that moment.

The question at issue, then, is: if those concepts are delusory, what are the *real* entities that make them up? What are the true conditioning causes? If my biases and my agency are the "line of ants," what are the *ants*? For Yogācārins, the causes of the world are mental events—seeds in the storehouse consciousness ripen into appearances; but what *causes* those seeds? Well, of course, *karma*. Actions that shape the mind: *karma, saṃskāra, cetanā*.

What does it mean, then, to take each momentary *cetanā* in this way, as one *ant* in an apparent line of ants? If we agree that the quintessential Buddhist *cetanā* is the vow, then perhaps the ideal colony is the monastic *saṃgha*. This suggests to me a compelling theory that Buddhist vows and Vinaya literature should be read primarily as tools for the effective organization of society, given the nature of the human minds out of which that society is inevitably constituted. Yet to elaborate this in detail would take us too far afield. In any case, before we can understand the workings of the collective of individuals, we must understand the collective *that is* the "individual." For the time being, therefore, my intent is to use the ant colony as an analogy for the individual, the collective activity of the many moments of *cetanā* that make up what we perceive as a person's intentional activities.

In addition to ants appearing visually as a whole mass from a distance, ants also appear to share a crucial *behavioral* similarity with masses of *cetanās*, which is that they are very clever, taken together, though individually, they are fools. It is only out of their collective behavior that the apparent intelligence of the colony appears. This apparent arising of complex intelligence out of the collective behavior of apparently simple ants is probably not what Vasubandhu was after in his analogy of the "line of ants" appearing as a "line" when there is no line, only ants. But it is possible, and the mere possibility points the way to a fruitful investigation of the analogy. The discussion from here to the end of the chapter is rooted in my own, anecdotal experience, and it should be taken as only speculative in its application to Vasubandhu's texts. I am shifting, thus, from a primarily interpretive analysis of Vasubandhu's views to one that is more constructive, and suggestive. My hope from here to the end of the chapter is to illuminate the potential, if as yet unrealized, ethical significance of views that Vasubandhu did clearly hold.

I submit the following story as suggestive of how we might read the analogy of the line of ants. I once spent a week in a turquoise-painted hotel room overlooking the Indian Ocean on the island of Lamu off the east coast of Kenya (nice place, I recommend it). One morning, I awoke to the smell of rain and saw, to my great surprise, that someone had painted a dark red stripe from one window, up the wall to the ceiling, over the ceiling, to the other window. Not only did this design choice seem alien, it seemed incredible that I had somehow not noticed it before. Did I come in late last night and fall asleep without even looking around the room? Why would the hotel have done this? They clearly took a lot of time, making the line straight, and the angles just so. As I was wondering this, staring at the line, my eyes refocused and the line dissolved into masses of moving ants. I realized with a shock that I was staring at an ant colony on the move to a new location after a rainstorm had flooded its previous home. Its path just happened to pass through my hotel room. Now I began to marvel anew at the precise shape created by this line of ants—precision that I had only moments before attributed to the attentive workmanship of the hotel's painter. This is a true story, and it proves that a line of ants can generate the appearance not only of a "shape," but of an intention as well.

We know (thanks to E. O. Wilson) that ants communicate with one another by scent. The reason the trail across my hotel room was so seemingly solid was that all of the ants were following scent trails left by previous ants. No individual ant ever intends to send a signal to other ants—each ant's limited genetic programming issues in mechanical behaviors that are well below anything resembling an "intention." Yet together it is difficult to deny the appeal of the term. A classic example is the ants' method of efficiently transporting food back to the nest, once it is found. Ants foraging for food lay pheromone trails, and they like to follow pheromone trails, the stronger the better. If they go back and forth on a trail, that doubles the strength of the trail, and makes it a preferred trail over one that's only been traveled once. Whatever path, among the many pheromone paths made by many foraging ants, happens to be the shortest path to the food, will have ants going back and forth more quickly than the others. More trips means a stronger pheromone path, which attracts more ants, and the process builds. The result is that eventually most of the ants are following the shortest path to the food. The simple behavior of each ant, replicated many times, *explains in its entirety* their behavior, without the need for any "intention" to bring the food home as efficiently as possible along a shared path. Thus, using Occam's razor, we can discount the possibility of an "intention" as a cause. There is no "intention" behind ant behavior.

If it is thought that there is no intention in the individual ant, but the ant's DNA (or body) contains the intention, this must be countered by an awareness that ant DNA came about through natural selection. It may seem inconceivable that ants could have settled upon this complex behavior (though it is simpler than it looks at first) without an intention. But this is the crux of what Daniel Dennett calls "Darwin's dangerous idea": we can explain apparent teleology via blind causes, over time.[48]

Ants then provide a wonderful example of action without an agent—it is only cause and effect. I would propose that in the "line of ants" analogy, where the apparent agency is only cause and effect—as each "ant" is analogized to a mental event—the *cetanā* is the activity of the ant *laying down pheromones*. It is *cetanā* that conditions the future tendencies, the shape of the *next* thought(s). *Cetanā* is the mental quality that connects the three times, that provides the link in the chain. In Abhidharma, it is *cetanā* that is the mental grasping that affirms, or does not, the self-identification with the mind's present activity. It either says "yes" or "no" or nothing to whatever the mind is doing; it either grasps the present thought as one's own identity, or it does not. That, for a Buddhist (as for a Sāṃkhya), is what it means to engage in *karma*. To lay metaphor on metaphor, we might say that what *cetanā* does is throw up its tag on the present thought, labeling the present experience with an identity marker. The next thought will follow, see the tag, and be attracted to it, as "my" identity. In this way, *cetanā* is not exactly "free" in any traditional sense, since it does nothing but enact a kind of "grasping" of the content of the present thought; it does not frame or choose the content, and it is conditioned by the previous tendencies of previous thoughts to place a mark on the way.

Central to Buddhist training is the ability to free oneself from one's previous identity-constructing patterns, which must mean being able to gradually transform the patterns laid by countless previous *cetanās*. It seems to me possible that, with training, one could learn to disassociate from particular mental events, to realize that one is no longer the person who committed a given act in the past, and one will no longer be this mental event in the future. Such a transformation might eventually allow one to refrain from "volition" entirely, and stop generating *karma*.

DEEP TIME ON THE BODHISATTVA PATH

It is remarkable what can be accomplished in a single human life (for impressive examples, see the obituary section in today's *New York Times*). Yet Buddhists speak of the countless rebirths in our past, as well as our present lives, as for the most part having been wasted, each good deed cancelled out by bad, each new skill and acquisition erased by death. The larger perspective drains meaning, as we cycle from rebirth to redeath. For Buddhists, the world does not preserve our accomplishments. But if they can be lined up, as in the Buddha's *Jātaka* stories, so that achievement builds upon achievement, our unending lives provide us the possibility of truly remarkable development, even if it must be built one mental moment at a time. This broadening of the frame provides for Mahāyāna—the path to Buddhahood—its distinctive vision.

Although it is not a strongly emphasized aspect of the Mahāyāna path, one meaning of the "Great Way's" *greatness* is its duration—that is, how long it takes to reach the goal of Buddhahood. The time it takes to complete the bodhisattva path is phenomenally longer than the path of the hearer. Jan Nattier, in *A Few Good Men*, emphasizes the machismo of the bodhisattva path expressed in the *Inquiry of Ugra* (*Ugraparipṛcchā*), which sets the Mahāyāna practitioner apart from his contemporaries.[49] The longer path is for those of great will, endurance, and aspiration. Yet paired with the greatness of sheer gumption that accompanies the Mahāyāna path is the greatness of the intended accomplishment. It is an obvious truism that a longer path provides more opportunities, but it is seldom noted just what is implied in changing the path from an immediate, meditative accomplishment to a practice that is intended to last, quite literally, countless lifetimes.[50]

Surely the best-known meditator in pre-tantric Mahāyāna was Asaṅga. The famous story of his meditative practices, which appears in his brother Vasubandhu's biography, is a wonderful exemplification of the virtue of endurance characteristic of the Mahāyāna path. Asaṅga is said to have spent twelve years meditating in a cave, but every three years he would give up. Each time, after meditating for a period of three years, he came down from his mountain retreat discouraged at having failed to receive a vision of Maitreya. Each time, he encountered someone who exemplified endurance, and so would return to his cave convinced that he should go on. The first vision was of a rock that had been worn away around a bird's nest just by the passing of the birds' wings; feather on rock, again and again, wore away the stone. The second vision was of drops of water, one at a time, wearing away stone. The third vision was of a man polishing pieces of iron into needles using just a cotton cloth. In each case, Asaṅga would return to his cave with renewed perseverance. These analogies exemplify the power of cumulative causality, of great results accrued from repeated, purposeful application in countless individual mental moments.

The sheer length of the path, as newly defined in Mahāyāna, provides an entirely different horizon of possibilities for personal transformation. Whatever possibilities are presented to a monk attempting to do his best to attain liberation in one life, his time is limited by the human lifespan. Once a practitioner accepts that the current lifetime is likely only one of many lifetimes (past, present, and future) spent gathering accomplishments toward liberation, there dawns a new possibility for openness and confidence about future achievement. If *nirvāṇa* is conceivably within your grasp in this lifetime, then ten or twenty lives more may well be enough, assuming your opportunities and your discipline hold out.

Along with this new confidence in accomplishment may come, as well, a new perspective on just what it is possible to attain. For if *nirvāṇa* is in your grasp, *why stop there?* This is, perhaps, the logic that led to acceptance of the path to Buddhahood and the expansive, visionary, bodhisattva attainments imaged in Mahāyāna literature. As the goal is expanded to include the total transformation of endless universes, the path of practice comes to be envisioned in a Buddhist version of what geologists call "deep time."

In his book *Time's Arrow, Time's Cycle*, Stephen Jay Gould writes about the discovery of "deep time" in geology, and how that discovery opened up, for Darwin, the possibility of the slow mechanism of evolution by natural selection. As a scientific discovery, "deep time" is merely a fact about the age of the earth: that it is more than four billion years old. Yet it is one thing to know this fact, and another to see its importance for understanding the workings of nature. Gould's book is a study of the difficulty and the promise of this earth-shattering temporal concept. Above all, the concept allows for the cumulative effects of extremely slow, but steady, causal processes. This is what deep time meant for Darwin: immense, transformative results can come from minute effects, massively repeated. The idea that breeding practices—selection—can change the appearance and behavior of animals only opens up into the idea of the differentiation of species if the small, visible transformations from one generation to the next can be imaginatively transposed into the massive differences between species. The transformation from ape to human that seems inconceivable when imagined as having taken place across one or ten generations and strains credulity in a hundred generations, becomes entirely believable, even comprehensible, given two hundred fifty thousand generations. The shift in scale opens up new vistas of transformation.

We can see Buddhist practitioners thinking in terms of cumulative causality in deep time as the target of meditative practice shifts toward a distant, rather than a near, future. Once framed by distant goals, our present actions take on a different cast. Our immediate actions are to be intended not only to allow us to reach those goals but, crucially, to condition ourselves to continue on the path toward them. The goal today is no longer simply to try to *act like* a perfect being ("What would Buddha do . . . ?"), but rather to try to *become* one. In the framework of deep time, this is not a presumptuous or unrealistic goal—it is, in fact, *far more pragmatic and realistic*, given its assumptions, than the idea of attempting, from where you are now, to emulate greatness. Am I capable of meditating with enough diligence, for enough time, in the proper way, to achieve enlightenment? Not likely. Am I capable of taking a step on the path, and trying to build a pattern of fruitful practice into my behavior? Unquestionably. And, in the context of deep time's message of cumulative causality, whatever I do to advance myself on the path, assuming I stay on the path, becomes a definite, pragmatic step toward even the most distant goal—it is, in fact, the only kind of step there is. Each mental event paves the way for the next, and together, over limitless eons, they pave the Great Way.

In this context, we can see the moral significance of Vasubandhu's insistence that the *present* is the only reality. Let us say that *cetanā* is best understood as a momentary measure of "pro-attitude" about what is occurring in the present mental moment.[51] It is not the action itself; it is not its content; it is only a part. It gains potential significance, however, from its being linked, causally, to future mental moments. Thus, ironically, whereas the momentary event is itself not only minute but *meaningless*, its momentariness and its causal potency are what make it *substantial*. Given this reading of the causal potential of the *cetanā*, the crucial moral question becomes how one is "taking" or "grasping" (*grahaṇa*) one's own present experience—secondarily how one interprets it conceptually, but primarily how, in each moment, one engages with (or disengages from) one's own mental representations. *Cetanā*—here the quintessence of *karma*—is limited to the present moment, but by the same token, it is always fully available. And the path it provides is slow and gradual, but extends from the restrictive cage of one's own attachments to the inconceivable liberation of a Buddha—with countless intermediate improvements along the way.

CONCLUSION: IDENTITY-CONSTRUCTION, CONTINGENCY, AND THE GOALS OF BUDDHIST ETHICS

My daughter Etta wants to play basketball today. Why? Well, it is a nice day, and she loves basketball. When we say, "She loves basketball," we are explaining her choice by appealing to a kind of stable state of affairs, which makes it clear she's going to want to play when she can. It is her disposition. I could say, by way of further explanation, that she plays after school every day with a regular group of playmates. I could say that basketball is her thing, and she's unstoppable. She brings her own basketball to school. But all of this is just a way to characterize a patterned set of desires.

Philosophers traditionally say that these are the "reasons" or the "justifications" for her choice to play basketball, but from the perspective of this chapter, *reasons* are only a shorthand—a construction—that makes useful, digestible sense of an extremely complex and intricate causal story.[52] Clearly the "nice day" is outside her control, and so cannot be seen as her own enactment. But what is *under* her control? For instance, why does she have her own basketball in the first place? Why does she have a group of playmates that she can rely on to have some kind of pick-up game every day after school? And most importantly, *why does she love to play basketball*? Considered from a causal perspective, a present disposition to play basketball is not something Etta *enacts*; it is not even a *thing*.

If we attempt to explain Etta's wanting to play basketball as an abstract fact, we are lost. There is a "brute fact" quality to the dispositional state of a person's mind that refuses explanation and, for some, satisfies the needs of explanation in itself.[53] At the same time, it is not only possible, but quite useful and instructive, to break down and describe the conditions out of which the love of basketball is constituted—even though they are multiple, perhaps endless. Our various modern academic disciplines—biology, psychology, sociology, history—have equipped us to begin to elucidate the causes.

First off, we have the body itself. Etta is healthy, and it is just part of a healthy ten-year-old human body-and-mind to love running around and trying stuff out—playing. So a significant set of conditions are those that keep the body up and running in this way and thus support the desire to play: regular exercise, nutrition, freedom from debilitating diseases and accidents, a good night's sleep.

These conditions are, of course, themselves conditioned. As a parent I can take some of the credit, for having provided food and insisting on sleep. I also bought the basketball. I might like to take credit also for my daughter's genetic heritage, though of course I "didn't build that."[54] Etta's health certainly relies upon genes from her mother and me. Her health is also indebted to the modern American medical practice of universal vaccination against common childhood diseases, and her terrific pediatrician has kept her occasional minor ailments from becoming a real pain and a real drain on her resources. She's never had a serious illness, but she did have an itchy foot problem one summer that I can imagine might have, in a previous generation, with lesser medical treatment and less comfortable shoes, diminished her love of running and jumping. So some credit for her desire to play has to go to the designers of athletic equipment, too. Each of these conditions rests on still others. My daughter has also had clean water, plentiful food, and safe streets. For these larger blessings I credit relatively good governance, together with a large slice of having-been-born-in-the-right-place-at-the-right-time.

The psychological conditions are also endless. In order to feel like playing today, Etta needs to be *in the mood* for it. Kids get tired, depressed, upset about this or that, or they just feel like doing something else. My daughter (these days) happens to be *always* in the mood to play pick-up basketball. So she's not (these days) susceptible to depression or the social concerns of other girls. Of course, in order to love the game Etta needs to be free of mental illness. But the fact that a girl of ten years old today *can* feel as free and comfortable as she does to play basketball in the playground with mostly boys is not something to take for granted; it is the result of more than a century of feminist struggle. It has deep, deep history, and on a planetary scale it is preciously rare. This brings us from psychological to social and historical conditions.

The fullness of Etta's enjoyment of basketball would probably not be possible without the psychological comfort that comes from social approval—approval from her peers, from her teachers, and from her family. In previous generations, it was far more difficult for women who enjoyed being athletes. Etta's great-grandmother—my grandmother—was a lover of basketball who wanted to be a gym teacher. Yet she was "diagnosed" with an overly large heart, and kept on bed rest for a time, though she suffered no symptoms. Her enormous heart did nothing to prevent her living past one hundred, but as a child her family required that she give up on her athletic dreams. Today, I cannot think of anyone who disapproves of my daughter playing basketball. But, truth be told, she is the only girl in her class who plays with this freedom from ambivalence; she is the only girl who dresses in basketball shorts and t-shirts. She complains that the other girls double-dribble and travel and do not see the big deal. This is not a sign of their lack of athletic ability (many play soccer quite well on the weekends); it is a sign of their lack of commitment on the play yard. A possible explanation is that they are hampered socially (or, they choose to appear so). They may care that they are perceived as girls. Etta is just a bit younger than they are—she is the youngest in her class—so that may contribute as a causal factor as well, if they are on their way to being preteens, and she is further behind them in this.

This is all, of course, thoroughly unscientific in its assessment. What are the real conditions for Etta's atypical unselfconsciousness? A Buddha would see all of these causes and conditions directly; I can only gesture and approximate. The point I am making is that our social sciences—especially psychology and sociology—provide us with tools to tell causal stories that the Buddha summarized as *karma*. They do not need to be exactly accurate to suggest that *there are some* conditions in operation of this kind.

In addition, we have the long history of the game of basketball, not just as a professional sport (important to its continued, broad acceptance), but particularly as a game among children. It is just fun to play. It is fun to bounce the ball, throw it in the hoop, try to steal the ball from another player, and so on. Just fun. But it did not arise out of nowhere. Children have played the game for more than a hundred years. The development of the ball, the selection of the proper height for the basket, the net so you can see when the ball's gone through, the rules against traveling and double-dribbling, and so on—all of this makes it *more fun to play*, so that by the time Etta was exposed to the game on the play yard she was, as an energetic, healthy kid, likely to enjoy it. Genes come in here too. Not just my grandmother, but my wife loved basketball. But that's just in the last couple of generations. If we are talking about the fun of throwing a ball, of play, of competition, it is difficult to disentangle the history of the game from the history of the human species as a whole, even from primates, or mammals. But basketball itself has a very recent, local history, having been invented by a late-nineteenth-century gym teacher as a game that rewards agility rather than strength. Etta is not tall or strong, but she is fast.

When we say that it is a disposition of Etta's that she *wants to play basketball*, then, we understand that this disposition is dependent upon, and in a sense constituted by, many additional qualities that we can safely attribute to Etta (she lives after the twentieth century, her parents approve, she is relatively healthy, she likes the experience of a game that doesn't require more strength than agility, there are welcoming pick-up games at her play yard, etc.), and that these are *also* dependent facts. And yet we have no trouble affirming that *love of basketball is a part of who Etta is, what she is like*. In this sense, she is who she is, and at the same time her identity is dependent upon contingencies: some just luck, some deeply embedded in the history of the world, in the nature of the cosmos—but all contingent, mostly good fortune.

We could imagine a world arising with Etta, but no basketball; she could find another sport. But how many of those contingencies could we hypothetically eliminate before we began to doubt we were still imagining *Etta*? Is it still Etta if we imagine her as a male soldier in Sparta in 500 BCE? The Buddhist view is that the contingencies that make up her identity are the results of her actions—her *karma*. And the world in which she finds herself, Vasubandhu tells us, is the collective result of the actions of the living beings born here.[55] Etta's specific *karma*, then, is to have all of the previous intentions of living beings lined up such that she is able to tag her own identity to the game of basketball.

The Buddhist notion that a person is constituted out of eighty-four thousand parts, each conditioned by morally significant acts performed in the past, understates the number. That means that much of who we are has been decided long ago, and one or two changes made today will not change everything. Yet once we are aware that our identities are shaped by causal stories in "deep time," we can shift our attention from what we cannot control to a skillful manipulation of what we can control.

In Buddhist practice, it is most often the simple *awareness* of the causal story that is emphasized because it motivates us to cultivate the ability to accept what we cannot control. This is an immediate psychological benefit of understanding dependent origination and impermanence. For instance, it is possible that, although Etta would be very upset if she were no longer living near a play yard with basketball hoops, she might be less upset if she saw the possibility of other activities that would build productively upon her basketball experience. She might be able to adopt a different identity-construction once she recognizes that *who she takes herself to be* is contingent upon many random, ever-changing factors.[56] And, whereas a ten-year-old's disappointment at having to switch sports is relatively inconsequential, the same structure applies, mutatis mutandis, to identities that are constructed based on choosing a career, falling in love, serving in the armed forces, feeling a patriotic connection to a state, and so on. In this view, nearly everything of moral importance to humans can be described, in similar terms, as contingently constructed out of vaguely biological and sociolinguistic patterns ("culture"), which have no essential nature in themselves (they are only causal patterns) but do *appear* as real—real enough to be affirmed as "me" by countless *cetanā*-events in the minds of sentient beings.

The difference between acknowledging, or not acknowledging, the causal contingency of the story that generates one's mental events and one's identity can be extremely significant. I have sometimes noticed my son being unusually possessive about a toy—refusing to share fairly, say—and then, after wondering why he was acting this way, realized that he had not yet had breakfast. As a parent, part of my job is, of course, to teach my children to play fairly. But another crucial job is to make sure my children are properly fed. My son's possessiveness about his toys is causally conditioned by the irritability that he feels due to being hungry. Once he is properly fed, the sense of injustice that he has about his rights to this particular toy dissipate; he is able to share.

The Buddhist tradition says that ordinary beings are like children, unable to see the causes and conditions of their desires and conceptual constructions. The essence of the Buddhist path is the cultivation of the ability to eliminate the conditions that bring about negative states of mind, in oneself and in others. It is to intervene at the causal level, rather than keeping one's attention on the abstract construction. To apply the teaching to the present example, we might say that even more important, for my son, than learning in the abstract how to share, would be to learn how to keep himself properly fed, and more broadly, to learn how to notice, and counter, the causes and conditions that bring about feelings of possessiveness.

To apply this example to the political realm, historians and social scientists who seek to explain the forces leading to nationalism may be aware of the contingent, "deep" historical nature of the construction of nationalist identities, but nationalists themselves are not. To affirm that nationalisms arise under certain kinds of historical circumstances (joblessness, hopelessness, humiliation, unacknowledged injustice, anxiety about the imminent demise of the social group, etc.) is to deny the "ultimate" legitimacy of all nationalisms. It is to say that there is no such thing as the *nationalist identity itself* that has a causal effect; the true causes are social, historical forces (which are, in principle, reducible to individual psychological responses to social conditions). To express this in the language of the Three Natures, we could say that since the *appearance* of nationalism is caused by means other than the way it appears, it is real only as an appearance and thus is ultimately empty of reality. Beings who imagine that they choose to act based upon nationalism are deluded not just about the nature of their nationalisms, but about their own motives. To intervene in nationalist disputes, then, one must address the causes and conditions that bring about these particular kinds of self-constructions. It is conceivable, for instance, that if one could intervene to undermine the conditions that produce joblessness, hopelessness, anxiety, etc., the nationalism itself would no longer arise. It is thus a Buddhist way of putting things to say that a person with a sense of security, hope for the future, a stable job, and confidence in the rule of law is not a nationalist.

If this seems condescending and disrespectful, well, remember that Milarepa would appeal to the same reasoning to criticize my selfish love for my children. The Buddhist perspective asks that we *all* admit that we are deluded, and work from there to solve problems pragmatically. Rather than negotiate among ideological principles, a Buddhist approach would seek to intervene to alter the causes and conditions of the problem. But we do not ordinarily consider all of our ideals "ideologies," and all of our views "problems." Does the Buddhist view that we are all deluded undermine all moral action? As I have suggested, I think it comes close to doing so. I admire the modern attempt to shape the Buddhist path into a foundation for political ethics, but I believe that a great deal of constructive work has yet to be done before this can be accomplished. If it is to be done, though, I think it would require a robust deployment of the historical and social sciences, as I have already begun to suggest, but in a way that these disciplines are hardly equipped to meet as of yet.

The Three Natures ideal focuses us on the unreality of everything but what can be discerned via measurable causes. This, I take it, is a deep motivation behind Buddhism's famous failure, in ethics, to account for "justice." Justice is an abstraction. Right action is not *morally just* action, it is action free from negative motives, which brings about greater freedom. Yet it seems to me that it is sensible to attempt to expand the range of responsible action by expanding our knowledge of cause-and-result patterns. After all, the Buddha recommends specific actions based in his awareness of the freedoms that they will produce for his listeners. Thus, perhaps the social sciences could be used as the "handmaiden" to Buddhist ethics, where they would be used to determine not the *justice* but the likely *results* of certain kinds of individual, social, or political actions. It is conceivable, at least in principle, to justify particular social interventions with this kind of Buddhist consequentialist reasoning. To generalize, then, Buddhist ethics should be expected always to counter ideological dogmatism, and to emphasize restraint from immediate, known, harmful "means" for distant ends, except where an action's pragmatic efficacy is well understood.

The modern advocacy of nonviolence seems to me a rare example of action based upon the kind of motivational structure I am proposing. One of the standard arguments for nonviolence, which goes back to the Buddha, is that violence comes about in dependence upon stinginess and selfishness, and without these mental poisons we would have no call for violence and war. Understanding the causes of violence helps to prevent violence from coming about:

> "And so, Ānanda, feeling conditions craving, craving conditions seeking, seeking conditions acquisition, acquisition conditions decision-making, decision-making conditions lustful desire, lustful desire conditions attachment, attachment conditions appropriation, appropriation conditions avarice, avarice conditions guarding of possessions, and because of the guarding of possessions there arise the taking up of stick and sword, quarrels, disputes, arguments, strife, abuse, lying, and other evil unskilled states.
>
> "I have said: 'All these evil unskilled states arise because of the guarding of possessions.' For if there were absolutely no guarding of possessions . . . would there be the taking up of stick or sword . . . ?"
>
> "No, Lord."[57]

Framed thus as a causal result of heedless selfishness, violence loses its justification. The Buddha's question—"If there were absolutely no guarding of possessions . . . would there be the taking up of stick or sword?"—suggests that a proper explanation of the *causes* of violence includes the state of mind called "guarding of possessions" or "defensiveness" (*ārakkha*),[58] but does not include "injustice"—or "justice," from that perspective. That is, the *real* causes of violence are always selfish, deluded emotional states. Since, as we have discussed at great length, mental objects have no causes except to the degree that they appear within mental events, and are taken as motivations for action, the causes of violence are always ignorant, emotional attachments to images and ideas, not the ideas themselves.

The advocacy of nonviolence, then, may be justified by a psychology of violence that claims that violent action is always motivated falsely. The history of the doctrine of nonviolence in political ethics reflects this kind of causal reasoning, deploying psychological and social scientific evidence in exactly this way. I will put off a full discussion of this topic, but a number of modern authors may be seen to argue in this way. The most famous of nonviolence advocates—Tolstoy, Gandhi, Martin Luther King Jr.—familiarly advocated nonviolence based on appeals to the humanity of the adversary, on the view that one cannot act violently without dehumanizing the other and thus blinding oneself to the truth.

It should not be surprising, then, if Buddhist ethics finds itself in concert with the social sciences that seek to uncover the causes and conditions of human decisions. One of the goals of Buddhist meditative practice is to turn this examination inward, to develop awareness of the grooves, the patterns of thought, through which one's own mind has grown accustomed to flow. One *cetanā* at a time, the meditator cultivates the ability *not* to lay down additional pheromones, so that not every future mind will stumble down the same paths. The social scientist, too, seeks to illuminate patterns of events in their historical and social contexts, perhaps with something like the implicit hope that as humans, by looking, we can learn to refrain from repeating these patterns. The rapid changes in societies in modernity, and the growth of the social sciences, have thus provided new ways of understanding the causes of human identities, and this, I believe, has contributed to the appeal of Buddhist causal approaches to life and meaning. In the next chapter, our conclusion, we will formalize this approach, and ask what benefit Vasubandhu's insights might provide to this developing way of viewing the world.

CONCLUSION

Buddhist Causal Framing for the Modern World

VASUBANDHU'S WORKS cohere within a view that I would like to characterize as "Buddhist Causal Framing." By this term I mean to indicate the unified perspective that is implicit in the doctrines of the Three Natures and the storehouse consciousness (*ālayavijñāna*), and which I have shown Vasubandhu drawing from the central goals of Abhidharma and the Buddha's core doctrines of impermanence, dependent origination, and no-self. The Buddha said that there is no self, and what appears to be the self is only an ever-changing mass (*kāya*) of separate entities. Those entities, taken together, appear unified and static, but they are in fact distinct and in constant flux, and only linked to one another through their joint participation in a complex of causes and results; each separate entity arises dependent upon what has come before, and provides a conditioning factor for what comes next. In speaking this way, the Buddha presented a clear dichotomy between what appears, and what is. What appears is the illusion of the self; what is is an ever-changing causal series.

Vasubandhu's Abhidharma works seek to articulate the distinction between entities that *seem* real, and those that truly satisfy the Buddha's reality requirements, which leads him to defend a universe of independent, momentary entities with definite causal results. Yet in the context of arguing for this view, Vasubandhu never closes a self-referential, ironic loop: the causality that is the foundation of his distinction between real entities and conceptual constructions cannot itself be established as a real entity. Causality, then, although it is the only legitimate condition for knowledge, is not itself knowable. It is only within a particular causal frame—determined, necessarily, by localized conceptual needs—that entities can be judged real or unreal. It is only as conceptual constructions, then, that entities can be determined real.

As a further irony, the *fact that* causality itself, though deemed arbiter, is only conceivable through "localized conceptual needs" is *itself* a claim pronounced in language, and so can only be a conventional, conceptual construction. After all, whose "needs" could they be, unless they are the needs of human persons, who are at the same time being claimed not to exist?[1] This seems like a damning internal contradiction, but, as Graham Priest has urged, this kind of contradiction *always* arises when we attempt to talk about the limits of knowledge and language.[2] Priest believes that, since the idea of inexpressibility is itself inexpressible unless we are willing accept the possibility of true contradictions, we must either accept that our knowledge is unlimited and our language unbounded, or accept the possibility of true contradictions. While Vasubandhu does not speak of true contradictions per se, he does affirm that all things have three natures—natures that are each simultaneously both real and unreal, both dual and unified. Vasubandhu does not abandon the law of noncontradiction; rather, he uses these "limit contradictions" to suggest the limitations of our conceptual capacities, and to propel his reader to seek a new view—a Buddha's view.

At the same time, to suggest that the only perspective that is not ironically self-undermining (if not outright false) rests on the far side of enlightenment is to grant new legitimacy to the local utility of the ordinary world's conceptual tools—for that is the only kind of legitimacy that conceptual tools can have. Vasubandhu argues in the VyY that causally relevant entities can be judged conventionally real, but no judgment may claim the authority of ultimate reality.[3] The notion that all entities as we understand them are at some level conceptual constructions allows the recognition that there is no good, final answer to the causal story of perception and the reality of the external world as it appears. Ground-level, realist physical causality is no longer required in a world of appearances, and appearances are much easier to account for than physical realities. Yet the lack of ultimacy does not disqualify or negate the localized utility of entities that are causal within their proper contexts. Entities may be ultimately unreal, but still *substantial*, and therefore pragmatically useful for those seeking advancement on the Buddhist path. And the frame, in which entities acquire their status *as* substantial, remains always and only a causal frame.

In Buddhist Causal Framing, then, the question that is asked of any entity or concept is *What is the causal story in which this entity operates, and what role does it play?* To take the paradigmatic example of the self: framed within the causal story of the aggregates, it must be denied, since it plays no verifiable causal role. From a causal point of view, there is no agent and no experiencer who plays an indispensable role in the causal story of the aggregated elements that make up the apparent self. Framed within the story of the aggregates, the self thus disappears. The exceptions that prove the rule of the ubiquity of Buddhist Causal Framing are the occasional episodes in Buddhist scriptures where the self is reified for the sake of those who are unable to handle the complex and frightening doctrine of the five aggregates. In some cases, as Vasubandhu explains in AKBh IX, the Buddha speaks of a self or person, but this is always with the purpose of eliminating more damaging views than selfhood, such as the failure to accept the truth of *karma* and rebirth. But to say that such assertions are made with a different purpose is to say that they are made from within a distinct frame of reference; the Buddha never affirms the self *within* the frame in which he affirms the aggregates, as though the self existed over and above the aggregates. In this way, the Buddha's teachings are always true within their particular frame of reference, their particular degree of depth, their particular level of analysis. At the level of personal existence, people are causally connected to their actions in previous lives. If people perform good deeds, they will end up in a better rebirth. This causal story is true, even though it lacks substantial truth from the perspective that recognizes that persons are conceptual constructions imposed upon the aggregates.

Throughout the AKBh, Vasubandhu asks the same questions not just of the self, but of every entity: *What is the supposed causal story in which it plays a role? What are the causal consequences of its presence and absence?* The effect of this analysis is to distinguish, ever more clearly, between entities that deserve their status as substantial participants in viable causal stories, and entities that can be accounted for merely as they appear, whether as mere objects of experience or as ostensibly necessary parts of dubious conceptual matrices. Vasubandhu targets his criticisms at the intellectual structures erected by the Vaibhāṣika tradition, in order to show that non-Buddhist reification results from a too-rigid adherence to the structures within inherited treatises and literalistic readings of scripture. And here non-Buddhist reification is reification of entities that play no notable *causal* role in the story of *dharmas* beyond their *appearance*.

In Yogācāra, then, every *appearance* is defined as a false nature, a conceptual construction, so that everything in our experience falls into this category. The causal story, the dependent nature, is outside of our experience. Even when we know that our experience is conditioned, it remains our experience. This is, in fact, the fundamental point, what it means to say that everything is *causally conditioned*: the world as we experience it is brought about not by any single event of reasoning or knowing, but by countless causes and conditions, which are unavailable to our immediate awareness. Things do not come about in the way that they appear to arise.

While this situation is an ontological fact with epistemological implications, the Buddhist tradition's emphasis is always ethical and pragmatic: we are called upon to do our best to *improve* our understanding and free ourselves from our most damaging delusions. But given that our appearances have causes that are distinct from how they appear, the only way we can change what we experience is by learning of, and focusing on, the truest causes and conditions we can know. The philosopher's job with respect to a conceptual construction is therefore different from what it would be with respect to a real entity. The job is no longer to decide how that thing acts and interacts with other entities, but rather to determine how it comes about that *we think this unreal thing is real*. We cannot fight an illusory man or scare away an illusory elephant. The same is true of changing anything in the world; change is not made by a single intentional act, directed at an apparent problem. Problems can only be undermined by accumulating the causes and conditions that prevent their continued arising, by placing a hand on a ringing bell.

Buddhist Causal Framing thus reflects several linked ideas:

1. To understand anything is first and foremost to understand its role within a well-defined series of causes and conditions;
2. Any entity whose causal relations can be explained fully by appeal to its component parts is only a *false conceptual construct* and does not itself have a claim to reality (within the causal frame that acknowledges its components);
3. While the story of a given set of causes and conditions may be reliable and valid (i.e., substantial) within a certain perspectival frame, no causal story is itself finally true (i.e., ultimate), since no causal story can itself be understood (in the terms of the first point)—every frame is, therefore, ironically self-undermining;

4. We seem to be individual, independent, intentional agents, engaging with the world and our own experiential contents—but this is impossible, since there is no place in the causal world for such a self;
5. Similarly, other people and the furniture of our experience appear stable and unchanging, tagged with specific meanings and identities—but this is also impossible, since (for instance) otherwise we could not experience them;
6. As with the things of the world, so too with our perspectives: to the degree that we can be aware of our concepts and perspectives, they do not exist as they appear (as abstract entities known or perceived by our minds), but are, like everything else, merely apparent conceptual constructions and not the causal reality;
7. If we are to correct our deluded perspectives, we cannot do it directly, intentionally, cognitively, by "convincing" ourselves; we must change ourselves indirectly, by studying, discerning, and manipulating, incrementally, the causes of our awareness;
8. As with ourselves, so too with the people and things of the world: to the degree that they are conceptual constructs, they are not susceptible to change, so we cannot change them in predictable ways by acting in accord with our conceptual constructions and abstract frameworks; we must understand the causes and conditions of the circumstances in which we are working, and address those causes we can effect directly, which often means working toward distant goals only incrementally;
9. The possibility of change is limited by the conditions in which action takes place, which means that in the short term there is very little that can be done; but causally real changes accumulate over time, so, given sufficient time, even apparently unyielding conditions can be changed—and time is limitless. So, although we are benighted, there is nothing we cannot accomplish by focusing on the immediate causes and results of our actions.

I name this perspective on causality "Buddhist" because it is so evidently a reflection of core doctrinal positions of Buddhism, and because it was developed in its clearest and most decisive form by Vasubandhu, the greatest mainstream Buddhist philosopher after the Buddha himself, as a reflection on Buddhist scripture. Yet it surely reflects the doctrinal standpoint of only a portion of Buddhist traditions, which have appeared in great variety since the Buddha's time.[4] And there is nothing in the above points that requires that advocates of Buddhist Causal Framing identify themselves religiously as Buddhists. Buddhist Causal Framing can certainly be articulated and advanced without adhering to the authority of the Buddha. As I intend the expression, it is a conceptual structure and method that can be employed without reference to Buddhist scriptures, and that has, in fact, appeared in many areas of thought outside of Buddhist intellectual worlds. The purpose of the next and final section, then, is to carve out what I see as an already resident space for Buddhist Causal Framing in the modern world, in order that we may better understand the conceptual nexus that it defines, and test the potential significance of Vasubandhu's distinctive contribution to the intellectual, artistic, and ethical worlds of our present.

THE UNITARY CAUSAL LINE AS A THEORY OF THE MIND AND THE WORLD

> After we came out of the church, we stood talking for some time together of Bishop Berkeley's ingenious sophistry to prove the non-existence of matter, and that every thing in the universe is merely ideal. I observed, that though we are satisfied his doctrine is not true, it is impossible to refute it. I never shall forget the alacrity with which Johnson answered, striking his foot with mighty force against a large stone, till he rebounded from it, "I refute it *thus*." This was a stout exemplification of the *first truths* of *Pere Bouffier*, or the *original principles* of Reid and of Beattie; without admitting which, we can no more argue in metaphysicks, than we can argue in mathematicks without axioms.
>
> —Boswell, *Life of Johnson*

Idealism is counterintuitive, if not self-defeating. Samuel Johnson's famous kick against a rock is taken by many as a decisive refutation of Berkeleyan idealism. Boswell reads it as a proof that reason is blind without a contribution from the empirical, which, once presumed, cannot be discarded. Yet Buddhism is founded upon the counterintuitive notion that we do not have a "self"—that the soul is an illusion generated for practical reasons as a conceptual construction imposed upon ever-changing component parts. Thus, it should not be a problem for Buddhists that the view espoused is counterintuitive, as long as it is sensible and coheres with Buddhist doctrine. And, for Buddhists, the empirical evidence is not as clear-cut as Johnson's kick seems to presume. In these ways, I would suggest that the Buddhist view was prescient of our own ambiguous relationship to empirical reality.

For how counterintuitive *is* this form of idealism, once we accept what modern science teaches us about the causes and conditions of the furniture of our world? Let us take Johnson's simple notion that there must be a physical world, since I can kick a rock with my foot, feel the resistance, and so on. There is elegance in the simplicity of this notion. Yet the simplicity of the idea that the solidity of a rock proves the physicality of the world is in serious jeopardy once we begin to describe the act of kicking a rock in the language of contemporary scientific explanations—our best current version of the empirical. In fact, it is not legitimate to help oneself to the "solidity" of a rock as though this were a simple thing. We know that, in fact, rocks and everything else in our world are made up of tiny component parts—molecules—which are in constant motion, themselves made up of atoms, with far more space between them than matter, which are themselves made up of subatomic particles or, if you like, superstrings. I take it the physicists are not yet satisfied that they have a complete theory of everything, but we know at least that rocks are not solid and unmoving in the way they appear to our senses. The resistance that a large stone puts up against my foot is explained by its mass, but its mass is in turn explained by superstring theory. If we wish to avail ourselves of the evidence of our senses, we must explain why it is that the rock appears solid *when it is not*, and the air appears as empty space, *when it is not.*

Granted, Johnson did not say, "I refute it by the fact that there is a rock that resists my foot by virtue of its solidity." This was his genius; his kick proves that there must be *something* that provides physical resistance, without pinning himself to exactly what it is. But if we allow that *this* is his argument, then Johnson is not refuting Kantian or Buddhist forms of idealism, which acknowledge that there is *something* that makes up the *noumena*, the "ultimate" cause. The problem is that *that something* is unknown to us, and is by its nature *unspeakable.* The form of idealism we are left with is in fact *confirmed* when Johnson has to kick, instead of speak, to make his point.

If Vasubandhu had been present, perhaps when Johnson kicked his rock, he might have had the opportunity to challenge him to kick a rainbow, or any other of the many examples of an illusion put forward by the Yogācāra tradition.[5] For the fact is that the world *is not as it appears.* The rainbow that seems to be hovering above the mountain is the result of the light being refracted through particles of water suspended in the air. But this doesn't happen *where the rainbow appears.* There's nothing up *there.*[6] Furthermore, the physics of light does not fully account for the differences we readily draw between a rainbow's color bands; those distinctions result from the structure of our perceptual apparatus, the ways we mix different signals in the brain, and, apparently, cultural training.

But of course this is just the beginning. I will not detail the positions widely held among psychologists and neuroscientists that the unity of the self is a useful psychological fiction, or that it is the fictive self constructed after the fact that enacts "the illusion of conscious will";[7] nor will I say anything of Nietzschean or Freudian "false consciousness," and the thousand ways that psychologists tell us, echoing the Buddha, that we are deluded by our desires. We do not need to know most of these complex and disconcerting truths to understand that the world as "given" to our experience, which our senses and our brains enact for us, is selective and delusory in a thousand ways.[8] All that we need is to know that the rock we kick with our foot is mostly empty space. Its identity *as a rock*, which even the dictionary tells us is solid, is no more real than a rainbow.[9]

Of course, to make this point is not to deny the genuine, causal differences between rocks and rainbows. But the only legitimate way to distinguish between them is *pragmatic*, and relative to our sensory experience. It is not the "rockness" that we feel, but the solid surface that our brains generate for us based upon manifold data from our tactile senses. Now, there are reasons for why our tactile senses generate data that lead to this kind of construction. We cannot make our foot pass through the rock, whereas a bird may seem to fly through the rainbow. Clearly the kinds of causes *behind* our sensation of the rock are different from those behind the rainbow. There are patterns in our tactile experience that we have learned to distinguish and label as "solid." But our tactile sense of a rock is fundamentally just as delusory as our visual sense of a rainbow, to the degree that we deduce from it solidity "out there," independent of our sensory experience. That pattern is caused by *something*—which is unknown as of yet, call it "superstrings"—acting in such a way as to create, for us, the experience we describe as "solid." But the only way to preserve solidity as a real thing is to describe it as a quality evident in objects like rocks, relative to objects like my foot.

To speak thus of the constructed, relative nature of the entities of our experience is not to deny the legitimacy of the objective world as described by modern science. On the contrary, it is to take such descriptions seriously, and to discern the epistemic place such descriptions consign for us. Current evolutionary theory provides a good explanation for why we see things as we do, and *it does not require that things be the way they appear*. All that is necessary for the evolutionary development of sensation is for it to provide a selective advantage for some species in competitive circumstances. Since it turns out to have been of great advantage to our evolutionary ancestors to see, better and better, over countless generations, we can see. But, given the range of body sizes and the kinds of bodily control that were available to our evolutionary ancestors, there is no reason to think it would have been advantageous to them to see *molecules*, let alone superstrings. Even if we can imagine such vision being possible, we cannot manipulate individual molecules.[10]

We can imagine a slightly different planet from ours, one with a higher likelihood of species dying or being damaged by exposure to localized nuclear radiation, providing conditions conducive to species developing the ability to "see" radiation. In such an environment, such a sensory capacity could be a significant advantage. If we had such a sensory capacity, we might have trouble falling asleep in a room without sufficient lead in its walls to block out the radiation's "light." In that case, whether we would be convinced by Johnson's "kick" might depend upon the iron content of the rock he kicked. Many stones that put up resistance to a kick are penetrable to deadly radiation.

The point is that evolution has picked out, and reified for us, certain significant patterns of qualities within our environment, since the sensory apparatus available to any given species is a causal result, over vast spans of time, of the massive accumulation of responses to environment. Significance, in this way, is always indexed to the capacities of the species to manipulate its environment. What we see—what exists for us—is only what we can engage with, causally, in some potentially beneficial way. The frame in which we find ourselves experiencing, and reifying, entities is the frame in which our ancestors have been most capable of manipulation.

This story focuses on perception, but the same point can be made, mutatis mutandis, with regard to conceptual-linguistic constructions overall. The formation of the thought "stone" in any given person at any given time is a causal result of the sensory capacities of our ancestors and their communal interactions around what they took to be stones, bequeathed upon their heirs through linguistic assimilation and education. The point is that we do not need there to be stones, per se, in the world (as, for instance, solid, unmoving objects), in order to account for the utility of the shared conception of stones. And, of course, a shared conception does not need to be shared *exactly*. Just as our sensory organs provide a vague representation of the solidity or smoothness of an object that does not reflect its precise surface, our words and concepts trade in vagueness about their objects, so that beneficial usage does not require perfection of conceptual reflection.

Philosophers of language distinguish between sociocultural "artifacts," such as dollars and pots, which most agree are conceptual constructions, and "natural kinds," which are often thought to exist independently. Yet awareness of the "deep time" causal processes that have led to human sensation, language, and culture provides a strong argument that everything that we take to be a "natural kind" is in fact just another kind of "artifact" (unless and until the physicists can ground all of the other sciences in a fundamental set of entities). Evolutionary causal processes in deep time therefore provide a modern translation of what Vasubandhu means when he says that beings in hell experience the same hallucination together because of the similarity of their endless karmic conditioning.[11] Part of what it is to be a human is to have certain perceptions and conceptions shared by other humans, which we inherit with our human body. Nothing that we experience is as it appears, and the real causes and conditions of our shared, delusory perceptions are unending, and indescribable. But they can be known better. And the first step in understanding those causes is to acknowledge that the way things appear is caused in a way that is different from the way things appear to be caused. The Buddhist tradition, and modern science, both seek to focus our attention on clarifying the real causes. Even the "appearance only" tradition, which is founded in the denial of the real existence of external objects, then, may be called "realistic" in the conventional sense that it demands that we accept our situation for what it really is.

This is not to say that Buddhism itself is "scientific" in its methods or outlook. Traditional Buddhist meditation, for instance, should be understood through the conceptual lens of "ritual" as much as "science of the mind." Still, it seems to me that a modern, scientifically educated rationalist has good reasons to hope that Buddhist ethical and epistemic discussions might provide useful engagements with a modern worldview.

Far from being a counterintuitive, solipsistic idealism, Vasubandhu's worldview resonates in a commonsense way with the unavoidable recognition that we are medium-sized beings living in a world beholden to the physics of subatomic particles. Buddhist Causal Framing places sensible conditions on the kinds of affirmation such a reality permits: we are subject to our own, necessarily limited, frames of reference, but *within* those frames we are responsible to the inputs of objectivity-testing, which can call the frames themselves into question.

Finally, as a mode of cultural analysis, Vasubandhu's "three natures" view suggests a cultural interpretation of the Yogācāra "storehouse consciousness" (*ālayavijñāna*), the mental source of the possibilities of experience and action. Culture conditions us and forms us, but we each contribute to its causal series, as a *cetanā* contributes to a mental stream. The better we understand our history and our humanity—and thus the better we understand the conditions that have contributed to what we take to be our identities—the better equipped we are to improve our own perspectives and to understand those of others. Vasubandhu sought, through the three natures, to sequester scripture's multiple forms from the specter of nihilism. An appeal to causality undermines the claims of both "reality" and "unreality" by recognizing that no matter what views appear, they are all conditioned. Perhaps a three natures approach to culture may help, through the same means, to sequester cultural relativism while yet preventing a return to the false reification of bias. After all, we all share the nature of being subject to causes and conditions, and we all share the causal stream that makes it fun to bounce a ball.

Unsurprisingly, I find Buddhist philosophical traditions compelling not just in their intellectual and historical contexts, but in ours as well. I hope the reader will agree, if not today, then perhaps—in part due to the causal condition of having (intentionally) read this book—in the future.

Appendix A

AGAINST THE EXISTENCE OF THE THREE TIMES

AKBh V.25–27 (295.2–301.16)

Does a past and future thing really exist, or not? If it exists, then you have to say that conditioned things [*saṃskāra*] are eternal, because they exist at all times. If, on the other hand, it does not exist, then how is one bound in it or by it, or freed?[1]

The Vaibhāṣikas do not accept that conditioned things are eternal, because that is the point of being conditioned.[2] Instead they clearly accept that **all times exist.** [I.25a1]

For what reason?

Because it is said. [I.25a2] Since the Lord said, "O monks, if past form did not exist, then the learned, noble hearer [*śrāvaka*] would not have been indifferent with regard to past form. Since there is past form, the learned, noble hearer is indifferent with regard to past form. If a future form did not exist, the learned, noble hearer would not have been pleased with regard to future form. Since there is future form" and so on.

Because of the two things. [I.25b1] As it is said, "The arising of consciousness is dependent upon two things." What are the two things? "Eye and forms, up to the mind and mental objects." Also, were there no past and future thing, the consciousness that has it as its object would not be dependent upon the two. So a past and future thing exists based on scriptural authority and from reason as well.

Because of the existent sense object. [I.25b2] Consciousness is engaged with an existent sense object, not a nonexistent one. And if a past and future thing did not exist, consciousness would have a nonexistent experiential object. Then there would be no consciousness either, because it would have no experiential object.

Because of the result. [I.25b3] And if there were no past, how could the result of virtuous or unvirtuous action come about in the future? For at the time the result comes about, [296] the cause of maturation does not exist. Therefore, according to the Vaibhāṣikas the past and future thing is indeed existent.

And, necessarily, they say, a good Sarvāstivāda must accept this. Because,

Since they say that these exist, they are esteemed Sarvāstivāda (Those Who Say Everything Exists). [I.25c–d1] For, the Sarvāstivādins are those who say that everything exists: past, future, and present. Whereas, Vibhajyavādins (Those who say there is a distinction) are anyone who speaks making the following distinction: "The present and the past *karma* whose results are not yet given exist, but the past whose results are given, and the future, do not exist at all."

How many are those called "Sarvāstivāda"?

They are of four kinds, (25) **called differentialists of: being, quality, position, and difference.** [I.25d2–26b]

Bhadanta Dharmatrāta is a being-differentialist. Indeed, he says: "A *dharma* proceeding through the times is different in being; it is not different in substance. Just as a golden pot, being broken, when it is changed, is different in shape; it is not different in color. And just as the milk being changed by curdling, loses its flavor, strength, and freshness, but not its color. So a *dharma* too, when it comes from future time to present time, loses its being in the future; not its being a substance. So when it goes from the present into the past time, it loses its being in the present, not its being a substance."

Bhadanta Ghoṣaka is a quality-differentialist. Indeed, he says: "A *dharma* proceeding through the times is past insofar as it is connected to the quality *past* but not insofar as it is cut off from the qualities *future* and *present*; is future where it is connected to the quality *future* but not cut off from *past* and *present*. So it is present, too, where it is not cut off from *future* and *past*. In this way, a man desirous of one woman is not devoid of desire for others."

Bhadanta Vasumitra is a position-differentialist. Indeed, he says: "A *dharma* proceeding through the times, reaching one position and then another, is taken as being one thing and then another due to its having another position, not another substance. Just as one and the same mark placed in the ones' space is called 'one' and in the hundreds' space a hundred, and in the thousands' space, a thousand." [297]

Bhadanta Buddhadeva is a difference-differentialist.[3] Indeed, he says: "A *dharma* proceeding through the times is called one or the other with reference to what is previous and later, due to it having another position, not another substance. Just as one woman is called mother or daughter."

These are the four kinds of Sarvāstivādins.

Among them, the first is dispatched by reference to the argument against the Sāṃkhyas, because it advocates [their] view of change. The second leads to a confusion of the times, because everything is connected to every moment. For how is it the same, where the man's desire is enacted for one woman and only possessed[4] for another? For the fourth, too, in any one time the three times obtain. In the past time, the previous moment and the later moment are past and future, and the middle moment is the present. So also in the future.[5]

Thus among all of them, **the third is the best,** [I.26c1] which is the position-differentialist. For him, indeed, **the times are arranged according to activity.** (26) [I.26c2–d] "When the *dharma* is not doing its activity [*kāritra*], it is future. When it does it, it is present. When, having done it, it is stopped, it is past." This encompasses everything.

But this must be said: If what is "future" exists substantially even as past, why is it called "past" or "future"? And, where it is said that "the times are arranged according to activity," what is the activity of the present *tatsabhāga* eye?[6]

Giving or taking the result.

In that case, there is the fallacy of mixing characteristics: even the past *sabhāgahetu*, etc., since it gives a result, may have its activity or have partial activity.

And this must be said: Where by that very nature the *dharma* exists eternally, in its doing its activity, **what is the obstruction** [I.27a1] by virtue of which, sometimes it does [its] activity, sometimes not? Suppose you say the conditions are not in place: no, because you have conceded that they always exist. And when the activity is said to be past, present, and future, **how can this be?** [I.27a2] [298] Does the activity, too, have another activity? In that case, it is not past, nor is it future or present. Then you would be saying that since it is unconditioned, it is eternal. Thus it cannot be said that a *dharma* is future when it does not perform [its] activity.

This would be a mistake if the activity were something else other than the *dharma*. But in fact **it is not something else,** [I.27a3] so this is not a mistake.

So then that very thing **is disconnected from the times.** [I.27b1] If the *dharma* itself is the activity, how can it be that this very *dharma*, existing by its own nature, is sometimes called "past," and sometimes "future"? This is not an acceptable arrangement of the times.

What is not acceptable about it? For a *dharma* is future if it is unborn. It is present if it is born and not destroyed. It is past if it is destroyed.

The response to that is as follows: If the past and the future exist substantially just like the present does, for something **existing in this way how can it be unborn or destroyed?** [I.27b2–c] For how can a *dharma* that exists by its very own nature be acceptable as "unborn" or "destroyed"?[7] What did it previously lack, by virtue of whose nonexistence it is called "unborn"? And what does it subsequently lack, by virtue of whose nonexistence it is called "destroyed"? Therefore it is not acceptable that it be here in the three times and also eternal.

If one does not want to say that having not existed, it exists, and having existed it does not exist again, and what one does say is, "Because of being joined with the qualities of conditioned things, there is no erroneous entailment of eternality," this is just words, because it is not connected to arising and destruction. To say that "it is eternally quasi-existent, and the *dharma* is not eternal" is an unprecedented expression.

Indeed, he also says:

> *Own-nature [*svabhāva*] always exists, but its existence is not accepted as eternal.*
> *Nor is there existence other than own-nature—an expression spoken by the Lord.*

[299] As to what is meant by "Because it is said": we too say that there is a past and future thing. But a past thing is what existed before. A future thing is what will exist when there is a cause. Each is said to exist just insofar as this is the case, but not also substantially.

And who says, "It exists as present"?

How else does it exist?

As past and future [*atītānāgatātmanā*].[8]

This is also established for you: "How is it called past and future if it exists eternally?"[9] Therefore, the Lord says, "the past thing exists, the future thing exists" in order to refute the view that denies cause and effect, and in order that one come to know that a previously existent cause existed, and a subsequently existent result will exist. This is because the word "exists" is used as a particle [*nipāta*].[10] Just as one says of a light that previously it is nonexistent and subsequently it is nonexistent,[11] and as in, "The light is extinguished, but has not been extinguished by me," the past and future thing too, is said to exist. For otherwise the existence of a past and future thing would not be acceptable.

What then of what the Lord said when speaking to the mendicants of the *Laguḍaṣikīyaka*, "Past action lost, destroyed, gone, changed—it exists!" Did he not in this passage intend that each of these actions existed previously?

With regard to that passage too, it was spoken with the special intent [*saṃdhāya*] that what was deposited within that causal series is capable of giving forth a result. For the alternative, that what is existing by its own nature is past, would not be acceptable.

And this is just what the Lord expressed in the *Paramārthaśūnyatā*, "The eye, coming into existence, does not come from anywhere, nor, being destroyed, does it go to a dumpsite [*saṃnicaya*] anywhere. For, O Bhikṣus, the eye, not having existed exists, and having existed goes away." And if there were a future eye, he would not have said that having existed it does not exist. If you say that "having not existed" refers to its having not existed in the present time: no, because there is no difference in meaning between the existence and the time. If, on the other hand, "having not existed" refers to its having not existed in its own nature, this establishes that the future eye does not exist.

As to the expression, "The arising of consciousness is dependent upon two things," this, first of all, needs to be considered: in the situation where the mental consciousness arises dependent upon the mind and *dharma*, is it that the *dharmas* are a condition as a producer [*janaka*] of the mind, or that the *dharmas* are merely experiential objects [*ālambana*]?[12] If, on the one hand, the *dharmas* are producer conditions, how can what will come about one thousand *kalpas* in the future, or not, bring about a present consciousness? And *nirvāṇa* does not make sense as a producer, since it is the elimination of all activity. If, on the other hand, the *dharmas* are merely experiential objects, we say that the past and the future are also experiential objects.

If they do not exist, how are they experiential objects?

With regard to this, we say: If an experiential object exists in this way, how can it be that that experiential object existed and will come to be? For it is not that someone remembering a past form or feeling sees that "it exists," but rather that "it was." For surely one remembers what is past just as one experiences it when present. And the intellect grasps the future just as it will be when present. And if it exists just as it is, you say it is present, otherwise not. It is established that nonexistents too are experiential objects.

If you should say that this means that this [past form] is dispersed [*vikīrṇa*]: [300] no, because one does not grasp it as dispersed. And if you should say that each and every physical form is divided into atoms, in that case you would be saying that atoms are eternal. And you would be saying that the mere separation and coming together of atoms attains existence. But "nothing comes into being, nor is destroyed" is upheld by the Ājīvikas.[13] And scripture [*sūtra*] opposes this: "The eye, coming into existence, does not come from anywhere," and so on. How can there be diffusion for feelings, etc., which are not collections of atoms? And they, too, are remembered as they were experienced at their arising. If they exist like that, then you are saying that they are eternal. If, on the other hand, they do not exist, it is established that nonexistents too are experiential objects.

If nonexistents too may be experiential objects, there must be a thirteenth sphere [*āyatana*].[14]

For the consciousness "there is no thirteenth sphere," what is the experiential object?

The experiential object is just those words [*nāma*].

So then you would accept that as just words [*nāma*], it does not exist. And for the sound, what is the not-yet-existent experiential object for one who takes it up?[15]

The sound itself.

Then someone who seeks the nonexistence of sound should just make a sound.[16] If you say it is in a future state, why is it not intellected, given that it exists? If you say this is because it is not present: no, because they are the same, except to the degree that they are distinct from one another by one being established as existing, having not existed.[17] Therefore, both the existent and the nonexistent are experiential objects for consciousness.

What then of the Bodhisattva's saying, "That I should know or see what does not exist in the world—this is not a possibility"?

There is a special intention [*abhiprāya*] here to mean, as in another passage, "They who are prideful see as existent appearances of what do not exist; but I see only what indeed is existent." For otherwise, with every thought having an existent experiential object, how could one have deliberation or differentiation? This one would be just like that one. If consciousness has an existent object it would also be pointless for the Lord to have said: "This Bhikṣu, my hearer, as to what I have said in the morning he pursues its distinctions until evening, and as to what I have said in the evening he pursues its distinctions until morning.[18] And what he knows is is, and is not is not, and is not highest is not highest, and is highest is highest."

As to the expression, "because of the result": no, because the Sautrāntikas do not accept that a result arises from a past action.

From what then?

As we will explain thoroughly in the refutation of the doctrine of self,[19] from a characteristic of the continuum that precedes it. But what is the capacity of an action, if you say that its past and future exist substantially, and its result exists eternally?

The capacity for production.

Then it is established that not having existed, production exists. Alternatively, strictly everything exists. In that case, what is the capacity of what? Vārṣagaṇya's position is illustrated thus: "What is is just that. What is not is not. The nonexistent does not come to be. What exists is not destroyed."

Then it is the capacity to make present.

What is this thing called "the capacity to make present"? Suppose you say it is the change to another state. It is an eternal continuity. And how can that be among the formless which changes it, which is its existence from not having existed?[20] If you say it is a difference in nature [*svabhāvaviśeṣaṇa*], then it is established that not having existed, it exists. Therefore this is not the proper tradition of the Sarvāstivāda, which says that past and future exist substantially.

But it is the proper one. Just as it is expressed in the *sūtra*, "everything exists," so it says.[21]

And how is it expressed in the *sūtra* that "everything exists"?

"Everything exists," O Brahman, meaning "the twelve spheres." Or the three times. But it is expressed just as it is.[22] In the case where the past and future thing does not exist, how is one bound [*saṃyukta*] in it or by it?

Where one has a sensory object due to a defilement because of the existence of an afflictive tendency which is the cause of this coming from that, one is bound to a thing because of the existence of defilements and afflictive tendencies.[23]

But the Vaibhāṣikas say that a past and future thing simply exists. With regard to which one is not capable, its nature must be acknowledged: **the basic nature is indeed profound.** (27) [I.27d]

In that case, it is not necessarily indeterminate. It is the way of things that what comes about, perishes. Form comes about, form perishes. It is the way of things that one thing comes about, another perishes. The future comes about, the present perishes. Time also comes about, because coming about is grasped in time. The times, too, come about, because future time is of multiple moments. This is come about through its connection with that, which is gone.

Appendix B

BRIEF DISPROOF OF THE SELF

AKBh III.18 (129.5–21)

Now, in this case outsiders [=non-Buddhists], having grasped upon the view of a self, say: "If it is accepted that a living being transmigrates to another world, then a self is proven."

One counters this: **There is no self.** [III.18a1]

What kind of self? That kind of internally functioning person does not exist, who is imagined to abandon these aggregates and appropriate others. Thus the Lord has said:[1] there is action and there is fruit, but no agent is perceived who casts off these aggregates and appropriates other aggregates, because this is counter to the stipulated meaning [*saṃketa*] of *dharma*. In this situation, the stipulated meaning of *dharma* is just what is dependently originated—elaborated as "when this exists, that arises."

But then what kind of self is not rejected?

But that which is only aggregates. [III.18a2] But if that which is only aggregates is figuratively called "self," it is not rejected. It is thus that the aggregates-alone transmigrates to another world. But it is not that a complete [*prāpta*] aggregates-alone transmigrates there. **Conditioned by defilements and actions, it proceeds to the womb as the intermediate-state continuum, like a light.** (18) [III.18b–d] For the aggregates are momentary; they are not able to transmigrate. But brought into being by defilements and actions, defilements alone approach the mother's womb as a continuum known as the "intermediate state." In this way, it is not a fault to say of a light, though momentary, that it moves to another place as a continuum. Therefore it is accepted that although the self does not exist,[2] the continuum of aggregates, conditioned by defilements and actions, enters the mother's womb.

Appendix C

DISCUSSION OF "VIEW" (*DṚṢṬI*)

AKBh I.41–42 (29.12–31.16)

Which of the eighteen *dhātus* are views [*dṛṣṭi*] and which are not views?[1] **Both the eye and the *dharmadhātu* are indicated to be views.** [I.41a–b1]

If you ask how many this is: **of eight kinds.** [I.41b2] Eight kinds of *dharmadhātu* are views: The five views starting with the view with respect to the existing body; worldly right view; the trainee's [*śaikṣī*]; and the post-trainee's [*aśaikṣī*] views. The rest are not views. Among these, the view with respect to the existing body, and so on, will be addressed in its time in the chapter on defilements [*anuśaya*].[2] The worldly right view, furthermore, is a good, defiled discrimination [*prajñā*], associated with the mental consciousness.[3] The trainee's [view] is [glossed as] the undefiled view of a trainee, and the post-trainee's is that of a post-trainee. Seeing *dharmas* through the views of defiled and undefiled ordinary persons, trainees and post-trainees is like seeing forms in clouds, without clouds, at night, and at daytime, [respectively.]

Now, why is the worldly right view said to be associated with the mental consciousness? Because: **a thought produced with the five consciousnesses[4] is not a view, because of being indeterminate** [*atīraṇa*]. (41) [I.41c–d] For a determinate [*santīrika*] view is arisen from close consideration [*upadhyāna*]. And this is certainly not the case for discrimination [*prajñā*] produced with the five consciousnesses. Therefore it is not a view. So too for the others: neither defiled nor undefiled discrimination [*prajñā*] is a view.

In that case, how is the eye, which is indeterminate, a view?

In the sense of seeing a form. For **The eye sees forms.** [I.42a]

If the eye sees, then so also the other sufficient conditions for consciousness should see.

Certainly not every eye sees.

Which does, then?

One with a corresponding [consciousness].[5] [I.42b1] It sees when it is accompanied by consciousness; otherwise it does not.

Then it should be said that just that consciousness sees, with the eye as the support.

It's not that with it as support, the consciousness [I.42b2–c1] sees, so it can be able to be unaware.[6]

Why?

It does not see form, they say, where there is something intervening. (42) [I.42c2–d] For, they say, it does not see a form covered by a wall, etc. For if the consciousness were to see, since it is not subject to resistance [*pratigha*], there would be no resistance where there is a wall, etc., so it would see even a covered form.

No, the eye consciousness does not arise with respect to something covered, so how will it see what does not arise?

How then does it not arise?

Since the eye is subject to resistance, the state of seeing something does not come about with respect to what is covered. So for the consciousness, too, it does not arise; it operates by means of a single sensory object, which joins it as support [*āśraya*].[7]

Why then would you say that the eye, like the bodily sense organ which meets its object, does not see it to the extent it is covered?

Because it is subject to resistance.

And how is something seen which has an interposition by glass, fog, veil, or water?

That is not a case where, because it is subject to resistance, an eye fails to see a covered form.

What is then?

The eye consciousness does arise in the case where sight has no impediment even with respect to a covered form. But where there is an impediment, it does not arise. In that case, because it does not arise, the covered thing is not seen.

What then of the *sūtra* that says, "Having seen forms with the eye . . . "?

Here the intent is [that one sees forms] *with this as support*—just as he says, "One should know *dharmas* with the mind [*manas*]," and the mind is not cognizing *dharmas*, because it is past.

What does then?

The mental consciousness. Or, the supported action is referred to figuratively as the support, as in "The stands cried out." And as in the *sūtra* that says, "Known by the eyes, forms are desired, beloved," and they are not cognized by the eyes. And it is said in the *sūtra*, "The eye, O Brahman, is the doorway for seeing forms"; by this is meant that by the doorway that is the eyes, the consciousness sees. In this case he does not say "doorway into seeing," because it does not make sense[8] to say, "The eye is the seeing for seeing forms." [31]

If the consciousness sees, what cognizes [*vijānāti*], and what is the difference between them?

Consciousness of a form just is "seeing" it. In this way, if it is said that some discrimination [*prajñā*] "sees," it also "discriminates"; and if it is said that some consciousness "sees" it also "cognizes."

Others say: If the eye sees, then what else, aside from the eye that is become the agent, may be called the "action of seeing"?

This is unacceptable.[9] For if it is granted that the consciousness cognizes, and in that case there is no difference between the agent and the action, then for the other case it should be accepted just as it is in that case. It is said that the eye "sees," because it is the support for the seeing eye-consciousness. Just as, it is said that a bell "resonates" because it is the support for the resonance.

But then it obtains that the eye cognizes, since it is the support for the consciousness.

This does not obtain. "The seeing consciousness" is a convention in the world. For when it has come about in this way, it is said that the "form is seen," not that it is "cognized." Also, the *Vibhāṣā* says, "'Seen' [*dṛṣṭa*] is said when the eye, completed, is experienced by the eye consciousness." Therefore it is said just that the eye sees, not that it cognizes.

But it is said that the consciousness "cognizes" form by the mere fact of its presence [*sānnidhyamātreṇa*], as the sun is the "maker of the day."

On this, the Sautrāntika says: Why carve the ether? For, conditioned by the eye and forms, the eye consciousness comes about. In that case, what sees, and what is seen? For it is passive [*nirvyāpāra*], merely *dharmas*, and merely cause and effect. With regard to this, figurative terms are used by choice with a conventional meaning: "Eye sees, consciousness cognizes"—one should not be attached to them. For the Lord said, "Do not be attached to the popular etymology, nor rush to accept the world's ideas."[10]

But this is the established position of the Kashmiri Vaibhāṣika: The eye sees, the ear hears, the nose smells, the tongue tastes, the body touches, the mind cognizes.

Appendix D

AGAINST THE ETERNALITY OF ATOMS (*PARAMĀṆU*)

AKBh III.100 (188.24–190.8)

Now, what are the destructions? **There are three repeating destructions: by fire, water, and wind.** [III.100a–b] Since in one absorption [*dhyāna*], living beings equally come together there, it is the "coming-together" [*saṃvartanī*, i.e., destruction]. The heat destruction is from seven suns; the water destruction is from rainwater; the wind destruction is from a tumult of wind. And thereby, not even the subtle parts of the receptacle worlds [*bhājana*] remain.

But with respect to this some non-Buddhists accept: "Atoms are eternal. They remain then."

Why do they accept this?

"Lest there be the appearance of coarse things without seeds."

Surely the seed is said to be the wind that has sentient beings' distinctive powers, born from *karma*. Or, the wind that is associated with the destruction will become its cause. The Mahīśāsakas cite a *sūtra*, "The seeds were carried by the wind from other worlds."

Even so, they do not accept that the arising of a sprout, etc., is from a seed, etc.

What then?

From just their own parts, and from theirs in turn, and so on down to atoms.

What is this capacity of a seed, etc., in a sprout, etc.?

Nothing anywhere aside from drawing together their atoms.

And why, again, do they accept this?

Because it is not logical to have an origin from a different class.

Why is it not logical?

Because it would have no rule [*aniyama*]. It will not come about because of a rule of capacities, as in the arising of sound and what is cooked. For the variegated is a quality but not a substance, because things of a similar class are seen to arise from substances of a similar class, such as a mat from grass, and a cloth from thread.

This is illogical.

What is illogical about it?

That something unproven is taken for the reason.

What about it is unproven?

"That a mat is from grass, whereas a cloth is from thread." For as they are brought together, they are taken as an idea [*saṃjñā*], like a line of ants.

How can that be?

Because one does not conceive of a cloth when there is contact with a single thread. For what in that case prevents the existing thing being conceived of as a cloth?

Given that it is incomplete, a part of a cloth should not be a cloth.

In that case, a cloth must be only an assemblage. What, other than a thread, is a part of a cloth? When looking at the contact among multiple things, where the contact is only among ten, one should conceive of a cloth—or never. For the sensory organ does not come into contact with an intermediary power. And when coming into contact by stages with parts that are being touched by the eye, there should not be cognition of parts. Therefore, because coming-into-contact by stages engages with parts, the thought is also with respect to parts, like a firebrand circle. The form of a thread does not appear in cloths that are manufactured out of different forms (colors), etc. If it has the nature of a variegated form, then there is an origin from a different class;[1] and if it is not variegated, one either does not see the thread among those next to it, or sees variegation.[2] Where the manufacture is also variegated, there is extreme variegation. Furthermore, given the difference in the shining of the glow in the beginning, middle, and end of a fire's radiance, it does not appear from contact with its form.[3] Also, given that atoms are imperceptible, perception is of assemblages [*samasta*], like their causal origin,[4] and like the perception of a mass of hair for those with diseased eyes. A singular, atom-like hair for them is imperceptible.

And since the specific idea of the atom applies only to the forms, etc., the destruction of the atom is established when they are destroyed.

Since the atom is a different substance from the substance of the forms, etc., its destruction is not established when they are destroyed.

Its being different does not make sense, as long as there is no way to differentiate earth, water, and fire from their forms, etc., and those things that are grasped through touching the eye are perceived. And since there is no thought of wool, cotton, safflower, and saffron [*kuṅkuma*], etc., when they are burnt,[5] the thought of them applies to differences of form, etc. The ascertainment of a pot with respect to what has arisen as cooked is due to the formation generality, like a line. Because there is no ascertainment for one not seeing the mark. What is the point of this childish prattling? Let it stand just so, uncontradicted.

Appendix E

THE *PROPER MODE OF EXPOSITION* ON CONVENTIONAL AND ULTIMATE

VyY 236–240 (P: 127b–129b)

When the Lord says in the *Paramārthaśūnyatā[sūtra]*, "Although *karma* exists and results exist, no agent is apprehended," what is this, ultimate or conventional?

What comes of this?

If it is ultimate, then all *dharmas* are without substance. If it is conventional, then since the agent too exists conventionally, it should not be said that the agent is not apprehended. If you say this:

Some ask: What is "conventional"? What is "ultimate"? Thereby, what exists conventionally? What exists ultimately?

Suppose we say that word and speech and imputation and designation [*tha snyad*] are convention [*kun rdzob*], and the specific character of *dharmas* is ultimate?[1]

Then, since *karma* and results both exist just as words, and also they exist just as their specific character, you have the problem of how their two existences are accepted. I exist conventionally as a person but not substantially, because of the imputation of that upon the aggregates. *Karma* and results exist substantially, conventionally. They do not exist ultimately, because they are objects of mundane knowledge. [237] Supreme [*dam pa*] is wisdom beyond the mundane, and its object [*don*] is the ultimate [*don dam pa*]. That object is not the specific character of those two, because that object is an inexpressible general character.[2]

Here, if you ask whether mundane and beyond-the-mundane awarenesses are epistemic means [*tshad ma*]:

What is beyond the mundane is only one. The mundane has divisions. Whatever is attained via the beyond the mundane, that is means of knowledge.[3] Other than that is not means of knowledge. As the verse of the Mahāsāṅgika says:

Eye and ear and nose, too, are not means of knowledge.
Tongue and body, too, are not means of knowledge.
If the sensory organs were means of knowledge,
There would be nothing to do on the noble path.

And other similar statements.

Also, for some Mahāyānists who say that whereas all things, in their natures as a specific character, simply do not exist, this argument will also arise: What is being taught, conventionally, in those expressions where the Lord speaks of the existence of a thing just as it is, in the words, "The very existence of *dharmas* is taught"?[4]

End of chapter 8.

As to what is expressed in "conventional" [*kun rdzob*]: whatever it is, where it is associated with the afflictions in every way, it is "speaking wrongly," and where it is associated with purification, it is "well spoken." If you say this:

If we limit ourselves just to the expression, is it well spoken or wrongly spoken? It must be definitively stated. Even if it is conventional, someone must definitively state it. Otherwise, it is being said that it has conventional existence even though it does not exist. Overall, since to denigrate all the afflictions and the purifications fails to settle what is definite and indefinite, [238] and since one would contradict one's own expressions oneself, it should not be said. If one says that it is a special intention [*dgongs pa can*], it will not purify this fault.

Now, if one does not accept that "conventional" is a mere word, how is the following verse established, which comes from the Mahāyāna?

All of these are mere words.
They are settled in ideas alone.
Outside of being expressed,
What is expressed does not exist.

If you ask this, we say:

Here there is the rejection that outside of being expressed what is expressed does not exist, but there is no substance to the inexpressible character. Therefore, that [passage] is just like this:

They are settled in ideas alone.

And saying this, what are called "ideas" are ideas arising from the mind. For, as the *sūtra* says:

It is conventionally designated just as it arises from an idea.

It is not suitable that the word itself resides within the word. This is also said, immediately after [the above]:

In whatever words

Whatever dharmas *are expressed,*

In them they do not exist.[5]

*That is the true nature [*dharmatā] of* dharmas.

If there were no *dharmas* with an inexpressible character, without saying "In them," he would say only the part, "they do not exist." [239] In the character of conceptual constructions—in just those expressible *dharmas* as they are conceptually constructed by fools—in *those* there is no existence. In them they do not exist [means that] *in words* they do not exist. As it is said:

In them they do not exist.

And as for:

*That is the true nature [*dharmatā] of* dharmas—

Whatever is said, here the inexpressible nature of the true nature is intended. Outside of mere words, there must be a true nature of some *dharmas.* Nonetheless:

Words themselves are empty of words, as well.

How is it acceptable that one says this, given that with the idea, "All this is only words," it is said that "Words too do not exist"? If you say this:

Where one has refuted the substantial nature of what is conceptually constructed, since the refutation is some expression which is conceptually constructed as having the self-nature of an expression, there will be a substantial nature to the reasoning. This too is not accepted:

All dharmas *are without words, and*

Are expressed with words.

If what is said here is simply nonexistent, what are those non-existent *dharmas* and words? Where all *dharmas* are inexpressible characteristics, by speaking as with the conceptual constructions of fools, following their understanding, it is suitable even for the Āryas to express with words what has no words. In this way, the following passage from the *Saṃdhinirmocanasūtra* applies:

> Noble son, "conditioned" is a term designated by the teacher. This term designated by the teacher is a conventional expression arising from [240] conceptual construction. And that which is a conventional expression arising from conceptual construction is a conventional

expression of various conceptual constructions that is not thoroughly established. Therefore, it is not conditioned. As with the conditioned, so it applies in the same way to the unconditioned as well.[6] Also, whatever is said about anything not included within the conditioned and unconditioned will also be like this. Moreover, an expression is not simply without substance. And what is that substance? It is that to which the Āryas, with Ārya knowledge and Ārya vision, are inexpressibly, perfectly and completely awakened.[7]

Appendix F

THE *TWENTY VERSES* ON APPEARANCE AND MEMORY

Viṃś 16–17b (8.22–9.8)

Existence or nonexistence is ascertained by means of knowledge [*pramāṇa*], and among all means of knowledge, perception is the best. So, where a thing does not exist, how can a thought with respect to it be a "perception"?

Perceptual thought is just as in a dream, etc., [16a–b1] even without the thing—as has been shown before. **And when it exists, the thing is not seen; how can it be considered to be perceived?** [16b2–d] And when there the perceptual thought "This is my perception" exists—at that point the thing is not seen, because it is discerned just by the mental consciousness, and at that point the eye consciousness is finished. How is it accepted as perceived? But especially for a momentary sensory object, at that point its form or taste, etc., is truly finished.

What is not experienced is not remembered by the mental consciousness. Thus, the experience of a thing exists necessarily, and the "seeing" [*darśanam*] is what is considered the perception of the form, etc., of the sensory object.

It is not established that it is a memory of the experienced thing, since [it is], **as already explained, an appearance with its image.** [17a–b1] Just as an appearance—an eye consciousness, etc.—arises even without the thing, with an image of the thing, so, it is said, **memory is from that.** [17b2] For from that—from the appearance—arises a mental consciousness with a construction of form, etc., taken as a memory, having just that image. So the perception of a thing is not established based upon the arising of a memory.

Appendix G

THE *THREE NATURES EXPOSITION*

TSN

1 Fabricated, dependent, and perfected:
So the wise understand the three natures as profound.

2 What appears [*khyāti*] is the dependent, because of being dependent on conditions.
How it appears is the fabricated, because of being only fabrication.[1]

3 The eternal nonexistence of the appearance as it appears:
That is known to be the perfected nature, because of being always the same.

4 What appears there? The unreal fabrication. How does it appear? As dual.
What, accordingly, is its nonexistence? There being no duality there.[2]

5 What is this unreal fabrication? Mind. For it does not exist at all in the way it is fabricated or in the way it fabricates a thing.

6 Mind is regarded as twofold, being cause and result:
The consciousness called "storehouse," and the seven called "activity."

7 It is called "mind" [*citta*] because of being "full of" [*citatvāt*] the seeds of defiled tendencies.
So for the first. But the second because of acting as "various" [*citra*] appearances.

8 In short, the fabrication of the nonexistent and the thought of three kinds:
Matured, thus being caused, or else appearing.

9 The first is the root-consciousness, for having the nature of maturation,
The other the activity consciousness, from the activity of the seeing intellect and what is seen.[3]

10 By virtue of reality and unreality, of duality and unity, of affliction and purity
And of nondifference in character, it is accepted that the natures are profound.[4]

11 Since it is grasped as existent while never existent as such,
The fabricated nature is considered to have the character of reality and unreality.[5]

12 Since it is known through the existence of an error, and not known as it appears,
The dependent nature is considered to have the character of reality and unreality.[6]

13 Since it exists as nonduality and is the very nonexistence of duality,
The perfected nature is considered to have the character of reality and unreality.[7]

14 By force of the fact that the thing is fabricated in a twofold manner [*dvaividhyāt*] and its unreality is a singular existent,
The fabricated nature is considered to have the nature of duality and unity.[8]

15 Because while it is perceived as a dual existent, its being a mere error is a singular existent,
The dependent nature is considered to have the nature of duality and unity.[9]

16 Since its singular nature as nondual is the nature of the existence of duality,
The perfected nature is considered to have the nature of duality and unity.[10]

17 The fabricated and dependent are known as afflicted natures.
Whereas the perfected is regarded as the nature of purity.

18 Because of [one] having the nature of an unreal duality and [the other] having the nature of its nonexistence,
the perfected is known to be nondifferent in character from the fabricated nature.

19 Because of [one] having the nature of a nonduality itself and [the other] having the nature of the nonexistence of duality,
The fabricated is also understood to be nondifferent in character from the perfected nature.

20 Because of [one] being an unreal existence how it appears, and [the other] having the nature of just that reality,
The perfected is declared to be nondifferent in character from the dependent nature.

21 Because of [one] having the nature of an unreal duality, and [the other] being the lack of the nature as it appears,
The dependent nature is also understood to be nondifferent in character from the perfected.

22 In accordance with different stages, the conventional properties of the natures
and their practical properties are explained for the sake of growth [in understanding].[11]

23 The fabricated is the conventional nature, later having the nature of conventions,
and then again is accepted as the nature of the destruction of conventions.

24 The dependent is undertaken initially having the nature of nonexistent duality,
Then it is undertaken as the nonexistent duality, the mere appearance there.

25 Then the existence of the nonexistence of duality, the perfected, is undertaken there,
For then it is just as it is, and it is said, "It is, it is not."

26 For these very three natures have the character of the unattainable nonduality,
Due to nonexistence, existence not in that way, and the nature of that nonexistence.

27 It is just as [something] made into a magical illusion with the power of an incantation [*mantra*] appears consisting of an elephant.
A mere appearance [*ākāramātra*] is there, but the elephant does not exist at all.

28 The fabricated nature is the elephant; the dependent is its appearance [*ākṛti*];
and the nonexistence of an elephant there is said to be the perfected.

29 In the same way, the construction of what does not exist appears consisting of duality from the root-mind.
The duality is utterly nonexistent. A mere appearance [*ākṛtimātraka*] is there.

30 The root-consciousness is like the incantation. Suchness [*tathatā*] is understood to be like the piece of wood.
Discriminative construction [*vikalpa*] should be accepted to be like the appearance of the elephant. The duality is like the elephant.

31 When there is understanding of how things really are [*arthatattva*], then at the same time there is knowledge, abandonment, and obtaining, [which relate] in proper order to the three characteristics.

32 It is acknowledged that here knowledge is nonperception; abandonment is nonappearance; and obtaining is direct and full awareness, apprehension without cause.

33 With the nonperception of duality, the dual appearance goes away; as a result of its removal one arrives at the perfected, which is the absence of duality.

34 So also in the case of the magical illusion: simultaneously there is the nonperception of the elephant, the removal of its [the elephant's] appearance, and the apprehension of the piece of wood.

35 As a result of the intellect being the cause of adverse thoughts, by seeing [its] objectlessness,
And thus by following the threefold knowledge, effortlessly entering into liberation,

36 As a result of perception of only mind, there is no perception of knowable things.
As a result of no perception of knowable things, there can be no perception of mind.

37 As a result of no perception of either [*dvayor*], there is perception of the *dharma* realm.
As a result of perception of the *dharma* realm, there can be the perception of sovereignty [*vibhutva*].

38 And having attained sovereignty, the goals of oneself and others accomplished,
The wise one obtains unexcelled enlightenment, with the nature of the three bodies.

NOTES

1. SUMMARIZING VASUBANDHU: SHOULD A BUDDHIST PHILOSOPHER HAVE A PHILOSOPHY?

1. I do not really believe in any strict calculus of the "greatness" of great philosophers, but this is a statement I like to make to challenge the casual certitude with which the top position is so often claimed for Nāgārjuna. Nāgārjuna definitely had a masterly philosophical idea in his Madhyamaka defense of the doctrine of emptiness, and he presented it with elegance and consistency. But to use the famous terminology of Isaiah Berlin, Nāgārjuna was a hedgehog—he knew one thing very well, and united everything under a single vision—whereas Vasubandhu, whose insights transformed every arena of philosophical investigation, was a fox—the one who "knows many things." Though, if the thesis of this book is correct, then perhaps Vasubandhu was, as Berlin says of Tolstoy, "by nature a fox, but believed in being a hedgehog" (Berlin 1978:24).
2. See Takakusu 1904 and Butön 2013:241–245.
3. There were at least two Vaibhāṣika commentaries on the AKK.
4. Takakusu 1904:293.
5. On Tibetan doxographies, see Cabezón 1990, Hopkins 1996, and Harter 2011. Cabezón explains how the classification of distinct philosophical schools according to the *siddhānta* (Sanskrit) or *sgrub mtha'* (Tibetan) scheme has had significant effects upon Tibetan readings of Buddhist doctrine, since it came to define what counted as Buddhist for Tibetans, and had an even greater authority than the classification of what texts were included in or excluded from the canon. I am arguing that we reflect this classificatory rigidity when we allow our interpretations of Vasubandhu to be stunted by the almost universal, but anachronistic, reliance on these categories. See Trivedi 2005 for a similar claim.
6. Skilling 2000:298.
7. In describing Vasubandhu's view, I start by explicating the philosophical articulation of the core doctrinal concerns of the AKBh. Since it is not possible to lay out every compelling philosophical argument in the AKBh, I have chosen to

begin with a series of linked arguments that are characteristic and representative, but that, most importantly, are aimed at refuting what Vasubandhu calls the distinctive doctrine of the Vaibhāṣika tradition, namely the view that the three times all exist (the source of the name "Sarvāstivāda"). These arguments make use of a number of other points from the AKBh, which I also elucidate when they come up. Since one of these references is to the famous ninth chapter, on the "Refutation of the Person" (see Gold 2011), I am able to establish these many arguments, taken together, as representing the key concerns of the author of the AKBh. The next chapter is a study of three passages that, together, fill out the motivational and theoretical implications of the views studied in the "three times" chapter. With the AKBh thus established as gravitational center, we can then measure the ways in which other works attributed to Vasubandhu are in its orbit.

8. Frauwallner 1951:1.
9. When Frauwallner claims that Paramārtha or his students could have been responsible for the integration of these two narrative strands, he is forgetting that Xuanzang, Butön, and Tāranātha all provide "combined" versions—none of which can be traced back to Paramārtha. If there was an erroneous combination, it had to be quite early, and Indic.
10. Still, Anacker (1998:24–25, n13) says that the Chinese gives indications that the author was aware of telling the story out of chronology, so this is only an error if there were, indeed, two separate Vasubandhus.
11. Jaini 1958:50ff. As one example, with regard to the view that claims that the meditative state called the "attainment of cessation" (*nirodhasamāpatti*) still has a mind, which the AKBh does cite but attributes to Vasumitra, the commentary says it is "non-Buddhist" (*abauddhīyam*). See Griffiths 1991:122–128 for a translation of the AKBh passage and a study of this issue, which has been claimed to be one of the central motivations for the famous Yogācāra assertion of the "storehouse consciousness" (*ālayavijñāna*). See Schmithausen 2007 for that argument. If it is right, then it does seem that to claim Vasumitra's view "non-Buddhist" blocks this particular Mahāyāna solution, and thus cuts off a path to the Mahāyāna that the AKBh had left open.
12. Frauwallner 1961:131–132. Frauwallner writes that this similarity in their biography makes their confusion all the more likely.
13. Here I am replicating the judicious reasoning of D'Amato (2012:40–41).
14. Schmithausen 1967.
15. Hirakawa et al. 1973.
16. Anacker 1972.
17. Skilling 2000.
18. For example, see the connection forged between the VyY and the MSABh in Horiuchi 2009. Although his analysis is in a somewhat different vein, I would specifically mention Corless (1989) here as an example of an author whose vision of philosophical unity for Vasubandhu I am extending in my work. As another recent example, Braarvig (1993:cxxix) suggests that although it is unlikely that Vasubandhu wrote the *Akṣayamantinirdeśasūtra* commentary attributed to him (the *Akṣayamantinirdeśaṭīka*) himself, because it contains quotations from works that postdate Vasubandhu, including works by Sthiramati, the commentary cites the AKBh in a way that suggests that the author of the *Akṣayamantinirdeśaṭīka*

associated Vasubandhu the author of the AKBh with the early Yogācāra. Braarvig thinks the commentary may have been begun by Vasubandhu and completed by Sthiramati.

19. Kritzer 2003a, 2003b, 2005. Here also Park (2007) must be noted as a gradualist counterpoint to Kritzer, and a strong supporter of continuity in Vasubandhu's oeuvre. I am very much indebted to Park's insightful analyses, especially for his pointing to the passage from the VyY that I study in chapter 4.
20. Jaini: "It does not contradict the fact of two (one elder and the other younger) Vasubandhus. The Vṛddhācārya Vasubandhu certainly existed, as is clear from the statements of Yaśomitra. He may well have been the author of a commentary to the Abhidharma-sāra of Dharma-śrī and also author of many Mahāyāna works" (1958:53).
21. Buescher (2013) is an exception here; he calls one Vasubandhu the "Kośakāra" for his having written the AKBh, and the other the "Bhāṣyakāra" for his commentaries on Yogācāra treatises. The latter is a confusing name, since the AKBh is, after all, a Bhāṣya. But it at least provides us a key to the identity of the "second" Vasubandhu as the author of Yogācāra commentaries. Unfortunately, although Buescher does distinguish these sets of texts stylistically and doctrinally, and although he is right to acknowledge the importance of the Yaśomitra passages (see below), his analysis fails to connect the "Bhāṣyakāra" Vasubandhu with the supposed reference of the Yaśomitra passages. The main wedge separating the Bhāṣyakāra from the Kośakāra in Buescher's argument relies upon Von Rospatt's point (1995:187, n408, cited in Buescher 2013:392) that the defense of momentariness in the MSABh neglects to take advantage of the AKBh's argument that destruction is not an effect (see chapter 4). Thus, if Vasubandhu wrote the MSABh after the AKBh, he must have decided not to include his own somewhat radical, if brilliant, innovation in this commentary on a Maitreya text. How do we weigh this evidence? If, as Kritzer believes, Vasubandhu was already a Yogācāra thinker when he composed the AKBh, there is nothing to prevent his having written the MSABh first. To me, it seems quite plausible that he might have chosen not to repeat an argument in a new context for a different audience. It seems, rather, an unduly centrifugal presumption to deduce distinct authorship from this. But if these commentaries are not "his," there is very little substance to the second "Vasubandhu."
22. Frauwallner 1951:21. Śāstrī (2008) provides an edition of Yaśomitra's commentary, the *Sphutārthā*.
23. Anacker 1998:24–25, n13. I find myself in general agreement with Anacker's commonsense approach in this footnote. Mejor (1989–1990), in his careful analysis of the Yaśomitra passages, points out that Yaśomitra seems to have used *sthavira* and *ācārya* interchangeably, and hypothesizes another intriguing explanation of the meaning of *vṛddhācāryavasubandhu:* perhaps, given that the second passage refers to a view that agrees with the position advocated in the commentary (and is seen as non-Vaibhāṣika), the point is just that this is what Vasubandhu used to think, meaning what he thought before (ostensibly) converting to Mahāyāna. Instead of "the elder Vasubandhu," perhaps we should speak of "the early Vasubandhu."
24. Skilling (2000:293) "cannot dismiss" these references to a previous Vasubandhu, though he admits that we have no known texts attributed to that Vasubandhu. Buescher (2013) dismisses Anacker's readings with little discussion, but his analysis, though truly state-of-the-art, provides no smoking gun.

The main question keeping the "two Vasubandhus" hypothesis afloat today is whether the commentator on various Yogācāra texts—the author of MSBh, MAVBh, MSABh, and DhDhVV—might be a different, though roughly contemporary, "Vasubandhu," known to be such by Yaśomitra. (The authorship of the TSN is also widely doubted, but there is little support among the doubters for its attribution to the "second" Vasubandhu, either.) The resolution of this question awaits a detailed, close reading of each relevant passage from the AKBh together with Yaśomitra's and Sthiramati's commentaries, elaborated in the context of the larger arguments made by the author of the AKBh, and placed side by side with a full assessment of the commentarial accomplishments of the above four works. Buescher does some of this work, pointing out that these commentaries represent a different style from Vasubandhu's other attributed works, and emphasizing the significance of a conspicuously missing argument (namely, Vasubandhu's characteristic defense of momentariness, on which see my chapter 4). Yet these texts are commentaries on other people's works (Maitreya's or Asaṅga's), and so might be expected to follow different genre norms than Vasubandhu's autocommentaries.

My feeling, as I detail in the paragraphs that follow, is that the significance of the Yaśomitra passages in question is tremendously overblown. As I've said, we have different texts that we need to try to collate (see Buescher for an entrée into the evidence so far), and we do not presume to say that all of them are definitively composed by one author. But so far we have no biographical information and no convincing story to tell about any "second" or "third" Vasubandhu.

25. AKBh III.15 (127.18). Śāstrī 2008:339.29: *pūrvācāryāḥ | yogācārā āryāsaṅgaprabhṛtayaḥ.*
26. Frauwallner 1951:21, 22.
27. Frauwallner 1951:22.
28. See Park's (2007) hypothesis of a unified tradition that was the source of both the Yogācāra and Dārṣṭāntika/Sautrāntika.
29. AKBh IV.4 (197.4ff) and AKBh VI.10 (338.5ff).
30. Takakusu 1904:272.
31. This point goes double if we allow for Mejor's reading (1989–1990) of "the old Vasubandhu" as referring to Vasubandhu (some Vasubandhu) before his ostensible conversion (see note 23 above) to Mahāyāna.
32. Here I am not attempting to leverage the weight of post-Enlightenment philosophical hermeneutics to accomplish much beyond affirming this platitude. The notion of the "hermeneutic circle" harkens back to the medieval interpretive theory, based upon the necessary coherence of scripture, which required one to move back and forth between part and whole. In Gadamer's *Truth and Method*, this process of return and renewal of understanding is transformed into a philosophy of meaning that advocates a never-ending movement toward a "fusion of horizons" of one's own interpretive presuppositions with those of the text (Mueller-Vollmer 1989:37). Both uses affirm the interpreter's ongoing responsibility to make sense of each new interpretive move in the light of all that has come before. I take from Gadamer that this means that we, as historically conditioned interpreters, should never imagine ourselves to be outside the process of interpretation, never objectively distinct from the "content" of the texts we attempt to disclose. Yet each textual moment is also an expression of a human moment, a historical event of intentional composition. My goal as an interpreter, approached at best asymptotically, is

to disclose the intentions embedded within the text. This includes a reading of context and content, but seeks to elucidate, further, the human yearnings enacted through the specific social means that have produced enduring text traditions. It is an imperfect process, tainted by subjectivity and the limits of the present interpreter. But to set one's sights lower than this would be to abandon the search for understanding. What it entails, at a minimum, is a commitment to a continual renewal of the interpretative impulse, and the continual shifting of perspectives, to explore ever further the possible motivations of each textual choice.

33. Far preferable is Deleanu's (2006) modest admission that it is impossible to account for all of the evidence. Ironically, this admission makes the "two Vasubandhus" hypothesis far less satisfying.
34. Frauwallner 1951:42, 49.
35. Frauwallner 1995:128.
36. Anacker (1998:25, n13) asks the same question. At AKBh I.26a (16.12) Vasubandhu's commentary mentions an Abhidharma text with six thousand verses called *Dharmaskandha*. This, too, may be the text misidentified as authored by Vasubandhu, but neither the AKBh nor Yaśomitra's commentary identify (any) Vasubandhu as its author.
37. A similar point can be made about the narrative of the author of the AKK/AKBh, since the central narrative is his intellectual development from curiosity about Vaibhāṣika to his Vaibhāṣika teachers' dismay at his having composed a commentary that counters their doctrine. If Vasubandhu did not compose both texts, the entire narrative is a fabrication. That may be, but if it is, it makes no sense to say that the "earlier Vasubandhu" composed one, and the "later Vasubandhu" composed the other. If the biography is a fabrication, we have no author information whatsoever about the root text, and only the name "Vasubandhu" as author information for the commentary.
38. Frauwallner 1951:27.
39. Frauwallner 1951:27–28.
40. Frauwallner 1951:29–30.
41. Frauwallner 1951:24.
42. I think it is equally possible that Paramārtha named the wrong Vikramāditya, or some other similarly misleading error is present here, but Frauwallner does not entertain these ideas.
43. In fact, it is well known to textual critics that alterations are far more likely when the topic is known and attended to carefully by a copyist, because such readers tend to call upon their own understanding to smooth away difficulties.
44. Anacker 1998:24.
45. Deleanu 2006:191.
46. This rhetorical convergence may account for the tendency, bemoaned by Buescher (2013), for scholars treating the question even after Jaini's critique to ignore Frauwallner's complex defense, in which he avers two separate Vasubandhus, each of whom was both Hīnayāna and Mahāyāna.
47. This reading suggests a possible interpretation of the name whereby to be a Vasubandhu is just to be a bridge-building boundary-crosser. Paramārtha's "Life of Vasubandhu" opens with a famous story, explaining the name of Puruṣapura, where the Vasubandhus' father lived. The name hails back to a battle between the great

god Viṣṇu and a demon, Indradamana, who had earned a boon that allowed him to be instantaneously healed of any wound, so Viṣṇu was unable to kill him with any weapon. The demon's sister Prabhāvatī gave away the secret, by dividing a lotus and walking between the parts; Viṣṇu is able to kill Indradamana by slicing the demon in two, and walking between the divided parts. This story, with the evident lesson of "divided we fall," then sets the stage for the naming of the three Vasubandhus with the same name. Is it over-reading to see Vasubandhu's life story, thus framed, as a Buddhist inversion of this tale, saying that if the goal is to prevent a Tīrthaka victory and the resultant destruction of the *dharma*, Buddhist scholastics must stand united?

2. AGAINST THE TIMES: VASUBANDHU'S CRITIQUE OF HIS MAIN ABHIDHARMA RIVALS

1. The main arguments for distinguishing the author of the verses from the commentary involve the difference in style and viewpoint. While of course verses and commentary reflect different styles, there are countless examples of authors who have written verse texts and autocommentaries, and indeed the same style of verse-with-commentary is evident in the Viṃś. A notable distinction may be made, however, between the Vaibhāṣika content of the verses and the predominantly Sautrāntika perspective of the commentary. I have already suggested a few reasons for not jumping to the conclusion of distinct authors based on this kind of doctrinal difference. In chapter 3, note 19, I give a further reason for suspecting that the author of the AKK verses shared the Sautrāntika perspective of the commentary in a number of significant instances, which is evident in the verse author's occasional placement of the term *kila*. In Butön's (2013:243) biography of Vasubandhu this term is highlighted as having been offensive to some of the Vaibhāṣikas even before they saw the AKBh.
2. Gethin 1992.
3. And, of course, this understanding fits with the wider use of the term *dharma* in the Indian cultural world in reference to the basic rules of the universe.
4. When arguing with opponents, Vasubandhu says that the scriptures (*sūtras*) and not treatises (*śāstras*) of Abhidharma philosophers are to be taken as authoritative evidence of the true nature of reality (AKBh 146.3–4: *sūtrapramāṇakā vayaṃ na śāstrapramāṇakāḥ*). This seems to be what he means when he adopts the name "Sautrāntika." Yet he also says that scriptures are sometimes meant to have a secondary meaning (*abhiprāya*), as opposed to Abhidharma, which is always direct and literal. (AKBh 133.15: *abhiprāyikaḥ sūtre lākṣaṇiko 'bhidharmaḥ*). See chapter 4 for further discussion of this issue.
5. AKBh 77.3: *ata evātra sūtre saṃskṛtasyotpādo 'pi prajñāyata ity uktam*. This topic is discussed in chapter 3.
6. AKBh 2.3–10.
7. "Abhidharma is flawless discrimination [*prajñā*] together with its retinue" (AKBh I.2 [2.3]: *prajñā 'malā sānucarā 'bhidharmaḥ*). This includes the entirety of the living being associated with that discrimination. The term *prajñā* is glossed as *dharmapravicaya*, which is explained in the commentary to II.24 as referring to the classification of *dharmas*. See Hall 1983:44–45, n3.

8. AKBh 460.1: *prāyeṇa hi kāśmīravaibhāṣikāṇāṃ nītyādisiddha eṣo 'smābhir abhidharma ākhyātaḥ*. This comment comes at the conclusion to the eighth chapter of a nine-chapter commentary, and it is thought by some that this indicates that the ninth chapter was composed separately. It may also be taken to signal the pivot, in the last chapter, from a focus on the Vaibhāṣika position articulated in the verses, to a focus on the mistaken views of other groups—specifically, the Vātsīputrīyas and Vaiśeṣikas.
9. On the *bhāṣya* style, see Tubb and Boose 2007:173ff.
10. Dreyfus (2003) provides a fascinating and insightful analysis of the functions of debate in Tibetan Buddhist intellectual traditions. Nance (2011) and Griffiths (1999) thoughtfully examine the purposes of commentaries for Buddhist, and more generally religious, text traditions.
11. The argument over the three times, the topic of this chapter, is a paradigm case.
12. Takakusu 1904:288.
13. A special issue of the *Journal of the International Association of Buddhist Studies* (2003:2) was dedicated to "The Sautrāntikas." See Kritzer 2003a and 2003b and Honjō 2003 for studies of Vasubandhu's views. My view, as will become clear in later chapters, coheres with Honjō's interpretation of the term as indicating a position that "does not recognize the authority of Sarvāstivāda Abhidharmaśāstras" (328). I am less certain that it indicates an adherence to "the Sarvāstivāda sect." In chapter 4, I explain further how Vasubandhu replaces views previously based upon authoritative passages from *śāstras* and *sūtras* with new interpretations based on reasoning that takes a more holistic approach to scripture.
14. Vasubandhu as a Sautrāntika is considered by many to have been a follower of the view of one Śrīlāta, none of whose works are extant; Yao 2005:97, 118, n2.
15. It is also possible to read this compound to mean that its advocates hold that "things always exist" or that "all things exist"—including things that are past and future. These alternate interpretations, for Vasubandhu, amount to the same view.
16. When I say the verse text is not unreadable without the commentary, I only mean that it is possible to translate the meaning of the verses into English without including text from the commentary. I do not mean that I have read the verses and discerned their meaning without glancing at the commentary; I do not assume that that would be possible. In fact, I am doubtful that such a hypothetical is sufficiently well articulated to be meaningful. If I am to read the verses without commentary, does that mean that I am to read it with, or without, any knowledge of the doctrinal positions to which it refers? If without such knowledge, then I would surely be unqualified to read even the commentary. The question is therefore just how much knowledge is allowed. Should we assume that a reader of these verses should be familiar enough with the *Vibhāṣā*, which it summarizes, to know all of the details of the various subschools of fourth-century Indian Vaibhāṣika and their arguments with competitor schools? If so, then in order to understand the verses we may find ourselves insisting that they provide no nontrivial new information. The point is the same as that emphasized in the opening chapter. In order to read Indian philosophy, it is necessary to enter into the hermeneutic circle. It is not possible to gain a scientifically exact, perfectly objective analysis of textual meanings that has not already assumed a foundation of references and norms.

17. Note that verses are in **bold** type, as they will be throughout. Commentary will be in regular type. I present these verses as they might have appeared prior to Vasubandhu's having written his commentary, but in fact we do not have a Sanskrit original for the verses without the commentary. The Tibetan translations do contain the verses independent of the commentary, but in the extant Sanskrit manuscripts these verses are broken up, embedded within many pages of commentary. The following is an agglomeration, then, of the Sanskrit from the commentary, which runs from AKBh 295.6 to 297.1. The Sanskrit phonological transformations that take place at word boundaries, called *sandhi*, are not in proper operation where the words have not been written or spoken together, so the syllable count in these verses is also improper. I insert hyphens (—) where commentary has broken into the verses, so that those with the requisite skills may hypothesize the proper implicit *sandhi* and versification: ***sarvakālāstitā—uktatvāt—dvayāt—sadviśayāt—phalāt |—tadastivādāt sarvāstivādā iṣṭāḥ—caturvidhāḥ*** || (25) ***te bhāvalakśaṇāvathā'nyathā'nyathikasaṃjñitāḥ |—tṛtīyaḥ śobhanaḥ—adhvānaḥ kāritreṇa vyavasthitāḥ*** || (26).
18. Verse agglomeration from AKBh 297.18–301.12 (see note 17 for an explanation of the inserted hyphens): ***kiṃ vighnaṃ—tat kathaṃ—nānyat—adhvāyogaḥ—tathā sataḥ | ajātanaṣṭatā kena—gambhīrā khaludharmatā*** || (27).
19. This verse presents, I believe, a significant challenge to those who would claim that the author of the AKK held an opinion of the Vaibhāṣikas significantly different from that of the author of the AKBh. It supports the analysis of the term *kila* I present in chapter 3, note 19.
20. Clearly it is past actions and their karmic results to which one can be "bound" and from which one can be "freed." The pronoun "it" is probably intended to pick up the topic of the surrounding chapter, which is the "afflictive tendencies" (*anuśaya*) that bind one to *samsara*.
21. Lit. "because they are bound to the quality of what is conditioned" (*saṃskāralakṣaṇayogāt*).
22. AKBh 295.2–6: *kiṃ punar idam atītānāgatam ucyate 'sty atha na | yady asti sarvakālāstitvāt saṃskārāṇāṃ śāśvatatvaṃ prāpnoti | atha nāsti | kathaṃ tatra tena vā saṃyukto bhavati visaṃyukto vā | na saṃskārāṇāṃ śāśvatatvaṃ pratijñāyate vaibhāṣikaiḥ saṃskṛtalakṣaṇayogāt | pratijñāyate tu viśadaṃ* ***sarvakālāstitā***.
23. A question that does not loom large, which we might think would, is: Why would anyone want to believe in things existing in the past and the future? What kind of a world is that? In this passage, the reasons adduced for believing in a "block universe" do not attempt to salve the vertiginous character of this view. Perhaps, since Vasubandhu's view of universal momentariness has no more claim to common sense than the Sarvāstivāda view, there is no advantage to his attempting to highlight the counterintuitive nature of either side.
24. AKBh 296.9–14: *bhāvānyathiko bhadantadarmatrātaḥ | sa kilāha | dharmasyādhvasu pravartamānasya bhāvānyathātvaṃ bhavati na dravyānyathātvam | yathā suvarṇabhājanasya bhittvā 'nyathā kriyamāṇasya saṃsthānānyathātvaṃ bhavati na varṇānyathātvam | yathā ca kṣīraṃ dadhitvena pariṇamadrasavīryavipākān parityajati na varṇam | evaṃ dharmo 'py anāgatād adhvanaḥ pratyutpannam adhvānam āgacchann anāgatabhāvaṃ jahāti na dravyabhāvam | evaṃ pratyutpannād atītam adhvānaṃ gacchan pratyutpannabhāvaṃ jahāti na dravyabhāvam iti.*

25. "Among them, the first is dispatched by reference to the argument against the Sāṃkhyas, because it advocates [their] view of change." AKBh 297.4: *eṣāṃ tu prathamaḥ pariṇāmavāditvāt sāṃkhyapakṣe nikṣeptavyaḥ.*
26. AKBh 159.18–22: *na tu khalu yathā sāṃkhyānāṃ pariṇāmaḥ | kathaṃ ca sāṃkhyānāṃ pariṇāmaḥ | avasthitasya dravyasya dharmāntaranivṛttau dharmāntaraprādurbhāva iti | kaścātra doṣaḥ | sa eva hi dharmī na saṃvidyate yasyāvasthitasya dharmāṇāṃ pariṇāmaḥ kalpyeta | kaś caivam āha dharmebhyo 'nyo dharmīti | tasyaiva tu dravyasyānyathībhāvamātraṃ pariṇāmaḥ | evam apy ayuktam | kim atrāyuktam | tad eva cedaṃ na cedaṃ tatheti apūrvaiṣā vāyo yuktiḥ.*
27. AKBh 101.19–102.17. See Hayes 1988, Katsura 2003, and Gold 2011 on this argument. Patil (2009) treats later developments in Indian thought, as this becomes a central set of arguments between Hindus and Buddhists.
28. On momentariness in Vasubandhu, see the discussion of AKBh 193.2–8 in chapter 4, and also Von Rospatt 1995, Katsura 2003, Bronkhorst 2006, and Gold 2011.
29. "The Sautrāntika says that each and every unconditioned thing is insubstantial [*adravya*]. For it is not a separate existent like form, feeling, and so on. Why? Space is only the nonexistence of a touchable. For in this way, where in the dark, physical resistance is not found, one says 'space.'" AKBh 92.3–5: *sarvam evāsaṃskṛtam adravyam iti sautrāntikāḥ | nahi tad rūpavedanādivat bhāvāntaram asti | kim tarhi | spraṣṭavyābhāvamātram ākāśam | tadyathā hy andhakāre pratighātam avindanta ākāśam ity āhuḥ.* See chapter 4 for an elaboration of the epistemological implications of this view.
30. It may be mentioned that the non-Buddhist Vaiśeṣika system contains a somewhat more developed view of substances and qualities that may yet elude Vasubandhu's attack here. See my discussion in chapter 3 of the argument at AKBh III.100, in which the non-Buddhist opponent claims that changes are attributed to qualities, which are attributable to groups of substances. That argument requires a different line of attack, which is not on the table at the moment.
31. AKBh 296.15–18: *lakṣaṇānyathiko bhadantaghoṣakaḥ | sa kilāha | dharmo 'dhvasu pravarttamāno 'tīto 'tītalakṣaṇayukto 'nāgatapratyutpannābhyāṃ lakṣaṇābhyām aviyuktaḥ | anāgato 'nāgatalakṣaṇayukto 'tītapratyutpannābhyām aviyuktaḥ | evaṃ pratyutpanno 'py atītānāgatābhyām aviyuktaḥ | tadyathā puruṣa ekasyāṃ striyāṃ raktaḥ śeṣāsv avirakta iti.*
32. La Vallée Poussin (1923–1925.4:55) translates here "possession de la concupiscence," and proposes the Sanskrit *rāga-prāpti*, with a reference to II.36. Although the Sanskrit is not precisely correct, LVP's reference to *prāpti* in II.36 is (characteristically) right on target. There (AKBh 62.16), Vasubandhu uses *samanvāgama*, the term here, as a defining term for one kind of *prāpti*. See note 34 for the implication of this terminological choice.
33. AKBh 297.4–6: *dvitīyasyādhvasaṃkaraḥ prāpnoti | sarvasya sarvakṣaṇayogāt | puruṣasya tu kasyāṃcit striyāṃ rāgaḥ samudācarati kasyāṃcit kevalaṃ samanvāgama iti kimatra sāmyam.*
34. This argument makes oblique reference to Vasubandhu's critique of the Vaibhāṣika belief in a separate entity called *prāpti*, or "possession," where he provides a parallel critique of the reification of a distinction without a difference (see note 32). Here, Vasubandhu's implicit point is that Ghoṣaka's argument relies upon an equivocation in the notion of "possession" that must fail if the Vaibhāṣika/

Sautrāntika is to admit the distinct, separate entity called *prāpti*, "possession." For in that case there could be no question that *prāpti* would be considered equivalent to active engagement; the latter can produce karmic results, whereas the former cannot. If, however, *prāpti* is a *dharma* that exists in all three times, then the very difference between the three times is granted equivalent existence in all of the three times, which is a vicious regress. Vasubandhu's implication, then, is that his own, nonrealist understanding of "possession" does better even at supporting one of the Vaibhāṣikas' own attempts to salvage their temporal theory (not that it does save the view): even within nonrealism, we can provide a way to distinguish among the daydreamer's mental events. This compact implication becomes evident only once the full argument here is understood.

35. AKBh 296.19–21: *avastha'nyathiko bhadantavasumitraḥ | sa kilaha | dharmo 'dhvasu pravartamāno 'vasthām avasthāṃ prāpyānyo'nyo nirdiśyate avasthāntarato na dravyāntarataḥ | yathaikā vartikā ekāṅke nikṣiptā ekam ity ucyate śatāṅke śataṃ sahasrāṅke sahasram iti.*
36. Here, *kāritra* means a specific activity that is the characteristic action of the *dharma*, its doing what it does.
37. AKBh 297.10–13: *tasya kila* ***adhvānaḥ kāritreṇa vyavasthitāḥ*** || (26) [I. 26c–d] *yadā sa dharmaḥ kāritraṃ na karoti tadā 'nāgataḥ | yadā karoti tadā pratyutpannaḥ | yadā kṛtvā niruddhas tadā 'tīta iti | parigatam etat sarvam.*
38. AKBh 297.13–14: *idaṃ tu vatkavyam | yady atītam api dravyato 'sty anāgatam iti | kasmāt tad atītam ity ucyate 'nāgatam iti vā.*
39. "What is the activity of the present *tatsabhāga* eye?" AKBh 297.15: *yady evaṃ pratyutpannasya tatsabhāgasya cakṣuṣaḥ kiṃ kāritram*. See notes in appendix A for some discussion of this argument.
40. The term "grasping" (*grahaṇa*, *pratigrahaṇa*), which becomes central to the Vaibhāṣika view of the distinction among the times, will be central as well to Vasubandhu's Yogācāra definition of the illusion of "duality." For Vasubandhu as a Yogācāra commentator, what the Vaibhāṣikas think of as the defining character of "presence" is the very essence of the reifying errors of the dualistic mind. In chapter 5 we will return to this Vaibhāṣika meaning of "grasping" as a causal result, made into the quintessence of error. To foreground the error of "grasping" is, potentially, to critique the erroneous belief in the illusion of the self. It is a fundamental mistake of deluded sentient beings to imagine that events that have limitless conditions are caused by one event, or oneself.
41. The arguments against *kāritra* here may be profitably compared to Vasubandhu's rejection (at II.46a) of the Vaibhāṣika position on the qualities of "arising," "endurance," "change," and "destruction" attributable to all conditioned things (*saṃskāra*). There, as here, the Vaibhāṣika is criticized for positing a concept (there, a "being," *vṛtti*) that seems to account for the issues in question but must itself be accounted for in the same way—opening up an infinite regress that can only be closed by arbitrary stipulation.
42. Akimoto 2004:110–111.
43. AKBh 297.17–298.3: *idaṃ ca vaktavyam | tenaivātmanāsato dharmasya nityaṃ kāritrakaraṇe* ***kiṃ vighnam*** [I.27a1] *yena kadācit kāritraṃ karoti kadācin neti | pratyayānām asāmagryam iti cet | na | nityam astitvābhyupagamāt | yac ca tat kāritram atītānāgataṃ pratyutpannaṃ cocyate* **tat katham** [I.27a2] [298] *kiṃ kāritrasyāpy anyad asti kāritram |*

atha tan naivātītaṃ nāpy anāgataṃ na pratyutpannam asti ca | tenāsaṃskṛtatvān nityam astīti prāptam | ato na vaktavyam yadā karitraṃ na karoti dharmas tadā 'nāgata iti.

44. AKBh 298.4–22: *syād eṣa doṣo yadi dharmāt kāritram anyat syāt | tat tu khalu* ***nānyat*** [I.27a3] *ato na bhavaty eṣa doṣaḥ | evaṃ tarhi sa eva* ***adhvāyogaḥ*** [I.27b1] *yadi dharma eva kāritraṃ kasmāt sa eva dharmas tenaivātmanā vidyamānaḥ kadācid atīta ity ucyate kadācid anāgata ity adhvanāṃ vyavasthā na sidhyati | kim atra na sidhyati | yo hy ajāto dharmaḥ so 'nāgataḥ | yo jāto bhavati na ca vinaṣṭaḥ sa varttamānaḥ | yo vinaṣṭaḥ so 'tītaḥ iti | etad evātra vaktavyam | yadi yathā varttamānaṃ dravyato 'sti tathā 'tītam anāgataṃ cāsti | tasya* ***tathā sataḥ*** *|* ***ajātanaṣṭatā kena*** [I.27b2–c1] *tenaiva svabhāvena sato dharmasya katham idaṃ sidhyaty ajāta iti yo vinaṣṭa iti veti | kimasya pūrvaṃ nāsīd yasyābhāvād ajāta ity ucyate | kiṃ ca paścān nāsti yasyābhāvād vinaṣṭa ity ucyate | tasmān na sidhyati sarvathā 'py atrādhvatrayam | yady abhūtvā bhavatīti neṣyate bhūtvā ca punar na bhavatīti | yad apy uktaṃ saṃskṛtalakṣaṇayogān na śāśvatatvaprasaṅga iti | tad idaṃ kevalaṃ vāṅmātram utpādavināśayor ayogāt | nityaṃ ca nāmāsti sa dharmo na ca nitya ity apūrvaiṣā vāco yuktiḥ | āha khalv api svabhāvaḥ sarvadā cāsti bhāvo nityaś ca neṣyate | na ca svabhāvād bhāvo 'nyo vyaktam īśvaraceṣṭitam.*

45. Here La Vallée Poussin (1923–1925.3:52–53, n2) imports the term *anyonya* from the description of the view into the list of names of views, making Buddhadeva a defender of *anyonyathātva*—a "mutual-differentialist." That term works to describe this relativistic view, but the wording we have in both Sanskrit manuscripts, which is also reflected in the commentaries and Tibetan translations (*pace* LVP), is *anyathānyathika*, a "difference-differentialist." What does this mean, exactly? Perhaps that there are different ways to differentiate between the different times, depending on your perspective. But perhaps the manuscript traditions for this passage have been corrupt since before they were translated into Tibetan, and LVP's version, based on the Chinese implication of *apekṣa*, "relation," is closer to the original.

46. AKBh 297.1–3: *anyathānyathiko bhadantabuddhadevaḥ | sa kilāha | dharmo 'dhvasu pravartamānaḥ pūrvāparam apekṣyānyo 'nya ucyate avasthāntarato na dravyāntarataḥ | yathaikā strī mātā vocyate duhitā veti.*

47. AKBh 297.6–8: *caturthasyāpy ekasminn evādhvani trayo 'dhvānaḥ prāpnuvanti | atīte 'dhvani pūrvapaścimau kṣaṇāv atītānāgatau madhyamaḥ kṣaṇaḥ pratyutpanna iti | evam anāgate 'pi.*

48. It is not insignificant that this argument is, in fact, placed first, before any of the others (see "Order of Exposition in AKBh V.25–27" earlier). The passage is a discussion of the question of the reality of the three times, but it might just as well be considered a discussion of the question of the meaning of the Buddha's having claimed that things exist in the three times. The key doctrinal importance of this discussion is thus highlighted from the start.

49. AKBh 295.9–12: *uktaṃ hi bhagavatā 'tītaṃ ced bhikṣavo rūpaṃ nābhaviṣyan na śrutavān āryaśrāvako 'tīte rūpe 'napekṣo 'bhaviṣyat | yasmāt tarhy asty atītaṃ rūpaṃ tasmāc chrutavān āryaśrāvako 'tīte rūpe 'napekṣo bhavati | anāgataṃ ced rūpaṃ nābhaviṣyat na śrutavān āryaśrāvako 'nāgataṃ rūpaṃ nābhyanandiṣyat | yasmāt tarhy asty anāgataṃ rūpam iti vistaraḥ.*

50. Alternatively, it is possible to read the Buddha here as saying, effectively, "As I am about to say, and I quote. . . ." This may seem like an absurdity for anyone to say, even a Buddha whose words deserve to be heard and remembered, yet it is not

difficult to imagine that such a passage might appear in a text that brings together different versions of a story or event.

51. AKBh 299.1–2: *vayam api brūmo 'sty atītānāgatam iti | atītaṃ tu yad bhūtapūrvam | anāgataṃ yat sati hetau bhaviṣyati | evaṃ ca kṛtvā 'stīty ucyate na tu punar dravyataḥ.*
52. AKBh 299.2–4: *kaś caivam āha | varttamānavat tad astīti | katham anyathā 'sti | atītānāgatātmanā | idaṃ punas tavopasthitam | kathaṃ tad atītam anāgataṃ cocyate yadi nityam astīti.* Note the use of *ātmanā*, meaning "with a nature of . . .," in this passage. Since it literally means "as a self," this term is used ironically by Vasubandhu to indicate the false appearance of an essential nature. Vasubandhu uses the same term in this way in TSN 4.
53. See my discussion of III.100 in chapter 3.
54. AKBh 299.4–6: *tasmāt bhūtapūrvasya ca hetor bhāvinaś ca phalasya bhūtapūrvatāṃ bhāvitāṃ ca jñāpayituṃ hetuphalāpavādadṛṣṭipratiṣedhārtham uktaṃ bhagavatā asty atītam asty anāgatam iti.*
55. This is called *satkāryavāda*, the view of the existent effect. See Larson 1979:10. Vasubandhu is clearly not attempting to address the complexities of this view here, so I see no need to delay the argument by delving into Sāṃkhya causal theory.
56. Dan Arnold (pers. comm.) says that Vasubandhu is here adopting the idea from Jain philosophers that the existential verb acts as a *nipāta*. The point is that the word connects other words, rather than affirming some new entity.
57. Lit. "it has nonexistence." The point here is that although you say this, you do not intend to say that the light has some reality as a nonexistent.
58. AKBh 299.6–8: *astiśabdasya nipātatvāt | yathā 'sti dīpasya prāgabhāvo 'sti paścād abhāva iti vaktāro bhavanti yathā cāsti niruddhaḥ sa dīpo na tu mayā nirodhita iti | evam atītānāgatam apy astīty uktam | anyathā hy atītānāgatabhāva eva na sidhyet.*
59. Vasubandhu noted the ambiguous nature of the word "is" fifteen hundred years before Bill Clinton's famous "It depends on what the meaning of the word 'is' is." Clinton's point was just that by the word "is," he meant that he was not presently engaged in inappropriate relations, and it was therefore not technically perjury to have allowed his listeners to assume incorrectly that he was denying past liaisons. Strange as it seems, this set of fine points reflects, in more than form alone, the relevant moral questions about the three times in Vasubandhu's Buddhist perspective. First, Vasubandhu's analysis reflects a similar assertion of the technical correctness of the Buddha's utterance, even if it is known to have been uttered in a context in which its proper meaning would be misinterpreted. Second, Vasubandhu's claim that past events may seem to exist—but do not—in the present tense use of "is" exactly reflects Clinton's claim that he was not (technically) denying past events by his denial of what "is."
60. AKBh 299.8–11: *yat tarhi laguḍaśikhīyakān parivrājakān adhikṛtyoktaṃ bhagavatā yat karmābhyatītaṃ kṣīṇaṃ niruddhaṃ vigataṃ vipariṇataṃ tad astīti | kiṃ te tasya tasya karmaṇo bhūtapūrvatvaṃ necchanti sma | tatra punas tadāhitaṃ tasyāṃ saṃtatau phaladānasāmarthyaṃ saṃdhāyoktam | anyathā hi svena bhāvena vidyamānam atītaṃ na sidhyet.*
61. For an intricate study of this term, see Broido 1985.
62. AKBh 299.12–16: *itthaṃ caitad evaṃ yat paramārthaśūnyatāyām uktaṃ bhagavatā cakṣur utpadyamānaṃ* [correcting *utyadyamānaṃ*] *na kutaś cid āgacchati nirudhyamānaṃ na kvacit saṃnicayaṃ gacchati | iti hi bhikṣavaś cakṣur abhūtvā bhavati*

bhūtvā ca pratigacchatīti | yadi cānāgataṃ cakṣuḥ syān noktaṃ syād bhūtvā na bhavatīti | varttamāne 'dhvany abhūtvā bhavatīti cet na | adhvano bhāvād anarthāntaratvāt | atha svātmany abhūtvā bhavati | siddham idam anāgataṃ cakṣur nāstīti.

63. AKBh 295.13–16: ***dvayāt*** [I.25b1] *dvayaṃ pratītya vijñānasyotpāda ity uktam | dvayaṃ katamat | cakṣū rūpāṇi yāvat mano dharmā iti | asati vā 'tītānāgate tadālambanaṃ vijñānaṃ dvayaṃ pratītya na syāt | evaṃ tāvad āgamato 'sty atītānāgataṃ yuktito 'pi.*
64. This is a description of the connection between the sixth link in the chain, the "contact" (*sparśa*) of sensory organ and sensory object, and the seventh link, "sensation" (*vedanā*). I discuss Vasubandhu's presentation of the twelve links in chapter 6.
65. The "experiential object condition" is one of the four kinds of conditions. See AKBh II.61–62 (97.22–100.17). Vasubandhu provides no technical definition for a "producer condition" (*janaka-pratyaya*), though this might be thought to correspond imprecisely to the "causal condition" (*hetu-pratyaya*), since at AKBh II.46 Vasubandhu argues that "producings" come about as a result of the assemblage of causal conditions.
66. AKBh 299.16–21: *yad apy uktaṃ dvayaṃ pratītya vijñānasyotpādād iti idaṃ tāvad iha saṃpradhāryam | yan manaḥ pratītya dharmaś cotpadyate manovijñānaṃ kiṃ tasya yathā manojanakaḥ pratyaya evaṃ dharmā āhosvid ālambanamātraṃ dharmā iti | yadi tāvat janakaḥ pratyayo dharmāḥ kathaṃ yad anāgataṃ kalpasahasreṇa bhaviṣyati vā na vā tad idānīṃ vijñānaṃ janayiṣyati | nirvāṇaṃ ca sarvapravṛttinirodhāj janakaṃ nopapadyate | athālambanamātraṃ dharmā bhavanti | atītānāgatam apy ālambanaṃ bhavatīti brūmaḥ.*
67. This could be taken as an equivocation, attempting to counter an argument that works for all senses by focusing only on the mental sense. But it could also be taken to be just an opening step in a multistage argument. First, show that for mental objects, the Buddha must mean only experiential objects, not producer objects; second, point out that if the Buddha meant the quote to apply this way to mental objects, we are entitled to read it in this way for all objects.
68. AKBh 145.5–13: *kathaṃ sahotpannayor janyajanakabhāvaḥ sidhyati | kathaṃ ca na sidhyati | asāmarthyāt | jāte dharme dharmasya nāsti sāmarthyaṃ pratijñā 'viśiṣṭam | yad eva hīdaṃ sahotpannayor janyajanakabhāvo nāstīti tad evedaṃ jāte dharme dharmasya nāstīti | anyonyajanakaprasaṅgāt tarhi | iṣṭatvād adoṣaḥ | iṣṭameva hi sahabhūhetor anyonyaphalatvam | iṣṭam idaṃ sūtre tv aniṣṭaṃ sparśavedanayor anyonyaphalatvam | cakṣuḥsaṃsparśaṃ pratītya utpadyate cakṣuḥsaṃsparśajā vedanā na tu cakṣuḥsaṃsparśajāṃ vedanāṃ pratītyotpadyate cakṣuḥsaṃsparśa iti vacanāt | janakadharmātikramāc cāyuktam | yo hi dharmo yasya dharmasya janakaḥ prasiddhaḥ sa tasmāt bhinnakālaḥ prasiddhaḥ | tadyathā pūrvaṃ bījaṃ paścād aṅkuraḥ pūrvaṃ kṣīraṃ paścād dadhi pūrvam abhighātaḥ paścāc chabdaḥ pūrvaṃ manaḥ paścāt manovijñānam ity evam ādi.*
69. In the light of Kritzer's thesis (2003a, 2003b, 2005) that Vasubandhu's identity as a Sautrāntika masked his true identity as an advocate of Yogācāra, it is of interest to note how this argument against mutual causality may serve as an intervention in the issues that shaped the Yogācāra-*vijñānavāda* as a doctrinal system.

    Lambert Schmithausen (2007; first published 1987) argued that the initial, crucial motivation for one of the defining Yogācāra doctrinal innovations—the "store consciousness" or "latent consciousness" (*ālayavijñāna*)—was the problem of continuity, as it applied specifically to the meditative state called *nirodhasamāpatti*.

One problem, to put it briefly—see Griffiths 1991 for a careful study—was that a consciousness needs to be caused by a consciousness, but this meditative state is defined as being completely free of the six sensory consciousnesses. So the question arose, How does consciousness start again once it has stopped? Schmithausen argued that the "store consciousness" or the "hidden consciousness"—the consciousness that's tucked away in the body—was first introduced to solve this problem. In reply to Schmithausen, Buescher (2008) has recently argued that, in fact, the passage that Schmithausen cites as the initial use of this new concept does not in fact need to be read as an example of the "latent consciousness" of full-blown Yogācāra-*vijñānavāda*. It is, instead, a continuation of what Buescher terms the "bi-polar *bīja*-model," wherein the two "seeds" of consciousness bring one another about through mutual causality. See D'Amato 2009 for a summary of Buescher's thesis.

If Buescher is right, then there were two potential solutions to the problem of continuity available to Buddhists of the emerging Yogācāra, one of which was the *ālayavijñāna* and the other of which relied upon mutual causality. In that case, Vasubandhu's argument against mutual causality here, and his linear approach to causality in general (see chapter 3), could work to preclude a key, previous solution to the problem of continuity and might be taken to push those who took this problem seriously toward the more mature *ālayavijñāna* as the only truly viable solution.

70. This strict refusal to grant causal efficacy to merely apparent objects is at the crux of Vasubandhu's Yogācāra distinction between the causal "dependent nature" (*paratantrasvabhāva*) and the merely experienced "fabricated nature" (*parikalpitasvabhāva*). His extensive defense of the Mahāyāna view that all things are "merely apparent" (*vijñapti-mātra*) also picks up on this understanding of what is "merely an experiential object" (*ālambana-mātra*). See chapter 5.
71. AKBh 295.17–19: ***sadviṣayāt*** [I.25b2] *sati viṣaye vijñānaṃ pravartate nāsati | yadi cātītānāgataṃ na syād asadālambanaṃ vijñānaṃ syāt | tato vijñānam eva na syād ālambanābhāvāt.*
72. This argument is replicated in the TSN and the Viṃś, which trace the Yogācāra path of mental cultivation whereupon once one has eliminated the reification of the mental object, the consciousness also goes away. Of course, the Vaibhāṣika point in this passage is a reductio—we know there is consciousness, so its objects must exist—but the logic in this passage that deduces the impossibility of consciousness without its object fits Vasubandhu's later view that even the subjective side of consciousness is an illusion. See chapter 5.
73. AKBh II.62.
74. I note this here because it distinguishes this argument from the other three arguments, which Vasubandhu addresses directly by saying: "As to what is meant by 'Because it is said . . . ' "; "As to the expression 'The arising of consciousness is dependent upon two things . . . ' "; and "As to the expression 'Because of the result.' "
75. AKBh 299.21–25: *yadi nāsti katham ālambanam | atredānīṃ brūmaḥ | yadā tad ālambanaṃ tathāsti kathaṃ tad ālambanam abhūt bhaviṣyati ceti | na hi kaścid atītaṃ rūpaṃ vedanāṃ vā smarann astīti paśyati | kiṃ tarhi | abhūd iti | yathā khalv api varttamānaṃ rūpam anubhūtaṃ tathā tad atītaṃ smaryate | yathā cānāgataṃ vartamānaṃ bhaviṣyati tathā*

buddhyā gṛhyate | yadi ca tattathaivāsti vartamānaṃ prāpnoti | atha nāsti | asad apy ālambanaṃ bhavatīti siddham.

76. It will not benefit the opponent to claim that the unicorn has its existence as an experience. Vasubandhu does not dispute the existence of the experience, only the object of the experience.
77. See II.62, where Vasubandhu discusses the *ālambana-pratyaya*, the mental-object condition, and also my section on I.41–42 in chapter 3.
78. In this way, the apparent "perception" of temporality is similar to the apparent "perception" of destruction, as argued in Vasubandhu's proof of momentariness. See chapter 4.
79. AKBh 295.20–296.1: ***phalāt*** [I.25c] | *yadi cātītaṃ na syāt śubhāśubhasya karmaṇaḥ phalam āyatyāṃ kathaṃ syāt | na hi phalotpattikāle* [296] *varttamāno vipākahetur astīti | tasmād asty evātītānāgatam iti vaibhāṣikāḥ.*
80. See Griffiths 1991.
81. That is, AKBh IX.
82. AKBh 300.19–21: *yad apy uktaṃ phalād iti | naiva hi sautrāntikā atītāt karmaṇaḥ phalotpattiṃ varṇayanti | kiṃ tarhi | tatpūrvakāt saṃtānaviśeṣād ity ātmavādapratiṣedhe saṃpravedayiṣyāmaḥ.*
83. This is Kapstein's elegant translation (2001a:374) of AKBh 477.9–20. I see no reason to change it.
84. AKBh 477.11–12, 477.15.

3. MERELY CAUSE AND EFFECT: THE IMAGINED SELF AND THE LITERALISTIC MIND

1. See Kapstein 2001a for a translation and Gold 2011 for a summary. Duerlinger 2003 is a book-length translation and study.
2. AKBh III.17 (129.5–21).
3. As Vasubandhu says when he cites this same passage in book IX, it is from the *Paramārthaśūnyatā.*
4. AKBh 129.5–11: *atredānīṃ bāhyakā ātmavādaṃ parigṛhyottiṣṭante | yadi sattvo lokāntaraṃ saṃcaratīti pratijñāyate siddha ātmā bhavatīti | sa eṣa pratiṣidhyate* ***nātmāsti*** [III.18a1] *kīdṛśa ātmā ya imān nikṣipaty anyāṃś ca skandhān pratisaṃdadhātīti parikalpyate | sa tādṛśo nāsty antarvyāpārapuruṣaḥ | evaṃ tūktaṃ bhagavatā asti karmāsti vipākaḥ kārakas tu nopalabhyate ya imāṃś ca skandhān nikṣipati anyāṃś ca skandhān pratisaṃdadhāty anyatra dharmasaṃketāt | tatrāyaṃ dharmasaṃketo yadutāsmin satīdaṃ bhavatīti vistareṇa pratītyasamutpādaḥ.*
5. Here Śāstri (2008) has an opposed reading: *etad saty apy ātmani* instead of *etad asaty apy ātmani.*
6. AKBh 129.12–21: *kīdṛśas tarhy ātmā na pratiṣidhyate |* ***skandhamātraṃ tu*** [III.18a2] *yadi tu skandhamātram evātmeti upacaryate tasyāpratiṣedhaḥ | evaṃ tarhi skandhā eva lokāntaraṃ saṃcarantīti prāptaṃ skandhamātraṃ tu nātra saṃcaratīti |* ***kleśakarmābhisaṃskṛtam | antarābhavasaṃtatyā kukṣimeti pradīpavat*** || (18) [III.18b–d] *kṣaṇikā hi skandhās teṣāṃ saṃcarituṃ nāsti śaktiḥ | kleśais tu paribhāvitaṃ karmabhiś ca kleśamātram antarābhavasaṃjñikayā saṃtatyā mātuḥ kukṣimāyāti | tadyathā pradīpaḥ kṣaṇiko 'pi saṃtatyā deśāntaram iti nāsty eṣa doṣaḥ | tasmāt*

siddham etad asaty apy ātmani kleśakarmābhisaṃskṛtaḥ skandhānāṃ saṃtāno mātuḥ kukṣim āpadyata iti.

7. Dhammajoti 2009:246–252.
8. Vasubandhu stages an argument against the Vaibhāṣikas about the relationship between *avidyā* and *prajñā* at III.29 (141–142). The opponent (probably Vasubandhu's own view) proposes that ignorance *just is* "wrong view," but the Vaibhāṣikas reject this position and hold that ignorance is its own, distinct *dharma*. Either way, ignorance and "wrong views" are both causally efficacious.
9. One of the characteristic doctrines of Buddhist epistemology, known from Dignāga on (but already evident in the AKBh passage to be studied here), is that it is a mistake to distinguish between the "agent" and the "action" of knowing. Whereas other traditions distinguish between the knower (*pramātṛ*) and the action of knowing (*pramiti*), the Buddhist epistemologists see the action itself as both, as Dunne explains (2004:49–50). Two recent, somewhat divergent, interpretations of Buddhist thought as responding to the issues in Donald Davidson's famous article "Actions, Reasons, and Causes" (1963) are Arnold 2012 and Coseru 2012. I will reflect upon this issue briefly—from what I take to be Vasubandhu's perspective—in chapters 4 and 5, but for now it should be stated that Vasubandhu does not deny the conceptual utility of the distinction between reasons and causes. The important point is that the strict delineation between a realm of causes and a realm of reasons, as Davidson and others (such as Sellars 1997) have required, is a manifestation of the delusion of sentient beings. The realms interconnect in ways we do not ordinarily see. In a Buddhist view, we take reasons to be the basis for our beliefs and actions, but we are often caused, karmically and through ignorance, to only apparently "reason" our way to our mistaken perspectives.
10. See Arnold 2012:34–35 for a brief discussion of this issue as it is taken up by Dharmakīrti.
11. AKBh V.7 (281.19–282.2): *ātmadṛṣṭir ātmīyadṛṣṭir vā satkāyadṛṣṭiḥ | sīdatīti sat | cayaḥ kāyaḥ saṅghātaḥ skandha ity arthaḥ | saccāyaṃ kāyaś ceti satkāyaḥ pañcopādānaskandhāḥ | nityasaṃjñāṃ piṇḍasaṃjñāṃ ca tyājayitum evaṃ dyotitā | etatpūrvako hi teṣv ātmagrahaḥ | satkāye dṛṣṭiḥ satkāyadṛṣṭiḥ | sarvaiva sāsravālambanādṛṣṭiḥ satkāye | ātmātmīyadṛṣṭir eva tu satkāyadṛṣṭir uktā | yathā gamyeta* [282] *satkāyadṛṣṭir iyaṃ nātmani nātmīye veti | yathoktaṃ ye kecid bhikṣavaḥ śramaṇā vā brāhmaṇā vā ātmeti samanupaśyantaḥ samanupaśyanti sarve ta imān eva pañcopādānaskandhān iti.*
12. AKBh 282.2–3: *tasyaivātmābhimatasya vastuno dhruvadṛṣṭir ucchedadṛṣṭir vā 'ntagrāhadṛṣṭiḥ | śāśvatocchedāntagrahaṇāt.*
13. I write of "substratum" here as a shorthand for the entities upon which the false appearance is mistakenly superimposed, but I hope the reader will keep in mind that there is never any intent, within Vasubandhu's writings, to suggest that the "substratum" is a solid, essential thing. That would negate the whole point of denying the apparent unity which is imposed upon the substratum. The paradigmatic "substratum" is the five ever-changing aggregates.
14. Clearly this refers to the five consciousnesses that accompany the five sensory organs and their objects—that is, all of the consciousnesses except the mental consciousness.
15. AKBh 29.20–30.3: *atha kasmāl laukikī samyagdṛṣṭir manovijñānasaṃprayuktaivocyate | yasmāt* ***pañcavijñānasahajā dhīr na dṛṣṭir atīraṇāt*** *||* (41) [I.41c–d] *santīrikā hi dṛṣṭir*

upadhyānapravṛttatvāt | na caivaṃ pañcavijñānasahajā prajñā | tasmād asau na (30) *dṛṣṭiḥ | ata eva cānyā 'pi kliṣṭā 'kliṣṭā vā prajñā na dṛṣṭiḥ | cakṣur idānīm asantīrakatve kathaṃ dṛṣṭiḥ | rūpālocanārthena | yasmāt* ***cakṣuḥ paśyati rūpāṇi*** [I.42a].

16. See chapter 4, where I discuss Vasubandhu's patterns of scriptural interpretation.
17. Taken as a *dharma* that is a particular modality of *prajñā*, *dṛṣṭi* should have only one essential nature (*svabhāva*), so to admit that this error is only "sloppy" would be already to move toward a figurative reading of the term and to reject it as a *dharma*.
18. Vasubandhu even quotes the Vaibhāṣika's source text, the *Vibhāṣā*, to support one of his points, although of course he does not rely upon this text as chief witness.
19. Although the AKK summarizes the position of the Vaibhāṣikas of Kashmir, the word *kila*, "so they say," appears eight times in the verses, and six of them provide telling hints that the author of the verses was *already* harboring the exact questioning, critical view that dominates in the AKBh. Butön's (2013:243) biography of Vasubandhu even contains an episode in which AKK is said by the Vaibhāṣika followers of Saṃghabhadra to "insult our philosophical system" by virtue of its repeated inclusion of this term.

    Overall, the eight instances of *kila* are, I believe, a significant indication that the author of the verses was *of the same view* as the author of the AKBh, namely, a skeptical reader of the system who nonetheless was highly motivated to expend a tremendous effort to examine its every detail. (1) At I.3 (2.22), the verse implies with its *kila* that Abhidharma is not an authority, but "they say" it is. This in itself tells us that the author of the verses considered that the ultimate authority must be the *sūtras*, not the *Vibhāṣā*—which is to say, he was a Sautrāntika. (2) At I.28 (18.14), the point of the *kila* is that "they say" the void of the space element is light and darkness, day or night. Vasubandhu's commentary denies the reality of the *dharma* called "space." (3) As we are currently discussing, at I.42 (30.10), "they say" that consciousness cannot be said to "see," because vision is blocked by intervening matter, whereas consciousness is not—a position against which the commentary argues forcefully. (4) At II.1 (38.11), the verse which has a "so they say" in it is about the "predominating influence" of the sensory organs (*indriya*)—which is just senseless from the Sautrāntika perspective, since this way of speaking affirms the reality of something that is not at all causally real. Consciousness really causes things to happen (as is claimed at II.2). (5) At III.25 (133.10), the verse says that "they" advocate the static, not the other (less literal-minded) interpretations of dependent arising (*pratītyasamutpāda*). I will discuss some of the diverse interpretations of dependent arising allowed in the AKBh in chapter 6. (6) At IV.27 (213.1), "they say" that you only have "undiscipline" for a day and a night; but for the Sautrāntika, this is wrong: you do not *take* anti-vows. A lack of discipline is just something that happens, or that you *do*. As a "lack," this issue parallels the arguments against nonexistent entities that I will discuss in chapter 4. So, the commentary says, undiscipline is not a special entity, it is just a form of volition. But of course, you *could* decide to be undisciplined for as long as you like. (7) At IV.31 (215.16), "they declare" a position on the meaning of partial Upāsaka vows which the commentary criticizes based on scriptural analysis. (8) At V.37 (307.6), "they" have specific meanings for the word *āsrava*. Perhaps this is mistaken because it is too literal-minded, but I am not sure what the problem is.

20. Śāstrī 2008:91.23.
21. AKBh 30.4–6: *yadi cakṣuḥ paṣyed anyavijñānasamaṅgino 'pi paśyet | na vai sarvaṃ cakṣuḥ paśyati | kiṃ tarhi* ***sabhāgaṃ*** [I.42b1] *savijñānakaṃ yadā bhavati tadā paśyaty anyadā neti | evaṃ tarhi tad eva cakṣurāśritaṃ vijñānaṃ paśyatīty astu.*
22. The word *sabhāga*, which I translate as "one with a corresponding [consciousness]" is a technical term in the Vaibhāṣika system for those *dharmas* that are active (i.e., present tense) objects of consciousness. AKBh I.39 (27.19–20).
23. This argument establishes that the notion of a "view" is *caused* by the consciousness, in accord with the logic of causality and knowledge articulated at the start of AKBh IX. As I will explain further in chapter 4, Vasubandhu believes that in order for something to be called *real* it must be a necessary condition for some causal result.
24. AKBh 30.7–12: ***na tadāśritam | vijñānaṃ*** [I.42b2–c1] *paśyatīti śakyam avijñātum | kiṃ kāraṇam |* ***dṛśyate rūpaṃ na kilāntaritaṃ yataḥ*** || (42) [I.42c2–d] *yasmāt kila rūpaṃ kuḍyādivyavahitaṃ na dṛśyate | yadi hi vijñānaṃ paśyet tasyāpratighatvāt kuḍyādiṣu pratighāto nāsti ity āvṛtam api rūpaṃ paśyet.*
25. It seems to me that there is no need to appeal to a Vijñānavāda explanation here, as Yaśomitra suggests (Śāstrī 2008:91–92), since the point is that the sensory organ provides the support (*āśraya*) for the consciousness—which is how the senses are said to operate at I.9c–d. But the argument is clearly tending toward a Vijñānavāda perspective.
26. AKBh 30.12–18: *naiva hy āvṛte cakṣurvijñānam utpadyata ity anutpannaṃ kathaṃ drakṣyati | kiṃ khalu notpadyate | yasya tu cakṣuḥ paśyati tasya cakṣuṣaḥ sapratighatvād vyavahite vṛtty abhāva iti vijñānasyāpy anutpattir āśrayeṇaikaviṣayapravṛttatvāt yujyate | kiṃ nu vai cakṣuḥ prāptaviṣayaṃ kāyendriyavat yata āvṛtaṃ na paśyet | sapratighatvāt | kācābhrapaṭalasphaṭikāmbubhiś cāntaritaṃ kathaṃ dṛśyate | tasmān na sapratighatvāc cakṣuṣa āvṛtasya rūpasyādarśanam | kiṃ tarhi | yatrālokasyāpratibandha āvṛte 'pi rūpe tatropapadyata eva cakṣurvijñānam | yatra tu pratibandhas tatra notpadyata ity anutpannatvād āvṛtaṃ nekṣate.*
27. AKBh I.43d (32–33) clarifies that it is when in contact (*spṛṣṭa*)—that is, with no interval—that the organs perceive their objects.
28. Here we see Vasubandhu using the hermeneutic strategy of requiring consistency of purpose in texts, which McCrae (2000:433ff) writes about in the case of the Mīmāṃsā.
29. AKBh 30.18–24: *yat tarhi sūtra uktaṃ cakṣuṣā rūpāṇi dṛṣṭveti | tenāśrayeṇety ayam atrābhisandhir yathā manasā dharmān vijñāyety āha | na ca mano dharmān vijānāti | atītatvāt | kiṃ tarhi | manovijñānam | āśritakarma vā āśrayasyopacaryate | yathā mañcāḥ krośantīti | yathā ca sūtra uktaṃ cakṣurjñeyāni rūpāṇīṣṭāni kāntānīti | na ca tāni cakṣuṣā vijñāyante | uktaṃ ca sūtre cakṣur brāhmaṇa dvāraṃ yāvad eva rūpāṇāṃ darśanāya ity ato gamyate cakṣuṣā dvāreṇa vijñānaṃ paśyatīti | darśane tatra dvārākhyā | na hy etad yujyate | cakṣur darśanaṃ rūpāṇāṃ darśanāyeti.*
30. AKBh I.17 (11.18–12.3).
31. An alternate reading adopted by Śāstrī (2008:92.9) and Pāsādika (1989:26) is "to be *cognized* by the eye," *cakṣurvijñeyāni*, which makes the figurative nature of the statement even more evident. The eye might conceivably have its own kind of knowledge, but not its own "cognition."
32. See Gold 2007, Tzohar 2011, and chapter 4.

33. AKBh 31.1–3: *yadi vijñānaṃ paśyati ko vijānāti kaś cānayor viśeṣaḥ | yad eva hi rūpasya vijñānaṃ tad evāsya darśanam iti | tadyathā kācit prajñā paśyatīty apy ucyate prajānātīty apy evaṃ kiṃcid vijñānaṃ paśyatīty apy ucyate vijānātīty api.*
34. Vasubandhu will also pick up this argument in Viṃś 16. See chapter 5.
35. Vasubandhu rejects the question.
36. AKBh 31.3–10: *anye punar āhuḥ | yadi cakṣuḥ paśyati kartṛbhūtasya cakṣuṣaḥ kā 'nyā dṛśikriyeti vaktavyam | tad etad acodyam | yadi hi vijñānaṃ vijānātītīṣyate | na ca tatra kartṛkriyābhedaḥ | evam atrāpi | apare punar bruvate | cakṣurvijñānaṃ darśanaṃ tasyāśrayabhāvāc cakṣuḥ paśyatīty ucyate | yathā nādasyāśrayabhāvāt ghaṇṭā nadatīty ucyata iti | nanu caivaṃ vijñānasyāśrayabhāvāc cakṣur vijānātīti prāpnoti | na prāpnoti | tad vijñānaṃ darśanam iti rūḍhaṃ loke | tathā hi tasminn utpanne rūpaṃ dṛṣṭam ity ucyate na vijñātam | vibhāṣāyām apy uktaṃ cakṣuḥ saṃprāptaṃ cakṣurvijñānānubhūtaṃ dṛṣṭam ity ucyata iti | tasmāc cakṣuḥ paśyatīty evocyate na vijānātīti.*
37. What Vasubandhu says is that the distinction between an eye that sees and an eye that does not see is simply whether the eye brings about an event of visual consciousness. There is no activity for the eye that is called "seeing" distinct from the eye simply *being an eye*, or doing what eyes do by their very nature. But if there is an eye consciousness caused by that eye, we say, figuratively, that that eye "sees," because it is the support for that conscious awareness. Arnold (2012:168–169) characterizes Dignāga as arguing, in a similar passage, that we can only take an awareness to be "*pramāṇa*" because of its "being contentful (*viṣayākāratā*)." This seems to differ from what Vasubandhu would say. For Vasubandhu, the point here is that there is *never really any content* (the content as it appears is an impossibility, since it appears present when it is past; see next note)—but we speak figuratively as though there is, since this is how it appears to mistaken awareness. But perhaps this is not a real disagreement, since Dignāga also says in this context that awareness is *pramāṇa* only figuratively.
38. This argument presages Vasubandhu's interpretation of mental "nonduality" in his Yogācāra works. There he explains that mind and mental objects appear to be distinct entities, whereas in fact mental objects are mere appearances within mental events, without which the mental events would not exist. This is why mental events are called "nondual." Here we see that even in the AKBh, Vasubandhu foregrounded the fact that the object of cognition does not even exist at the same time as the mental event of which it is an object.
39. This critique of the distinction between action and agent resembles, though not perfectly, the "duality" we see criticized in Yogācāra texts such as the opening of the DhDhVV—as we will discuss in chapter 5. In the DhDhVV, the linguistic divisions among entities are said, similarly, to be false. Yet the specifics denied are not action and agent, but action and object. This extension reflects the denial of the separate existence of external objects for Yogācāra-Vijñānavāda.
40. The context here makes it clear that the mention of conventional terms used "by choice" or "as one pleases" (*chandataḥ*) refers to the Buddha's own figurative use of conventional terms.
41. AKBh 31.10–16: *vijñānaṃ tu sānnidhyamātreṇa rūpaṃ vijānātīty ucyate | yathā sūryo divasakara iti | atra sautrāntikā āhuḥ | kim idam ākāśaṃ khādyate | cakṣur hi pratītya rūpāṇi cotpadyate cakṣurvijñānam | tatra kaḥ paśyati ko vā dṛśyate | nirvyāpāraṃ hīdaṃ dharmamātraṃ hetuphalamātraṃ ca | tatra*

vyavahārārthaṃ cchandata upacārāḥ kriyante | cakṣuḥ paśyati vijñānaṃ vijānātīti nātrābhiniveṣṭavyam | uktaṃ hi bhagavatā janapadaniruktiṃ nābhiniviśeta saṃjñāṃ ca lokasya nābhidhāved iti | eṣa tu kāśmīravaibhāṣikāṇāṃ siddhāntaḥ | cakṣuḥ paśyati śrotraṃ śṛṇoti ghrāṇaṃ jighrati jihvā āsvādayati kāyaḥ spṛśati mano vijānātīti.

42. Here we see the Vaibhāṣika view that consciousness must play the role of a kind of subjective (Cartesian?) "seer" in cognition set up as a counterargument, refuted by the strict view that all things are "only cause and effect," not agent-and-object. See Williams (1998b:233–235) for an argument from the late Indian Buddhist philosopher Śāntarakṣita that resembles this one, used to defend the controversial doctrine of self-cognition (*svasaṃvitti*). At VII.18, Vasubandhu denies one of the foundational arguments for self-cognition—that for a Buddha's omniscience to work, a single cognition must be able to cognize all cognizables, including itself. Yao (2005:44–49) provides a study of this and related arguments and sees Vasubandhu as essentially accepting the Sarvāstivāda view that the Buddha's omniscience is not taken to see all things simultaneously. We may say that Vasubandhu goes further, though, by denying the implicit structure of consciousness that would distinguish, ontologically, between cognition and what is cognized.
43. "Where is this authority established? In the treatise. We have scriptures as means of knowledge; we do not have treatises as means of knowledge." AKBh 146.3–4: *kva caiṣa niyamaḥ siddhaḥ | śāstre | sūtrapramāṇakā vayaṃ na śāstrapramāṇakā.*
44. In his comment on the opening of Vasubandhu's Triṃś, Sthiramati explains: "[A word] is used figuratively with regard to something which is not there, as when [one calls] a Bahīkan [person] an ox." Lévi 1925:16: *yac ca yatra nāsti tat tatropacaryate | tadyathā bahīke gauḥ*. See Gold 2007:142ff for a brief discussion of this passage. For an in-depth study of *upacāra* that places Vasubandhu's usage in its proper context, see Tzohar 2011.
45. AKBh II.46 (76.20–21): *tad etad ākāṣaṃ pāṭyata iti sautrāntikāḥ*. The discussion of the characteristics of conditioned things is AKBh II.45c–46.
46. AKBh II.46 (79.22).
47. As Roy Tzohar has pointed out, the implications of the interactions among these various elements were only cashed out explicitly by Vasubandhu's great commentator, Sthiramati. But I hope to have shown that a careful reading even of this early passage displays Vasubandhu's intertwined interests in hermeneutics and philosophy of mind. Tzohar 2011:200: "While all these elements—upacaras, the non-existence of objectified phenomena, and their underlying causal reality—are present in the AKBh (often even in a single passage, as in AKBh 1.42), only in Sthiramati's TriṃsBh are they explicitly tied together theoretically, joining to form a cohesive account of the relation between language and reality."
48. Meyers (2010) studies Vasubandhu's discussion of seed-to-sprout causality as a model of "organic" as opposed to "mechanistic" causality. This is an important distinction for modern interpreters, who too readily think that a causal story is one in which results are determined, inevitably, by causes. I will discuss the issue of freedom and determinism in chapter 6. Here the issue is not the mechanistic vs. organic, but linear vs. part/whole causality.
49. For a translation of the argument as it appears in the Viṃś, see Kapstein 2001b. I provide a brief summary in chapter 5.

50. As I gather, this does not mean that all beings manage to achieve meditative absorption during these intermediate periods. Rather, only beings in absorption survive in *this* universe, but countless other universes are at different stages in the cycle of development and destruction, so there are ample opportunities for rebirth in one's appropriate form.
51. AKBh 188.24–189.6: *atha katīmāḥ saṃvartanyaḥ* | [189] ***saṃvartanyaḥ punas tistro bhavanty agnyambuvāyubhiḥ*** | [III.100ab] *ekatra dhyāne sattvāḥ samaṃ saṃvartante etasyām iti saṃvartanī* | *saptabhiḥ sūryais tejaḥsaṃvartanī bhavati varṣodakenāpsaṃvartanī vāyuprakopād vāyusaṃvartanī* | *tābhiś ca bhājanānāṃ sūkṣmo 'py avayavo nāvaśiṣyate* | *atra tu kecit tīrthakarā icchanti* | *paramāṇavo nityās te tadānīṃ śiṣyanta iti* | *kasmāt ta evam icchanti* | *mā bhūd abījakaḥ sthūlānāṃ prādurbhāva iti.*
52. AKBh I.43 (33.2–3): *na spṛśanti nirantare tu spṛṣṭasaṃjñeti bhadantaḥ* | *bhadantamataṃ caiṣṭavyam.*
53. Though to be more accurate it seems that they in fact used the same metaphorical notion of the eye—meaning the mind—that Vasubandhu says the Buddha adopts, when they say that the image is constructed in the "eye" of the beholder.
54. AKBh 189.6–8: *nanu ca sattvānāṃ karmajaḥ prabhāvaviśiṣṭo vāyurbījam uktam* | *saṃvartanīśīrṣavāyur vā tasya nimittaṃ bhaviṣyati* | *vāyunā lokāntarebhyo bījānyāhriyanta iti mahīśāsakāḥ sūtre paṭhanti.*
55. Some Indian creation stories do, however, have the universe proceeding from a cosmic egg.
56. He does this in his disproof of a creator god as well. See Gold 2011.
57. AKBh 189.8–13: *evam api na te bījādibhyo 'ṅkurādīnām utpattim icchanti* | *kiṃ tarhi* | *svebhya evāvayavebhyas teṣām api svebhyaḥ* | *evaṃ yāvat paramāṇubhyaḥ* | *kim idaṃ bījādīnām aṅkurādiṣu sāmarthyam* | *na kiṃcid anyatra tatparamāṇūpasarpaṇāt* | *kiṃ punaḥ kāraṇaṃ ta evam icchanti* | *na hi vijātīyāt saṃbhavo yukta iti* | *kasmān na yuktaḥ* | *aniyamo hi syāt* | *śaktiniyamān naivaṃ bhaviṣyati* | *śabdapākajotpattivat* | *citro hi guṇadharmo dravyaṃ tu naivam* | *samānajātīyebhyaḥ eva hi dravyebhyaḥ samānajātīyānāṃ dṛṣṭa utpādas tadyathā vīraṇebhyaḥ kaṭasya tantubhyaḥ paṭasyeti.*
58. See my conclusion for an elaboration on a reading of Vasubandhu's view as a way of structuring relations among scientific theories.
59. In AKBh, the question of just what kind of cause can produce just what kind of result is debated in the context of the discussion of an "equal and immediately preceding condition," *samanantarapratyaya*, at II.62. See Griffiths 1991.
60. On the contrary, he adopts this rule as part of his causally based definition of a logical reason, a "cause" (*hetu*; *gtan tshig*). See chapter 4.
61. AKBh 189.14–18: *idam ayuktaṃ vartate* | *kim atrāyuktam* | *yad asiddhaṃ sādhanāyodāhriyate* | *kim atrāsiddham* | *anyo vīraṇebhyaḥ kaṭo 'nyaśca tantubhyaḥ paṭa iti* | *ta eva hi te yathāsaṃniviṣṭās tāṃ tāṃ saṃjñāṃ labhante* | *pipīlikāpaṅktivat* | *kathaṃ gamyeta* | *ekatantusaṃyoge paṭasyānupalambhāt* | *ko hi tadā sataḥ paṭasyopalabdhau pratibandhaḥ* | *akṛtsnavṛttau paṭabhāgo 'tra syān na paṭaḥ* | *samūhamātraṃ ca paṭaḥ syāt* | *kaś ca tantubhyo 'nyaḥ paṭabhāgaḥ.*
62. AKBh 189.18–21: *anekāśrayasaṃyogāpekṣaṇe daśāmātrasaṃyoge paṭopalabdhiḥ syān na vā kadācit* | *madhyaparabhāgānām indriyeṇāsaṃnikarṣāt* | *kramasaṃnikarṣe cāvayavānāṃ cakṣuḥsparśanābhyām avayavavijñānaṃ na syāt* | *tasmād krameṇa saṃnikarṣād avayavivyavasāyād avayaveṣv eva tad buddhir alātacakravat.*

63. This refers back to where the opponent said that there can be no birth from a different class. If a variegated form arises from threads of individual colors, then this rule is violated.
64. The point seems to be that if one sees an individual thread, one must be able to distinguish different shades or colors—which means one sees a variegated form even when the thread is all the same color.
65. AKBh 189.21–24: *bhinnarūpajātikriyeṣu tantuṣu paṭasya rūpādyasaṃbhavāt | citrarūpāditve vijātīyārambho 'pi syāt acitre ca pārśvāntare paṭasyādarśanaṃ citradarśanaṃ vā | kriyā 'pi citrety aticitram | tāpaprakāśabhede vā 'gniprabhāyā ādimadhyānte tadrūpasparśayor anupapattiḥ.*
66. This view of perception as always a false construction will be useful to keep in mind in the upcoming chapters, as we see Vasubandhu advancing the utility of perceptually-based reasoning even while allowing that perception employs false constructions.
67. Things arise from multiple causes coming together.
68. AKBh 189.24–190.2: *paramāṇvatīndriyatve 'pi samastānāṃ pratyakṣatvaṃ* [190] *yathā teṣāṃ kāryārambhakatvaṃ cakṣurādīnāṃ ca taimirikāṇāṃ ca vikīrṇakeśopalabdhiḥ | teṣāṃ paramāṇuvad ekaḥ keśo 'tīndriyaḥ.*
69. A more literal reading here would be "there is no thought of them with respect to burnt wool, cotton, safflower, and saffron, etc."
70. AKBh 190.2–190.8: *rūpādiṣv eva ca paramāṇusaṃjñāniveśāt tadvināśe siddhaḥ paramāṇuvināśaḥ | dravyaṃ hi paramāṇur anyac ca rūpādibhyo dravyam iti na teṣāṃ vināśe tadvināśaḥ siddhyati | ayuktam asyānyatvam yāvatā na nirdhāryate kenacit imāni pṛthivyaptejāṃsi ima eṣāṃ rūpādaya iti | cakṣuḥsparśanagrāhyāṇi ca pratijñāyante dagdheṣu corṇākarpāsakusumbhakuṅkumādiṣu tadbuddhyabhāvād rūpādibhedeṣv eva tadbuddhiḥ | pākajotpattau ghaṭaparijñānaṃ saṃsthānasāmānyāt paṅktivat | cihnam apaśyataḥ parijñānābhāvāt | ko vā bālapralāpeṣvādaraḥ iti tiṣṭhatu tāvad evāpratiṣedhaḥ.*
71. Against Schmithausen (1967), who sees unity between the AKBh, the Viṃś, and the Triṃś, but holds with Frauwallner's "two Vasubandhus" thesis in distinguishing, doctrinally, the Asaṅga commentaries, I believe that the MAVBh, the MSBh, and the TSN all cohere with the causal linearity thesis advanced here. It is, of course, in principle possible that followers or imitators of Vasubandhu adopted his arguments and his approach. My point is to show the conceptual unity of these texts, which display a consistent intellectual agenda.

4. KNOWLEDGE, LANGUAGE, AND THE INTERPRETATION OF SCRIPTURE: VASUBANDHU'S OPENING TO THE MAHĀYĀNA

1. AKBh 299.1–2: *vayam api brūmo 'sty atītānāgatam iti | atītaṃ tu yad bhūtapūrvam | anāgataṃ yat sati hetau bhaviṣyati | evaṃ ca kṛtvā 'stīty ucyate na tu punar dravyataḥ.*
2. The question of the relation between Buddhist epistemology and the path to liberation is complex and contested. See Kapstein 2001c, Jackson 1995, and works cited therein for a range of problematics. My approach here is to suggest that the basic concepts in Buddhist epistemology are an expression of Vasubandhu's understanding of how knowledge operates in relation to basic Buddhist doctrine and its sources in the *sūtras*. If this is so, we have a full justification of the importance

of Buddhist epistemology not as a tool for attaining higher knowledge, but as a working out of intellectual problems that stem from the interpretation of Buddhist scripture.

3. NBh pp. 23.14–24.2: *yajjātīyasyārthasya sannikarṣāt sukham ātmopalabdhavān tajjātīyam evārthaṃ paśyann upādātum icchati seyam ādātum icchā ekasyānekārthadarśino darśanapratisandhānād* [24] *bhavantī liṅgam ātmanaḥ | niyataviṣaye hi buddhibhedamātre na sambhavati dehāntaravad iti.* Kapstein (2001:378ff) provides a translation of this passage, and Uddyotakara's brilliant, innovative subcommentary, also studied in juxtaposition with AKBh IX.
4. Here we see the assumption of newness as intrinsic to knowledge that is central to Buddhist epistemologists later on as well. When knowledge is understood as an event rather than a disposition, it is crucial that something be previously unknown for it to be considered an event of "knowing" (*jñāna* or *pramāṇa*). This suggests that a better translation for these terms might be "realizing" or "dawning."
5. On the issue of continuity among Buddhists, see Griffiths 1991 and other sources noted in chapter 2, note 69. This passage, and Vasubandhu's attention to it, show that the issue was of great importance to Buddhist defenses against non-Buddhists. If the Yogācāra-*vijñānavāda* represented a stable resolution to this problem, then it makes sense to see this tradition's emergence as not just an internal development of Buddhist doctrine, but at least in part a reformation in response to external critiques.
6. See Kapstein 2001a:367. I am not claiming that the chapter as a whole is intended as a response to this passage, but Vasubandhu is clearly aware of the content of the argument—whether in Vātsyāyana's words or not, I cannot say.
7. AKBh 472.15: *smṛtiviṣayasaṃjñānvayāc cittaviśeṣāt.*
8. AKBh 472.20–22: *na hi tayoḥ saṃbandho 'sti akāryakāraṇabhāvād yathaikasaṃtānikayoḥ | na ca bhrūmo 'nyena cetasā dṛṣṭam anyat smaratīti | api tu darśanacittāt smṛticittam anyad utpadyate.*
9. This refers to anything outside of the Buddha's teachings, and shows the final chapter to be in fact an extended commentary on the final verse of chapter VIII.
10. AKBh 461.2–4: *kiṃ khalvato 'nyatra mokṣo nāsti | nāsti | kim kāraṇam | vitathātmadṛṣṭiniviṣṭatvāt | nahi te skandhasaṃtāna evātmaprajñaptiṃ vyavasyanti | kim tarhi | dravyāntaram evātmānaṃ parikalpayanti ātmagrāhaprabhavāś ca sarvakleśā iti.*
11. As Franco (2001:291, 296) points out, Dharmakīrti essentially reduces the Buddha's teachings to the *anātman* doctrine. This is a natural extension of Vasubandhu's emphasis.
12. I call this a formal proof, but I do not intend to suggest that he has adopted the structure of a *prāmāṇika* syllogism. I say "means of knowledge" for *pramāṇa* for ease of comprehension (relative ease). I do not have a strong attachment to this translation.
13. This introduces a second example of inference, this time to prove the point at hand.
14. Vasubandhu uses the term *niścaya*, "determination" only very occasionally, and always to refer to the elimination of doubt. In a couple of instances it refers to the stages on the path in which various kinds of doubt are eliminated, and in others to ordinary certainty (for instance, a lack of doubt that the one you are shooting at is a living being).
15. AKBh 461.4–20: *kathaṃ punar idaṃ gamyate skandhasaṃtāna evedam ātmābhidhānaṃ vartate nānyasminn abhidheya iti | pratyakṣānumānābhāvāt | ye hi dharmāḥ santi teṣāṃ*

pratyakṣam upalabdhir bhavaty asaty antarāye | tadyathā ṣaṇṇāṃ viṣayāṇāṃ manasaś ca | anumānaṃ ca | tadyathā pañcānāṃ indriyāṇām / tatredam anumānam sati kāraṇe kāraṇāntarasyābhāve kāryasyābhāvo dṛṣṭo bhāve ca punarbhavas tadyathāṅkurasya | saty eva vābhāsaprāpte viṣaye manaskāre ca kāraṇe viṣayagrahasyābhāvo dṛṣṭaḥ punaś ca bhāvo 'ndhabadhirādīnām anandhābadhirādīnāṃ ca | atas tatrāpi kāraṇāntarasyābhāvo bhāvaś ca niścīyate | yac ca tatkāraṇāntaraṃ tadindriyam ity etad anumānam | na caivam ātmano 'stīti nāstyātmā. More-or-less the same argument is made in much shorter form with reference to the unreality of the unconditioned at AKBh II.55d.

16. The fragments that exist are sufficient to show that Vasubandhu's work was a strong precedent to Dignāga in Buddhist *pramāṇa* studies. Anacker (1998:31) credits Vasubandhu's writings with "the dawn of Indian formal logic." The main fragments are the sections from his *Vādavidhi*, cited by Dignāga and Jinendrabuddhi extant in Tibetan translation, collected in Frauwallner 1957, and introduced and translated in Anacker 1998:31–48. I will discuss one fragment below. It is of course possible to doubt that these fragments were written by the person who composed the AKBh, but as my first chapter explains, I am pursuing the assumption of continuity among these works. Verhagen (2008:253–258) provides an edition of the section from the VyY on the three *pramāṇas*.
17. Vasubandhu appeals to the three means of knowledge in several passages in the AKBh, and also in the Vyākhyāyukti. In this he is in agreement with a number of Yogācāra texts, as observed by Tucci (Verhagen 2008:245). It would appear that Yogācāra philosophers before Vasubandhu were already interested in establishing a Buddhist approach to *pramāṇa*.
18. Though perhaps not. Vasubandhu identifies two categories of objects, one for each *pramāṇa*, and does not allow that a third type of object exists which might be unidentifiable by the two *pramāṇas* he mentions.
19. Thus, Dignāga was not the first to suggest that different *pramāṇas*—different means of knowledge—come to know different sets of objects.
20. Woodward 2003:37.
21. This doctrine would appear to be a formalization of the understanding of the real as what has causal efficacy. Anacker (1998:32) cites Vasubandhu's *Vādavidhi* as the first Indian text to suggest that a proof requires invariable concomitance (*avinābhāva*) between the reason and the proven property. For Vasubandhu, like Dharmakīrti, that necessary concomitance is rooted in causality, understood in this simple, manipulationist mode. Wiggle one thing and the other changes. This is what Vasubandhu says is lacking in the quest for a proof of a self. This is simply an extension, for him, of saying that there is nothing that can only be explained as having been caused by a self.

    Although I do see a direct line here from Vasubandhu to Dharmakīrti, I would emphasize that I do not intend to impose on Vasubandhu a reification of causal powers or an empiricist foundationalism, as are often attributed to Dharmakīrti. We will see shortly that Vasubandhu's understanding of causal relations coheres with Woodward's relativistic approach, according to which what is termed a "cause" is always relative to the investigative framework. Like any other imposition across *dharmas*, causality is a conceptual construction, and not substantial. This is true even though it is only through appeals to causality that inference provides us the means for calling some entities substantially real.

22. AKBh III.26b–c.
23. As discussed in chapter 2, Vasubandhu also refuses to accept that the future must exist as an object of a Buddha's awareness. He says that Sautrāntikas hold that merely by intending it, the Buddha knows whatever he chooses to know, but they do not base this on any particular causal story of how a Buddha knows the future. Rather, they base this view on the scripture that says that the qualities of a Buddha's awareness are incomprehensible. AKBh 99.10: *tasmāt sarvam icchāmātreṇa bhagavān jānātīti sautrāntikāḥ | acintyo hi buddhānāṃ buddhiviṣaya ity uktaṃ bhagavatā.* See below for discussion of the incomprehensible (*acintya*).
24. This is clear also in the proof of momentariness (see below). Yet Vasubandhu's commonsense, relative preference for the evidence of perceiving something over inferring it (which often relies on the analysis of perceptions in any case) should not be taken to indicate a deeper claim to anything resembling empiricist foundationalism. Perception may be the best mode of knowledge, and it may be the source of a Buddha's perfect knowledge, but it does not give us perfect, direct, or even accurate knowledge. As we have seen in chapter 3, Vasubandhu believes that we fail to see things as they are even through perception. If atomic *dharmas* are imperceptible, he argued, then perception cannot give you knowledge of *dharmas.* We do not perceive what we think we perceive. Nonetheless, as I read Vasubandhu, even if perceptual knowledge is shot through with false conceptualization, it is the basis for our knowledge of the world and its living beings, and we cannot pretend to do without it. Inference relies upon and builds upon perceptual knowledge, but only by moving yet a further step into conceptual construction and away from causal reality.
25. That is, it is the source of the line that extends through Dignāga to Dharmakīrti and on. It is not the first Buddhist text to present *pramāṇa* discussions, however. See Verhagen 2008:244–247 and sources cited therein.
26. Frauwallner 1957:135–136: *de 'dra ba dang med na mi 'byung ba'i chos nye bar ston pa gtan tshigs so zhes pa ni | don gang sgra mi rtag pa nyid la sogs pa bsgrub par bya ba de 'dra ba ste | de'i rigs can med na don gang zhig 'gar yang 'byung ba ma yin pa ste | rtsol ba las byung ba nyid ni mi rtag pa nyid lta bu dang du ba ni me lta bu'o zhes pa de ni de 'dra ba med na mi 'byung ba'i chos can te | de nye bar ston pa ni 'dis nye bar* [136] *bstan par bya'o zhes pa'i tha tshig go || dper na brtsal ma thag tu byung ba nyid kyi phyir zhes pa 'di lta bu la sogs pa ste de ni gtan tshigs so || gang gis nye bar ston pa ma yin pa de ni gtan tshigs ma yin te | dper na sgra mi rtag ste mig gis gzung bya nyid kyi phyir zhes pa 'di lta bu la sogs pa'o.*
27. It proves a philosophical problem for Buddhists to account for certitude under an epistemology that denies the reality of conceptual constructions. See Arnold 2005, 2012. Reading through Vasubandhu, I find the basic Buddhist view to be that concepts are not real because they are not causally viable except to the degree that they are made up, constructed, by mental events. This means that ideas themselves are not causes; the minds that hold them are. But this talk of "holding" imports the basic illusion of selfhood into our talk *about* concepts. There is no agent, no subject who "holds" an idea. The mental event that constructs an appearance is the "holding." As I will explain in chapter 5, Vasubandhu argues that, like hairs that appear before diseased eyes, the appearance of "holding" an idea is a delusory by-product of the perceptual structure of awareness (see also Gold 2006 for more detail

on this). Thus, there is no distinction between "reasons" and "causes," because "reasons" are real only as mental events. There is, thus, no distinct "logical space of reasons" (Sellars, cited in Arnold 2005:54 and throughout Arnold 2012)—but until liberation, it unavoidably appears as though there is.

28. Cardona (1967–1968:352) shows that the grammarians used these concepts to establish a causal relationship between words or grammatical forms and the resultant arising of understanding of their meanings. Vasubandhu applies the process in a quite similar way to perception—establishing a causal relationship between its causes and the resultant awareness.
29. To put it another way, we could say that the requirement of a linear approach to causality transforms *anvaya* and *vyatireka* into the structure for a hypothetical manipulation. This is Vasubandhu's understanding of the Buddhist doctrine of the impermanence of all conditioned things: if something is permanent, it cannot be engaged with the flow of causes, and therefore it cannot be a true, substantial existent. The converse is that every substantial existent can be detected in some hypothetical manipulation.
30. Let us postpone the discussion of the implications of the ontological status of causality itself as, ironically, a mere conceptual construct that nonetheless verifies the substantial nature of entities. Ultimately, Vasubandhu finds this paradox best addressed in the Yogācāra rejection of the very concept of "reality." For the time being, it only means that to say that something is unreal or uncaused does not mean it does not occur, only that it fails to meet the criterion of substantiality. Things surely pass out of existence. But their "nonexistence" is not a substantial thing.
31. Matilal 1977:81.
32. Williams (1998a:78–80) discusses the nonexistence of negation in the Tibetan interpretation of Śāntideva; we may move this idea back to Vasubandhu. Williams makes it clear that Śāntideva shares Vasubandhu's view that negation is in the mind, even to the point of affirming the inherent conceptual connection between the negation and the negandum.
33. AKBh 193.10–14: *dṛṣṭo vai kāṣṭhādīnām agnyādisaṃyogād vināśaḥ | na ca dṛṣṭād gariṣṭaṃ pramāṇam astīti | na ca sarvasyākasmiko vināśaḥ | kathaṃ tāvat bhavān kāṣṭādīnām agnyādisaṃyogād vināśaṃ paśyāmīti manyate | teṣāṃ punar adarśanāt | saṃpradhāryaṃ tāvad etat | kim agnisaṃyogāt kāṣṭhādayo vinaṣṭā ato na dṛśyante utāho svayaṃ vinaṣṭā anye ca punar notpannā ato na dṛśyante | yathā vāyusaṃyogāt pradīpaḥ pāṇisaṃyogād dhaṇṭāśabda iti | tasmād anumānasādhyo 'yam arthaḥ.*
34. AKBh II.55 (91.14–21). In this passage there is an even stronger point to be made about the connection between Vasubandhu's denial of nonexistents and his view of the unitary causal line. For the reason the Sarvāstivādins give that *nirvāṇa* must be a cause is that it is the experiential object of the Buddha's awareness. In answer, Vasubandhu makes the distinction, discussed in chapter 2 with regard to past and future experiential objects, between "producer conditions" and merely experiential objects. The latter, he says, are not properly causes. Here he uses slightly different terms: instead of distinguishing a "producer condition" (*janakaḥ pratyayaḥ*) from a "merely experiential object" (*ālambanamātra*), he quotes the Buddha's claim that the conditions "for arising" (*utpādāya*) are impermanent, and says that this is not the same as saying that all conditions are impermanent. The

point is the same: the Buddha did not intend to say that objects of awareness, which are named "experiential object conditions" of that awareness, must be producers of that awareness. Hence, they do not need to exist in order to be mental objects. Conversely, to return to the point at hand, nonexistent entities can be known, even by a Buddha, without being, thereby, substantial. This point, and its connection to the argument over the three times, is confirmed when, in answer to the objector's concern, "If the unconditioned were simply nonexistent, then awareness of space and *nirvāṇa* would have nonexistent experiential objects," Vasubandhu replies, "We will consider this in the context of considering the existence of past and future." AKBh 93.13–14: *yady asaṃskṛtam abhāvamātraṃ syād ākāśanirvāṇālambanavijñānam asadālambanaṃ syād | etad atītānāgatasyāstitvacintāyāṃ cintayiṣyāmaḥ.*

35. Von Rospatt (1995) shows that the argument from the unreality of a nonexistent is Vasubandhu's distinctive contribution to the history of the doctrine of momentariness.
36. It would be admissible to take the sixth case of *yaś cābhāvas tasya kiṃ kartavyam* as an instrumental, which would give us, "What result is to be made by that which is nonexistent?" or "What can that which is nonexistent do?" Presumably, however, this is not quite Vasubandhu's point, since under such a reading the nonexistent would be the cause. I take the argument to be that the nonexistent is either the result in question or, possibly, that neither cause nor result are relevant to something that does not exist.
37. AKBh 193.4–9: *syād etad eva yadi sarvasya kṣaṇikatvaṃ sidhyet | siddham evaitat viddhi | kutaḥ | saṃskṛtasyāvaśyaṃ vyayāt ||* (2) [IV.2d2] *ākasmiko hi bhāvānāṃ vināśaḥ | kiṃ kāraṇam | kāryasya hi kāraṇaṃ bhavati | vināśaś cābhāvaḥ | yaś cābhāvas tasya kiṃ kartavyam | so 'sāv ākasmiko vināśo yadi bhāvasyotpannamātrasya na syāt paścād api na syād bhāvasya tulyatvāt.*
38. AKBh III.59d; see chapter 2.
39. This is true about this passage, even though, as mentioned above, Vasubandhu generally shares in the Yogācāra tendency of appealing to three *pramāṇas*. See Verhagen 2008:244–247.
40. Without Dignāga's innovative terminology, on which see Arnold 2005:13–31.
41. Without Dharmakīrti's innovative definitions, on which see Dreyfus 1997: esp. 65–67. This does not, however, make Vasubandhu into an empirical foundationalist, since for him causality itself is a useful, but ultimately false, conceptual construction.
42. I believe Dignāga's *apoha* theory derives its impetus here as well, from Vasubandhu's theory of the inferential construction of nonexistence, though to explain that complex theory would take us too far afield. For the current state of the art, see Siderits et al. 2011. The Nyāya, for their part, took the opposite path. They came to reify the nonexistent, to add it to their list of entities. For to admit to the conceptual construction of nonentities was to give in to the Buddhists, who (with Dignāga) used this to construct a nonrealist theory that supported the entire edifice of language and conceptualization.
43. Woodward 2003:85.
44. Woodward 2003:18.
45. Woodward 2003:90.
46. This is Vasubandhu's understanding of the Buddhist doctrine of the impermanence of all conditioned things: if something is permanent, it cannot conceivably be

engaged with the flow of causes, and therefore it cannot be a true, substantial existent. The converse is that every substantial existent can be detected in some hypothetical manipulation.

The fact that causality is a dependence relation whose postulation requires only hypothetical, not actual, intervention helps to address a number of misunderstandings of Vasubandhu's reductionist approach, especially as it applies to abstract entities. As just one example, Vasubandhu denies that a soul must exist to exercise "ownership" over experiences, or that "ownership" exists in the abstract, over and above the owner and the entity owned. He says, instead, that the relationship between owner and owned is causal—the owner is the one who milks the cow, and takes it to market, and so on.

Jonardon Ganeri's recent book cites, favorably, later Nyāya philosophers who criticize this idea of Vasubandhu's that ownership can be reduced to causal relations between owner and owned. As they say, ownership is not any particular action or set of actions, but rather a capacity that an owner has, to do what he likes with his property. To push the point, then, Ganeri writes, "A capacity might go unexercised, so there may be no causal connections corresponding to it" (2013:176). Now that we know that Vasubandhu sees causality as a dependence relation determinable through a merely hypothetical intervention, and not any actual set of events, the fact that the capacity of ownership may be unexercised is irrelevant to the validity of the claimed causal relation. Granted, we speak conventionally as though there is some "ownership" that Chaitra has, over and above Chaitra's various relevant acts and decisions about his cow. But you cannot say that an appearance is a reality by appealing to a mere convention.

47. A particularly clear example is found in Madhava (Stoker 2004), but the point could be made just as well about the distinction between Mīmāṃsā and Vedānta, or about the distinction between *āstikas* and *nāstikas*. Scriptural interpretation, and the methods of justifying scriptures, are crucial issues that determine philosophical positions.
48. "The knower of the text is beloved of the gods, but is not a knower of meanings! The Lord says the meaning is the refuge." AKBh 76.24–25: *granthajño devānāṃ priyo na tv arthajñaḥ | arthaś ca pratiśaraṇam uktaṃ bhagavatā.*
49. AKBh III.30b.
50. AKBh 143.17. Interestingly, he also accuses his opponents of doing the same (which they would, presumably deny), saying that they would accept an emendation of the text, or a figurative interpretation.
51. AKBh 64.7: *lobhasyāvinodanaṃ.*
52. AKBh 468.1–8; Kapstein 2001a:360–361, section 6.3. Pāsādika (1989:128) identifies the source in the *Bhārahārasūtra.*
53. This is a claim that I have begun to document using statistical analysis of scriptural citations and arguments in the AKBh, but it is not yet decisively proven. The sources to exemplify Vasubandhu's approach to scriptures used in what follows are primarily drawn from the section of the AKBh with the longest, most densely packed series of scriptural citations, which is verses 4–44 of chapter III.
54. Kapstein 2001a:359.
55. AKBh 91.23: *sūtrāṇi ca bahūny antarhitānīti katham etan nirdhāryate nokta iti.* This AKBh passage is proposed by an opponent; but Vasubandhu makes the same point himself in the KSP and the VyY.

56. AKBh 124.11–12.
57. AKBh 123.14–17.
58. AKBh 128.14.
59. AKBh 133.15. Cox (1992) reads this as only a principle of Vaibhāṣika scholasticism, but I take it that it coheres with Vasubandhu's overall approach even as a Sautrāntika. Abhidharma is intended to determine the definitive truth—what is substantially real. This point describes the purpose of this type of text, quite aside from declarations of the authority of any given text of the genre.
60. AKBh IX (466.5–471.21) explains the Buddha's reasons for famously having refused to address certain difficult topics, calling them "undeclared" (*avyākṛta*). See Kapstein 2001a:363–366 for a translation. There are, in fact, many reasons for the Buddha's having refrained from speaking forthrightly. Nance (2012:135) provides a translation from Vasubandhu's VyY of the "eight purposes for rhetorical strategies" in the Buddha's discourses. The lesson from all of this is that when something is "unsaid," it is for a specific reason: nonspeech has an intention just like speech does. Things that are not spoken of are not necessarily ineffable.
61. AKBh 115.4–5. As another example of this, two competing *sūtras* are in evidence at AKBh 143.2ff, where the Sautrāntikas have it out with the Sarvāstivādins about the nature of contact. One *sūtra* says that the coming together of the three kinds of *dharmas* for each sense (organ, object, and consciousness) just is the contact (143.17: *ya eṣāṃ trayāṇāṃ saṃgatiḥ saṃnipātaḥ samavāyaḥ sa sparśaḥ*), and the Sautrāntika takes this on its face as a definition of contact as just the activity of the distinct entities. The other *sūtra* passage (143.8–10) contains a list of "six sixes" (*ṣaṭṣaṭko*) which include the organs, objects, and consciousnesses along with the "six contacts" (*ṣaṭsparśakāyāḥ*), "six feelings," and "six thirsts"—which the Sarvāstivādins take as evidence that these are distinct things. Vasubandhu's reply is that if these are taken as a list of six separate things, then the six feelings and the six thirsts should be distinct from even the *dharmāyatana*, which is absurd.
62. AKBh 131.12–14.
63. Did the Buddha have to have "acted locally?" There is no reason, in principle, that a Buddha could not foresee that his words would be written down and misinterpreted by textual literalists in the future—which he did less than he perhaps could have to prevent. But the Buddha took it as his responsibility to focus on transforming the minds of his students, even if that meant confusion for his students' students' students' students' students. This may be a reasonable choice, if made on the assumption that the decline of the *dharma* is unavoidable.
64. Kapstein 2001a:359.
65. VyY 227.9–18: *gzhan yang theg pa chen po sangs rgyas kyi gsung ma yin no zhes zer na | sangs rgyas kyi gsung gi mtshan nyid ci yin zhes brgyal zhing brtag par bya'o || smras pa | sangs rgyas kyi gsung nyid du sde pa bco brgyad dag gis yongs su bzung ba gang yin pa'o zhe na | 'o na don dam pa stong pa nyid la sogs pa'i mdo sde bdag med pa dang ldan pa 'phags pa kun gyis bkur ba'i sde pa dag gis khas mi len pa dag dang | srid pa bar ma do dang ldan pa srid pa bdun zhes bya ba de lta bu la sogs pa sa ston pa'i sde la sogs pa rnams kyis khas mi len pa gang yin pa de dag sangs rgyas kyi gsung du mi 'gyur ro.*
66. Conze 2001:97.

67. See Gold (forthcoming) for my discussion of the Yogācāra response to the interpretation of Mahāyāna scriptures, in which Vasubandhu played a key clarifying role.
68. This point is made by Cabezón (1992) in his pioneering study of the VyY.
69. VyY 236.18–237.3: *nged ni gang zak kun rdzob tu yod kyi rdzas su ni ma yin te | phung po rnams la de'i ming gdags pa'i phyir ro || las dang rnam par smin pa dag ni kun rdzob tu rdzas su yod | don dam par ni med de | 'jig rten pa'i shes pa'i yul yin pa'i phyir ro | dam [237] pa ni ye shes 'jig rten las 'das pa yin te | de'i don yin pas don dam pa'o || de gnyis kyi rang gi mtshan nyid ni de'i yul ma yin te | de'i yul ni brjod du med pa'i phyi'i mtshan nyid yin ba'i phyir ro.*
70. VyY 237.6–13.
71. VyY 237.15–19: *yang theg pa chen po pa kha cig thams cad rang gi mtshan nyid du ni med pa kho na yin la | kun rdzob tu ni bcom ldan 'das kyis chos rnams yod pa nyid du bstan to zhes sgra ji bzhin pa nyid kyi don yin par brjod pa gang yin pa de dag la ji skad bstan pa'i rtsod pa 'di yang 'byung bar 'gyur ro.*
72. VyY 239.18–22: *brjod du med pa'i mtshan nyid dag chos rnams thams cad yin na ni | byis pa rnams kyis kun tu brtags pa bzhin du brjod pas | rjod par byed pa de'i rjes so 'brangs nas 'phags pa rnams kyis kyang min med pa rnams ming gis yongs su brjod pa yin par rung ngo.* This point is the culmination of Vasubandhu's argument in this passage from the VyY, translated in appendix E. See also Cabezon 1992 on the VyY's view of Buddhist scripture.
73. This sentence, from Vasubandhu's VyY quotation, is different from SNS.
74. VyY 239.22–240.10: *de ltar na dgongs pa nges par 'grel ba'i mdo las | rigs kyi bu 'dus byas zhes bya ba de ni ston pas btags pa'i tshig yin te | ston pas btags pa'i tshig gang yin pa de ni kun tu [240] rtog pa las byung ba tha snyad du brjod pa yin la | kun tu rtog pa las byung ba tha snyad du brjod pa gang yin pa de ni kun tu rtog pa sna tshogs kyi tha snyad du brjod pa gtan yongs su ma grub pa'i phyir 'dus byas ma yin no || 'dus byas ji lta ba bzhin du 'dus ma byas kyang de bzhin no zhes de bzhin du sbyar ro || 'dus byas dang 'dus ma byas su ma gtogs pa gang ci brjod kyang de yang de dang 'dra ba nyid du 'gyur ro || de yang brjod pa ni dngos po med pa can yang ma yin te | dngos po de yang gang zhe na | 'phags pa rnams kyis 'phags pa'i shes pa dang 'phags pa'i mthong bas brjod du med par mngon par rdzogs par sangs rgyas pa gang yin pa ste.*
75. Siderits (2009) discusses a similar point regarding the difficulty of speaking of ultimate and conventional realities—within the same frame of reference or in the same sentence. I read Vasubandhu's solution as something akin to what Siderits calls "panfictionalism" and attributes to Jñānaśrī—the view "that anything expressible is a conceptual fiction" (67). The difficulty with this solution, as Siderits notes, is that it must somehow still maintain distinctions within the conventional—a problem that I see Vasubandhu addressing through appeals to manipulationist causal framing and the pragmatics of scriptural interpretation.
76. Dunne 2004 and McClintock 2010. Dreyfus (1997) refers to "ascending scales of analysis."
77. AKBh 126.7: *ata eva coktaṃ bhagavatā acintyaḥ sattvānāṃ karmavipāka iti.*
78. AKBh 121.5: *acintyo hi dharmāṇāṃ śaktibhedaḥ.*
79. AKBh 99.10: *tasmāt sarvam icchāmātreṇa bhagavān jānātīti sautrāntikāḥ | acintyo hi buddhānāṃ buddhiviṣaya ity uktaṃ bhagavatā.*
80. Kapstein 2001a:357–367.

5. VASUBANDHU'S YOGĀCĀRA: ENSHRINING THE CAUSAL LINE IN THE THREE NATURES

1. For translations of the KSP, see Lamotte 1936, Anacker 1998:83–156, and Pruden 1987. Studies of the relation between KSP and other texts attributed to Vasubandhu include Hirakawa et al. 1973, Yoshihito 1993, and Skilling 2000.
2. AKBh IV.3 (194.14–18): *nāsti saṃsthānaṃ dravyata iti sautrāntikāḥ | ekadiṅmukhe hi bhūyasi varṇa utpanne dīrghaṃ rūpam iti prajñapyate | tam evāpekṣyālpīyasi hrasvam iti | caturdiśaṃ bhūyasi caturasram iti | sarvatra same vṛttam iti | evaṃ sarvam | tadyathā 'lātam ekasyāṃ diśi deśāntareṣv anantareṣu nirantaramāśu dṛśyamānaṃ dīrgham iti pratīyate sarvato dṛśyamānaṃ maṇḍalam iti | na tu khalu jātyantaram asti saṃsthānam.*
3. As Anacker (1998:130–131, n12) has noted, *lham pa* is probably a mistaken translation of *vṛtta*, which means "circle," here, as it is in two passages in the Tibetan translation of the AKBh (Hirakawa et al. 1973:340).
4. Anacker (1998:131, n12) takes these as "concave" and "convex."
5. KSP D.135r7–v4: *phyogs gcig gi sgor 'dus pa mang por snang ba la ni ring po'i blo 'byung | thung du la thung* [135v] *du'i blo 'byung | thams cad nas mnyam bar snang ba la ni lham pa'i blo 'byung | khor yug nas mnyam pa la ni zlum po'i blo 'byung | dbus na mang po la ni mthon po'i blo 'byung | nyung ba la ni dma' ba'i blo 'byung | phyogs gcig gi skor snang ba la ni phya le ba'i blo 'byung | phyogs sna tshogs kyi sgo la ni phya le ma yin pa'i blo 'byung ngo |. . . . kha dog kho na yul gi khyad par gnas pa la ring po la sogs pa'i blo dag 'byung ste | dper na shing dang bya dang | grog ma la sogs pa'i dngar ka dag la 'byung ba lta bu ste.*
6. This may not be true for all theories of language, but it ought to be for the AKBh. AKBh I.14 (10.16) has the third *skandha, saṃjñā*, "idea," as the grasper of concepts, including such examples as "long" (*dīrgha*) and "short" (*hrasva*).
7. AKBh II.47a–b (80.24–25): *vāṅnāmni pravarttate nāmārthaṃ dyotayati naiva ghoṣamātraṃ vāgyena tu ghoṣeṇārthaḥ pratīyate sa ghoṣo vāk.*
8. AKBh II.47a–b (81.21): *atrārtheṣu kṛtābadhiḥ śabdo nāma . . .*
9. For this reason, Vasubandhu's position in the AKBh might be subject to Arnold's (2012:140–141) critique of Dharmakīrti that while he would like to have reduced linguistic events to causal stories, in fact his causal stories always appeal at some point to a human subject. The KSP is not, however, subject to this critique.
10. By calling the false projection "subjectivity," I am emphasizing the subjective component in the denial of duality here, but of course duality has two sides (which is the point of its name), and Vasubandhu does spend a good deal of his time disproving the mistaken construction of mental *objects* as well as *subjects*. The error of "duality," though, is not the mistake of reifying any particular mental object or momentary subject, per se; it is, rather, a mistake implicit in the *structure* of awareness and language. Modern theorists following Brentano talk about the "intentionality" of language and consciousness, by which is meant the "aboutness" that makes consciousness and meaning what they are; consciousness is always consciousness *of* something, and words are always *about* something. For Vasubandhu's Yogācāra, as we will see, the term "duality" (*dvaya*) picks out this "aboutness" of consciousness and language and calls it a fundamental error that appears in every conceptual-linguistic moment until enlightenment. Things appear "dual" when in fact they are "only cause and effect."

11. See Schmithausen 1984, Aramaki 2000, and Buescher 2008 on this passage. It is Schmithausen's thesis that this was the "initiatory passage" of the *vijñapti-mātra*, a view with which Buescher disagrees. See chapter 3, note 71. As will become clear, the key point for me here is that the term *vijñapti-mātra* is being used to deny the distinction between mind and mental objects.
12. Here I am referring to Vasubandhu's citation of the SNS at the pinnacle of his scriptural hermeneutics (see chapter 4). For his use, and transformation, of the discussion of the elephant analogy from SNS I, see Gold 2006.
13. SNS VIII.7 (91.2–3): *ci'i phyir tha dad pa ma yin zhe na | gzugs brnyan de rnam par rig pa tsam du zad pa'i phyir te.*
14. SNS VIII.7 (91.7–8): *sems de nyid kyis sems de nyid la ji ltar rtog par bgyid lags.*
15. SNS VIII.7 (91.8–17): *byams pa de la chos gang yang chos gang la 'ang rtog par mi byed mod kyi | 'on kyang de ltar skyes pa'i sems gang yin pa de ni de ltar snang ngo | byams pa 'di lta ste dper na | gzugs la brten nas me long gi dkyil 'khor shin tu yongs su dag pa la gzugs nyid mthong yang gzugs brnyan mthong ngo snyam du sems te | de la gzugs de dang | gzugs brnyan snang ba de don tha dad par snang ngo || de bzhin du de ltar skyes pa'i sems de dang | ting nge 'dzin gyi spyod yul gzugs brnyan zhes bya ba gang yin pa de 'ang de las don gzhan yin pa lta bur snang ngo.*
16. AKBh 31.11–13: *kim idam ākāśaṃ khādyate | cakṣur hi pratītya rūpāṇi cotpadyate cakṣurvijñānam | tatra kaḥ paśyati ko vā dṛśyate | nirvyāpāraṃ hīdaṃ dharmamātraṃ hetuphalamātraṃ ca.*
17. Dignāga claims that "self-cognition" (*svasaṃvitti*) must be present within a mental event if it is to account for the subsequent arising of memory. If by this he means self-cognition to be a separate entity, he would seem to have forgotten, or betrayed, this argument of Vasubandhu's. The doctrine of self-cognition is elaborated upon by Dharmakīrti and his successors, and is a topic of wide-ranging discussion in the contemporary study of Buddhist philosophy. See, for instance, Arnold 2012: esp. 158–198, Coseru 2012, Williams 1998b, and Yao 2005. Vasubandhu does not take up the problem introduced and expanded upon by these authors, traditional and modern. In addition to his evident displeasure with the argument from memory, see his response to the issue of the Buddha's omniscience, at AKBh VII.18, which I discussed in chapter 3, note 42. Vasubandhu's view is straightforwardly that subjectivity is a false construction, which falls away at enlightenment. Once the duality between subject and object dissolves, the self-awareness of consciousness does not arise, since nondual awareness is inconceivable. Memory, however, is sufficiently supported by ordinary causality. The prior awareness is a support (*āśraya*) for the later consciousness, just like any other mental consciousness. See below for further discussion of Vasubandhu's disproof of subjectivity, and for his treatment of the memory argument in the Viṃś.
18. On this move from the meditative context to a global metaphysical claim, see Griffiths 1991 and Schmithausen 2005.
19. SNS VII.8 (91.18–24): *bcom ldan 'das sems can rnams kyi gzugs la sogs par snang ba sems kyi gzugs brnyan rang bzhin du gnas pa gang lags pa de 'ang sems de dang tha dad pa ma lags zhes bgyi 'am | bka' stsal pa | byams pa tha dad pa ma yin zhes bya ste | byis pa phyin ci log gi blo can rnams ni gzugs brnyan de dag la rnam par rig pa tsam de nyid yang dag pa ji lta ba bzhin mi shes pas phyin ci log tu sems so.*

20. Viṃś 3.2: *mahāyāne traidhātukaṃ vijñaptimātraṃ vyavasthāpyate*. See Rahder 1926:49 for the *Daśabhūmikasūtra* source.
21. In addition to sources mentioned in the "Doctrinal Positions and Works" section of Gold 2011, see Siderits 2007:146–173 for an insightful summary of the argument discussed in this section, and Kapstein 2001b for a close analysis of the argument about perceptual objects. Beginning here, several pages from Gold 2011 have been edited for integration into the present work, and are printed here with the kind permission of the Stanford Encyclopedia of Philosophy.
22. See Gold 2011 for a discussion of the question of Yogācāra as "idealism."
23. The work is generally described as a defense of the Yogācāra school of Mahāyāna Buddhism, in contradistinction to the Madhyamaka school. But during Vasubandhu's time there was no division between Yogācāra and Madhyamaka; on the contrary, the SNS claims to "clarify the intent" of the Mahāyāna overall, and eliminate disputation. Although Asaṅga and Vasubandhu do call into question certain alternative interpretations of Mahāyāna (see Gold forthcoming), these intra-Mahāyāna disputes do not arise in the Viṃś. My understanding, therefore, is that the Viṃś sees the defense of "appearance only" as a clarifying defense of Mahāyāna overall.
24. Failure to appreciate this fact lies at the root of many of the most common critiques of Vasubandhu's argument, both traditional and modern. See for instance Sarachchandra 1976 and Feldman 2005.
25. See Gold 2006, and sources cited therein, for further discussion of Vasubandhu's use of the dream example.
26. This is what Siderits (2007:157) calls Vasubandhu's use of the "Principle of Lightness," or Occam's razor. It may also be recast as a declaration that the doctrine of appearance-only solves the continuity problems associated with the causal relationship between physical and mental entities.
27. The alternative to this quandary would be to deny *karma* and be stuck with a different quandary, what Owen Flanagan (2009) calls "the really hard problem" of how to find meaning in a physical world whose causes are *not* indexed to human intentions.
28. Kapstein (2003b) introduces and translates Vasubandhu's mereological argument in full. I provide a bit more detail in Gold 2011 than I do here.
29. Viṃś 6.29–30: *na tāvad ekaṃ viṣayo bhavaty avayavebhyo 'nyasyāvayavirūpasya kvacid apy agrahaṇāt.*
30. Viṃś 6.30–7.1: *nāpyanekaṃ paramāṇūnā pratyekam agrahaṇāt.*
31. Viṃś 8.22–9.1: *pramāṇavaśād astitvaṃ nāstitvaṃ vā nirdhāryate sarveśāṃ ca pramāṇānāṃ pratyakṣaṃ pramāṇaṃ gariśṭam ity asaty arthe katham iyaṃ buddhir bhavati pratyakṣam iti* | ***pratyakṣabuddhiḥ svapnādau yathā*** [16a–b1] *vināpy artheneti pūrvam eva jñāpitaṃ* | ***sā ca yadā tadā*** | ***na so 'rtho dṛśyate tasya pratyakṣatvaṃ kathaṃ mataṃ*** || (16) [16b2–d] *yadā ca sā pratyakśabuddhir bhavatīdaṃ me pratyakṣam iti tadā na so 'rtho dṛśyate manovijñānenaiva paricchedāc cakṣurvijñānasya ca tadā niruddhatvād iti* | *kathaṃ tasya pratyakṣatvam iṣṭaṃ* | *viśeṣeṇa tu kṣaṇikasya viṣayasya tadānīṃ niruddham eva tad rūpaṃ rasādikaṃ vā.*
32. Viṃś 16–17, 9.1–8: *nānanubhūtaṃ manovijñānena smaryata ity avaśyam arthānubhavena bhavitavyaṃ tac ca darśanam ity evaṃ tad viṣayasya rūpādeḥ pratyakṣatvaṃ mataṃ* | *asiddham idam anubhūtasyārthasya smaraṇaṃ bhavatīti* | *yasmāt* | ***uktaṃ yathā tadābhāsā***

vijñaptiḥ [17a–b1] *vināpy arthena yathārthābhāsā cakṣurvijñānādikā vijñaptir utpadyate tathoktam* | *smaraṇaṃ tataḥ* | [17b2] *tato hi vijñapteḥ smṛtisaṃprayuktā tatpratibhāsaiva rūpādivikalpikā manovijñaptir utpadyata iti na smṛtyutpādād arthānubhavaḥ sidhyati.*

33. As discussed in chapter 4, Vasubandhu preserves the notion of perception as a valid means of knowledge, especially for a Buddha, but in several places—as here—he considers it essential to use reason to test and contextualize what we think we perceive.
34. Vasubandhu does not use the term "emptiness" in this characteristic, Mahāyāna inflection in his corpus, except in the MAVBh (on which, see below), so it should not be assumed that this now common usage would be natural to him. But there is a clear continuity between my usage here, and below, of the term "emptiness," based in the MAV, and the lengthier but conceptually equivalent term "lack of own-being" (*ngo bo nyid ma mchis pa*) which appears in the SNS—a text that Vasubandhu cites and uses extensively. I have taken the liberty of simply referring to the concept in this shorter, more familiar, way. For discussion of this continuity, see below and Gold (forthcoming).
35. This is not to say that Vasubandhu was skeptical of Buddhist doctrine overall—quite the contrary—but he did believe that even Buddhist doctrine needed to be tested, to see how, and when, it was most literally true, and when it needed to be taken with a grain of salt. See chapter 4.
36. Sthiramati's famous commentary on the *Thirty Verses* does include extensive philosophical defenses of the doctrines advanced in the verses. But Vasubandhu's own arguments, if he had any, are lost. The verses include only definitions and lists of terms. The *Three Natures Exposition* is also a systematic survey with none of Vasubandhu's (or anyone else's) commentarial defenses. It is possible, of course, that one or both of these works is/are misattributed to Vasubandhu. The *Three Natures Exposition* is certainly quite different in style from his other works. Philosophically, however, it follows quite logically from his other works, as I argue here.
37. I have not made Vasubandhu's approach to the path a focus in this work, though it is surely a scholarly desideratum. Tzohar 2011 contains an insightful discussion of the Triṃś, which parallels my analysis here.
38. TSN 154.1–6: *kalpitaḥ paratantraś ca pariniṣpanna eva ca* | *trayaḥ svabhāvā dhīraṇāṃ gaṃbhīraṃ jñeyam iṣyate* || (1) *yat khyāti paratantro 'sau yathā khyāti sa kalpitaḥ* | *pratyayādhīnavṛttitvāt kalpanāmātrabhāvataḥ* || (2) *tasya khyātur yathākhyānaṃ yā sadāvidyamānatā* | *jñeyaḥ sa pariniṣpannaḥ svabhāvo 'nyathātvataḥ* || (3).
39. The interconnected, unified character of the three natures is especially clear in verses 10–16, where the identity of each nature is played against the others in such a way as to display their conceptual dependence. See below, and the notes to appendix G, where I discuss these interconnections in detail.
40. TSN 154.7–8: *tatra kiṃ khyāty asatkalpaḥ kathaṃ khyāti dvayātmanā* | *tasya kā nāstitā tena yā tatrādvayadharmatā* || (4).
41. Although I am satisfied with my past translation of the term *dvayātmanā* (here "as dual") with the phrase "as a dual self," this was something of a creative translation, and here I do not want to mislead the reader as to my intentions, which I argue for in detail in Gold 2006. The word *ātman* means "self"; it is what is denied by the Buddha. Thus the word *dvayātmanā* means, literally, "with a dual self" or "with

the self of duality." But in addition to the meaning "self," the term *ātman* also means, more broadly, "nature" or "essence," so it is quite often used idiomatically to mean "with the nature of *x*." This is a particularly common meaning in śāstric commentarial literature, but it may appear in verse as well. For this reason, most translators of the TSN read the verse to say that the unreal fabrication appears "as dual," or "with a dual nature," leaving aside any implicit meaning of "self." In the next line, however, the verse uses *advayadharmatā*, which I translate here as "there being no duality," to refer to the appearance's fundamental lack of a false, dual nature. The alternation between *ātmanā* (lit. "with a nature"/"with a self") and *dharmatā* ("true nature") enlivens the dead metaphor of *ātmanā*. There is an undeniable pun on the term *ātmanā*. The "dual self" (*dvayātman*) is the essential nature of the duality between subject and object, which generates, for living beings, the false belief in a self (*satkāyadṛṣṭi*—see chapter 3). It is directly contrasted with the "nondual true nature" (*advayadharmatā*). This punning meaning on "self" makes sense of both instances where Vasubandhu uses the term *ātmanā* in the TSN, as opposed to the instances where instead he uses the term *ātmika*, which has the same idiomatic meaning, but no implicit pun. As a further defense of this reading, I would point to the following passage from AKBh II.46, where Vasubandhu uses the term *ātmanā* with exactly the same implicit pun—the falsely imposed "nature" is the nature of a self: "How, when the *dharmas* of birth of birth, etc., have been made unified, does a *dharma* come about as a ninth nature (*ātmanā*)?" (AKBh 75.15–16: *jātijātyādīnāṃ caikatra dharme katham kṛtā ātmanā navamo hi dharma utpadyate.*) Since this is only a pun, though, and not a direct philosophical statement, here I leave the "dual self" in the notes.

42. TSN 154.18.
43. As I will discuss below, this amounts to saying that in order to free oneself of the false construction of self, to free oneself of the false imposition of "duality," one must overcome the experience of consciousness as "intentional" in the philosophical sense of being "about" its experiential objects.
44. See Gold 2006 for detailed treatment of duality in early Yogācāra. See sources cited therein for a diversity of opinions on this complex topic.
45. AKBh 31.15–16. Discussed in chapter 3.
46. DhDhVV 71–72: *chos nyid kyi mtshan nyid ni* | ***gzung ba dang*** | ***dzin pa dang*** | ***brjod par bya ba dang*** | ***rjos par byed pa khyad par med pa'i de bzhin nyid de ni chos nyid kyi mtshan nyid do*** | *gzung ba dang 'dzin pa'i khyad par med pa gang yin pa dang* | *brjod par bya ba dang* [72] | *rjod par byed pa khyad par med pa gang yin pa de ni de bzhin nyid yin la* | *de yang chos nyid kyi mtshan nyid yin no* || *khyad par med pa nyid ni rim pa ji lta ba bzhin gnyis su med pa'i phyir dang* | *brjod du med pa'i phyir te* | *gang la khyad par yod pa ma yin pa de ni khyad par med pa zhes bya bas so.*
47. Although I have presented conceptual duality as distinct from conceptual-linguistic duality, it seems possible to me that conceptual-linguistic duality is always the target for Yogācāra thinkers, and that the ostensible bifurcation of the world into *x* and not-*x* is considered a "duality" only because it is always the case that one or the other is intended. Since Vasubandhu's distinctive innovation is to foreground perceptual duality, I will not pursue the evidence of conceptual vs. conceptual-linguistic dualities here. Let me also acknowledge that the root verse in this passage does equate the nondifference of "grasper and grasped" with the

nondifference of "expression and expressed," and so does seem to be a central inspiration for Vasubandhu's commentarial uniting of the perceptual with the conceptual-linguistic forms of nonduality, as I will discuss below.

48. TSN 154.9–10: *asatkalpo 'tra kaṣ cittaṃ yatas tat kalpyate yathā | yatā ca kalpyaty arthaṃ tathātyantaṃ na vidyate* || (5).
49. TSN 154.11–18: *tad dhetuphalabhāvena cittaṃ dvividham iṣyate | yad ālayākhyavijñānaṃ pravṛttyākhyaṃ ca saptadhā* || (6) *saṃkleśavāsanābījaiś citatvāc cittam ucyate | cittam ādyam dvitīyaṃ tu citrākārapravṛttitaḥ* || (7) *samāsato 'bhūtakalpaḥ sa caiṣa trividho mataḥ | vaipākikas tathā naimittiko 'nyaḥ prātibhāsikaḥ* || (8) *prathamo mūlavijñānaṃ tad vipākātmakaṃ yataḥ | anyaḥ pravṛttivijñānaṃ dṛśyadṛgvittivṛttitaḥ* || (9).
50. In this way, the storehouse consciousness may be read to provide a far more robust account of personal continuity than could be achieved by simply calling the self an illusion. Conventionally speaking, we are who we are from moment to moment, and from life to life, because of the storing and subsequent activation of this subliminal store consciousness. Some Yogācāras even say that the purificatory transformation of this storehouse consciousness into a series of seeds devoid of negativities constitutes the attainment of Buddhahood. So the storehouse consciousness certainly accounts for some aspects of personal identity over time. Since the karmic "seeds" are momentary, like everything else, and the *ālayavijñāna* is nothing but those seeds, there is no ultimately real identity to the storehouse. But it provides a useful analogy.
51. TSN 156.3–10: *māyākṛtaṃ mantravaśāt khyāti hastyātmanā yathā | ākāramātraṃ tatrāsti hastī nāsti tu sarvathā* || (27) *svabhāvaḥ kalpito hastī paratantras tadākṛtiḥ | yas tatra hastyabhāvo 'sau pariniṣpanna iṣyate* || (28) *asatkalpas tathā khyāti mūlacittād dvayātmanā | dvayam atyantato nāsti tatrāsty ākṛtimātrakam* || (29) *mantravan mūlavijñānam kāṣṭhavat tathatā matā | hastyākāravad eṣṭavyo vikalpo hastivad dvayam* || (30).
52. Kaplan (1990) provides a useful modern analogy, the hologram, which was of course not available to Vasubandhu. In Gold 2006 I argue that Vasubandhu chose the magical illusion analogy for its ability to express the illusion of selfhood.
53. Gold 2006.
54. MAVBh 17.4: *vaktāraṃ cāsmadādibho*. D'Amato (2012) provides an excellent translation and study of the MAV/MAVBh. I have benefited from his readings, but I have added changes of my own.
55. This is not to say that Vasubandhu was among the first to hear the text. The commentary allows the interpretation that its author was one among several people to whom Asaṅga spoke the text, successively, at different times.
56. I adopt a rather simplistic naïveté for the sake of clarity. The author of the MAV may indeed have been someone other than Asaṅga. Perhaps Asaṅga found the text in a cave, or forgot where he had originally heard it after remembering it in a dream—either of which might account for his faith in the revelation. Perhaps his real master swore him to secrecy.
57. MAV I.1 (17.16–17): ***abhūta-parikalpo 'sti dvayan tatra na vidyate / śūnyatā vidyate tv atra tasyām api sa vidyate*** || (I.1).
58. The term "emptiness" (*śūnyatā*) is the famous, central term of art for the Madhyamaka tradition founded by Nāgārjuna. It has been argued that the opening verses of the MAV are an attempt to provide a reading of this term from a Yogācāra

perspective, but this is hardly an arbitrary shift in terminology; the MAV uses the term "emptiness" to refer to what the SNS (VII.31 [86.1]) calls "lack of own-being" (*ngo bo nyid ma mchis pa*).

59. MAVBh 18.1–4: *tatrābhūtaprikalpo grāhya-grāhaka-vikalpaḥ | dvayaṁ grāhyaṁ grāhakañ ca | śūnyatā tasyābhūtaparikalpasya grāhya-grāhaka-bhāvena virahitatā | tasyām api sa vidyata ity abhūtaparikalpaḥ.*
60. This expression is ordinarily translated "subject and object." D'Amato (2012) does so, and I am not intending to register a complaint about that translation. I only preserve the more technical vocabulary so as to highlight the terms as a grammatical pair, as I explain below.
61. Admittedly, sometimes the term *dvaya* in the verses just refers to "two" of something (I.25, II.11). Yet there are several instances in which the verse text of the MAV uses *dvayam* to describe something metaphysically basic, and false. In those cases, we generally find it, as in this case, in close proximity to *bhāva-abhāva* or *sat-asat*; and these are exactly the contexts in which Vasubandhu glosses the term as "grasper and grasped" (I.1–2, I.13). In the TSN, we find the pattern of *dvayam* paired with *sat-asat* and *bhāva-abhāva* repeated over and over, but no use of *grāhya-grāhaka*. We do, however, find the use of *dṛṣyadṛgvitti*, which has the same meaning, as we will see, of consciousness and its object.
62. MAV I.2a–b (18.8): ***na śūnyaṁ nāpi caśūnyaṁ tasmāt sarvvam vidhīyate.***
63. A quick example on hand from the *Vajracchedika-sūtra* (Conze 2001:34–35): "Great, O Lord, great, O Well-Gone, would that Heap of merit be! And why? Because the Tathagata spoke of the 'heap of merit' as a non-heap. That is how the Tathagata speaks of 'heap of merit.'"
64. In none of these cases is the pair of terms referred to as a *dvayam*, a "duality," though they are referred to as "twofold" (*dvidhā*, at V.24)—they are, after all, two words. There is also an instructive use of the term *grahaṇa* at III.20.
65. This provides a parallel to TSN 9 if we read *dṛśyadṛgvitti* as three separate entities.
66. MAV III.17c–d (45.9): ***grāhaka-grāhya-tad-grāha-bījārthaś cāparo mataḥ.***
67. MAV III.4–5a (38.10–12): ***samāropāpavādasya dharmma-pudgalayor iha | grāhya-grāhakayoś cāpi bhāvābhāve ca darśanaṁ ||*** (III.4) ***yaj-jñānān na pravartteta tad dhi tatvasya lakṣaṇaṁ.***
68. Each also appears in the lists from MAV V.23–26.
69. MAV III.16b1 (44.5): *ātmadarśanam*. D'Amato 2012:152.
70. At AKBh II.59, Vasubandhu argued against *grahaṇa* as a mode of causality at a temporal distance. This is a different kind of false conception of "grasping," but, to characterize it as yet another version of this same illusion of false causality, it too expresses Vasubandhu's preference for causality understood in direct, causal lines.
71. A final meaning for *grahaṇa* that may be worth considering as we attempt to make sense of the attribution of the *grāhya-grāhaka* gloss to Vasubandhu is the meaning given the term by the Vaibhāṣikas in their discussions of causality and temporality. Vasubandhu had critiqued a vagueness in Vaibhāṣika terminology that seemed to allow for the same entity to be present at two separate moments (see chapter 2). According to Akimoto (2004), the Vaibhāṣika Saṃghabhadra responded to Vasubandhu's critique by insisting that entities exist in the past just until the moment of their "taking" (*grahaṇa/pratigrahaṇa*) their causal result, when they become present—thus removing the apparent problem. With such a view in

mind, we might see Vasubandhu's gloss on "nonduality" as grāhya-grāhaka as an updating of his AKBh argument, deploying a Yogācāra counter to the Vaibhāṣika terminological fix. For if causal series are by their nature "nondual," there is no possibility that an entity could be a "taker" that "takes" its causal result in order to become present. Once present, it is a different entity than it was when past; the series of entities are not "taker and taken," but merely cause and effect. This familiar argument would work quite well against the revised Vaibhāṣika view; but it is only a hypothetical. I have never seen it in any Buddhist text.

72. This claim is based upon a reading of deep, conceptual similarities and motives, but I do not hold that this counts as a "scientific proof" that the extant Yogācāra commentaries were necessarily composed by the same hand as the AKBh. My first chapter is intended to call such certainty into question. My point is, rather, that there is a distinctive, common complex of ideas and philosophical motivations identifiable across the works discussed here. As of yet I see no good reason to deny this "Vasubandhu complex" a single authorship, but should that become necessary, the conceptual nexus will remain. Buescher (2013) displays stylistic differences between MSABh and AKBh as evidence against a common authorship, but as I have said above, I do not consider this sufficient to rule out common authorship. As Corless (1989) argues, we are right, after all, to attribute both the *Tractatus* and the *Philosophical Investigations* to the same "Wittgenstein."
73. On the contrary, although he defends the use of perception and inference in order to clarify our understanding, from the perspective of ultimate reality, he is skeptical of all "epistemic means" (*pramāṇa*). In the VyY he cites approvingly the scripture that says, "If the sensory organs were epistemic means, there would be nothing to do on the noble path." See appendix E.
74. *Pace* Sellars (1997), who expands upon Kant's notion that "intuitions without concepts are blind" to argue that nothing is "given" to awareness that is not already structured for awareness. Vasubandhu would agree, at least as it applies to ordinary sentient beings. See below.
75. Monier-Williams 1993:372; Tubb and Boose 2007:225–226; and Cardona 1967–68:320.
76. For a useful introduction to "intentionality" as a philosophical term, see Jacob 2010. If it seems unlikely that a Buddhist scholastic would have come up with this concept, recall that Brentano's term is based on a medieval European scholastic one.
77. This is perhaps even broader than Searle 1992. This is not the place to attempt to locate Vasubandhu's position in the forest of contemporary views on "intentionality."
78. Searle (1992:20): "Because mental phenomena are essentially connected with consciousness, and because consciousness is essentially subjective, it follows that the ontology of the mental is essentially a first-person ontology. Mental states are always somebody's mental states. There is always a 'first person,' an 'I,' that has these mental states."
79. Recall Vasubandhu's point that the distinction between what the eye "sees" and what the mind "sees" does not represent an ontological difference. There need be no unique ontology to the first-personal perspective if it is just a story that is told "about" an eye-consciousness—a tag with which it is labeled—when its image is reconstituted within a mental consciousness.
80. See Sharf 1998 for a parallel argument regarding religious experience.

81. The Buddhist view is that we are "programmed" by our *karma* to experience the world as we do.
82. It would appear that Bhāviveka was the first to launch a Mahāyāna critique of Yogācāra, in order to establish the Madhyamaka tradition as dominant—a doxographic project that took some time to gain traction, but did so, eventually, in Tibet. See Eckel 2008 on Bhāviveka and Vose 2009 for a study of the story in Tibet.
83. Garfield 2002:176: "External objects are nonexistent. But their conceptual construction by the mind is real. That construction, being itself purely mental, is not dual: it does not resolve into subject and object simply because there is nothing to be found on the object side—there is only the conceptual activity of the subject, which is mistaken for an independent object."
84. TSN 156.21–24: *cittamātropalambhenajñeyārthānupalambhatā* | *jñeyārthānupalambhena syāc cittānupalambhatā* || (36) *dvayor anupalambhena dharmadhātūpalambhatā* | *dharmadhātūpalambhena syād vibhutvopalambhatā* || (37).
85. This argument also echoes the Viṃś, in which Vasubandhu argues against the viability of anything that might be called the real "grasped" objects of perception. The argument in the Viṃś is causal as well: since there can be no sensible account of the causal relation between physical and mental events, the traditional Buddhist understanding of sensation must fail. It follows from that argument, furthermore, that the unreality of perceptual objects leads to the unreality of the perceiving consciousness.
86. With regard to *nirvāṇa*, the term *upalambha* is clearly metaphorical, used for poetic assonance; there is no possibility of sensory grasping of knowledge by an omniscient Buddha.
87. Although the notion of "the emptiness of emptiness" as expressed in Madhyamaka is a unique structure, the self-referential, self-undermining logic of which it is an instance appears across Mahāyāna literature and is only one of many examples of philosophers' attempts to address the "limit paradoxes" or "limit contradictions" that arise when we try to speak of the limits of thought and language. On the Madhyamaka doctrine of the "emptiness of emptiness," see Huntington 1989, Garfield 1994, Arnold 2005, and Siderits and Katsura 2013. Mark Siderits (pers. comm.) thinks that my reading of TSN places Vasubandhu quite close to Candrakīrti. On limit paradoxes, see Priest 2002.
88. Viṃś 10.30: *sarvathā sā tu na cintyā.*
89. Viṃś 11.1: *sarvaprakārā tu sā mādṛśaiś cintayituṃ na śakyate* | *tarkāviśayatvāt.*
90. Viṃś 11.4–5: *buddhānāṃ hi sā bhagavatāṃ sarvaprakāraṃ gocaraḥ sarvākārasarvajñeya jñānāvighātād iti.*
91. VyY 239.15–16: *chos rnams thams cad ming med cing* || *ming gis yongs su brjod pa yin.*
92. VyY 239.18–22: *brjod du med pa'i mtshan nyid dag chos rnams thams cad yin na ni* | *byis pa rnams kyis kun tu brtags pa bshin du brjod pas* | *rjod par byed pa de'i rjes so 'brangs nas 'phags pa rnams kyis kyang min med pa rnams ming gis yongs su brjod pa yin par rung ngo.*
93. The discussion that follows refers to the central verses of the TSN, which I have provided with detailed, interpretive annotations in appendix G. The SNS is the source that describes emptiness with the terminology of "the lack of own-being of *dharmas*" (VIII.31 [86.1]: *chos rnams kyi ngo bo nyid ma mchis pa*).
94. See appendix G for a complete translation.
95. Apte 1992:648.

96. This paragraph refers to Vasubandhu's commentary on MAV III.16c–d (44.15–21). D'Amato's translation (2012:152–153) reads: "Form [i.e., the first of the five aggregates] is threefold. Form as it is imagined is the imagined nature of form. Form as it is conceptually discriminated is the dependent nature of form, because this is how the conceptual discrimination of form comes about [i.e., through dependence on causes and conditions]. The actual nature of form is the perfected nature of form [i.e., its emptiness or absence of subject–object duality]. And the same applies to the aggregates other than form, viz., feeling, [conceptualization, dispositions, and consciousness]; to the spheres; to the sense bases; etc. Thus the tenfold skillful reality is viewed in terms of the fundamental reality since the aggregates, etc., are included in the three natures."
97. The great Madhyamaka philosopher Candrakīrti famously claimed that an ordinary cowherd is privy to all the worldly conventions (*lokaprasidda*) that can constitute genuine knowledge. Perhaps this claim was motivated by frustration with the well-known tendency within all academic communities to reify jargonistic terms and concepts. If the idea is taken too seriously, however, it denies the pragmatic benefits of expertise and theoretical framing. After all, not all cowherds affirm Buddhist doctrine or practice. See Cowherds 2011 for a contemporary discussion of the Madhyamaka attempt to untangle this issue.
98. Thus, although the frame is relativistic, it depends for its viability upon the ostensibly objective data available through its application to pragmatic goals. The ultimate "pragmatic" goal for Buddhists is, of course, liberation.

6. AGENCY AND THE ETHICS OF MASSIVELY CUMULATIVE CAUSALITY

1. It may be argued that *karma* for Buddhists is not *intended* to be fair; the pathetic and unjustified suffering that results from its lawlike operation may be taken to be the very quintessence of the First Noble Truth. We ought to want to escape from *saṃsāra*, it may be said, precisely *because* it is unfair. Yet even so, *karma* is anything but arbitrary. Pleasant experiences result from well-intentioned, good deeds, and unpleasant experiences result from evil deeds. *Karma* is wonderfully "just" in the sense that the punishment always fits the crime. One of the strategies used to combat anger in both the Theravāda tradition of the *Visuddhimagga* and the Mahāyāna tradition of the *Bodhicaryāvatāra* is to recognize that one's enemy will be punished whether or not one intervenes: if they've done something wrong, they have it coming, so you can relax and let *karma* take its course. Our main problem indicated by the First Noble Truth, then, is not the *injustice* of *karma*, but rather its tragic *justice* meted out when we act childishly, out of our ignorance and our inability to control our impulses. Perhaps the real injustice of *karma* is that it continually punishes as adults those who are at heart only minors. The Buddha, in his compassion, teaches us how to act our age and stay out of trouble. That is a far cry from saying that the whole system of *samsara* is corrupt.
2. See, for an introduction, Siderits 2007:69–84.
3. For a readable introduction to Abhidharma categories of mind, including an insightful analysis of the foundational importance of the *kleṣas*, see Dreyfus and Thompson 2007.

4. Under such a reading, Buddhism is broadly consequentialist, as Goodman (2009b) argues convincingly.
5. By "moral nihilism" I mean the view that everything of moral significance is an illusion—or, to say the same thing, that morality itself is unreal.
6. The sixth-century Madhyamaka philosopher Candrakīrti's famous affirmation of the "emptiness of emptiness," which undermines all claims to ultimate reality, including the claim that would undermine them all, is sometimes read as throwing one *back* into conventional reality. If ultimate reality is empty of ultimate reality, then there is no purchase to the "only" in what was previously taken to be "only" conventional reality. This perhaps reaffirms conventional reality, reality as we ordinarily understand it. It is difficult to reconcile such a view, however, with the Madhyamaka philosophers' continued advocacy of practices such as philosophical analysis and meditation, which are clearly intended to liberate the mind from certain specific conventions. For an elaboration on this and related problems for Madhyamaka ethics, see Cowherds 2011.
7. Quoted in Patrul 1998:88.
8. This translation of the title is from Thanissaro 1997b. Further citations will be from Walshe 1995, abbreviated as SPS.
9. SPS 99.
10. SPS 100.
11. SPS 101.
12. For an overview of Plato and Augustine on self-mastery, see O'Connor 2005.
13. As Meyers (2010:261) points out, however, free will and Buddhist liberation are not at all the same thing; the main freedom in consideration in the Nikāyas is not metaphysical "freedom of choice" but "freedom of control." She also (2010:22) makes the interesting point that if we consider "freedom" to be the ability to choose among multiple courses of action, we might find the "liberated" being to be less free, in the sense of having to choose always the *best* action, the action that advances the path.
14. The word "damaged" is from Thanissaro 1997b. Walshe (1995a:547, n139) correctly comments that the passage literally says the king is "uprooted and destroyed," indicating "that Ajātasattu was inhibited by his kamma from obtaining the results that would otherwise have accrued."
15. SPS 94.
16. A classic statement of this argument is Van Inwagen 1975.
17. For a summary of libertarian views of free will, see O'Connor 2002.
18. Siderits 2007:69–84.
19. Goodman 2009b:150; Griffiths 1991.
20. This clever translation is adopted by Meyers (2010).
21. The view I advocate, then, agrees in structure with where Meyers (2010) points out that a nondeterministic metaphysics is not required for one to believe in the ability to choose one action over another.
22. Meyers 2010:253: "An intending (*cetanā*) is a kind of exertion, a movement of the mind towards a particular object or end, but the fact that intendings are present in all states of consciousness, including those that we would consider 'unconscious,' means that an intending is not, in itself, indicative of choice or control and that *karma* is not always subject to free will."

23. For this way of putting the point, I am indebted to Christopher Knapp (pers. comm.). The same conclusion is drawn by Meyers (2010).
24. A possible counterexample here might be the Ājīvikas, but given how little we know about their beliefs, I am inclined to assume that their determinism was similar to that of the Sāṃkhya, as described in the next paragraph: objects, but not subjects, are causally determined.
25. Miller (1986:151–152): "Arjuna, the lord resides / in the heart of all creatures, / making them reel magically, / as if a machine moved them. | (18.61) With your whole being, Arjuna, / take refuge in him alone— / from his grace you will attain / the eternal place that is peace. / (18.62) This knowledge I have taught / is more arcane than any mystery / consider it completely, / then act as you choose / (18.63)." See Malinar 2008 for an analysis of the complex Sāṃkhya theory that makes this an arcane mystery, not a self-contradiction.
26. An alternative, which does mesh in certain ways with the structure of the *Mahābhārata*, is that urging and convincing is an important part of the proper lead-in to warfare, and indeed any of a king's important acts. My sense is that the urging has an important causal impetus, but only because it places before the king the reasoning and the motivation for making the right choice.
27. One reading of the notion of determinism operating at an "ultimate" level when free will operates at the "conventional" level would be to say that we are thrown "back" into the conventional once we see the impossibility of altering things at the ultimate level. This might be thought to counteract the utility of Abhidharma analysis, a view of Mahāyāna that Vasubandhu rejects in the VyY. See chapter 4.
28. Whitney 1885:47.
29. Though *cetana* as an adjective is not common in Buddhist texts.
30. "These ten *dharmas* are omnipresent in every mental moment." AKBh 54.19: *ime kila daśa dharmāḥ sarvatra cittakṣaṇe samagrā bhavanti.*
31. AKBh 54.20: *cetanā cittābhisaṃskāro manaskarma.*
32. AKBh 10.20.
33. Rabten 1992:114. Batchelor translates *cetanā* here as "intention."
34. AKBh IV.1b (192.9): ***cetanā tatkṛtaṃ ca tat.***
35. Meyers 2010:174.
36. "*Cetanā* is that by which the course of action is brought to completion. *Āśaya* is its purpose/intention [*abhiprāya*], 'I will do such and such, and I will not do such and such.'" AKBh 271.11–12: *cetanā yayā karmapathaṃ niṣṭāpayati* | *āśayas tadabhiprāya evaṃ caivaṃ ca kuryām evaṃ caivaṃ ca na kariśyāmīti.*
37. AKBh 192.23: *cittavaśena kāyasya tathā tathā saṃsthānaṃ kāyavijñapti.* Note that this definition applies only to "bodily informative action" (*kāyavijñapti*), not all bodily *karma.*
38. AKBh 195–196. This passage is complex, and although I believe I have fairly expressed an implication of the *jaḍatvāt* on 196.1, it is admittedly somewhat ambiguous.
39. At AKBh III.25a, Vasubandhu says that the official Vaibhāṣika position is that the true meaning of *pratītyasamutpāda* is that they represent twelve distinct states of the five aggregates (133.10: *āvasthikaḥ* ***kileṣṭo*** *'yaṃ*). This verse is one of the instances, which we listed in chapter 3, note 19, where the verses use the term *kila* to indicate traditional Vaibhāṣika doctrines with which the author has some disagreement.

According to La Vallée Poussin (1923–1925.2:66, n. 5), Vasubandhu's Vaibhāṣika rival Saṃghabhadra attributes the alternate view here to "Le Sautrāntika," meaning Vasubandhu. This is evidence of the unity of authorship for the verses and the commentary. ("Saṃghabhadra: Les maîtres d'Abhidharma disent que c'est en considérant les « états » (*avasthās*) que le Bouddha enseigne le Pratītyasamutpāda. Le Sautrāntika (=Vasubandhu) ne le croit pas, et c'est pourquoi il met dans sa stance le mot *kila* [que nous traduisons: « d'après l'Ecole »].")

40. AKBh III.21b.
41. "The situation of the virtuous, etc., actions in the previous life is what they call conditioning [*saṃskāra*]—by whose action the result is here." AKBh 131.22–23: *pūrvajanmany eva yā puṇyādikarmāvasthā seha saṃskārā ity ucyante yasya karmaṇa iha vipākaḥ*. The point seems to be that under this interpretation, we call previous actions "conditions" to the extent that they ripen into results here. Such a reading localizes the intentions of the Buddha to make a specific point, and reminds us that, for Vasubandhu (as against the Vaibhāṣikas), we should not expect to find a singular explanation of *saṃskāra* or any of the twelve links.
42. AKBh 134–135.
43. Pruden 1988–1990 has "consciousness" for *bhava* here: 2:407.
44. A corollary piece of evidence here is that a defilement cannot cause a thing. If the twelve links represented only blind, mechanistic causality, there would be no reason that defilements should *only* cause actions. The current structure suggests that a defilement is just understood as the cognitive and emotional content that prompts deluded actions.
45. An entire scritpural "basket" (*pitaka*) is dedicated to the monastic vows.
46. This is implicit in the *Sāmaññaphalasutta* when Ajātasattu is unsatisfied by his conversation with Pūraṇa Kassapa, who holds the Ājīvika view of "nonaction" (*akarma*) (SNS 93–94).
47. Vasubandhu uses the word *paṅkti* for a line of ants. This analogy is clearly what Śāntideva has in mind in his *Bodhicaryāvatāra* VII.101, as the commentator Prajñākaramiti understood. Williams's suggestion (1998a:105, 113–114) that this refers to "a caste line" is therefore probably mistaken.
48. Dennett 1995.
49. Nattier 2003.
50. The path of the bodhisattva takes three "countless" eons, where an eon is one Brahma-lifetime, and the word "countless" is a not literally infinite, but a very large, finite number. Following Kapstein's notes on Dudjom (1991.2:9–10, n109), I calculate Vasubandhu's explanation of the term (AKBh III.93d–94a) to add up to 10^{59}.
51. Meyers 2010:174.
52. The idea that reasons and causes are two discrete regions of analysis, but that, contrary to Davidson, this does not prevent reduction, may be taken to be yet another expression of the Three Natures view: what Sellars calls the "logical space of reasons" is the fabricated nature; the "causes" are the dependent nature; and the fact that the "logical space of reasons" is only a construction, a delusion brought about by causes and conditions, is the perfected nature.
53. Swinburne (1991:76) considers it a satisfying "terminus for explanation" if we can provide a "personal explanation" of an event that includes a person's ability and

desire to act. We do not need to reach behind the desire and explain that, too. This is key to his proof of the existence of God, since he argues that God's will and ability to make the world explains it, whereas no scientific explanation could ever be similarly complete. Vasubandhu would answer that every person's desires are, by their nature, conditioned, so to ascribe desires to God would be to define God as conditioned. (See Gold 2011 for Vasubandhu's disproof of the existence of God.) He might also add that it is crucial to the illusion of self that we do not question its apparent unity, in which it appears to us as though it were uncaused and eternal. Once we know that our apparent identity is causally conditioned, we must change our view of the nature of the self. It is, therefore, only delusion that makes Swinburne's explanatory criterion appear "satisfying."

54. This from Barack Obama's famous July 13, 2012, campaign speech in Roanoke, VA, in which he was pointing out that people who start businesses rely upon others who have paid for road construction, education of workers, and so forth. Obama's opponents criticized this acknowledgment of causal indebtedness as un-American.
55. AKBh IV.1 (192.5): ***karmaja lokavaicitryaṃ.***
56. This is the secret moral of the opening line of every *Jātaka* tale, every story of the Buddha's previous lives: "Once, the bodhisattva was a Brahmin living in Benares"; "Once, the bodhisattva was king of the monkeys"; "Once, the bodhisattva was in hell." Contrary to our ordinary practice, the Buddhist tradition extends personal identity across lives. What is significant about us—what is valuable about us—is the set of moral choices of which we are capable, rather than our status within a particular body within the cycle of *saṃsāra*.
57. MNS 224–225.
58. "Defensiveness" is Thanissaro's translation (1995a). Walshe (1995b:564, n334) cites other translators' choices as "watch and ward," "protection," and "safeguarding."

CONCLUSION: BUDDHIST CAUSAL FRAMING FOR THE MODERN WORLD

1. This question is pursued by Siderits (2009).
2. Priest 2002: e.g., 252.
3. See chapter 4 and appendix E.
4. I do believe, however, that Vasubandhu's position is a faithful synthesis of mainstream Buddhism for most of its history in India, the land of its birth. As mentioned in chapter 4, Indian Buddhist philosophy after Vasubandhu was dominated by the *pramāṇa* schools, which come under direct influence of his perspective, and the *tantras*, the practice of which explicitly manipulates conceptual constructions in a mind-only frame.
5. Westerhoff 2010.
6. Here we might add that even this way of speaking of space—as a location in which objects may be said to exist—is mistaken from the perspective of general relativity.
7. Wegner 2002:263: "The experience of consciously willing an action is something that happens in a virtual agent, not in a brain or in a mind." Westerhoff (2010) details a wide range of correlations between the best contemporary cognitive science and the elements in a traditional Buddhist list of examples illustrating the illusory nature of experience.

8. Here it is worth mentioning the oft-noted convergence between Buddhism and psychotherapy. What I would add to this well-studied issue is a convergence in the approach to causality and the mind. To put a fine point on it, the secular, psychological mode of description *is* Buddhist Causal Framing as defined above. Remember that the key for BCF is always to return to the core question of the *causal story* in which entities participate. It hardly needs mentioning that the common psychological story of the development of the personality, the person's identity, challenges the unity of the person by recognizing the conditioning roles played by relationships with parents and siblings and teachers, for instance, in the formation of character. Not only does this recognition play a role in identifying the fact of, and the nature of, the identity's construction, but it is also used to revisit those conditioning factors, reevaluate them, and manipulate their influence so as to transform the personality. What seems an intractable nature, what appears as a solid and indelible identity to the patient, is of course conditioned—and subject to further conditioning. This is, essentially, point 4: the self appears as an unchanging entity, acting independently and intentionally, but it is not, and cannot be, given what we know about its history and its development.

   Furthermore, the way that the various sets of points flow—4, 5, and 6 from 1, 2, and 3, and 7, 8, and 9 from 4, 5, and 6—is readily exhibited in a psychological worldview. The recognition of the long, incremental and cumulative, conditioned history of the mind shapes the psychotherapeutic approach to changing it. Even if I am aware of the destructive patterns of my mind, I can only change them gradually, one moment at a time. Inclinations and tendencies are not transformed by individual decisions, but by repetitive exercises in transformative choices. I cannot decide not to be an addict; I can choose not to drink today. Or, to be more accurate, I can "decide" to *not be* an addict, but that decision is not sufficient to *make me* not an addict. Conditions trump intentions. Psychological thinking (especially behaviorist therapy) in this way adopts the perspective of Buddhist Causal Framing in its suggestion that our best rational choices, placed before us, provide *causal conditions* for our healing. But our behavior, even when we exhibit our strongest effort, is not "rational"; it does not exist as it appears. The self is a construction, and must be reconstructed through slow accruals of mental action.

9. Not every dictionary. For instance, not Johnson's. Johnson's dictionary (1755) defines "stone" as "a mineral not ductile or malleable" (324), which provides a different set of qualities, more legitimately supported by pragmatic, physical examination, than "solidity." We are still left with the question of just what it *is*, though, that puts up resistance to the doctor's foot, so we look up "mineral" and find "matter dug out of mines" (217). That is a rather pragmatic definition. So, we turn to "mine," where we find, "a place where minerals are dug" (217). I do believe at rock bottom we have found a rainbow.

10. There are, of course, many capacities that have come about that are not advantageous. I assume that molecular-level vision would be expensive to maintain, and difficult to generate randomly, and so would not arise unless it conferred a significant advantage.

11. "Because it is under the influence of the ripening of their similar, own *karma*." Viṃś 4.16–17: *samānasvakarmavipākādhipatyāt*.

APPENDIX A. AGAINST THE EXISTENCE OF THE THREE TIMES

1. Clearly it is past actions and their karmic results to which one can be "bound" and from which one can be "freed." The pronoun "it" is probably intended to pick up the topic of the surrounding chapter, which is the "afflictive tendencies" (*anuśaya*) that bind one to *samsara*. The *tatra tena vā*, which I translate "in it or by it," is repeated at the end of this passage, where the question is reiterated in reverse as "by it or in it," *tena tasmin vā*.
2. Lit. "because they are bound to the quality of what is conditioned" (*saṃskāralakṣaṇayogāt*).
3. Here La Vallée Poussin (1923–1925.3:52–53, n2) imports the term *anyonya* from the description of the view into the list of names of views, making Buddhadeva a defender of *anyonyathātva*—a "mutual-differentialist." That term works to describe this relativistic view, but the wording we have in both Sanskrit manuscripts, which is also reflected in the commentaries and Tibetan translations (*pace* LVP), is *anyathānyathika*, a "difference-differentialist." What does this mean, exactly? Perhaps that there are different ways to differentiate between the different times, depending on your perspective. But perhaps the manuscript traditions for this passage have been corrupt since before they were translated into Tibetan, and LVP's version, based on the Chinese implication of *apekṣa*, "relation," is closer to the original.
4. Here Vasubandhu uses *samanvāgama*, which is his conventional replacement for *prāpti* in II.36 (as noted by LVP; see chapter 2, note 32).
5. The point is that whether the *dharma* is past or future, its relations to other *dharmas* are the same—so this fails to distinguish between *dharmas*.
6. Vasubandhu is applying his mastery of the complex Vaibhāṣika causal system. He refers to a *potential* cause, the *tatsabhāga*, which is not engaged in its causal activity, and asks of it what makes it present when it is present. According to the notion of *kāritra* on the table, a present entity must be engaged in *some* activity ("giving or taking a result") to be called "present." Even as a merely "potential" cause there must still be some activity that makes it present. So, if even a potential cause (*tatsabhāga*) has an activity, then an actual *sabhāga* cause must have two separate activities that make it present. That would be strange enough (already causal overdetermination), but the trick here, I gather, is that the way a *sabhāga* cause works—which is what the *tatsabhāga* potentially could have been—is that it "gives forth" its result when it is *in the past*. "Giving" causes are past conditions of present results (AKBh II.59). That means that the two activities for the same entity are *at different times*. If "activity" distinguishes the times, then this entity transcends the times.
7. A possible reading of this is that Vasubandhu is asking, "How can its own nature not exist yet or be yet-to-exist, if the thing itself exists?" An alternative translation would separate the passage into distinct phrases and take it as a word-by-word gloss: "['Existing in this way' means that] the *dharma* is existing by its very own nature. ['How can it be' means,] How can this be established? ['Unborn or destroyed' refers to] what is called unborn, or is called destroyed."
8. Is this comparable to TSN 4, *dvayātmanā*?
9. This is given as a quotation that the Vaibhāṣika accepts as authoritative.

10. Dan Arnold (pers. comm.) says that Vasubandhu is here adopting from Jain philosophers the idea that the existential verb acts as a *nipāta*. The point is that the word connects other words, rather than affirming some new entity.
11. Lit. "it has nonexistence." The point here is that although you say this, you do not intend to say that the light has some reality as a nonexistent.
12. The "experiential object condition" is one of the four kinds of conditions. See AKBh II.61–62. Vasubandhu provides no technical definition for a "producer condition" (*janaka-pratyaya*), though this might be thought to correspond imprecisely to the "causal condition" (*hetu-pratyaya*), since at AKBh V.46 Vasubandhu argues that "producings" come about as a result of the assemblage of causal conditions.
13. Ājīvikas were a non-Buddhist heterodox (non-Hindu) school whom Buddhists generally depict as fatalists.
14. Here the discussion shifts to the topic of Buddhist doctrine. The Vaibhāṣika challenges Vasubandhu's analysis by pointing out that there is no proper doctrinal structure for the mental perception of a nonexistent. On the contrary, the objects of the mental sense organ are *dharmas*, which are the entities of Abhidharma analysis. This challenge allows Vasubandhu immediately to turn the tables and show that for many examples of supposedly systematic thinking within the Vaibhāṣika, they must appeal to mere linguistic constructs, and not real *dharmas*, as mental objects—which is exactly what Vasubandhu believes.
15. The "one" here probably refers to the "consciousness" above—since the issue under discussion is the experiential object that is taken up by a consciousness.
16. This is rather a convoluted point, but as I take it Vasubandhu is making fun of the Vaibhāṣika's apparent failure to distinguish between the sound of a word and its meaning, which ought to be the mental object for the mind that takes it up. Here Vasubandhu is saying that, according to their system, in order to call to mind a future sound, which does not yet exist (because it is future), one makes a sound (speaks a word).
17. That is, a real distinction could be asserted only if one says that one exists where the other does not. Since the Vaibhāṣika asserts that all things exist even in the future, this distinction cannot be made between future and present *dharmas*.
18. I have had some difficulty with this sentence.
19. That is, in AKBh IX. See the penultimate section of chapter 2 in this book for discussion.
20. If a thing is changed so that it comes into being, this is an acceptance of the expression that Vasubandhu is pushing here, that "not having existed it exists."
21. That is, so the Sarvāstivāda tradition says.
22. This is Vasubandhu's ironic statement of Vaibhāṣika literalism: *yathā tu tad asti athoktam*. It is clearly ironic because it follows two quite different interpretations of the same passage.
23. Afflictive tendencies (*anuśaya*), when activated, become defilements (*kleśa*), which affect one's experience, especially if one acts on them. The more general point is that one can give a causal account of being metaphorically "bound" by one's actions in a way that prevents one from having to affirm that the past actions are literally doing the binding directly (and so must exist). See chapters 2 and 6 for my discussion of Vasubandhu's view that *karma* works through mediated stages and the gradual accumulation of tendencies.

APPENDIX B. BRIEF DISPROOF OF THE SELF

1. As Vasubandhu says when he cites this same passage in book IX, this is from the *Paramārthaśūnyatā*.
2. Here Śāstrī (2008) has an opposed reading: *etad saty apy ātmani* instead of *etad asaty apy ātmani*.

APPENDIX C. DISCUSSION OF "VIEW" (*DṚṢṬI*)

1. In the *dhātu* system, there are eighteen elements that make up all of the *dharmas*: six sensory objects, six sensory organs, and six consciousnesses. Here one sensory organ, the eye (*cakṣu*), and one sensory object, the mental objects (*dharmadhātu*), are classified as kinds of "view" (*dṛṣṭi*). Not all mental objects are views, though; eight kinds of mental objects are named, and the rest are said not to be views.
2. These first five are treated at AKBh V.7 (281.19–282.2). See chapter 3 for my translation and study of this passage.
3. The *prajñā* is one of the ten *mahābhūmis*, which are always-present aspects of mind.
4. Clearly this refers to the five consciousnesses that accompany the five sensory organs and their objects—that is, all of the consciousnesses except the mental consciousness.
5. This bold passage is my translation of one word, *sabhāga*, which is a technical term referring to *dharmas* that have an *active (i.e., present tense) corresponding object*. See AKBh I.39 (27.19–20).
6. The Vaibhāṣika argument will be that if the consciousness is what "sees," it must be aware of every visual object—but that is clearly not what happens in visual consciousness. So this view must be rejected in order to make it possible that the visual consciousness is unaware of objects that we ordinarily cannot see.
7. It seems to me that there is no need to appeal to a Vijñānavāda explanation here, as Yaśomitra suggests (Śāstrī 2008:91–92), since the point is that the sensory organ provides the support (*āśraya)* for the consciousness—which is how the senses are said to operate at I.9c–d. But the argument is clearly tending toward a Vijñānavāda perspective.
8. Here we see Vasubandhu using the hermeneutical strategy of requiring consistency of purpose in texts, which McCrae (2000:433ff) writes about in the case of the Mīmāṃsā.
9. Vasubandhu rejects the question.
10. The context here makes it clear that conventional terms used "by choice" or "as one pleases" (*chandataḥ*) refer to the Buddha's own figurative use of conventional terms.

APPENDIX D. AGAINST THE ETERNALITY OF ATOMS (*PARAMĀṆU*)

1. This refers back to where the opponent had said that there can be no birth from a different class. If a variegated form arises from threads of individual colors, then this rule is violated.

2. The point seems to be that if one sees an individual thread, one must be able to distinguish different shades or colors—which means one sees a variegated form even when the thread is all the same color.
3. Given that fire's radiance is so diverse and variegated, there is no unified "color" or "form" that could be said to be the single cause of the appearance of fire. We do not, therefore, "see" a fire; we see lots of separate things and construct the "fire" conceptually.
4. Things arise from multiple causes coming together.
5. A more literal reading here would be "There is no thought of them with respect to burnt wool, cotton, safflower, and saffron, etc."

APPENDIX E. THE *PROPER MODE OF EXPOSITION* ON CONVENTIONAL AND ULTIMATE

1. Based on the next passage, I am following Lee's suggestion (2001:236, n1722) and leaving out the *ma*. With it, the passage would read: "the specific character of *dharmas* is *not* ultimate." This might be taken to apply to the specific character of the *dharmas* designated by conventional language, but then how do we explain the subsequent critique of two kinds of existence applying to the same entity?
2. Here "those two" refers to *karma* and results.
3. Here the claim seems to be that of course a Buddha's awareness is nothing but "means of knowledge," but the only awareness that should count as "means of knowledge" for ordinary beings is the awareness that *follows from* the transcendent vision of Buddhahood.
4. This sentence introduces the discussion that continues to the end of this appendix.
5. Difficult to convey in English is the idea here, clearly expressed in the Tibetan (one imagines expressed even more clearly in the original, lost Sanskrit), that the *dharmas* have no existence in, or with reference to, the words. All of the singulars have been translated as plural to match English idiom. A literal translation of this line would be "It is not that it exists there" or "It is not that it has it."
6. This sentence is different from SNS.
7. Here "Buddhahood" (*sangs rgyas pa*) is used verbally to indicate the substantial truth behind the language of the Āryas. I translate it as "awakened," but it is clear that what one is awakened "to" or "into" is the inconceivable nature of Buddhahood.

APPENDIX G. THE *THREE NATURES EXPOSITION*

1. Since the first quarter-verse clearly fits with the third and the second with the fourth, I have reordered the verse: a–c–b–d.
2. The verse uses the expression *dvayātmanā*, which I translate here as "as dual" to refer to how the illusory duality appears, and then uses *advayadharmatā*, which I translate here as "there being no duality," to refer to the appearance's fundamental lack of a false, dual nature. The alternation between *ātmanā* (lit. "with a nature"/"with a self") and *dharmatā* ("true nature") enlivens the dead metaphor of *ātmanā*.

3. Possibly "the activity of the seen, the seeing, and the cognition"—taking *vitti* separately from *dṛg*.
4. Here we begin the section that most evidently integrates the three natures and shows how they are paradoxically inconceivable.
5. From one perspective, we might see this as just expressing a general fact about a constructed error. It is real from its mistaken, constructed perspective, and unreal from the perspective of truth. But the grasping is not denied its reality. The verse does not say that there is *real* reality and *unreal* reality. It says that there are two ways to look at this entity—so it is both real *and* unreal. This means that the assignment of *unreality alone* is as much a mistake as the assignment of reality alone. If we take it from the SNS that the fabricated nature represents the doctrines of the Śrāvakayāna, this verse expresses that it is essential to employ, but not be attached to, those doctrines.
6. The dependent nature is the causal story of how the subconscious mind brings about the appearance of what appears to exist. This verse tells us that the causal story is real, but the appearance is not. This verse thus confirms that the causal story of the mind, which is the story of how we end up with the fabricated world as it appears, is opaque to us. Notice that if the *Three Natures* were providing a phenomenological description of the mind, we would expect to find out that the dependent nature does not *appear* at all. But in fact what the verse says is that the dependent nature appears under an error—it is as though error disguises the dependent nature, so it appears as something that is not there. But this is not the same thing as saying that the dependent does not appear at all. It appears. It is, in fact, *all that appears*, because there is nothing else that *can* appear. It is the only real, causal series. But it is only known *through the existence of an error*; how it appears is false. This verse therefore brings together the *viewing-as* an error with the *viewing-of* the mental causal story itself.
7. The perfected nature for the TSN is the absence of a real *svabhāva* where it appears to exist, in the fabricated nature. This definition weds the perfected to the fabricated—it is not as though the perfected is some *additional* reality, behind or above the fabricated. It is an inherent characteristic of *the fabricated itself*. The real-and-unreal character here is not, therefore, merely a logical problem of the form $(-x) = -(x)$. One of the basic points of Yogācāra is the affirmation of the reality of nonexistence not as a thing, but as an appearance. We saw this affirmed in the opening verse of the MAV. Here the existence *as nonduality* is therefore affirmed as a thing with as much "reality" as anything else. Again, the point of there being *both* reality and unreality is affirmed as against a simple reduction of these two to a single description.
8. There are three quite interesting points here. First, note that construction takes place in a dual manner, or through the rule or application of two. The word *vidhi* means, centrally, a grammatical rule, so we may take it that fabrications are conceptual-linguistic dualities. Second, we have the idea that whereas reality is a dual construction, unreality is singular. We see this point in the next verse as well. What's the point here? We may have a trick, an attempt to sound profound in the context of a need to find a way that this is unitary. More likely, though, is that the unreality of the fabricated nature is the perfected nature, the inconceivable ultimate that is always and everywhere the same—so, unified. This is affirming,

then, that the perfected is one of the natures of the fabricated (its nature as unified). Third is the notion that the correct view includes both duality and unity: so, while we normally would say that Yogācāra holds to the view that all things are nondual, in fact the more appropriate point would be to say that things are beyond duality and unity. This verse thus launches the recursive logic of nonduality.

9. Here we have a similar point to the previous verse, where the unreality of the construction was said to be a "singular existent" (*ekabhāva*); here the fact of it being an *error* is said to be a "singular existent." This is probably, again, a reference to the perfected nature, the ultimate, unitary emptiness. But we might also point out that the dependent nature is unitary here in the sense that it is a single causal stream that is only "dual" in how it is perceived. The error is itself "singular" even though it appears as "dual." It is a unitary causal line that only appears as subject and object, action and agent. This is a central point that is expressed in the magical illusion analogy, encompassed in the notion that the duality is analogized to the elephant alone, not to the elephant-and-the-audience. The elephant's reality is the "dual" nature of reality, the subject/object structure, which is generated (split) out of a single stream of awareness. See Gold 2006 for more on this point.
10. This verse is further confirmation that, for Vasubandhu, the perfected nature *may not be taken to be* the ultimate nature outside of, or over and above, the dependent and the fabricated natures. Clearly the three are intertwined. There is no way to speak of the perfected nature outside the duality of which it is the unitary nonexistence, and in which it exists. There is an alternative reading here that would make it "the nonexistence of duality" instead of "the existence of duality." This is a somewhat more disappointing reading, since it makes the two perspectives essentially the same (-x) = -(x). Again, we have the point that nonduality is unitary.
11. Here Vasubandhu shifts gears, to talk about the *conventional* meanings of the three natures, which he calls a practical, or introductory (*praveśa*), perspective on them. The verses that follow provide, for each nature, its different stages of contemplation. These verses thus locate the "progressive model" of the three natures as a useful method of contemplation, which is nonetheless subordinate to the "pivot model," wherein all three natures are descriptions of the same reality. These terms for different ways of interpreting the Three Natures are from Sponberg 1983; see also D'Amato 2012:15–16. I am only partly content with the idea of a "pivot" between fabricated and perfected with the dependent as the ground of both, since these verses place the nature of the perfected within the fabricated and vice versa. Perhaps the "crystalline model" or the "integrated model" would be better. But whatever term is used, the key for Vasubandhu is that all three are thoroughly integrated aspects of the same reality.

BIBLIOGRAPHY

Akimoto Masaru. 2004. "Buddhist Definition of Existence: Kāritra to Arthakriyā." In *Three Mountains and Seven Rivers: Prof. Musashi Tachikawa's Felicitation Volume*, ed. Shōun Hino, 107–116. Delhi: Motilal Banarsidass.

Albahari, Miri. 2002. "Against No-Ātman Theories of Anattā." *Asian Philosophy* 12:5–20.

——. 2006. *Analytical Buddhism: The Two-Tiered Illusion of Self.* New York: Macmillan.

Anacker, Stefan. 1972. "Vasubandhu's *Karmasiddhiprakaraṇa* and the Problem of the Highest Meditations." *Philosophy East and West* 22:247–258.

——. 1998. *Seven Works of Vasubandhu, the Buddhist Psychological Doctor.* Rev. ed. Delhi: Motilal Banarsidass.

Apte, Vaman Shivaram. 1992. *The Practical Sanskrit-English Dictionary.* Repr. Kyoto: Rinsen Book Company.

Aramaki Noritoshi. 2000. "Toward an Understanding of the *Vijñaptimātratā*." In *Wisdom, Compassion, and the Search for Understanding: The Buddhist Studies Legacy of Gadjin M. Nagao*, ed. Jonathan A. Silk, 39–28. Honolulu: University of Hawaii Press.

Arnold, Dan. 2005. *Buddhists, Brahmins, and Belief: Epistemology in South Asian Philosophy of Religion.* New York: Columbia University Press.

——. 2012. *Brains, Buddhas, and Believing: The Problem of Intentionality in Classical Buddhist and Cognitive-Scientific Philosophy of Mind.* New York: Columbia University Press.

Berlin, Isaiah. 1978. "The Hedgehog and the Fox." In *Russian Thinkers*, ed. Henry Hardy and Aileen Kelly, 22–81. Isaiah Berlin: Selected Writings. New York: Viking.

Bhattacarya, Kamaleswar, trans. *The Dialectical Method of Nāgārjuna: Vigrahavyāvarttanī.* Ed. E. H. Johnston and Arnold Kunst. 2nd ed. Delhi: Motilal Banarsidass.

Braarvig, Jens, ed. 1993. *Akṣayamatinirdeśasūtra.* 2 vols. Oslo: Solum Forlag.

Broido, Michael. 1985. "Intention and Suggestion in the *Abhidharmakośa*: Sandhābhāṣā Revisited." *Journal of Indian Philosophy* 13:327–381.

Bronkhorst, Johannes. 2006. "Systematic Philosophy Between the Empires: Some Determining Features." In *Between the Empires: Society in India, 300 BCE to 400 CE*, ed. Patrick Olivelle, 287–313. New York: Oxford University Press.

Buescher, Hartmut. 2008. *The Inception of Yogācāra-Vijñānavāda.* Beitrage zur Kultur- und Geistesgeschichte Asiens. Vienna: Austrian Academy of Sciences.

——. 2013. "Distinguishing the Two Vasubandhus, the Bhāṣyakāra, and the Kośakāra, as Yogācāra-Vijñānavāda Authors." In *The Foundation for Yoga Practitioners: The Buddhist* Yogācārabhūmi *Treatise and Its Adaptation in India, East Asia, and Tibet*, ed. Ulrich Timme Kragh, 368–396. Harvard Oriental Series 75. Cambridge, MA: Harvard University Department of South Asian Studies and Harvard University Press.

Butön Rinchen Drup. 2013. *Butön's History of Buddhism in India and Its Spread to Tibet: A Treasury of Priceless Scripture*. Trans. Lisa Stein and Ngawang Zangpo. Boston: Snow Lion.

Cabezón, José Ignacio. 1990. "The Canonization of Philosophy and the Rhetoric of Siddhānta in Tibetan Buddhism." In *Buddha Nature: A Festschrift in Honor of Minoru Kiyota*, ed. Paul J. Griffiths and John P. Keenan, 7–26. San Francisco: Buddhist Books International.

——. 1992. "Vasubandhu's *Vyākhyāyukti* on the Authenticity of the Mahāyāna Sūtras." In *Texts in Context: Traditional Hermeneutics in South Asia*, ed. Jeffrey R. Timm, 221–243. Albany: State University of New York.

Cardona, George. 1967–1968. "*Anvaya* and *vyatireka* in Indian Grammar." *Adyar Library Bulletin* 31–32:313–352.

Conze, Edward, trans. 2001. *The Diamond Sutra and the Heart Sutra*. New York: Vintage.

Corless, Roger J. 1989. "On the Continuity of Vasubandhu's Thought: A Suggestion from the Continuity of Wittgenstein's Thought." In *Amalā Prajñā: Aspects of Buddhist Studies*, ed. N. H. Samtani and H. S. Prasad, 455–462. Delhi: Indian Books Centre.

Coseru, Christian. 2012. *Perceiving Reality: Consciousness, Intentionality, and Cognition in Buddhist Philosophy*. New York: Oxford University Press.

Cowherds. 2011. *Moonshadows: Conventional Truth in Buddhist Philosophy*. New York: Oxford University Press.

Cox, Collett. 1992. "Mindfulness and Memory: The Scope of *smṛti* from Early Buddhism to the Sarvāstivāda Abhidharma." In Gyatso 1992:67–108.

D'Amato, Mario. 2005. "Three Natures, Three Stages: An Interpretation of the Yogacara Trisvabhava-Theory." *Journal of Indian Philosophy* 33:185–207.

——. 2009. Review of Hartmut Buescher, *The Inception of Yogācāra-Vijñānavāda*. H-Buddhism, H-Net Reviews, May 2009. http://www.h-net.org/reviews/showrev.php?id=24596 (accessed July 18, 2013).

——. 2012. *Maitreya's Distinguishing the Middle from the Extremes (Madhyāntavibhāga) Along with Vasubandhu's Commentary (Madhyāntavibhāga-bhāṣya): A Study and Translation*. Treasury of the Buddhist Sciences. New York: American Institute of Buddhist Studies.

Davidson, Donald. 1963. "Actions, Reasons, and Causes." *Journal of Philosophy* 60:685–700.

Deleanu, Florin. 2006. *The Chapter on the Mundane Path* (Laukikamārga) *in the* Śrāvakabhūmi: *A Trilingual Edition (Sanskrit, Tibetan, Chinese), Annotated Translation, and Introductory Study*. Studia Philologica Buddhica. Tokyo: International Institute for Buddhist Studies.

Dennett, Daniel C. 1989. *The Intentional Stance*. Cambridge, MA: MIT Press.

——. 1991. *Consciousness Explained*. Boston: Little, Brown.

——. 1995. *Darwin's Dangerous Idea: Evolution and the Meanings of Life*. New York: Simon and Schuster.

Derge Tanjur. 1982–1985. *Bstan 'gyur (sde dge)*. Tibetan Buddhist Resource Center W23703. 213 vols. Delhi: Delhi Karmapae Choedhey, Gyalwae Sungrab Partun Khang.

Dhammajoti, K. L. 2009. *Sarvāstivāda Abhidharma*. 4th rev. ed. Hong Kong: Centre for Buddhist Studies, University of Hong Kong.

Dreyfus, Georges B. J. 1997. *Recognizing Reality: Dharmakīrti's Philosophy and Its Tibetan Interpretations*. Albany: State University of New York Press.

——. 2003. *The Sound of Two Hands Clapping: The Education of a Tibetan Buddhist Monk*. Berkeley: University of California Press.

Dreyfus, Georges, and Evan Thompson. 2007. "Asian Perspectives: Indian Theories of Mind." In *The Cambridge Handbook of Consciousness*, ed. Philip David Zelazo, Morris Moscovitch, and Evan Thompson, 89–114. Cambridge: Cambridge University Press.

Dudjom Rinpoche, Jikdrel Yeshe Dorje. 1991. *The Nyingma School of Tibetan Buddhism: Its Fundamentals and History*. Trans. and ed. Gyurme Dorje and Matthew Kapstein. 2 vols. Somerville, MA: Wisdom Publications.

Duerlinger, James. 2003. *Indian Buddhist Theories of Persons: Vasubandhu's "Refutation of the Theory of a Self."* London: RoutledgeCurzon.

Dunne, John. 2004. *Foundations of Dharmakīrti's Philosophy*. Studies in Indian and Tibetan Buddhism. Somerville, MA: Wisdom Publications.

Eckel, Malcolm David. 2008. *Bhāviveka and His Buddhist Opponents*. Harvard Oriental Series 70. Cambridge, MA: Harvard University Press.

Feldman, Joel. 2005. "Vasubandhu's Illusion Argument and the Parasitism of Illusion Upon Veridical Experience." *Philosophy East and West* 55:529–541.

Flanagan, Owen. 2009. *The Really Hard Problem: Meaning in a Material World*. Bradford Books. Cambridge, MA: MIT Press.

Franco, Eli. 2001. "Dharmakīrti's Reductionism in Religion and Logic." In *Le parole e i marmi. Studi in onore di Raniero Gnoli nel suo 70º compleanno*, ed. Raffaele Torella, 285–308. Rome: Instituto per l'Africa e l'Oriente.

Frauwallner, Erich. 1951. "On the Date of the Buddhist Master of the Law Vasubandhu." Rome: Istituto Italiano per il Medio ed Estremo Oriente.

——. 1957. "Vasubandhu's Vādavidhi." *Wiener Zeitschrift für die Kunde Süd- und Ostasiens* 1:104–146.

——. 1961. "Landmarks in the History of Indian Logic." *Wiener Zeitschrift für die Kunde Süd- und Ostasiens* 5:125–148.

——. 1995. *Studies in Abhidharma Literature and the Origins of Buddhist Philosophical Systems*. Trans. Sophie Francis Kidd. Albany: State University of New York Press.

Ganeri, Jonardon. 2013. *The Concealed Art of the Soul: Theories of the Self and Practices of Truth in Indian Ethics and Epistemology*. New York: Oxford University Press.

Garfield, Jay. 1994. "Dependent Co-origination and the Emptiness of Emptiness: Why did Nāgārjuna Begin with Causation?" *Philosophy East and West* 44:219–250.

——. 2002. *Empty Words: Buddhist Philosophy and Cross-Cultural Interpretation*. New York: Oxford University Press.

——. 2009. "Vasubandhu's *Trisvabhāvanirdeśa* (*Treatise on the Three Natures*)." In *Buddhist Philosophy: Essential Readings*, ed. William Edelglass and Jay Garfield, 35–44. New York: Oxford University Press.

Gethin, Rupert. 1992. "The *mātikās*: Memorization, Mindfulness, and the List." In Gyatso 1992:149–172.

Gold, Jonathan. 2006. "No Outside, No Inside: Duality, Reality, and Vasubandhu's Illusory Elephant." *Asian Philosophy* 16.1:1–38.

——. 2007. "Yogācāra Strategies Against Realism: Appearances (*ākṛti*) and Metaphors (*upacāra*)." *Blackwell Religion Compass* 1.1 (Jan.): 131–147.

—. 2011. "Vasubandhu." *Stanford Encyclopedia of Philosophy*, ed. Edward N. Zalta. http://plato.stanford.edu/vasubandhu/ (April 2011).

—. Forthcoming. "Without Karma and Nirvāṇa, Buddhism Is Nihilism: The Yogācāra Contribution to the Doctrine of Emptiness." In *Madhyamaka and Yogācāra: Rivals or Allies?*, ed. Jay Garfield and Jan Westerhoff. New York: Oxford University Press.

Goodman, Charles. 2009a. "Vasubandhu's *Abhidharmakośa*: The Critique of the Soul." In *Buddhist Philosophy: Essential Readings*, ed. William Edelglass and Jay Garfield, 297–308. New York: Oxford University Press.

—. 2009b. *Consequences of Compassion: An Interpretation and Defense of Buddhist Ethics*. New York: Oxford University Press.

Griffiths, Paul J. 1991. *On Being Mindless: Buddhist Meditation and the Mind-Body Problem*. LaSalle: Open Court.

—. 1992. "Memory in Classical Indian Yogācāra." In Gyatso 1992:109–131.

—. 1994. *On Being Buddha: The Classical Doctrine of Buddhahood*. Albany: State University of New York Press.

—. 1999. *Religious Reading: The Place of Reading in the Practice of Religion*. New York: Oxford University Press.

Gyatso, Janet, ed. 1992. *In the Mirror of Memory: Reflections on Mindfulness and Remembrance in Indian and Tibetan Buddhism*. Albany: State University of New York Press.

Hall, Bruce Cameron. 1983. "Vasubandhu on Aggregates, Spheres, and Components: Being Chapter One of the *Abhidharmakosa*." PhD diss., Harvard University, Cambridge, MA.

—. 1986. "The Meaning of Vijñapti in Vasubandhu's Concept of Mind." *Journal of the International Association of Buddhist Studies* 9.1:7–23.

Harter, Pierre-Julien. 2011. "Doxography and Philosophy: The Usage and Significance of School Denominations in Red mda' ba gzhon nu blo gros' Ornament of the Proofs of Consciousness." *Revue d'Etudes Tibétaines* 22 (Nov.): 93–119.

Hayes, Richard P. 1988. "Principled Atheism in the Buddhist Scholastic Tradition." *Journal of Indian Philosophy* 16:5–28.

Hirakawa, Akira, et al. 1973. "Introduction." In *Index to the Abhidharmakośabhāṣya (P. Pradhan edition), Part I: Sanskrit-Chinese-Tibetan*, ed. Akira Hirakawa, Shunei Hirai, So Takahashi, Noriaki Hakamaya, and Giei Yoshizu, i–xliv. Tokyo: Daizō Shuppan Kabushiki Kaisha.

Honjō Yoshifumi. 2003. "The Word *Sautrāntika*." *Journal of the International Association of Buddhist Studies* 26:321–330.

Hopkins, Jeffrey. 1996. "The Tibetan Genre of Doxography: Structuring a Worldview." In *Tibetan Literature: Studies in Genre*, ed. José Ignacio Cabezón and Roger R. Jackson, 170–186. Ithaca, NY: Snow Lion Publications.

Horiuchi, Toshio. 2009. "Vasubandhu's Relationship to the *Mahāyānasūtrālaṃkārabhāṣya* and *Laṅkāvatārasūtra* Based on Citations in the *Vyākhyāyukti*." [Studies in Philosophy] 哲学・思想論集 34:101–108.

Huntington, C. W. 1989. *The Emptiness of Emptiness: A Study of Early Indian Mādhyamika*. With Geshe Namgyal Wangchen. Honolulu: University of Hawaii Press.

—. 2002. "Was Candrakīrti a Prāsangika?" In *The Svātantrika-Prāsaṅgika Distinction: What Difference Does a Difference Make?*, ed. Georges Dreyfus and Sara McClintock, 67–91. Somerville, MA: Wisdom Publications.

Jackson, David P. 1995. "The Status of Pramāṇa Doctrine According to Sa skya Paṇḍita and Other Tibetan Masters: Theoretical Discipline or Doctrine of Liberation?" In *Papers in*

Honor and Appreciation of Professor David Seyfort Ruegg's Contribution to Indological, Buddhist, and Tibetan Studies, ed. T. Skorupski and U. Pagel, 85–129. The Buddhist Forum 3 (1991–1993). New Delhi: Heritage Publishers.

Jacob, Pierre. 2010. "Intentionality." *The Stanford Encyclopedia of Philosophy*, ed. Edward N. Zalta. http://plato.stanford.edu/archives/fall2010/entries/intentionality/.

Jaini, Padmanabh S. 1958. "On the Theory of the Two Vasubandhus." *Bulletin of the School of Oriental and African Studies* 21:48–53.

——. 1992. "*Smṛti* in the Abhidharma Literature and the Development of Buddhist Accounts of Memory of the Past." In Gyatso 1992:47–65.

Jha, Gaṅgānātha, ed. 1939. *Gautama's Nyāyasūtras with Vātsyāyana-Bhāṣya* 2. Poona Oriental Series 58. Puna: Oriental Book Agency.

Johnson, Samuel. 1755. *A Dictionary of the English Language: In Which the Words Are Deduced from Their Originals, Explained in Their Different Meanings, and Authorized by the Names of the Writers in Whose Works They Are Found*. Dublin: W. G. Jones.

Kaplan, Stephen. 1990. "A Holographic Alternative to a Traditional Yogācāra Simile: An Analysis of Vasubandhu's Trisvabhāva Doctrine." *Eastern Buddhist* 23.1:56–78.

Kapstein, Matthew T. 2001a. "Vasubandhu and the Nyāya Philosophers on Personal Identity." In *Reason's Traces*, 347–391. Somerville, MA: Wisdom Publications.

——. 2001b. "Mereological Considerations in Vasubandhu's 'Proof of Idealism.'" In *Reason's Traces*, 181–204. Somerville, MA: Wisdom Publications.

——. 2001c. "Introduction: What Is 'Buddhist Philosophy'?" In *Reason's Traces*, 3–26. Somerville, MA: Wisdom Publications.

Katsura, Shoryu. 2003. "Some Cases of Doctrinal Proofs in the *Abhidharma-kośa-bhāṣya*." *Journal of Indian Philosophy* 31:105–120.

Kiblinger, Kristin Beise. 2004. "Using Three-Vehicle Theory to Improve Buddhist Inclusivism." *Buddhist-Christian Studies* 24:159–169.

Kochumuttom, Thomas. 1982. *A Buddhist Doctrine of Experience: A New Translation and Interpretation of the Works of Vasubandhu the Yogācārin*. Delhi: Motilal Banarsidass.

Kritzer, Robert. 2000. "Rūpa and the *Antarābhava*." *Journal of Indian Philosophy* 28:235–272.

——. 2003a. "General Introduction." *Journal of the International Association of Buddhist Studies* 26:201–224.

——. 2003b. "Sautrāntika in the *Abhidharmakośabhāṣya*." *Journal of the International Association of Buddhist Studies* 26:331–384.

——. 2005. *Vasubandhu and the* Yogācārabhūmi: *Yogācāra Elements in the* Abhidharmakośabhāṣya. Studia Philological Buddhiaca 18. Tokyo: International Institute for Buddhist Studies.

Lamotte, Étienne. 1935. *Saṃdhinirmocana Sūtra: L'explication des mystères*. Louvain: Université de Louvain.

——. 1936. "Le traité de l'acte de Vasubandhu: *Karmasiddhiprakaraṇa*." *Mélanges Chinoise et Bouddhiques* 4:151–264.

Larson, Gerald James. 1979. *Classical Sāmkhya: An Interpretation of Its History and Meaning*. Delhi: Motilal Banarsidass.

La Vallée Poussin, Louis de. 1923–1925. *L'Abhidharmakośa de Vasubandhu*. 6 vols. Société Belge d'Études Orientales. Paris: Geuthner.

——. 1928–1929. *Vijñaptimātratāsiddhi: La siddhi de Hiuan-Tsang, traduite et annotée par Louis de la Vallée Poussin*. Paris: Geuthner.

——. 1933. "Le petit traité de Vasubandhu-Nagarjuna sur les trios natures." *Mélanges chinois et bouddhiques* 2:147–161.

Lee, Jong Cheol. 2001. *The Tibetan Text of the* Vyākhyāyukti *of Vasubandhu. Critically Edited from the Cone, Derge, Narthang, and Peking Editions.* Tokyo: Sankibo Press.

Lévi, Sylvain. 1925. *Vijñaptimātratāsiddhi: Deux traités de Vasubandhu, Viṃśatikā (La vingtaine) accompagné d'une explication en prose, et Triṃśikā (La trentaine), avec le commentaire de Sthiramati.* Paris: Libraire Ancienne Honoré Champion.

Lusthaus, Dan. 2002. *Buddhist Phenomenology: A Philosophical Investigation of Yogācāra Philosophy and the* Ch'eng Wei-shih lun. New York: RoutledgeCurzon.

Malinar, Angelika. 2008. *The Bhagavad Gītā: Doctrines and Contexts.* Cambridge: Cambridge University Press.

Mathes, Klaus-Dieter. 1996. *Unterscheidung der Gegebenheiten von ihrem wahren Wesen (Dharmadharmatāvibhāga): Eine Lehrschrift der Yogācāra-Schule in tibetischer Überlieferung.* Swisttal-Odendorf: Indica et Tibetica.

Matilal, Bimal K. 1977. *Nyāya-Vaiśeṣika.* A History of Indian Literature 6.2. Wiesbaden: Harrassowitz.

McClintock, Sara. 2010. *Omniscience and the Rhetoric of Reason: Śāntarakṣita and Kamalaśīla on Rationality, Argumentation, and Religious Authority.* Studies in Indian and Tibetan Buddhism. Somerville, MA: Wisdom Publications.

McCrea, Lawrence. 2000. "The Hierarchical Organization of Language in Mīmāṃsā Interpretive Theory." *Journal of Indian Philosophy* 28:429–459.

Mejor, Marek. 1989–1990. "The Problem of Two Vasubandhus Reconsidered." *Indological Taurinensia* 15/16:275–283. Retrieved from indologica.com (June 2013).

Meyers, Karin L. 2010. "Freedom and Self-Control: Free Will in South Asian Buddhism." PhD diss., University of Chicago.

Miller, Barbara Stoler, trans. 1986. *The Bhagavad-Gita: Krishna's Counsel in Time of War.* New York: Bantam.

Mimaki, Katsumi, Musashi Tachikawa, and Akira Yuyama, eds. 1989. *Three Works of Vasubandhu in Sanskrit Manuscript: The Trisvabhāvanirdeśa, the Viṃśatikā with Its Vṛtti, and the Triṃśikā with Sthiramati's Commentary.* Tokyo: Centre for East Asian Cultural Studies.

Monier-Williams, Monier. 1993. *A Sanskrit-English Dictionary.* Delhi: Motilal Banarsidass. 1st ed., Oxford University Press, 1899.

Morris, Michael W., and Richard P. Larrick. 1995. "When One Cause Casts Doubt on Another: A Normative Analysis of Discounting in Causal Attribution." *Psychological Review* 102.2:331–355.

Morris, M. W., and R. E. Nisbett. 1993. "Tools of the Trade: Deductive Schemas Taught in Psychology and Philosophy." In *Rules for Reasoning*, ed. R. E. Nisbett, 228–258. Hillsdale, NJ: Erhlbaum.

Mueller-Vollmer, Kurt, ed. 1989. *The Hermeneutics Reader: Texts of the German Tradition from the Enlightenment to the Present.* New York: Continuum.

Mukhopadhyaya, Sujit Kumar. 1939. *The Trisvabhāva-nirdeśa of Vasubandhu.* Calcutta: Visvabharati.

Nagao Gadjin, ed. 1964. *Madhyāntavibhāga-bhāṣya.* Tokyo: Suzuki Research Foundation.

——. 1991. *Mādhyamika and Yogācāra: A Study of Māhāyana Philosophies.* Trans. Leslie Kawamura. Albany: State University of New York Press.

Nakamura, Hajime. 1987. *Indian Buddhism: A Survey with Bibliographical Notes.* Delhi: Motilal Banarsidass.

Nance, Richard. 2012. *Speaking for Buddhas: Scriptural Commentary in Indian Buddhism.* New York: Columbia University Press.

Nattier, Jan. 2003. *A Few Good Men: The Bodhisattva Path According to the Inquiry of Ugra (Ugraparipṛcchā)*. Honolulu: University of Hawaii Press.

Obermiller, E. 1931–1932. *History of Buddhism by Bu-Ston*. 2 vols. Tokyo: Suzuki Research Foundation Reprint Series 5/Heidelberg: Harrassowitz.

O'Connor, Timothy. 2002. "Libertarian Views: Dualist and Agent-Causal Theories." In *The Oxford Handbook of Free Will*, ed. Robert Kane, 337–355. New York: Oxford University Press.

——. 2005. "Free Will." *The Stanford Encyclopedia of Philosophy*, ed. Edward N. Zalta. http://plato.stanford.edu/entries/freewill/.

Park, Changhwan. 2007. "The Sautrāntika Theory of Seeds (*bīja*) Revisited: With Special Reference to the Ideological Continuity Between Vasubandhu's Theory of Seeds and Its Śrīlāta/Dārṣṭāntika Precedents." PhD diss., University of California, Berkeley.

Pāsādika, Bhikkhu. 1989. *Kanonische Zitate im Abhidharmakośabhāṣya des Vasubandhu*. Göttingen: Vandenhoeck and Ruprecht.

Patil, Parimal. 2009. *Against a Hindu God: Buddhist Philosophy in India*. New York: Columbia University Press.

Patrul Rinpoche. 1988. *The Words of My Perfect Teacher*. Trans. Padmakara Translation Group. Boston: Shambhala.

Powers, John, trans. 1995. *Wisdom of Buddha: The Saṁdhinirmocana Mahāyāna Sūtra: Essential Questions and Direct Answers for Realizing Enlightenment*. Berkeley: Dharma Publishing.

Pradhan, Prahlad, ed. 1975. *Abhidharmakośabhāṣyam of Vasubandhu*. Ed. Prahlad Pradhan. Tibetan Sanskrit Works 8. Patna: K. P. Jayaswal Research Institute.

Priest, Graham. 2002. *Beyond the Limits of Thought*. New York: Oxford University Press.

Pruden, Leo, trans. 1987. *Karmasiddhiprakaraṇa: The Treatise on Action by Vasubandhu*, by Étienne Lamotte. Berkeley: Asian Humanities Press.

——, trans. 1988–1990. *Abhidharmakośa Bhāṣyam*, by Louis de la Vallée Poussin. Berkeley: Asian Humanities Press.

Rabten, Geshe. 1992. *The Mind and Its Functions*. Trans. Stephen Batchelor. Mont Pèlerin, Switzerland: Rabten Choeling.

Rahder, J., ed. 1926. *Daśabhūmikasūtra et Bodhisattvabhūmi: Chapitres vihāra et bhūmi*. Paris: Geuthner.

Rescher, Nicholas. 2001. *Cognitive Pragmatism: The Theory of Knowledge in Pragmatic Perspective*. Pittsburgh: University of Pittsburgh Press.

Sarachchandra, Edirivira R. 1976. "From Vasubandhu to Śāntarakṣita: A Critical Examination of Some Buddhist Theories of the External World." *Journal of Indian Philosophy* 4:69–107.

Śāstrī, Dwārikā Dās, ed. 2008. *The Abhidharmakośa and Bhāṣya of Ācārya Vasubandhu with Sphutārthā Commentary of Ācārya Yaśomitra*. 2 vols. 2nd ed. Varanasi: Bauddha Bhāratī.

Schmithausen, Lambert. 1967. "Sautrāntika-Voraussetzungen in *Viṃśatikā* und *Triṃśikā*." *Wiener Zeitschrift für die Kunde des Süd- und Ostasiens* 11:109–136.

——. 1984. "On the Vijñaptimātra Passage in *Saṃdhinirmocanasūtra* VIII.7." *Acta Indologica* 6:433–455.

——. 1992. "A Note on Vasubandhu and the *Laṅkāvatārasūtra*." *Asiatische Studien/ Études Asiatiques* 46:392–397.

——. 2005. *On the Problem of the External World in the Ch'eng wei shih lun*. Studia Philologica Buddhica Occasional Paper Series 13. Tokyo: International Institute for Buddhist Studies.

——. 2007. *Ālayavijñāna: On the Origin and the Early Development of a Central Concept of Yogācāra Philosophy*. 2 vols. Studia Philologica Buddhica 4. Repr. Tokyo: International Institute for Buddhist Studies.

Schwyzer, Hubert. 1997. "Subjectivity in Descartes and Kant." *Philosophical Quarterly* 47:342–357.

Searle, John. 1992. *The Rediscovery of the Mind*. Cambridge, MA: MIT Press.

——. 2001. *Rationality In Action*. Cambridge, MA: MIT Press.

Sellars, Wilfrid. 1997. *Empiricism and Philosophy of Mind*. Cambridge, MA: Harvard University Press.

Sharf, Robert H. 1998. "Experience." In *Critical Terms for Religious Studies*, ed. Mark C. Taylor, 94–116. Chicago: University of Chicago Press.

Siderits, Mark. 1997. "Buddhist Reductionism." *Philosophy East and West* 47.4:455–478.

——. 2003. *Personal Identity and Buddhist Philosophy*. Aldershot: Ashgate.

——. 2007. *Buddhism as Philosophy: An Introduction*. Indianapolis: Hackett.

——. 2009. "Is Reductionism Expressible?" In *Pointing at the Moon: Buddhism, Logic, Analytic Philosophy*, ed. Mario D'Amato et al., 57–69. New York: Oxford University Press.

Siderits, Mark, and Shōryū Katsura. 2013. *Nāgārjuna's Middle Way:* Mūlamadhyamakakārikā. Classics of Indian Buddhism. Somerville, MA: Wisdom Publications.

Siderits, Mark, Tom Tillemans, and Arindam Chakrabarti, eds. 2011. *Apoha: Buddhist Nominalism and Human Cognition*. New York: Columbia University Press.

Skilling, Peter. 2000. "Vasubandhu and the *Vyākhyāyukti* Literature." *Journal of the International Association of Buddhist Studies* 23.2:297–350.

Sponberg, Alan. 1983. "The *Trisvabhāva* Doctrine in India and China." *Ryūkoku Daigaku Bukkyō Bunka Kenkyūjo Kiyō* 22:97–119.

Srivastava, R. P. 1973. *Contemporary Indian Idealism*. Delhi: Motilal Banarsidass.

Stoker, Valerie. 2004. "Conceiving the Canon in Dvaita Vedānta: Madhva's Doctrine of 'All Sacred Lore.'" *Numen* 51.1:47–77.

Swinburne, Richard. 1991. *The Existence of God: Revised Edition*. Oxford: Clarendon Press.

Takakusu J., trans. 1904. "The Life of Vasu-bandhu by Paramārtha (A.D. 499–569)." *T'oung Pao* 5:269–296.

Thanissaro Bhikkhu, trans. 1997a. "*Maha-nidana Sutta*: The Great Causes Discourse (DN 15)." *Access to Insight* (June 8, 2010). http://www.accesstoinsight.org/tipitaka/dn/dn.15.0.than.html.

——, trans. 1997b. "*Samaññaphala Sutta*: The Fruits of the Contemplative Life (DN 2)." *Access to Insight* (Jan. 30, 2010). http://www.accesstoinsight.org/tipitaka/dn/dn.02.0.than.html.

Tola, Fernando, and Carmen Dragonetti. 1983. "The *Trisvabhāvakārikā* of Vasubandhu." *Journal of Indian Philosophy* 11:225–266.

——. 2004. *Being as Consciousness: Yogācāra Philosophy of Buddhism*. Delhi: Motilal Banarsidass.

Trivedi, Saam. 2005. "Idealism and Yogacara Buddhism." *Asian Philosophy* 15.3:231–246.

Tubb, Gary, and Emery Boose. 2007. *Scholastic Sanskrit: A Handbook for Students*. Treasury of the Indic Sciences. New York: American Institute of Buddhist Studies at Columbia University.

Tzohar, Roy. 2011. "Metaphor (Upacāra) in Early Yogācāra Thought and Its Intellectual Context." PhD diss., Columbia University, New York.

Van Inwagen, Peter. 1975. "The Incompatibility of Free Will and Determinism." *Philosophical Studies* 27:185–199.

Verhagen, Peter C. 2005. "Studies in Indo-Tibetan Buddhist Hermeneutics (4): The *Vyākhyāyukti* by Vasubandhu." *Journal Asiatique* 293.2:559–602.

—. 2008. "Studies in Indo-Tibetan Buddhist Hermeneutics (6): Validity and Valid Interpretation of Scripture According to Vasubandhu's *Vyākhyāyukti*." In *Buddhist Studies: Papers of the Twelfth World Sanskrit Conference*, ed. Richard Gombrich and Christina Scherrer-Schaub, 233–258. Delhi: Motilal Banarsidass.

Von Rospatt, Alexander. 1995. *The Buddhist Doctrine of Momentariness: A Survey of the Origins and Early Phase of This Doctrine up to Vasubandhu*. Alt- und Neu-Indische Studien 47. Stuttgart: Steiner.

Vose, Kevin. 2009. *Resurrecting Candrakīrti: Disputes in the Tibetan Creation of Prāsaṅgika*. Studies in Indian and Tibetan Buddhism. Somerville, MA: Wisdom Publications.

Walshe, Maurice, trans. 1995a. "Sāmaññaphala Sutta: The Fruits of the Homeless Life." In *The Long Discourses of the Buddha: A Translation of the* Dīgha Nikāya, 91–109. Boston: Wisdom Publications.

—. 1995b. "Mahānidāna Sutta: The Great Discourse on Origination." In *The Long Discourses of the Buddha: A Translation of the* Dīgha Nikāya, 223–230. Boston: Wisdom Publications.

Wegner, Daniel M. 2002. *The Illusion of Conscious Will*. Cambridge, MA: MIT Press.

Westerhoff, Jan. 2009. *Nāgārjuna's Madhyamaka: A Philosophical Investigation*. New York: Oxford University Press.

—. 2010. *Twelve Examples of Illusion*. New York: Oxford University Press.

Whitney, William Dwight. 1885. *The Roots, Verb-Forms, and Primary Derivatives of the Sanskrit Language*. London: Trübner and Co.

Williams, Paul. 1998a. *Altruism and Reality: Studies in the Philosophy of the* Bodhicaryāvatāra. London: Curzon.

—. 1998b. *The Reflexive Nature of Awareness: A Tibetan Madhyamaka Defense*. London: Curzon.

Wood, Thomas E. 1991. *Mind Only: A Philosophical and Doctrinal Analysis of Vijñānavāda*. Honolulu: University of Hawaii Press.

Woodward, James. 2003. *Making Things Happen: A Theory of Causal Explanation*. New York: Oxford University Press.

Yao, Zhihua. 2005. *The Buddhist Theory of Self-Cognition*. Routledge Critical Studies in Buddhism. New York: Routledge.

Yoshihito G. Muroji. 1993. *Vasubandhus Interpretation des Pratītyasamutpāda: Eine kritische Bearbeitung der Pratītyasamutpādavyākhyā (Saṃskāra- und Vijñānavibhaṅga)*. Alt- und Neu-Indische Studien 43. Stuttgart: Steiner.

Zahavi, Dan, and Josef Parnas. 1998. "Phenomenal Consciousness and Self-Awareness: A Phenomenological Critique of Representational Theory." *Journal of Consciousness Studies* 5:687–705.

INDEX